I0134205

BENEATH A FALLING STAR

(Third Book of the Kahana Chronicles)

III

A family historical novel by
Allen E. Goldenthal

Copyright © 2020

All rights reserved – Allen E. Goldenthal

No part of this book can be reproduced or transmitted in any form or by any means, graphic, electronic, or mechanical, including photocopying, recording, taping or by any information storage retrieval system, without the permission of the publisher in writing.

VAL D'OR Publishing

ISBN: 978-0-6488083-1-2

AUTHOR'S NOTE

Over the past twenty-two years since this series began, the Kahana Chronicles has become far more than a simple history of one family, my family, but instead a shining beacon that signals hope for all of mankind, as it emphasizes that no matter what the odds against any one of us, as long as we are willing to persevere, to face our adversaries with courage, grit and determination, to challenge evil no matter how overwhelming it may appear, we will prevail even under the most difficult and horrific of circumstances. That is the vital message for us to find and share from the historical events, both fortunate and disastrous, faced by the Kahana. It is a revelation, a discovery that binds us with the common thread that all families can come together in the hope and creation of a better future. We must learn from our past.

Each novel has been a story of survival based in its own time, not always successful, but never lacking in determination and strength of will to fight for that which is most important; freedom. And it is freedom, which is without question our greatest treasure, our dearest possession, yet taken for granted repeatedly, as we never realize its true value until we have lost it. There is a cost for freedom. It demands blood, loss and sacrifice, and only then can we truly appreciate the tremendous cost that has been paid by those that came before us. As long as the spirit of the Kahana exists, there will always be those that are willing to fight for truth, honour, liberty and freedom. Those willing to sacrifice everything for the sake of others. That is the essence and spirit of true heroes.

But there also comes a time when the lines between what is right and what is wrong are blurred to such a degree that even the wisest among us cannot determine if the path chosen has been the correct one. We hope, we pray, and if fortune smiles upon us, then we can sometimes turn even a wrong decision into the right choice. It is not without a high cost and often mixed with pain and suffering, but it is possible. What you will read in *Beneath A Falling Star* is one such time when even those with the purest of heart and intentions could not distinguish right from wrong and a time when those we have raised and praised as heroes were in reality the greatest villains of all. For that has been the curse of the Jews since the dawn of time, that even though Moses gave us the word of God, we have always chosen instead to follow the words of men.

God told us not to make kings, but we did not listen. God told us to be a light unto the world but again we did not listen. God warned us to be patient and, in His time, he would deliver everything that he had promised but we could not wait because we desired everything on our own time. Sadly, we have let ourselves follow fools dressed as wisemen, charlatans that possessed silver tongues greased with the oil of their own anointing. It is only through His mercy and His benevolent spirit that we still survive, forgiven for all the times we have been led astray by those that we have credited as our leaders. This book will reveal the truths behind such a time when men that should have known better, chose to follow the lies of one man that even today is acclaimed as one of Judaism's greatest Sages. A man, and I am loathe to even call him that, who almost single-handedly extinguished the Jewish nation and brought us to the point of extinction. My ancestor knew better. He knew that there was wisdom in the Book of Ecclesiastes; a time to fight and a time to make peace but sadly his voice was not loud enough to drown out the war cries from a man that ashamedly only loved himself and cared little for the hundreds of thousands he sacrificed. So, I warn all of you now who are about to read this book, if you do not wish to have your beliefs shaken, if you consider the history you have been spoon fed since birth as the only nourishment your soul requires, and if you prefer to keep your eyes shuttered against the horrors of obvious truths, then you should put this book down immediately and not read any further. Sometimes the truth is painful and only those with the intestinal fortitude to face the reality that this world is not always as it has been portrayed will be able to bear the brilliance of the sun's purifying rays of enlightenment.

I dedicate this book to my ancestors, those that have come before me in whom I delight and have such pride, knowing that through the centuries they have possessed the morality, the clarity of vision, the integrity and faith to do what was right in the eyes of the Lord. They certainly were not saints, and as the books in the Kahana Chronicles series have highlighted they often committed sins that they openly admit to but they faced their admonishments and punishments and even ultimately their deaths with courage and an understanding that all men must be eventually held accountable for their actions. I have never concealed or attempted to hide their Zadokite or Karaite roots, the foundations for their fundamental beliefs and logic. They knew that for every lie they exposed, it could only be undone through great sacrifice. Often that sacrifice was paid in blood. And certainly, there is no denying that we have not seen eye to eye with our rabbinical brethren. We have hurled stones at each other for over a thousand years. This story is not intended to be one of those stones but in fact a chance to bridge our differences. To have an understanding and united vision recognizing that the greatest enemies to our people have not always come from without but have often come from within.

We can only continue to evolve as 'the Chosen People' if we acknowledge that being chosen is not a privilege but a burden that weighs heavy upon our shoulders and must be carefully balanced with truth, dignity, honesty and under the microscope of self-examination, otherwise it will literally haunt us and come crashing down upon our heads. Carrying that tremendous burden has been the primary responsibility of the Kahana throughout the centuries. But it is all our duty as human beings to accept this burden, to share our mandate to spread the word of God and recognize that in our constant battle for freedom we must never surrender quietly to evil.

NB: Throughout this book you will find paragraphs, sentences and quotes that are *italicized*. The italicization is intentional, and its significance will be fully explained in my address at the end of the book. Pay close attention to these italicized quotes.

"The greatest lie is the one you convince everyone to believe in the name of God."

-Elioneai ben Yosef

(136 ACE)

PROLOGUE

What is left, if not the ashes of our own hubris? We have been oppressed, scourged and downtrodden for over sixty years since our defeat but our prayers to the Almighty to free us from this Roman domination fall upon deaf ears. How long can we stay the hands of those calling for insurrection before they set ablaze what remains standing in the ashes from our last doomed effort to win our freedom. I beseech all those calling for war that we must wait, and let the Lord deliver us when He decides the time is ripe. These so-called leaders, the inheritors of the mantle from the Pharisee rabble are in the streets preaching to us that the time has come for the final battle, let them stand in the front line against our greatest enemy rather than encourage others onward to their deaths. Do they not understand? We are staring in the face of termination, the complete and utter annihilation of our existence, and they persist in preaching this nonsense of the Lord guaranteeing a victory. Have they learned nothing from our mistake sixty years ago? Do they not realize that now is the time we can achieve more with the sweet taste of honey than the bitter edge of cold steel. Let these new-age Pharisees delude themselves into believing it is so, but be aware that there is no victory to be gained by our deliberate deaths. There is no promise that we will return and touch this earth ever again after we have left it even though they preach of some false belief in resurrection. These are their lies, which are now prevailing and render us divided as a people. It is imperative that we over-come our own mistruths, falsehoods and religious deceptions before we can ever believe that the Lord will send us His messiah! This is not that time!

Sixty years ago, my grandfather said these same words from the Temple steps and they slew him for speaking out against their misdeeds and lies. Not the Romans, not even the Zealots, but these very same Pharisees that could not bear to hear his words of truth and reconciliation. My grandfather, Jeshua ben Gamaliel, of the House of Phiabi, your High Priest, the Lord's chosen spokesperson, slain for speaking the words of the Lord by those possessing blackened evil hearts. My grandfather was not a man that openly sought violence but nor was he one that would shirk in his responsibilities to fight for freedom for his people. From the Temple Mount he led the army of God against the Romans and he brought the enemy to its knees and to a point of conciliation. A threshold where they had suffered such great losses and humiliation that they sent word to him that they were finally willing to negotiate a truce. A truce where we would have had our nation back a long time ago, our Temple would still be standing, and perhaps even our own king to rule over us once again. But the agent of the Pharisees, a man that they still laud for his greatness because if they did not, then they would have to admit their sins in all that befell us, permitted the Idumeans to enter the Temple during the night and through this subterfuge they subdued my grandfather and his men. And then John of Gischala, the leader of these fanatical rabbis had my grandfather, a holy man, the true High Priest of Israel beheaded, ending any chance of a peaceful solution to the war.

Yes, his blood is on your hands, you men parading around as paragons of virtue, calling yourself teachers of truth, but the reality is you are no more than butchers and your hands run deep in blood. Now once again you attempt at rekindling the fire to see if you can scorch what little remains from our last defeat. Have you learned nothing? Do you hate your own people so much that you will lead us down this path once again? Have you no conscience, or do you only hear the sounds from your own voices, the meaningless chorus of cackling geese.

I pray that all good people put their faith in God and not these men parading around in their long gray robes pretending to have heavenly knowledge. I only returned from Baghdad, years after my grandmother fled there with my father when he was still a young boy following his father's execution because I thought there was a golden opportunity for our nation. Now I fear you have trodden too far down the path to find redemption. Put not your faith in men but only in God. For God is both the beginning and the end and there shall be no others to speak for him. No second book of unwritten laws that only these liars and basest of creatures say that they have been given access to by angelic messengers. This litany of oral traditions which only they claim they have the power and authority to interpret. How convenient that the common man cannot see these for himself and make up his own mind on the meaning of what the Lord has given directly to us. Trust me when I say, there was no such thing as an unwritten law but only the one set of laws which Moses carried down the mountain side. Remember this, he was the only man that has ever spoken directly to the Lord, and he would most certainly challenge these modern day Korahites that dare to proclaim otherwise. Do not be swayed by them. Do not listen to their false words no matter how tempting they may be for they are no more than the serpent in the garden.   But this time there is no Garden of Eden that we will lose but instead it will be our land, our homes and our lives. Do not be led into temptation but show God you have the strength to endure until He delivers you with His mighty hand.

Elioneai ben Yosef

High Priest of Israel

5th of Tammuz 3892

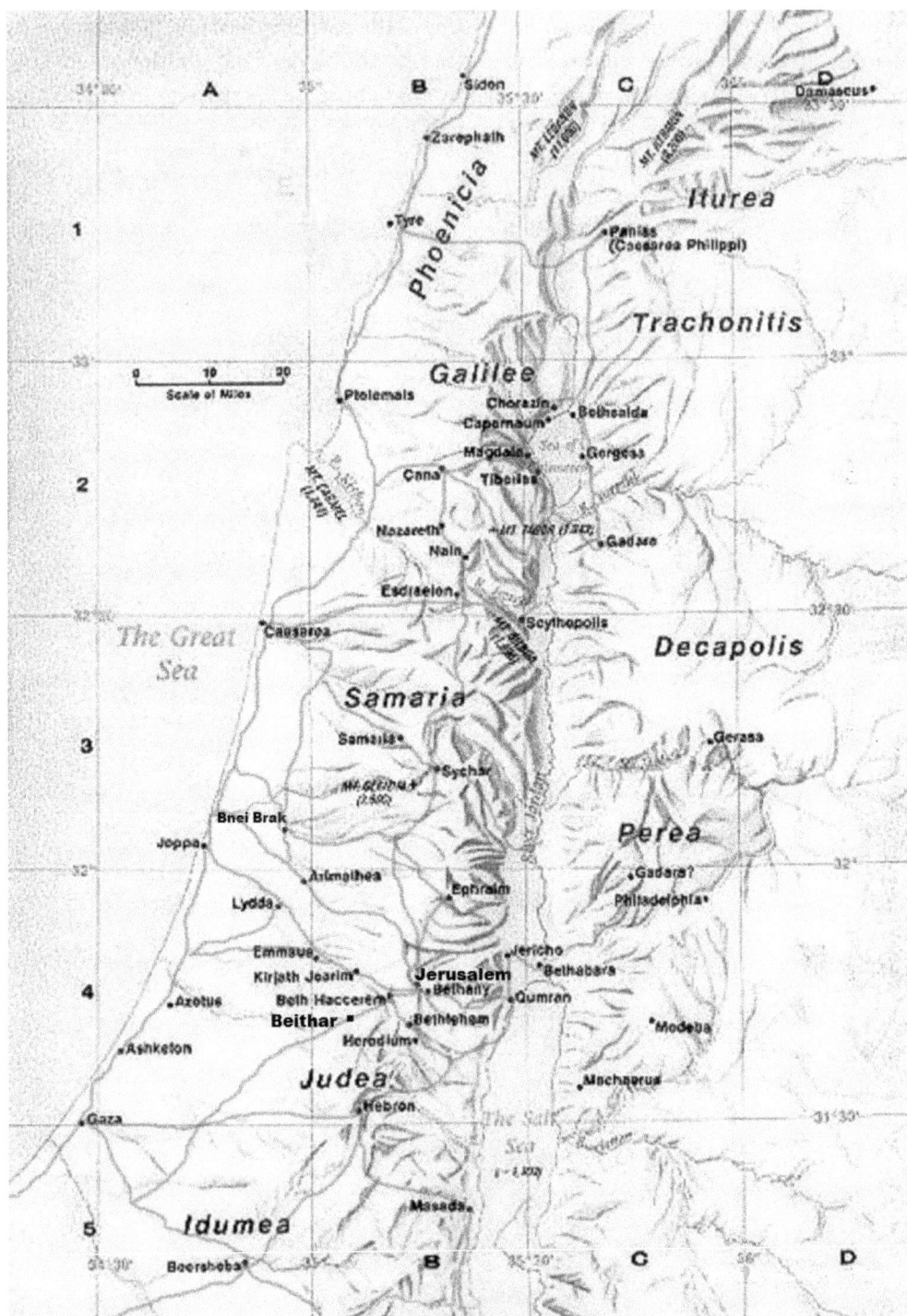

Chapter One

The Road North: 1st Day of Adar 3896 (136 ACE)

Without a single cloud in the sky providing any relief, the broiling sun took unfair advantage of our situation of taking the inland road and beat down upon us relentlessly. The excruciating heat raised a stench from the land to a level where I could hardly breath without feeling the urge to gag in reflex. It left the taste of rotting flesh sitting thick upon the base of my tongue. Not even the scarf from my turban could prevent the foul, fetid fumes from filling my nostrils, my head swirling with an unfamiliar nausea, that made me dizzy as I rocked in the saddle. Looking to my left, I could see from the expression on my eldest son's face that he too was already overwhelmed by the noxious fumes, his chin slumping to his chest as he closed his eyes and prayed, we would pass through this valley of death soon.

"Stay strong, Joseph," I encouraged him to try and clear his mind of everything he saw on either side of the road. "I assure you, once we reach Galilee the air should be fairly normal again." It was little consolation since the border of Galilee was still days away. "Why don't you do me a favor and go back to the wagons and check on how your mother and brother are doing? Make certain they don't need any help."

Immediately obeying my instructions, my eldest son urged his mule towards the rear of the long caravan, towards the specific wagon decorated with a striped linen cover, unlike the other wagons. Azariah, who rode behind the wagon, waved as soon as he saw his older brother approaching. Joseph quickly dismounted and hopped into the back of the wagon without saying a word to his young brother. Those riding close to the wagon could hear the repeated sounds of his retching shortly after his disappearance behind the flaps.

I turned my head to the right to see the captain of my guard bearing a broad smile across his face. "I see that you found my son's turning green amusing, my old friend."

"I laugh not at your son but at you, Excellency. I think that perhaps you feared seeing your son vomit, which is why you hastened him to check on the wagons," Jacob laughed. "It would appear you are looking green and quite close yourself to doing the same."

"Only you, my friend, would find watching the High Priest of Israel, casting the contents of his breakfast on the ground funny, Jacob," I responded. "But I will give you credit. With thousands of dead bodies, bloated and rotting in the fields to either side of the road the fact that you can still find something worth laughing about is astounding. I wish I could do the same."

"I have done my share of crying, Excellency. My eyes are so sore and dry from the number of tears I have shed that I can cry no more. But if I am to go on, then I must find something at which to laugh or the sadness will drag me down into a despair from which I fear that I would never recover."

"You are right my friend, as always," I concurred with him. "I too have spent the last four years crying and I pray that I will never have to cry another day in my life but I fear that will not be possible. I think we have just begun our torment and it will not end until the day our people are able to return to Jerusalem."

Jacob pulled on the point of his black beard thinking about what I had to say. Over the years I have come to realize he only does that when his mind is troubled. "Do you think that such a day will ever come again, Excellency?"

I had to think long and hard about an answer for that question. Never before had we been banished from our own capital by any of our enemies in the past. The Babylonians never did it, the Greeks never banished us, and even the Romans did not pass such a decree when we fought them more than sixty years ago. This was unlike anything I had encountered before. Other civilizations had suffered expulsions, never to return to their homes. I had no idea what was in store for us and I feared that 'unknowing' more than anything else I could imagine. "I will be honest with you Jacob. Only God knows the answer to that question," I responded. It wasn't much of an answer, but it was the only response I could think of. "When we returned to the city with my family ten years ago, I had no idea that I would ever be leaving again. It certainly wasn't my intention. I had come to restore the priesthood to our Holy City and begin negotiations with the Romans regarding the rebuilding of our Temple. Now I fear that has all been lost to us because of my foolishness."

"Excellency! How can you even think of blaming yourself for the destruction that occurred?" My captain was actually shocked that I could disparage myself and take the blame for our people's demise.

"Because I knew this would happen," I responded somewhat aggressively. "I knew and I did nothing to stop it. I had a chance; a real opportunity and I did not stop it!"

"What nonsense is this," Jacob chastised me. "You cannot take the blame for this devastation. You did everything you could!"

"Not nonsense, truth," I insisted. "I'm telling you the truth Jacob. I had the opportunity and I failed to do what needed to be done. It was right there in the Book of Daniel and I failed to convince the people to rely on the Lord. I knew it from the beginning, and I failed to act."

"How so, my Lord," Jacob could not accept my guilt and challenged my response, refusing to believe that in some way I was responsible.

"Daniel tells us so right in Chapter 2. He said that only the Lord has the power to break the Iron Kingdom. We know that kingdom to be the Romans. But God will only do that on his time and not ours. We have no say when that will happen which is made even clearer in Chapter 7. For beginning with the nineteenth sentence, we can know that Rome would stamp the residue of our land into dust if we revolted. Such a thing they did when we lost the first war sixty years ago and they have continued to do so ever since they conquered us. So, it is written. All God asked from us through Daniel, His prophet, was to wait. Nothing more, just wait! And we could not do that!"

"How do you know this, Excellency," Jacob was intrigued as he moved his pony closer to my mule so that he could hear better.

"I know because I am still the High Priest of Israel, which means on occasion the Lord, Our God, still talks to me at times. He came to me in a dream, and He explained to me the meaning of the first prophecy. It is the eleventh ruler of Rome that we were to fear the most, but he was also the key to unlocking the prophecy. I knew that horn that rose last was the Emperor Hadrian."

I watched as Jacob counted out on his fingers, only to look up at me with a look of surprised disagreement, thinking that he had caught me in an error. "But Excellency, Hadrian is the fourteenth Emperor of Rome. Pardon my outspokenness but you are obviously mistaken."

"I will admit Jacob that I shared the same doubts myself at first," I confessed to him. "But then I thought even more about what Daniel had said regarding his dream. How well do you recall your stories from the Tanach?" I asked him.

"Not very well," he admitted.

"So, I will tell you then. This last horn forced the shedding of three earlier horns. Do you not think that was mentioned for a reason?"

Jacob was about to answer but I waved my hand for him to remain silent as the question was purely rhetorical. Let us look at the history. Is that not what Hadrian had actually done? The Flavians conquered this land and there is no denying we have suffered for six decades because of it but still even they had ordained that in time our rights and privileges would be eventually restored to us. That is part of the reason I returned to Jerusalem. Already there were rumors of talks taking place of restoring a limited Jewish government. In time, I knew they would likely grant us permission to rebuild the Temple. The damage inflicted upon us by Vespasian and his two sons, Titus and Domitian, appeared to finally be coming to an end. It was the time to rejoice I thought, but then Hadrian became Emperor and he blew into Jerusalem like an ill wind, dismissing all of the improvements in our relationship that had taken place. Instead, this new Emperor talked of turning Jerusalem into a purely Roman city. To erect a temple dedicated to Jupiter on the Temple Mount. Where I had assumed that we had fulfilled our time and obligation against the curse those three Emperors inflicted upon us, we now faced a new and far more serious threat from Hadrian. A threat that made what the Flavians had done pale in comparison. So, as you can see, the Emperor Hadrian displaced the three Flavian Emperors as if all they said and all they had done and all they promised, never mattered. He scorned any thought of returning control of our city, of our Judea, dismissing every promise we may have had in writing from the Roman Senate regarding the restoration of our land. I knew then and there that he was no longer the fourteenth emperor but the eleventh as described in the prophecy. The generation of a new horn that displaces three previous ones. All that we endured and negotiated over six decades mattered little, now that the existence of Vespasian and his sons had been displaced by a much greater evil."

Jacob nodded his head in agreement. "Now I understand, Excellency. What you have said makes sense."

"I remember it well. It was Hadrian's thirteenth year as Emperor and he was preparing to leave Alexandria and sail back to Rome after his eastern journey through the Empire. Before departing he gave his final instructions to Rufus, the procurator of Judea, who took great pleasure in telling me what they were as we returned to holy Jerusalem. It was clearly evident to me that Hadrian intended to do everything that was mentioned in the prophecy. He intended to challenge our ancient prophets and interfere with our sacred laws. He would prevent us from converting any pagans to Judaism by forbidding us to perform circumcision on any of the converts. He also intended to change the name of our Holy city from Jerusalem to Aelia Capitola, dedicating the city to himself. He agreed that we should be permitted to build a new Temple, but just not in his city. But even as Rufus told me all these things, I knew there was far more to all these decisions than I could explain at the time. It was as if I was suddenly caught in a game of chess, and they were baiting me to make the next move. "What they did not know was that God had spoken to me through the prophecies of Daniel. "I knew then that all we had to do was wait until Hadrian passed away. His days were numbered though I knew not the number of years involved. All I knew was that the prophecy clearly revealed to me that this Emperor was the last obstacle before the land would be returned to us and then we would be able to rebuild the Temple on the Mount where it belonged. I could only guess that it would be seventy years from the time the Temple fell. I presumed that God in his mysterious ways would bring these changes about in the same length of time that we were exiled in Babylon. For such is the way of Our Lord."

"Excellency, are you saying that Hadrian will be dead in two more years?"

"I am Jacob," I was confident in my calculations.

"Praise be the Lord," Jacob exclaimed loudly, his words easily overheard by the rest of the guard riding along with us, who then repeated the same refrain.

"And now you know why I blame myself, Jacob. All I had to do was keep our people at peace for eight years until the prophecy was fulfilled and I failed. It was my responsibility to do so, and I could not complete the simple task Yahvu had given me. Because of my failure we have been practically exterminated as a people. Our opportunity to rebuild the Temple is lost for an eternity. I am now returning to Baghdad disgraced in the eyes of my ancestors. They will refer to me as the last High Priest who brought about the greatest disaster on our people."

"That is not true, Excellency," Jacob immediately came to my defense. "It was as you said, Excellency, a game of chess being played and no matter what move you made they were going to counter it because they had already anticipated all the possible counters you possessed. You were fighting against unknown forces you weren't even aware of. Invisible players that were making moves you couldn't even see."

"Do you really believe that Jacob? It was a thought in the back of my mind that had always troubled me from the time that Rufus confided in me. I always felt he was taunting me. That he had some secret means by which they could manipulate the situation no matter what I said or what I did. That always troubled me, but I could never explain that pervasive feeling of being in the dark and I never could uncover what was his secret strategy that he possessed. Did Rufus really have someone working on the inside and keeping me continually off balance?"

Jacob suddenly looked a little defensive as he saw the look on my face as I thought heavily on the matter. "I swear to you, Excellency, nothing you ever said to me passed from my lips to anyone else."

"Relax Jacob, I have never doubted you," I reassured him. "Anyway, you were never privy to the manner of secrets I am referring to. For example, why did he bother to mention the erection of a statue to Jupiter on the Temple Mount if he actually never did so? Even their ruling on who could be circumcised was suspect. The number of proselytes to Judaism are minimal, yet they made it sound like they were preventing thousands from having the option to become Jewish. They even mentioned extending the rule to all our newborns but never did. He was toying with me, keeping me focused on matters that never materialized but meanwhile they had another strategy in play. It was if he only wished to antagonize me, knowing exactly which issues to press upon in order to obtain a reaction, yet whatever minions he had acting were doing something else, completely unrelated to his threats."

Jacob pulled on his beard again, that tell-tale sign that I he was nervous and troubled. "Just a thought Excellency, but do you think that perhaps it was always his intention to provoke us and force us to go to war. That he purposely said things which would light the fires of revolt beneath our feet?"

"It does sound like that," I admitted. "But why would Rome want a war? What would they possibly gain for provoking us to fight?"

"Perhaps there was something that made the Emperor hate our people beyond even our comprehension and he intended to push us to war so he could annihilate us completely," Jacob suggested. "I know that does not make sense, but…"

"It may not be that unreasonable as you think," I replied calmly. "It was not as if we made his ascent to the throne easy for him. But the hate would have to be of such an intensity that I can't even conceive of any justification of that magnitude."

"I guess we have always been a thorn in his side from day one," Jacob commented.

"A thorn is a major understatement, my friend but still not any worse than many of the other nations," I figured. "What we are talking about is a hatred that   borders on the pathological."

"Perhaps he blames us for the death of his predecessor. He and his uncle were very close from what I was told," Jacob recounted some past history that could explain the bad blood between Hadrian and us Jews.

I reflected upon Jacob's train of thought. "Although I was still a young boy, I do remember some part of that war that we were involved in and which took place in Mesopotamia. Trajan, I recall, had taken Ctesiphon and I was in Babylon, a teenager eager to defend our cities from the invaders but my father had other plans. He invited me to attend the council meetings that were taking place in the palace. He said he wanted me to see how those with the wisdom of age dealt with a threat versus the impetuousness of my youth. It was typical of my father but in retrospect, it was a good lesson. I remember all the different leaders in their colourful dress and armor from around the eastern world. They all looked so different and yet we were one people. I felt strange, seeing this gathering of leaders from all the different communities within the Empire as well as the King's military advisors, realizing I was completely out of my depth. One thing that was clear to me is that it was obvious early on that they shared a common hatred of everything Rome represented.

Thinking back to that time, I remember all of the propaganda the Romans disseminated through the towns and villages as they advanced, claiming that they had come only to provide the people with liberty and freedom from oppression. It made no sense. Why should we forfeit the freedoms and the equality that we already enjoyed under the rule of the Parthians to embrace the known servitude that other nations had to endure under the heavy hand of Rome. It was all a lie. Trajan came as a conqueror, not as a liberator. Many of these generals fighting for the Parthians could recall episodes of brutality against their own people in the past at the hand of Rome and they had no reason to believe Rome had changed since then."

"But I also recall that we did not challenge him as he sailed down the Tigris and took city after city," Jacob interrupted me. "We let him take our cities and as a result many people suffered and died."

"It was all part of the plan," I explained. "I remember them discussing the strategy back in those meetings."

"How so, Excellency?" Jacob was eager to hear more.

"I'm getting to it," I held up the palm of my hand to suggest he remain patient. "It was not as if our King had not attempted to negotiate several times with the Roman invader. He offered Trajan the opportunity to redraw the borders, giving the Roman Empire all of Southern Armenia but Trajan refused. Osroes even offered to change the king in Armenia to one that would be more inclined to deal with Rome but again, that offer was turned down. Despite their refusals, it never occurred to the enemy how strange it was that they were sailing down the river and they never met any significant resistance. In his arrogance, Trajan actually believed that the million-man army of Parthia was terrified of the presence of a few Roman legions. They assumed we were petrified by fear to face our invaders. It was foolish if not ignorant, but such words throughout history define the Romans best."

"But he took Ctesiphon, the capital city," Jacob insisted. "Was it not foolish on our part to let him take our capital.

"It only lulled him further into a false sense of security. He was met with some opposition in Ctesiphon, enough to convince him that he won a great battle and that he was now master of the world. He even invoked the Senate in Rome to name him as Trajanus Parthicus, as if the war was over. Meanwhile, I remember my father saying that we had him exactly where we wanted him. He was confined within Ctesiphon, whereas we were free to plan and prepare for the coming spring."

"I never realized that we let him occupy Ctesiphon intentionally," Jacob admitted. "No one ever told me that part of the story before."

"And why would you know?   Had my father not brought me to the meetings of all the officials I would not have known it myself.   I learned a valuable lesson at that time.   That lesson being, 'inaction is often the greatest weapon you have in your arsenal'. And it is a lesson I have never forgotten. There is a time for resistance and a time of quiescence, the latter to be used when your enemy expects conflict, and the former to be used when he expects it least.   It causes confusion, it instills doubt, and it makes your enemy second guess everything that they do."

Jacob appeared quite impressed by that lesson as he nodded his head in appreciation.   "I must remember that," he commented.   "Just in case we ever find ourselves in a similar situation."

"So, while Trajan wintered in Ctesiphon, we plotted. "Our clever courtesans in Ctesiphon fawned all over the Roman Emperor, while reporting everything he did, every decision he made back to us.   We knew exactly what he planned to do next.   He wanted to relive the Glory of Alexander the Great and that meant he was intending to come next to Babylon. Again, he was met with little resistance. While he and his six legions enjoyed all the beauty that Babylon had to offer the Parthians stirred the people in each of the cities that the Romans had passed through along the way to revolt.   As soon as the insurrections began, Osroes sent his troops to take out each garrison that Trajan had posted. While the Roman Emperor slept in the same bed where Alexander slept, we took back Nisbis, Edessa, and Seleucia, slaughtering every last man Trajan had left behind."

"But that situation did not last for long," Jacob interjected, knowing that Trajan managed to retake those cities.

"I see you do know your history, Jacob," I complimented him.   "But what did he gain?   He sent his general Appius Maximus to retake Edessa, only to have the general and his entire legion obliterated by the Parthian infantry. Lusius Quietus won back Nisbis but at a heavy price.   Ericius Clarens and Julius Alexander managed to take back Seleucia, only to find they needed to abandon the city and retreat under the pressure of a second wave of attacks. Trajan pulled his entire army back to Ctesiphon and then marshaled it against Hatria, only to find after a long siege he was unable to take that city.   The war from his perspective had become a disaster and was quickly turning into a nightmare."

Jacob grinned as soon as I mentioned nightmare.   He knew what was coming next.   It was a favourite story in Parthia that had been retold repeatedly for almost twenty years since it occurred.

"While everything in Mesopotamia fell into disarray, and Trajan was now trapped with his army thousands of miles from Rome, my father set his plan in motion. You see, Osroes never intended to defeat Rome on the battlefield, he wanted to destroy it from within and he knew that my father was the one man that could make that happen. While the Romans were well into their second year of the Parthian campaign, my father, Joseph ben Jeshua of the House of Phiabi, used his authority as the one true High Priest of Israel to send out messages to all the Jewish communities under the oppressive yoke of Rome. Once you tally them all, you appreciate that there were dozens of cities in the Roman Empire with huge Jewish populations. He urged each community to prepare themselves for their coming liberation. He would provide them the signal when to launch the revolts in each of their communities at the proper time. For now, all they had to do was wait, prepare and be patient."

"So, what was the signal, Excellency?"

"Yes Father, what was the signal?" having overheard part of the conversation while riding to the front of the caravan on his mule, Joseph wanted to hear the story again, even though he had probably heard it a hundred times by now.

"How is your mother?" I wanted to know first before I continued the story.

"Like mother," my son replied sarcastically.

"What is that supposed to mean," I snapped back.

"You know," Joseph rolled his eyes. "It's too hot. It's too smelly. Why did we have to find the bumpiest road to take? What else could I possibly mean."

"Good," I commented. "That means she's alright then. Nothing I need to worry about.

"Except Azariah wants to know why he has to ride at the back and listen to her all day."

"Because he's the youngest and that's his job." We all laughed knowing that it was more a punishment than a job, but someone had to be there to take care of mother's needs.

"So go on with the story, Father. I enjoy this part. Do you not know it already, Jacob?"

My captain of the guard wasn't much older than my eldest son. They had grown up together in our household and were almost like brothers themselves.

"I have heard it told but not this version by Elioneai the High Priest," he admitted. "So, I'm very interested to hear it told from your father's point of view, being that it was his father that organized the entire revolt."

"Organized is not the precise word I would use," I corrected him. "I would say more like instigated, even initiated but certainly what was to follow could hardly be accused of being organized. That is definitely not the word I would use."

"How would you describe it then, Excellency?"

"More like absolute unleashed mayhem!"

"I wish we could have succeeded in doing it again, this time," Joseph sighed regrettably.

"Really son," I questioned him. "Have you not taken a good look at the bodies strewn across the fields that we've been passing? Can you not hear the women and children wailing in the distance for husbands and fathers that will never be coming home? Or perhaps the stench of rotting Jewish corpses hasn't turned your stomach enough for you to realize the futility and stupidity of our repeated battles with Rome. We are on the verge of extinction and unless we find a way to survive peaceably within all these kingdoms and empires, I'm afraid we won't survive another century."

"If you don't mind my disagreement, I think you may be slightly exaggerating Father," Joseph countered. "We have survived practically every empire that has existed since the dawn of time, and we are still here. All of them have crumbled into dust but we still remain. That is God's promise to us. To keep us as an everlasting sign of his omnipotence."

"If you think that entitles your generation to be as foolish as this one, then I'm warning you son, even God has limited patience. He will only suffer fools for so long before he finds another people to give his commandments. Remember my words that I say to you today, there will be others. The Nazoreans, the Mineans, and even the Samaritans are just waiting to knock the crown from atop our heads. And they are just the beginning, for I foresee many others that will lay claim to our inheritance if we do not safeguard it properly." I shook my head not knowing what to do about the impetuousness of this next generation. They jump carelessly into every dangerous and precarious situation with both feet forward, never thinking through the impact and consequences of their actions. It is as if they believe they are invulnerable and nothing can stop them, not even the sharp point of a Roman blade. I thought the disaster that had just befallen us would at least cause my son to hesitate and tread more carefully, but I'm afraid he and his companions still dream of revenge, when they should just be thinking on how they can survive and perpetuate our race. This is the main reason why I'm taking my family back to Babylon. There is nothing left here for us now. Jerusalem is in ruins. We've lost over half a million people in the three and a half years we fought, and now the Romans are finding and detaining anyone that may have been involved. That means not even myself or my family would be safe if we remained here much longer. In Babylon I will find my sons good wives and they can start raising a family of their own. Perhaps that will teach them responsibility and they will abandon any more fanatical ideas of fighting for freedom and finally come to appreciate the sanctity of life.

"Excellency? Excellency are you alright?" Jacob's voice broke through my thoughts, and I realized I had let my mind drift far from the discussion at hand.

"My apologies. Where was I?"

"You were just about to talk about what grandfather did," Joseph reminded me.

"Ah, yes. That's right. So, my father sent messages to every Jewish community throughout the Empire to prepare for the uprising. The moment Trajan's forces began their preparations for their return to Rome, that would be the signal for the revolt to start. We knew that within the week it would take Trajan to begin their march back to Antioch, we could have every community between Syria and Iberia notified and mobilized to launch an attack against the local garrisons. What we didn't know is that the stress of his failure to take Parthia was already taking its   toll on Trajan health. No sooner had he reached Antioch, after the long march from Babylon, he found himself paralyzed on one side of his body. This had not been anticipated and it meant others would begin to think they had a better plan. So, some of those that my father had recruited to start local uprisings saw Trajan's infirmity as a sign of being something much larger than simply creating a bit of urban chaos as my father had intended and advised. They took Trajan's failing health as a sign from the Almighty that the Empire was ready to fall. You must appreciate that even in the time of Moses, getting Jews to actually agree on something and stick to a plan is almost impossible. Practically every Jew wants to be a general rather than a soldier and follow orders. What happened next was not as my father had intended at all."

"Nevertheless, Excellency, it taught the Romans a lesson they sorely needed because of their unbridled pride and arrogance," Jacob announced excitedly, knowing how the story ended.

"The uprisings were only intended to teach the Romans to stay at home and to abandon any future attempts to conquer the world. If he could not control the unrest within his own Empire, surely, he would recognize the futility of trying to keep conquered people thousands of miles away under control. But as usual, we seem to have made it a habit of underestimating our brethren in North Africa. They are a completely different breed of Jew from us here in the Levant. More savage, more brutal and once the blood lust is stirred within them, they cannot stop."

"That is for certain," Jacob agreed. "I once courted a girl from a Carthaginian family. Barely escaped that relationship with my life. The girl attacked like a wild leopard."

"I don't remember you being with any Carthaginian girl," Joseph interrupted the captain's reminiscence.

Shrugging his shoulders, Jacob laughed at his friend's inference. "You think you know everything about me," he quipped. "I admit we spent a lot of time together, but I also have a life of my own when I'm out soldiering. I met her when I was away doing my military training. She was absolutely beautiful. Her skin was brown like carob seeds, with hair like red silk and piercing green eyes."

"It sounds like you still lover her," Joseph responded as he listened to Jacob's description.

"Never found another woman that compared to her," Jacob sighed. "Couldn't marry anyone else but I couldn't marry her either. We would have ended up killing one another and I had enough fighting in the army without having to endure it at home as well."

"Sound more like she frightened you," I added my opinion. "You must have a spine like steel if you intend to marry a domineering woman. Especially one from North Africa!"

"I thought it would be the opposite," Joseph surmised. "I would have thought you'd have to be spineless in order to get along."

"Remind me son that later we must have that talk about marriage and selecting the right wife for you. I think it is long overdue if that's what you think. Give a brazen woman a spineless man and she'd just chew him up and spit him out. She would continue to do that for so long before she decides she's better off just throwing him out of the house and finding another man. A woman like that is looking for someone that will go toe to toe with her and not back down."

Joseph looked over at his longtime friend, scanning him up and down while he made a clucking sound with his tongue.

"And what is that supposed to mean," Jacob was curious.

"It means what it means," my son responded.

"You are beginning to sound more and more like a High Priest," Jacob cautioned him.

"You mean wise beyond my years?"

"No, I mean you are starting to act judgmental," Jacob replied.

"Oh, so that's what you think of me," I laughed knowing that my Captain had just let slip a sentiment that he probably wished he could retract.

"Of course, I didn't mean you, Excellency," he fumbled around searching for something pithy to say but his tongue was tied in knots.

"It's alright Jacob," I reassured him. "I'm supposed to be judgmental. You might say it is my job. After all, God didn't make the sons of Aaron high priests just so they could light candles and say a few prayers. We're here to judge. That's what we do. That is why we sit on all the courts of law in all our communities. Or at least I hope we still do, now that all of this has happened. I'm not too sure what our purpose will be from now on. I believe our future has changed."

"Excellency," Jacob was quick to respond. "You are the Kohen Gadol. You are the patriarch of our people. Yes, we are returning to Mesopotamia, but I swear to you, as God is my witness, sometime in the future your family will return to the Holy Land. We will rebuild the Temple and it will be even more glorious than the second Temple.

"I appreciate your enthusiasm," I praised him for his faith. "I too pray it will be so. I truly do, but to even think of such things when we are surrounded by death and destruction, pains me so and weakens my spirit."

"Then finish the story, Father. It only proves that we will return and rebuild because that is what we always do. Even if we have to fight a hundred wars in between, we always come back."

"Alright Joseph, I will finish the story but only because Jacob has never heard me tell it. So, like you past girlfriend Jacob, those from the colonies in North Africa can be a wild and terrifying lot."

"That's for certain," Jacob commented spontaneously, unable to hold back his words.

"My father sent them word to start an uprising, but never did he think that they would start a war. It was in the African province of Cyrenaica where the revolt was suddenly unleashed with a most terrifying and horrific intensity. Young Jewish rioters took to the streets of the provincial capital of Cyrene but rather than just being an unruly mob, somehow, they encountered a very determined man named Lukas, who saw this as an opportunity to create something far more than just a disturbance. I know very little of his background, but he had the mind of a military strategist and the heart of a lion that was bursting with hatred towards the Romans. Whatever his motivation, he was able to mold that mob into a fighting force that annihilated the Roman garrison within a day. Then he set the people against anything that was Greco-Roman, their statures, buildings, temples and government buildings. Everything was fair game as he left a trail of destruction wherever he took his rebels.

He forced the Romans in the city to fight as gladiators in the city's coliseum, much as they had done to the Jewish prisoners over the years. But once there was nothing left to destroy in Cyrene, no further resistance or opposition for the angry mob to tear to pieces, Lukas set his sights on Egypt, where my father's letter to the Jews of Alexandria had already spurred them to rebel against the Roman authorities. By the time Lukas and his blood thirsty civilian army reached that outskirts of the Egyptian city, the Roman Governor Marcus Rutilius Lupus had fled from the city along with his soldiers. Lukas was able to easily ignite old hatreds among the Alexandrian Jews towards their Gentile neighbors and immediately turned the city into a mirrored reflection of what he had accomplished in Cyrene. He set the city to the torch and even had the audacity to destroy Pompey the Greats tomb. By this time, the numbers of dead Romans and Greeks were numbering in the tens of thousands.

Upon hearing of the events that had transpired in Cyrenaica and Egypt, the Jews living on the Island of Cyprus quickly turned their modest uprising into another bloody revolt. There, they found their own version of Lukas, a man called Artemio. Under his command, they burnt the capital city of Salamis to the ground. And then something happened that my father did not anticipate. In his overwhelming desire to safeguard Judea, which had suffered so terribly in the first war, he did not send a letter to the council in Lydda to invoke any sort of civil unrest in the province. But news manages to travel swiftly and when the Jews of Judea, Samaria and Galilee heard what had happened around the Great Sea, two Jews named Julianus and Pappos, gathered their own rebel forces and seized the city of Lydda, making it their revolutionary capital.

I need you to open your mind and appreciate the absolute genius of my father's plan. Although he did not foresee this outcome, thinking only that the mobs would create sufficient headaches for the Emperor that he would never think of invading Parthia again in his lifetime, it was suddenly feasible that these revolts could actually earn us our freedom. The Roman army at that time was stretched very thin with its forces spread thinly across Mesopotamia and in Britannia, where they were clashing with the populations of both those lands. Now, in an effort to restore peace in the Empire, Trajan would have to reassign some of those legions he was dependent on for his own survival and reassign them to the various areas of the uprising. In desperation, Trajan dispatched his own Praetorian Prefect Quintus Marcius Turbo with several legions under his command to put down the revolts in both Egypt and Cyrene. It took almost two years of bitter fighting before Turbo could claim victory but, in that time, Lukas and a remnant of his army had fled to Judea, where they intended to join forces with Julianus and Pappos.

By the fall of that year Turbo had completed his mopping up task in North Africa and General Quietus who had successfully retreated with those legions under his command from Mesopotamia, both of them now entered Judea with their armies in tow. In addition to their forces, Trajan ordered the transference of the VI Ferrata Legion to Judea. Once united, they placed Lydda under siege, attempting to starve the rebels into submission. Within the city, Rabbi Gamaliel, the second of that name, was present, and urged on the rebels even though he knew it was a desperate situation and in spite of the fact that he had always been a peace-loving man. It wasn't until the bone gnawing months of winter were almost over that the city finally fell. Rabbi Gamaliel fortunately had died several weeks before the eventual collapse and conquest of Lydda, so he did not suffer being tortured like those captured. Thousands of the rebels and hundreds of the defenders of the city were crucified, their bodies lining all the roads extending in every direction from Lydda.

When the revolts were finally suppressed, they say that there were two hundred and twenty thousand Greeks and Romans slaughtered in Egypt and Cyrene, and a further two hundred and forty thousand of the Gentiles perished in Cyprus. I cannot attest to how accurate the count may be, but I do know that we did not suffer losses anywhere close to the Gentiles. In truth, I can actually reflect back and say that as far as my father's plan went, it had been very successful. He did not calculate on a war of liberation; his only intent was to send a message to Trajan that we will no longer tolerate his oppression. Of course, the message may have been lost on the emperor because he never made it back to Rome, dying instead in Cilicia during his retreat. That part of the plan my father had not calculated. Hadrian was now crowned emperor.

Hadrian made it clear that he intended to treat us Jews differently, which was encouraging to both myself and my father. Just one year after his victories in Mesopotamia and Judea, Quietus fell out of favor with the new Emperor and was executed because he objected to the leniency that Hadrian displayed outwardly towards the Jews. The emperor ordered the release of Julianus and Pappos from prison. We even declared it a holiday on the 12th of Adar in Judea, two days before the festival of Purim, to celebrate their release, calling it the 'Day of Trajan'. What happened to them afterwards, I do not know. They both seem to have disappeared. Some say it was a ruse by Hadrian to suppress any further agitation and thoughts of insurrection by his Jewish subjects and that he later had both Julianus and Pappos slain in secret. From the events of these past few years, I would think it highly probable.

But as I reflect back, to recollections of that time, Hadrian even discussed the rebuilding of the Temple soon after his ascent to the throne. It was to be the dawn of a new age of reconciliation. His intent seemed genuine. In fact, prior to this war, when he was residing in Alexandria, he held regular meetings with Rabbi Joshua ben Hanania, where he repeatedly remarked and spoke of his respect and tremendous fondness for the Jewish people. His own confidant, Aquilius Antinous was likely the cause for his affinity. Aquilius, it is said was actually a Jew from Bythia, which makes sense, for how else could you explain that he was able to translate passages of the Torah into Greek for Hadrian. As both his confidant and advisor, Aquilius spoke in our favour repeatedly."

Both Joseph and Jacob began to snicker at the mention of the name Antinous.

"What do you find so amusing," I questioned them both.

"I'm sorry Father, but it was your use of the word confidant," Joseph apologized. "Everyone knows he was Hadrian's homosexual lover."

"It matters not," I commented. "Advisor, friend, lover, what they did was between them and my only concern was why after Antinous drowned did Hadrian's attitude towards us change so dramatically. We had no hand in the young man's death. A purely accidental death they concluded, yet following that event, Hadrian changed every edict he made that had benefited us. As much as I say there was no connection, every instinct in my body tells me there must have been one!"

"I have not heard you mention that before," Joseph responded to his father's suggestion. "Where did you get that idea from?"

"As usual, it came as a voice in the night. I prayed to God to give me some insight into the madness that befell us all and led us into this war, and in response I heard the name Antinous repeated when I was about to fall asleep."

"But what can we do about it now, Excellency, we are already on the road back to our homes in Babylon?" Jacob questioned. "It is too late to save anyone now. The slave sales are taking place in Hebron and Gaza. That is the other direction, and we could not possibly purchase the freedom of all of them."

"There is no one to save except my own peace of mind," I clarified my concern. "I need some answers before we return home."

"Pardon my saying so, Excellency, but if we wanted answers then we probably should have stayed in Jerusalem a little longer. I doubt we will find out anything of relevance along the way."

"Maybe not or perhaps destiny draws us this way," I suggested rather cryptically.

"Exactly what does that mean?" Joseph insisted on knowing.

"It means I heard a rumour, and we are going to check it out before we cross the provincial border."

"Well, that explains why you had us take the inland road rather than the coastal highway," my Captain had deduced that my selection of road north was not un-intentional. "The king's coastal road would have been much smoother and faster and with the winds blowing off the sea we wouldn't have been suffocating as much from this putrid air. So, are we to expect trouble along the way?"

"I doubt it, but it wouldn't hurt to ensure your men are prepared just in case."

"Are you going to tell us more about this rumour?"

My eldest son had always been the most impatient of the two boys. It's why I sent Azariah to the back of the caravan to watch over his mother. "No! I think I'm going to wait and see if it is true first."

"And what do you intend on doing to prove it is true," he continued his questioning.

"I intend to do nothing. If it is true, then I expect it will make itself known to me."

"Are we looking for a burning bush, Father," my son laughed, thinking his question had been most humorous.

"Perhaps we are," I responded, saying nothing further.

.

Chapter Two

The Road To B'nai Brak:

The caravan proceeded northwards, following the winding road as it traversed through small villages and towns, some of them consisting of only a few shanties and mud huts, therefore hardly worth even labeling them as a village. I was terribly saddened to see that the remaining inhabitants consisted primarily of the old and debilitated, the injured and the sick, the war having taken from them the best and most capable from both the last and the next generation. At least there were still the young children visible, running and playing as children do even in the worst of times, but now being cared for by their grandparents, their parents lost to the war and the purge. But children meant there would still be a lifeline within our Holy Land. A new generation to come and one after that and so on. L'oylum Va'ed, as our expression claimed; forever and ever. All had not been lost. We would repopulate our land as we had done so many times before. Jerusalem may have become the abomination of desolation but eventually our Holy City would return to our control. Rome would not last forever. Every empire eventually crumbles into dust and is blown away by the wind. That is the reality; that is the promise which God made to us and He will never forsake us. Perhaps that is why so many nations have been determined to obliterate us, to wipe our existence from the face of the earth, because our existence reminds them of how fleeting their own lifespan is in the overall scheme of time. They measure their civilizations on a scale of hundreds of years, whereas my people measure existence against a framework of passing civilizations.

Egypt watched as we slaved upon their pyramids, only to witness their monuments become worn away by wind and sand but we persisted. The Assyrians and the Babylonians came, only to discover their civilizations were measured in a few centuries, yet we remained. The Persians and the Greeks came, bringing their enlightenment to the world only to find the candle shedding that light melted away so that their memories are barely illuminated, as we raised our own kingdom on this Earth once again. Now it is the Romans and the Parthians, and we will watch them both pass before our eyes like fluttering moths, attracted to the flames until they get too close and their wings are singed. All have come and all have gone in the blink of an eye, but we remain. Can they not see that is the way it is meant to be? Others will come and they will attempt to exterminate us but no matter how often they come, they will not succeed. Only when we reach the end of time will they recognize the futility of opposing an unseen power far greater than the sum of our people. But unfortunately for them, that revelation will come too late to have been of any benefit.

I do not know why it seems that we suffer continually for our beliefs. Why the world becomes so upset that we follow a different path. You would think that we are so minor in manipulating world events that we would not even be given notice, but here we are once again, taking on the present masters of the world, against phenomenal odds and surviving to tell the tale. That is not to say that God commends us for what we have done. No, he condemns us harshly and makes us pay with excruciating hardship and pain because clearly it was not his intention that we do these things without His approval. Therein lies the problem because so many took up the cause, to fight for the liberation of the people, strapping a sword to their belt, only to lose their lives because they thought and honestly believed they had been directed to do so by Him. How could we have been so wrong. One thing our history has taught us is that many will share in the benefits of the One but just as equally, many will be made to suffer for the One as well. The world is a dichotomy, and the Almighty lets us choose without interference. For when he sent us Moses to follow, He blessed us exceedingly, rewarding us with His favour and His love. Yet at the same time he sent us Dathan, and those that followed Dathan were punished severely. Why does He test us constantly if He already knows we are subject to human frailties and foibles. When a good King sat on the throne in Judea, the Lord lavished us with peace and prosperity, but then would come a king that was evil and corrupt and as a nation we all paid the price for that one individual. If there is a lesson to be learned here, then I cannot determine what it is. I know He is telling me that once again it was necessary to punish us for our sins but how could a revolt against the Romans be anything but a good thing if it was done to preserve our religious freedom and restore the Temple? Or was this to be my undoing. Did I bring this tragedy down upon our heads because I, Elioneai ben Yosef of the House of Phiabi, the family of Aaron, the one true High Priest of Israel refused to give my support to the rebels? Because I did not believe strongly enough that the Almighty would deliver us in our hour of need? Tell me truthfully Lord, are the deaths of over half a million Jews because my faith failed you? Please Lord, I'm begging you, tell me!

I was so caught up in the web of my thoughts that the reigns of my animal had gone limp in my hands. I wasn't even aware that my mule was continuing down the road of its own accord. It was then that I felt the reigns being pulled suddenly free of my hands as the mule was brought to a sudden halt.

"Excellency," Jacob's voice suddenly broke through my suspended state of my mind. "Are you all right? Is something wrong?"

I shook my head, wrenching myself back to reality. "I'm fine," I responded. "Just a little tired I guess."

"Or a lot tired," Jacob snapped his comment back quickly. "You almost trampled the old lady under you mule's feet."

I looked ahead and saw that he was right. There, standing but inches away in front of my animal was an old lady that I had not even noticed. How could I have been so stupid as to place this woman's life in danger because I was too busy wallowing in self-doubt? As much as I must have appeared frightened for the sake of the old lady's well-being, the fact that she was almost trampled didn't appear to phase her at all."

"A blessed holy charm to assure you safety on your journey, my Lord?" she held up several small bags dangling from her fingers for me to observe.

"Do you know..." I interrupted Jacob before he could finish making his pronouncement.

"Yes, I am just a weary traveler on the road with my merchant caravan," I informed her so that Jacob was aware that I did not wish to have my identity disclosed.

"So, what do you have there?" I asked as sincerely as I could, intending to sound like an interested customer.

Then the gray-haired woman, probably mid-fifties in my assessment stepped to the right side of my mule so that I could see the items more closely. There were a variety of trinkets, some appearing to be little bags containing small pieces of parchment, other items looking to be no more than a few beads strung along on a thin red thread, while a few of the other items appeared to be miniature carvings of mythological creatures. Those last few items were unexpected. I would not have thought anyone would have considered them suitable for religious   tokens. "So how much are you looking for in return for each type," I asked.

Now the woman seemed much younger in the manner in which she moved, excited by the prospect of a potential sale. "The beads are a zuz for one string," she responded, "but the prayer bags and zodiac symbols, they are two zuz each."

"Two denarii," I responded. "That is a lot for a piece of paper with some writing from some unknown scribe."

"Not some unknown," she lectured me, "But a great Sage. The greatest of our time!"

"I'm afraid dear madame that there are no great sages left. The Romans have slaughtered most and those they haven't are prohibited from teaching the religion any longer."

Jacob was about to signal the caravan to move on when the woman suddenly reached upward and grabbed the halter of my mule. "I speak the truth my Lord. He has come back to us and has sworn to help restore our community. He blesses these charms for us to sell. He gives us hope."

"And in return, how much does he take," I asked rather sarcastically, knowing full well that of all the learned men I have met in the past, it is only the rare exception that performs any religious duty for free."

"It is not like that, my Lord. He asks for nothing personally. Only that a third of the profits from what we sell is given to re-establish the school in B'nai Brak. It is a worthy cause my Lord."

"Yes, it is," I nodded in agreement. "So, what blessings do you have on those pieces of parchment for a weary traveler like myself."

The smile on her face practically stretched from ear to ear. It was obvious that she was not selling too many of the trinkets recently and I would be having a significant impact on her livelihood by buying one.

"There are blessings to ensure you have a safe journey. That is this one," she pointed to one of the small pouches hanging from her right index finger. "But there are others to guarantee that your travels for business will be   successful and this one to protect you from illness."

"What is the use of these zodiac signs," I inquired. "Did he bless those too?"

"Of course," she was quick to reply. "It is our most sacred and honoured duty now to restore the population having lost so many of our sons in the war."

"So, what will these little images do, make you fertile?" I said somewhat in jest.

"Not only fertile but you pick the sign of the month that you want to have the child and charm will make it come true." I could tell that she strongly believed in what she was saying.   Her belief in this Sage was extraordinary.

"And what do the beads on the threads do?" I pretended not to know of their origins; a fable invented Ben Shetah almost three hundred years ago.

"These will protect you from demons," she answered, her voice almost a whisper as if she was afraid she would be overheard by evil forces.

"Demons?" I scoffed.   "I don't believe in demons."

"Not so loud, my Lord."   She placed a finger to her lips, warning me to speak the word quietly.   "I can assure you they exist.   The Sage saw them with his very own eyes at Beithar.   It was not the Romans that slaughtered our brave young men but their demon allies.   No army of men could have defeated us so the Romans made a pact with the demon hordes."

"But this Sage, he managed to escape?" I asked more out of curiosity to see if she could shed any light on how that was possible.

"It was a miracle," she exclaimed.   "It was days before the demons rose up out of the ground to kill our poor boys. Our holy Sage was asleep in the room that he shared with one of the other great men of the Sanhedrin, when suddenly there appeared a bright light that filled the room.   He opened his eyes thinking that the Romans had set fire to their fortress but instead he saw the angel Gabriel standing before him."

Jacob cleared his throat loudly while rolling his eyes upward as he did so, signaling that he had listened to enough of this nonsense but I flashed him a stern look to be quiet and let her finish. I was very interested in what she had to say.   "Go on," I insisted.

She ignored my Captain's rude interruption and continued, "He trembled in fear before the Lord's messenger, knowing that Gabriel's role is to herald the dead entering into Heaven.   'Have you come to tell me that we are all going to die here at Beithar,' he asked.   The angel shook his head and told him that it was not his time to die and he was sent to usher him to safety because God had much more for him to do before he departed this world. 'But what about everyone else,' the Great Sage inquired but Gabriel shook his head.   He could only ferry one person from the fortress.   'Not even my companion?' he pleaded for the safety of the other rabbi that still remained asleep in the room.   But again, the angel shook his head, saying that once the demons are raised from their domain in Ghenna, it is a requirement that they must satiate their blood lust before they can be returned from whence they came.   Only in the final battle at the End of Days will it be possible to slay the forces of Hell.   This was not to be that time," he said.

"But how could this Sage you speak of, escape?" I needed her to keep talking until she had revealed everything to me. "Beithar was surrounded. The Romans had sealed off all the routes in and out months earlier. So, I don't understand how he could escape from the city. It was impossible!"

The woman laughed at my confusion. "You know nothing of angels my Lord. Gabriel simply picked the Sage up under the arms and flew him out of the city. Angels have wings, you know."

"Of course! I should have known better. How could I forget, the answer was so simple. Angels have wings, everyone knows that. And then what?"

"He was found lying face down in the middle of the road to B'nai Brak by some of the townsfolk. They thought he was dead because even after they prodded him, he did not move. So, then they poured some water over his head and suddenly he revived. At first, he did not know who he was or even where he was. When the people asked him how it came to be that he was lying in the middle road, he could not tell them. They suggested that perhaps he had encountered robbers along the road and they left him there thinking that they had killed him. But when they examined his face, neck and hands they could find no marks or wounds to suggest so. Then he suddenly shouted the word Beithar, catching them all by surprise. 'What is the news of Beithar?' he inquired. The city has fallen they told him. Everyone was slain they said, at which point he rent his clothes and spread the dust of the road upon his head, crying as he did so. That is when he remembered how he came to be on the road, and they brought him into B'nai Brak where he has remained ever since."

"It is an incredible story," I said to the woman.

"And every word of it the truth, my Lord. I swear I have told it exactly as it was told to me."

"Of that I have no doubt. There can be no doubt that such a man is certainly blessed by God," I commented.

"His entire life he has been a man of God," the woman continued to tell his story. "Just as David was raised by God from being a lowly shepherd boy to be king over our nation, so to was he taken from watching over his master's flock of sheep to be a holy shepherd over the people. Now you can see how his blessing over these items are guaranteed to provide you with the benefits they promise along your journey."

"I have no doubt about it," I concurred. "I would appreciate if I could talk to the people that found him on the road," I noticed that she frowned, suspecting that I didn't fully believe what she had described to me but needed further confirmation. "Please don't misunderstand me. It is not because I have any doubts about what you told me. I'm hoping that they can perhaps add more details that you may not have known. The more I can learn about this miracle, the more I will be able to assess if B'nai Brak is now truly a blessed place. It will help me decide if I should also invest in this school, you say is being built."

"Not being built," she corrected me. "The school has been built for a long time but now it is his plan to turn it into an academy for the training of new Rabbis. It will rival Jamnia."

"A rival to Jamnia, I am impressed." I tried to sound excited. "That will be quite an achievement. So, do you know the names of the people that found him? It will be important in making my decision about what to do if I can hear what they have to say."

She scratched the top of her head through the blue scarf that she was wearing in an attempt to recall their names. "There was Shimon bar Benjamin. He's one of the butchers in the city. But I don't buy my meat from him. I don't trust his scales. I think he has weighted them in some manner. The portions get smaller while the price keeps going higher. Asshur ben Ishmael. He doesn't do much at all if you ask me. He says he is involved with trading, but I've never seen him work a day in his life. Spends most of his time sitting outside the synagogue gossiping like an old woman." She laughed at the comment she just made. "Not that I spend all my time gossiping," she tried to assure me. And Menachem...ben...ben...I'm not certain who his father is. But you can find him working at the mill. There was a fourth man, but he wasn't from around here. Just stayed the day to make certain that the Sage was alright and then he went on his way. But he wouldn't be able to tell you anything different from the other three, so I guess it's not that important that you speak to him."

"That is a shame," I said. "Who knows what this fourth man had to say. Perhaps he had other knowledge to divulge. He never gave a name you say. How odd."

"It was not as if we didn't ask," she replied. "But each time we did, he would simply tell us that he was 'the other' man. I guess he wished to keep his name a secret for some reason."

I bowed my head in gratitude to her for the information she provided. She had done me a greater favour than she could ever realize.

"Hey, what about buying one of the charms, my Lord," she reminded me of her original purpose in stepping in front of my mule.

"What if I was to buy all of them?   Would five shekels be enough to purchase everything?"

"Five shekels, my Lord," the woman was practically ecstatic.   "That will be more than enough," she responded.   It was probably more money than she had seen in a very long time.

I reached into my purse and pulled out five tetradrachms from Tyre and handed them to the old woman. Almost immediately she put each one in her mouth to see if she could bite into it.   As soon as she finished teething on each one, that huge grin that I had witnessed earlier was now spreading from ear to ear. She removed all the trinkets from her hands and fingers and handed them to me.   I looked back at Jacob to see the look of shock and concern on his face.   He thought I had gone mad.   "One more thing," I spoke to the woman more seriously this time.   "Is there a priest still in charge of your synagogue?"

"Yes, my Lord," she responded.

"Since you have nothing left to sell, can you do me the favour and go directly to the synagogue and let the priest know he will be having guests tonight. Tell him Elioneai ben Yosef, High Priest of Israel will be lodging in the synagogue annex with my family and colleagues.   We will need a bed for seven of us while my captain and his men will set up barracks in a neighbouring field."

From the look on her face, I thought the woman might be having a heart attack. Never in her wildest dreams did she think the man buying all her blessed items would be the Kohen Gadol, even though without a Temple, there was no such thing as a Kohen Gadol any longer. "Are you alright?" I asked her as the shock slowly faded from her face.

"Yes, yes, Excellency," she practically stammered as she wobbled on her feet. "Please excuse any insult this foolish old woman may have committed to offend you." She reached towards me to grab my robe, placing it to her lips and kissing its fringes.

"You have done me no offense," I told her.   "Instead, you have done me a great service."   I placed my right hand gently atop her head.   "A blessing upon your house and may any of the losses you have suffered as a result of this war be replenished. Blessed is Our Lord, King of the Universe."

"Baruch atah adonai, melech ha oylum," the woman repeated as tears streamed from her eyes. "I will tell the priest immediately," she said as she took off practically at a running pace towards the city. She was definitely younger than she looked.

"Do you mind telling me what that was all about, Excellency," Jacob stared at me as if I had lost my mind.

"What?" I asked nonchalantly as if I didn't have a clue as to what he might be referring to.

"Excellency, help me understand. You just gave this woman five tetradrachm for a bunch of useless trinkets and mindless scribbles on paper. Are you feeling alright? Perhaps we have spent too much time in the sun and you need to rest."

"I am feeling better than I have in a long time, Jacob. Don't you worry. The Almighty has sent me the sign I prayed for. He did not abandon me. This woman was sent by God in answer to my beseeching Him to provide an answer in my hour of desperation."

Now Jacob was looking extremely worried. "Excellency, let me help you back to the wagon. Perhaps you need to lay down for a while. "

"Don't patronize me, Jacob. Instead, tell everyone to dismount and find me some rocks. I wish to set up a shrine on this spot." My request left my Captain even more dazed and confused.

"I don't understand Excellency. What are you not telling me?"

"For months now I have been concerned that the deaths of my people have been the result of my failure to support them in their war against the Romans. I had come to the point that I believed if I had just given them my blessing the outcome of the war would have been different."

"That is ridiculous, Excellency," Jacob tried to assure me. "Even if they didn't have your blessing, they still had received the same from the other high priest."

"My cousin is nothing but a fool and an impostor. Eleazar is as much a High Priest as you are," I corrected him.

"I did not say he was the High Priest, Excellency. I just inferred he was a high priest and that meant they had someone from your family to deliver the blessing whether it was of any value or not. Our soldiers fought bravely and without fear because they still had a blessing from the House of Phiabi. You are not trained as a warrior Excellency so I'm not expecting you to fully comprehend what I am about to say. As a soldier, when we go to battle, if we believe that we have received a sign or omen from God, it does not matter who instilled that belief into us, only that we believe it to be true. So, whether Eleazar ben Azariah was the anointed Kohen Gadol of God or not, the fact was that he gave them the priestly blessing and in the minds of the warrior, that is all that matters."

"You have missed my point," I tried to make him understand. "It was not about what any of the soldiers believed, it was what in my mind I believed to be true. I had come to think that I had failed them and that I could have made a difference. That somehow victory or defeat rested entirely upon my shoulders, and I was too frightened to take that responsibility. To think that the deaths of all those men, woman and children could have been prevented if I had only acted more forcefully in either direction is a terrible burden to bear. Perhaps if I had tried harder, I could have stopped the war all together. On the other hand, perhaps if I became more involved after the war broke out, I could have assured them a victorious outcome. In either scenario, I am left to question if I could have done more."

"So now you are saying, Excellency, because of two handfuls of worthless charms and tokens you have your answer from God? Is this what you are telling me?" Jacob sounded very dubious about my belief either way. It always amazed me how others could not see what those in my family could always see so clearly. My father tried to explain it to me that it was one of the many gifts that God had given to the sons of Aaron. The ability to see with clarity through the smoke and lies and obfuscation that others built their existence upon. Where others see only the clouds, we could see the sun that shone just as brightly behind them. Without that clarity, I found that we spent more time trying to explain a multitude of things to others rather than actually doing something. It looked like this time would be no different.

"What I hold in my hand is evidence. Now I understand that whatever path I chose it was not going to make any difference."

Jacob looked even more confused, now that I had provided him with an answer. "I don't quite understand, Excellency," he struggled with my enigma.

"Trust me. Once we have stayed several days in B'nai Brak you will understand completely. Now have your men dismount and find me some suitable stones as I requested."

Calling the High Priests guard to gather around him, their Captain explained the latest task that he had been assigned. Many had never seen a stone shrine built before and therefore had no idea what kind of stones were required. Jacob relied on his knowledge of what he had seen in the past. They were to be broad and flat, heavy enough that they could not be easily removed, and colourful enough that they attracted attention.

The townspeople gathered around as I knelt in my striped robes on the ground and started piling the stones into a spiraling tower about six feet high. Most had no clue as to what I was doing but they were polite and said nothing. It was only when a young boy, perhaps no more than seven years old, finally asked a question and broke the eerie silence. "Mister, what are you doing?" That is when everyone else in the crowd began to mumble, indicating that they had the very same question on their minds.

"Be it known that on this spot, the Lord Most High, sent Elioneai ben Yosef, High Priest of Israel and of the House of Phiabi, a message in answer to his prayers through the embodiment of one of your very own citizens. Though she may not have realized what she had said or done, let all come to know that Yahvu has found favour in His eyes for B'nai Brak and your city will exist forever as it is. Even when others come to rule over the land in the future, they will not dare to change the name of your city for fear that they will be cursed. Thus, with this shrine, the Lord extends his protection over you now and forever. Know that your children and your children's children and their children long afterwards will always be safe as long as they remain connected to this soil." Having pronounced the blessing of the shrine, I rose from the ground and remounted my mule. The people were excited by the revelation of good news after having suffered so much over the past several years. You could see the joy in their faces, and the sheer relief of finally hearing some good news. If we were to survive as a people, then not only their souls had to be nurtured but their spirits also had to be raised.

Chapter Three

The Synagogue of B'nai Brak:

As we rode through the streets, the caravan was met with a hail of Hallelujahs and joyful Shalom Aleichems voiced enthusiastically by the people that had come out to greet us. I had not realized that my actions via the shrine I erected had sparked a festival that night. It was already planned that the citizenry would feast and drink long into the wee hours of the morning. It was to be a celebration of the likes they had not experienced since before the war. Meanwhile, my wagons and entourage continued to make its way to the city's old synagogue with the help of numerous people pointing us in the right direction.

Standing in the courtyard, nervously waiting for us was the local priest. He was as thin as a rake, looking frail as if he had not had a decent meal in ages. His beard was white, reaching his chest but neatly trimmed. He wore a white linen cap and a simple white linen robe that reached down to his cloth shoes. From the way his hands fidgeted, I doubt he had too many guests of my stature. It was obvious the woman I encountered had done as she was instructed. "Hail and welcome to you Elioneai ben Yosef, Son of Aaron, in the name of God to our humble synagogue. Peace be with you."

"And Peace be with you too, brother" I responded. "Are you Kohen or Levite?" I asked as was the common courtesy to determine how we would address each other throughout the evening.

"I am your loyal servant, a humble Levite, Master. My name is Yehonatan ben Matthias. My family has lived here and cared for this synagogue for centuries."

"No need for calling me Master. You are my right hand and my equal in piety. The Lord has ensured that the tithes apply to both our families. We are weary from our travels. I hope we will not be too much of an intrusion and a burden for you during our stay."

"There is plenty of room in the synagogue's annex building," Yehonatan indicated, pointing to the enormous empty building erected immediately along-side the main synagogue structure.

"It is quite large," I commented, curious as to its origins because the truth was that the building practically dwarfed the synagogue that it was intended to be an appendage to.

"When the Pharisaic sages first arrived at B'nai Brak over a century ago, they had no school built yet for their students. The synagogue had an old, much smaller annex building which they expanded, calling it a temporary accommodation until such time they could build their school. Of course, the school never got built, so the annex continued to expand and continued to grow while it served us over the years."

"Well, it will serve us well during our stay. I thank you very much Yehonatan for your hospitality."

"It is my honour, pleasure and duty to serve you Excellency," the elderly man bowed his head.

"Please, we are family, are we not, cousin? Elioneai will suffice. Is there a laver of water where we can wash the dust of the road from our hands?"

"Of course, Excellency. All has been prepared." I gave Yehonatan a cold stare and then burst into laughter. "I mean, Elioneai," he corrected himself and then laughed as well. "Follow me and I will show everyone where they can wash and then I will take you to your rooms." For an elderly man he moved quite spritely as he marched in front of us. I motioned for Joseph and Azariah to go fetch everyone else from the wagons so that they could wash away the dirt accumulated from their days of travel, at which point I trailed after Yehonatan as he led me towards the location of the laver.

Fed from a cold underground spring, the water in the laver was crystal clear and refreshing. I readily splashed it on my face and across the back of my neck, letting the droplets trickle beneath my tunic. The cool water instantly provided some relief from the grueling heat of the day. Before long I could hear the rest of my party arriving.

"Yehonatan, permit me to introduce my darling wife, Deborah."

"It is a pleasure Madame to have the wife of the High Priest stay with us." Yehonatan bowed, making no effort to extend his hand or in any way make physical contact with my wife. The Levites had been taught to consider all woman to be unclean unless they knew specifically the timing of their cycle. Not a question you could actually ask when first meeting someone. It did not dawn on him that I was bound by the same restriction and I held Deborah's hand when she stood by my side. My wife was used to our priestly custom so she paid it no mind.

"And these are my two sons. My eldest Joseph and his younger brother Azariah." Yehonatan exchanged greetings and then they each seized each other above the wrists of the right hand in the customary salutation.

"And this is…"

The Levite did not even let me finish as he raced forward to greet his next guest, staring upwards in fascination as he began to speak. "This man or giant or should I say giant of a man, can only be the famed Abba Saul bar Nash," he announced excitedly. "It is an honour good Sir. What they say is true. You truly are the tallest man in all of Israel."

"Perhaps even the tallest man in the world," I suggested. I was not exaggerating. Abba Saul stood almost eight feet tall, with long gangly arms and legs that never seemed to end. Even though he was not a rabbi, he was still very well respected among scholars of the Torah. He had been a young boy at the time that the Temple was destroyed but his mind has remained sharp, and he can still recall watching many of the religious services that took place in the Temple. In many ways he was considered the antithesis or bane of all the learned rabbis he ever engaged with. There was a phrase that he was best known for uttering, that being, *"Morality Is greater than learning."* It was his way of telling all of those pompous and self-glorifying rabbis that doing what was right was more important than just moving their lips and telling all the people what God wanted them to do. Many resented him for it because it implied they were hypocrites, but none would dare say a word because of his close relationship to the past presidents of the Sanhedrin and then the Rabbinical Council and lastly with Rabbi Simeon ben Gamaliel, who disappeared into hiding during the war and still has not been seen. I had the pleasure of enjoying Abba Saul's company in Jerusalem and when he mentioned that he would like to see the Jewish schools or yeshivas we had established in Babylon, I invited him to journey with us.

After Abba Saul finally managed to tear his arm away from the surprisingly firm grip of Yehonatan who still stood in awe, I introduced the others that traveled in our party. "This is Simon Ben Azzai and that is Simon ben Zoma. Both of these men are experts in what is known as theosophic Judaism. They claim to see things that lay behind the words of the Torah," I explained to the priest. "Secret messages and secret codes delivered by God and waiting to be deciphered."

Yehonatan found the description amusing as he greeted the other two rabbis.

"You believe that God has been cryptic regarding his messages to us through the Torah. Hiding His true teachings intentionally. Is that correct?"

"Not necessarily cryptic, only that He wanted us to see more. To expand our senses in order to appreciate what he has given us," Ben Zoma replied.

"I am not certain that I understand," Yehonatan apologized.

"For example," Ben Zoma tried to explain. "We all believe God gave to Moses ten commandments on Mount Sinai. Correct?"

"Yes, that is true." Yehonatan responded immediately. "Are you implying there were more?"

"Well, what about the commandment that you must do all ten of these. Not nine out of ten or eight out of ten. Ten meant ten. So even though the eleventh commandment wasn't written, we take it for granted that it exists. True?"

"True," Yehonatan replied hesitantly. "But do we really need another commandment to tell us not to overlook any of the ten. Wouldn't it be understood to be naturally implied?"

I immediately slapped my forehead but tried to conceal my action doing so. I knew exactly how this discussion was going to go now that Yehonatan had asked that question. I had been through this same discussion numerous times.

"People don't always see the obvious," Ben Azzai piped in his comment.

"It cannot be expected that the people will know God's intentions unless you actually determine what is the Lord's intentions. And to do that you must see what the Lord has hidden in His own words to guide us clearly."

Yehonatan glanced over at me as if to ask if these two were actually serious about this or merely having a jest at his expense. I rolled my eyes upwards as if to say that now that he had opened this Pandora's box, he had to see it through.

"Or what about I am the Lord your God and you shall have no other God but me," Ben Zoma continued. "Is that really two commandments or are they just part of one? If just one, then what happened to the other commandment that would be missing if that is the case because then there would only be ten. Did we lose one? But if they are two separate commandments, why repeat them. Is there something else that the Lord wants us to understand by them. Is he implying that there are other deities, perhaps not as powerful as he is, but still in existence? Or is it a reference to an entire realm of supernatural beings, such as angels and demons that are often mistaken for being as powerful as God? Unless we analyze what has been said very carefully, we may never know His true intent. There are so many mysteries that need to be followed; so little time."

I could see that Simon ben Azzai was already preparing to add his own opinion to this discussion but I felt it necessary to put an end to it as soon as possible, otherwise we would never eat. "Ben Azzai has his own insights by which to compare the two points of view. But I must warn you, if you listen to them for too long it will corrupt your own way of thinking. Perhaps you can engage in a discussion of such matters at a later time. Yet I do find these theosophical discussions very interesting at night, when one is not yet ready to sleep. It helps me close my eyes far more easily. So, I've invited them to ride along with us until we reach the border." Everyone had a little laugh at my joke regarding my companions, even though it was at their expense, and I was being serious. They practically cured my insomnia.

"Greeting good Sirs," Yehonatan welcomed them to his abode, pointing to the laver where they all could wash. Do you need time to rest or shall we begin to eat as soon as you have put your belongings in your rooms?"

"I think we are all looking forward to some good food and some good wine," I answered on behalf of my party. "The sooner the better."

Having said that, Yehonatan took us into the Annex where we were assigned our rooms and left our belongings behind as we followed him down a passageway and into the expansive dining area of the synagogue.

"I'm impressed once again," I admitted to him. "It is not customary for these small-town synagogues to have a rectory with both a galley and dining hall intended to serve so many guests." We all sat down around a long cedar wood table with benches on either side. Several of the women from the village had come to cook our food tonight in the well-equipped kitchen and were now emerging from the galley with trays and trays of food.

"As I mentioned, Exc…"

I held up my finger to silence him mid-sentence.

He knew immediately why I had stopped him. "As I mentioned Elioneai, it was the intention that the synagogue serve as the temporary residence for all the students belonging to the rabbis. Not only did they expand the annex but they had to increase the size of all the ancillary service areas as well."

The town's woman spread the plates of food all around the table. There were a variety of vegetables, cheeses and fish, all prepared and seasoned with the utmost care. Having been on the road so long everything they offered I knew would taste phenomenal.

"Shall you say the blessings, Yehonatan," I asked and instructed at the same time.

Reciting the three blessings over bread, wine and food from the earth, it was time to eat.

"Absolutely delicious, Yehonatan. I must admit that you eat very well here."

The Levite laughed at my comment. "I eat very well here because of my special guests," he insisted. "Most nights my meal consists of a little cheese on bread with a cup of water. I am left to prepare my own meals, though on some occasions I will admit the townspeople do bring me food. But from what I heard on the streets, the citizens of B'nai Brak say that you did a very special thing for them today and in gratitude they wanted to show their appreciation. Believe me when I say, we will consider ourselves lucky if we should eat this well tomorrow. As for your men outside, have no worries. They won't be eating as well as us but they will be taken care of and their animals will receive fresh water and hay."

"I don't know how I will ever repay you for your kind hospitality Yehonatan. I am certain all of my companions feel the same way. This meal is a most delightful surprise."

"A toast to our Levite host," Abba Saul raised his cup to the priest. We all followed suit and raised our cups. "May the Lord bless you all the days of your life. May He who created the fruit of the vine make your remaining days just as fruitful."

"Amen," we all said in unison.

"Of course, fruitful can be interpreted in several ways," Ben Zoma began his usual introspection of the possible meanings of Abba Saul's blessing. "Now he could be referring to the seasons the vine cycles through during its lifetime, thereby he is wishing you a very long life. Or he could be using the term fruitful as in meaning prolific, so now he is wishing upon you many wives and many children."

"Not to mention," Ben Azzai interrupted, "He could be indicating the stage of life you are in as in the cycle of life of the budding flower, followed by development of the fruit, only to followed by the shriveling of the plant once it is past its time. A reflection of how life begins tasteless, only to become sweet and then sour in our old age."

"Now you can understand why I have these two as my companions on the road, Yehonatan. Even on the most boring of days they can manage to make it challenging. Honestly, I think I will be sad when we have to part on our separate ways," Upon reflection, I know that I truly meant it. They had provided me with insights that I had never considered before.

"Which brings me to a question Elioneai, if you don't mind me asking."

"You are our host, Yehonatan. You can ask of me whatever you wish," I replied.

"That being the case, then I have two questions."

Spoken like a true Levite I thought to myself. One is never enough.

"Why are you here and why did you really set up the shrine along the road into B'nai Brak?"

Obviously, the priest guessed that my trip had nothing to do with exchanging pleasantries for the evening. He may have been elderly, but his mind was astute. I watched as he reached under his linen cap to wipe the sweat from his brow and I knew immediately that he was concerned about his own welfare and continued status as the local priest.

"Be reassured Yehonatan, my visit has nothing to do with you if that is what you were thinking. I am here simply because of a rumor." There was the sound of several surprised 'ahhhs' from my companions. Even my wife and sons were caught unawares by my answer. "I am sorry everyone for not having confided in you earlier. I know that this may have caught you off guard and now you are wondering what plan I may have conceived in my mind that I have involved you in without your consent. I could not say anything until I was certain, so I chose not to say anything at all."

"Certain of what?" Abba Saul was quick to ask before the others could even say a word.

"This rumor said that there was someone in this town that could not possibly be here. Or should I say more correctly, should not be here."

My answer had definitely grabbed their attention. "All that remains is for me to confirm my suspicion. Yehonatan, who is the Sage that the woman was referring to that has returned to your town? It is obvious that he has all your townspeople excited about the rebuilding of a rabbinical school here, so I suspect the rumor I heard is true."

The Levite looked surprised that I would even ask that question, his expression indicating that he had taken it to be a well-known and widespread fact. "It is Akiva ben Joseph, of course. Surely you would all know that. How else could he be here? Why would you call it a rumor?"

"How else indeed?" I questioned in return.

"Akiva is alive?" Abba Saul sounded equally shocked and surprised as I was when I first heard it said, practically falling out of his chair as the information sunk in.

"An impossibility," Ben Zoma refused to believe it at first but then his mind attempted to analyze the situation. "Except an impossibility means it could be the result of a miracle. Only a miracle could create an impossibility. But a miracle implies it is for the good of all not just the good of one. Of course, a school is for many but not as many as the ones that were lost." Simon ben Zoma wrestled with the conundrum of separating a miracle from the impossible and it was clearly obvious his mind was struggling with reality.

"Brother," Simon ben Azzai interceded. "What if it was not a miracle but simply good fortune. Akiva has lived his entire life as if he was born beneath a lucky star. The man has gone from being a simple, illiterate and uneducated shepherd to being the most respected mind for the interpretation of the law. Not to mention rich beyond most men's wildest dreams. To go from nothing to everything certainly implies he is blessed with luck!"

"Luck is simply an excuse for being unable to determine what has actually happened," Ben Zoma fought back. "It could only have been a miracle because no one escaped alive from Beithar."

"At least no one of importance, you mean," Abba Saul corrected him. "Those of no consequence were taken for the slave markets."

"Father," Joseph tugged at the sleeve of my robe. "Why did you not mention this earlier to me? You must have known that everyone in the caravan was questioning why you decided to take the inland road, but no one dared to ask."

"If you had asked," I responded, "What was I to say? That I have been made aware of a rumor of something that should not have been possible. That I needed to see with my own eyes and hear with my own ears if it was true. You all would have thought me mad. Even I was beginning to think that I was suffering from dementia, the stress of guilt weighing too heavily on my mind."

"Is this guilt you speak of why you set up that shrine?" Abba Saul wanted to know. "Personally, I can see absolutely no reason why you should feel guilty, Excellency," Abba Saul confronted me. As a close friend, I had previously expressed my dark thoughts to him.

"I think you know why. Because in our time of need, I was not equal to being the man my father was when we went to war twenty years ago." I choked on the words as I tried to release them from my mouth. "He wasn't even trying to start a war and he managed to bring the Roman Empire to its knees. This time we went to war and I could not give it my blessing or support."

"Because you thought we could achieve our goals without shedding our own blood. Simeon ben Gamaliel thought the same way. So did many of the others. Choosing peace over war is not a sin." Abba Saul was not prepared to listen to my second guessing of my past decisions.

"But I am left wondering if we could almost destroy Rome with the High Priest's support and direction when we weren't even at war, as was the case with my father, what could have been achieved if I had lent my support in a real war such as the one we just faced. It has haunted me ever since the tide of battle turned against us. Perhaps God abandoned us because I did not provide my support."

"Now you are thinking like some of the others, "Abba Saul scolded me. "You think the Lord really creates the reality of this world based on what you think? Those like Akiva, I know think that way. That if they decide something is good based on the teaching of the Torah then God must listen to them. No! You are wrong! We do not create God in our own image. God does as He believes. We either accept it or we admit that we are like Elisha ben Abuyah and don't believe in God at all. For you to think that you had the power to sway God one way or another is not only supreme arrogance, it is downright heresy!"

"But why have I felt so lost for so long," I questioned. "Why did I feel as if I had abandoned my people in their hour of need?"

"Because of whom and what you are," Abba Saul calmed down and answered in a quieter tone. "The moral nature of man must always prevail," Abba Saul consoled in his customary manner, "And you Excellency are a moral man. If you cannot be true to your nature, then you are doomed to wander in darkness. Every moral man seeks a solution other than warfare because that is God's way. Even when it is only the slimmest of possibilities, you are bound to seek it. And that is how you know that you are created in God's image and not the opposite as those others choose to believe. You were true to your nature, a nature nurtured in the image of the Lord of the Universe, and therefore no fault can ever be counted against you."

"Can the fight for our freedom always be reduced so simply to a moral issue of right and wrong? I would think that in the desire to be free is also instilled within us by God and therefore there will always be shades of gray that require us to perform acts that cannot be deemed as moral and perhaps may even border on being sinful. Is that not so Abba?"

He stroked his long gray beard, an indication that all that knew him had grown accustomed to seeing, suggesting that he was about to say something profound. "You know Excellency that I have been around for a very long time. I was there when the Temple fell, and Titus burnt it to the ground. Some even suggest I am old enough that I was there when the Babylonians burnt the first Temple to the ground." Everyone around the table laughed at his joke. "I witnessed the self-imposed exile of some of the wisest and brightest minds of our people after the war as they headed eastward to Mesopotamia also wondering if it would have been different if they only did a little more. Their minds filled with regret but never with solutions. They could escape from the reality by leaving but in the end, there was no changing of what had occurred. No matter how they analyzed it, the only time we were able to have our homeland back, govern ourselves and rebuild our Temple was when we chose not to fight and let God return us from exile peacefully."

"But that was because of Cyrus," Ben Zoma interjected.

"Who's to say Cyrus was not an instrument of God," Abba Saul responded.

"A worthy point," Ben Zoma admitted.

"So, in that time as well, the best of us, our leaders, our teachers, they went into exile and sat by the rivers in Babylon while others stayed behind in what was left of our country to deal with the destruction and the decimation. None to guide them, no one to help keep their faith strong, yet those that remained behind did so on their own and after seventy years they were released from their isolation when the others finally returned."

I began to nod my head. I knew exactly where Abba Saul was heading with this story and it helped to clear my head of the webs of doubt that had settled there.

"Titus destroyed our second Temple and many went East in exile as in the past but I remained behind because like my father and his father before him, there always had to be someone to bury the dead. And I have buried more dead in my lifetime than any man should ever have to do. People would see me walking with my shovel across my shoulder and say, "Their goes Abba Saul, I wonder how many of our young boys the Romans have killed today? But in my mind, I said life is a circle and what I was doing was no different from my ancestor that did so six centuries earlier. I only had to wait and those in the East will return and we will once again build our Temple in a time

43

of peace. And then you returned to Jerusalem, Excellency, and that day I wept for joy because I knew the time was at hand. I began to count down the years to our redemption. The ninth of Av in the year 3830 it fell which meant the Lord would have us rebuild it in the seventieth year after its destruction, just as he had done before. According to the Mineans that would be the year of 140 or only twelve more years after your arrival. Then even the Emperor Hadrian came to our part of the world in the year 3890 and I knew it was now the Lord's intention to return our kingdom into our hands by the year 3900. I rejoiced for once again we would be delivered from evil."

"And then something happened," Ben Zoma suggested there was a reason the prophecy failed.

"Yes," Abba Saul was convinced. "Something happened. Something I can't explain that I can't account for, but it turned the entire world upside down. What should have happened didn't, what should never have happened did, and once again I found myself surrounded by bodies needing burial. Some people even began to refer to me as the angel of death, but no one ever took into consideration how many tears I shed for every young Jewish boy that I put into the ground."

"I agree," I confessed my own thoughts on the matter. "I'm not certain how, but it felt as if someone was pulling all the strings and we were merely puppets dancing to the puppeteer's commands."

"Surely you cannot believe this war was avoidable," Ben Azzai challenged my thoughts on the matter.

"I did," I answered firmly. "With all my heart and all my soul. I was there when Hadrian made his proclamations challenging our right to circumcision, our need for the Temple Mount to raise our new Temple. It was unbelievable. Weeks before he had promised me that we could rebuild our nation exactly as we had hoped and then suddenly the lad drowns and Hadrian became a completely different person. It was if I was dealing with two entirely different people. It made no sense. But I believed I could still convince him to return to his prior stance if I was given enough time. All I needed was time!"

"I don't know what confidences you shared with the Emperor in private," Abba Saul continued, "But I can tell you from having lived my life so close to death all the time that there is nothing moral about war. The true immorality is when you don't know when to stop fighting. When you don't recognize that you are on the losing side and you have the opportunity to stop any further suffering. Or to the contrary, when you are on the winning side, then it is necessary that you must also have the moral fortitude and empathy to know when to stop the unnecessary slaughter of any further innocents."

"Exactly what are you trying to say, Abba Saul?" His last comment had confused me. I now couldn't decide if he was approving or condemning my failure to act because I believed I still could convince the Emperor not to push us in that direction.

"I will get there, be patient," he snapped at me. "Like I said, I was there when the Temple fell, watching from the lower city, a child exposed to all the horrors of war but my only safety was to stay by my father and he was a very busy man during those last few days when the Temple still stood. The Romans watched as Eleazar Ben Yair's men rained down arrows upon John of Gishchala's men who in turn shot their arrows down on Simon ben Gioras and his men. Titus could hardly believe what he was seeing as his enemies were bent on their own self destruction. One man finally decided it was enough, that there was not any further sense in fighting for freedom if we were already so bent on killing each other. That man, Excellency, was your grandfather. He possessed the moral conviction and common sense to recognize that those who called themselves God's freedom fighters were nothing more than murderous tyrants bent upon ruling over the remains of a fallen nation, no matter how many innocents had to die. Even though he knew that he would earn the ire of all these false messiahs, these would-be kings of death and mayhem, he made a secret arrangement through Joseph ben Matthias, to permit Titus and his army into the Temple grounds to put an end to the fighting, an end to the war and spare the lives of any further innocents that were caught between these warring factions. The deal was that Jerusalem would be spared, the Holy Temple would be preserved, and discussion of making Agrippa, King over Judea would begin. It was everything we could have hoped for when we first went to battle against the Romans. Thousands would have been saved. Judea once again would by a satrap ruled by its own king and Rome would leave us live in peace under those conditions." Abba Saul looked wistfully skyward as the trail of tears traced their way across his cheeks. It was an all too painful memory that he was now reliving in its entirety.

"Do you need some water, Abba Saul?" Yehonatan stood and ran over with the jug to fill his cup.

"No! I need some wine," he bellowed. "Give me more wine and lots of it," he demanded. Putting down the jug of water, Yehonatan retrieved the decanter of wine and began to pour it slowly into the cup at which point Abba Saul seized the decanter and put it to his lips and gulped back mouthfuls of the sweet tasting wine. He banged the practically empty decanter down on the tabletop and began to speak once more. "You know why I never became ordained as a Rabbi?" he asked all of us around the table.

We all shook our heads. It was common knowledge that Abba Saul had studied with some of the greatest of the early sages but for some reason during all that time, he never asked to be ordained, even though some of his teachings and comments have been preserved and taught to others. "I will tell you why! Because I learned at that time you could not be both a moral person and a Rabbi simultaneously. The two are directly in opposition because as soon as you have gained power over others, able to tell them how to live their lives, it is human nature that you seek out more power. Those with a little power are never satiated. Of course, there are the occasional exception. Simeon ben Gamaliel and his father were such exceptions, but they saw all the rabbis that surrounded them in the same manner that I did. Did you ever wonder why I served their meals every day? It was so we all could talk freely and express our worries concerning those that desired to call them- selves the Great Men of the Sanhedrin."

It seemed that Abba Saul was ignoring the fact that he had two such Rabbis sitting at the table with us. Or perhaps he did know it and he didn't care if his comments stung them deeply.

"I think you may have drunk too much wine Abba Saul and may regret what you are saying, tomorrow," Ben Zoma tried to caution him politely.

"I haven't drunk enough!" the wizened old scholar rejected the accusation. "Both you and Simon ben Azzai will pour endlessly over the Torah trying to find secret messages from the Almighty because accepting at face value what God had to say is too mundane for your liking. Others pour over the words because they feel if they can manage to unlock the occult power of the holy words then they themselves would have mastery over the arcane world. I saw it was true during those last days of Jerusalem during the first war. It wasn't Eleazar or John or even Simon that fueled the intensity of the blood lust among their men. It was those that called themselves holy men with their honey-sweet words of everlasting paradise in a world without pain, without suffering, where every whim would be granted and every man would be forgiven for every sin he ever committed as long as he refused to put down his sword and continued the battle and welcomed death. All that they ever desired and failed to receive on earth would suddenly be granted in the picture of the heaven that they painted for them. It no longer mattered how great the trail of destruction they left behind on this plane of reality because this world that we live in was never intended to be anything but a temporary place for those that were righteous in the eyes of God. They twisted every teaching that the Torah actually stated, convincing our warriors that death was not the end but in fact should be greeted with open arms as the beginning of life. It was a lie, for nowhere in the holy text are such things written but it was a convincing lie that easily blinded young men seeking honour and glory in this world so they could fulfil every desire in the next. These lies made them blind to the reality of their situation and once these learned men, with their sanctimonious speeches had gained control of their minds and implanted their own thoughts, then it was easy for them to suggest that anyone caught advocating surrender was a traitor and deserved to die. It mattered not what status that person might be, male, female or even a child, old or young, only that they advocated peace and that undermined the theocracy that these so-called holy men desired to create."

Ben Azzai looked extremely agitated. "Are you suggesting that all these wars, are the results of us? Not the Romans, but us Rabbis!"

I must admit that I had never seen Abba Saul like this before. When he turned to face Ben Azzai directly, the expression on his face was so terrifying that Ben Azzai slunk back into his chair and wasn't about to say another word.

"If the shoe fits," was all that he said to Ben Azzai and those few words said everything. He then sat back in his chair and directed his comments towards me. "Now as for you grandfather, Jeshua ben Gamaliel, he was one of those that they directed their hate and hostility towards because he knew the weaknesses in their arguments, the falseness of their claims and they resented him more than anyone else because of it. If anyone had the ability to stop the bloodshed and end the war it was Jeshua ben Gamaliel, the High Priest of Israel. I may have only been a young boy, but I still remember the day they seized him and under the direction of John of Gischala, the rebels beheaded him on the steps of the Temple for everyone to see. Your grandfather bared his neck and showed the cowards where to strike with their blade. He embraced death willingly, not because he believed that he would be going to a better place but because he knew he would be free of the deceit and immorality, the licentiousness and depravity of those proclaiming themselves to be leaders of the Jews."

"Not that he would have believed in a heaven anyway," I added, as a Zadokite it was not within our beliefs. Abba Saul did not appreciate my interruption, staring me into silence as he had done earlier to Ben Azzai.

"As for those same rabbis that urged the men of Israel to commit such an unforgivable and immoral sin, they would later praise John for what he did, claiming he was the true hero of that ill-fated war. The murderous Zealots who raped and killed their own people were proclaimed to be warriors of God and standard-bearers of our religion. Eleazar ben Yair, was hailed as a patriot of Judea beyond human measure, meanwhile his men poured their arrows down upon the hapless citizens of Jerusalem like a relentless rain. And let us not forget Simon ben Gioras, whom the rabbis chose for a messiah except for the fact that the Romans took him to Rome in chains where they finally executed him. So much I say for false messiahs. Bah! I have had my fill of them! They are like the dew on the ground, appearing everywhere at the dawn but evaporating in the blink of an eye when you need it most.

So don't any of you dare to tell me to be silent, lest I regret what I say on the morrow. My only disappointment is that I haven't said enough during all these intervening years during which I have borne witness. I remained quiet, letting bad men call themselves good men though I knew it was morally wrong but now my days of saying nothing are over. Are you all understanding the point that I am making?"

We all nodded but truth be said, I was wondering how Abba Saul was going to connect all this to the fact that I mentioned that it felt as if we were steered into this war by some other force beyond our control.

"Furthermore, it was never your father's intention, Elioneai ben Joseph, to restart a war between our people and the Romans. I was always in communication with him during that time. So, I know it to be true. It was only his intent to teach Trajan a lesson, a warning not to grasp for more than his hands could actually hold. Yosef ben Jeshua was well aware that the majority of our people lived within the borders of the Roman Empire. We were the one most at risk if there was to be an outbreak of bloodshed, not him because he was living in Babylon and safe from harm. So, he would never intentionally put us in harm's way. That being the case, you can believe me when I say that he had no intention for us to turn acts of civil disobedience into outright warfare because he knew it would not end well for us. He only wished to hasten the Emperor's return to Rome and make him regret that he ever set foot in Parthia. But sometimes fate can be a cruel harpy, often determining its own path as was the case when Trajan died during his retreat. Who could have foreseen such an event but many a Jew took it as a sign that God was raining down his wrath upon Rome and once convinced of that misconception, there was no opportunity for your father to reign in the chaos that had been unleashed because of this unanticipated event.

Yosef ben Jeshua had never intended to be responsible for the death of a million souls, whether they be Gentile or Jew. But an insanity had taken hold and it could not be stopped. Nor was it his intention to let Judea become involved in these skirmishes, ensuring that the Jews here did not follow in the footsteps of Alexandria and Cyprus. Fortunately, your father was able to dispatch sufficient communications to ensure that the numbers of men supporting Julianus and Pappus, never reached a critical mass where they considered themselves powerful enough to be actual freedom fighters. At the same time, he was able to convince the Emperor Hadrian that they should not be executed when captured, so that they were not seen as martyrs and the flames of resistance would burn themselves down to smoldering cinders naturally. That was what your father did, may the Lord bless him and protect him. He kept Judea from being destroyed and all the Jews banished as they did in Cyprus."

"Do you know what happened to Julianus and Pappus then," my youngest son Azariah asked.

"They met the fate that all rebels meet I'm afraid," Abba Saul explained. "It was just long after everything had settled down and they had been forgotten.

"So, are you saying that I was right in resisting the war effort?" I was still not quite certain what Abba Saul wanted me to learn from his telling of this history lesson.

"There are several points that should be learned from what I have just said," Abba Saul instructed. From the first war you learn that there are those people that will make every effort to control how you think and act. Most often they disguise themselves as the most honourable and respected of men. They are the snake from the Garden of Eden and the Lord warns us always to be aware of their presence. The snake is always there behind the scenes and always working against those that are morally upstanding. When evil is not identified, it will always manage to drown out the voices of the righteous. Those that follow a proper moral path are quickly silenced. Do you understand what I am saying Excellency?"

I nodded my head in acknowledgment. "Yes, I understand you perfectly. In fact, I used the analogy of the snake quite often in my own teachings. I'm glad we share that lesson in common."

"As for the war against Trajan, it was not until your father could exploit a weakness that he could make his voice heard. Tremendous damage had already been done in Cyrene, Alexandria and Cyprus. He could do nothing to stop the massacres that took place in those communities. Only because the leaders in Judea did not incorporate the same venomous ferocity as their counterparts elsewhere was Yosef ben Jeshua able to restore the calm. Your father provided just in time, a strong, rational voice to restore the peace, but in order to do so he still needed allies within the province to deliver his messages. Do you now see the message from this story now, Excellency?"

"Yes, it is crystal clear," I responded. "I could not do it alone because there is always someone pulling in the opposite direction."

"The world is a balance," Abba Saul continued. "I'm certain my colleagues, Ben Zoma and Ben Azzai will agree." Looking over at the two rabbis, I could see that they were perfectly aligned with what had just been said. "So, if you are on the one side of the balance, Excellency, who was on the other side. If you can find the evidence for this last 'truth' then you will be released from the self-guilt you have wrapped around your shoulders and wear as a coat of shame."

"The statements by Abba Saul were very profound. I knew exactly what he was referring to and exactly what I had to do next. "Joseph and Azariah, I need you to find where Rabbi Akiva is residing. You will deliver a message to him."

"Yes father, we will see to it first thing in the morning," my eldest son responded.

"No!" I disagreed. "You will go to his residence this evening. You will tell him that he is to meet with Elioneai ben Yosef, High Priest of Israel, in the morning, in this synagogue at the fourth hour after the dawn. You will take Jacob and a few men with you so that he takes this summons very seriously. Jacob will secure his home to ensure Akiva does not decide to leave the city during the night."

"What if he has other commitments at that time," my eldest son asked.

"This is not up for debate, Joseph. No excuses, he will attend. Otherwise, I will have Jacob drag him here. That is my final word on the matter."

Both of the Simons appeared somewhat shocked by my instructions but I could see that Abba Saul bore a broad smile, meaning that he was satisfied that I had completely understood the message from his reminisces. Sometimes one has to look into the shadows in order to find the brightest light.

"Excellency," Ben Zoma sounded nervous. "Am I mistaken, but it almost appears as if you are arresting Rabbi Akiva. Perhaps a little more diplomacy is in order if all you seek is for him attending an audience."

"Why not just invite him to join our dinner," Ben Azzai suggested as a possible alternative. "After all, we should be rejoicing in his miraculous survival, not acting as if he committed some heinous crime. Is that not right," Simon ben Azzai searched the faces of everyone around the table to see if the others were in agreement with his position. Ben Zoma was in complete agreement but it was obvious to everyone else, placing Akiva under arrest was exactly what I was doing.

Looking from one of my sons to the other, Ben Azzai hoped to at least have them acknowledge that this was not the way it should be done. "Rabbi Akiva is a great man," Simon ben Azzai continued in his defense. "Perhaps the greatest mind of us all. A man beloved by God. You cannot treat him this way, like a common criminal, without any evidence to justify your actions. I protest this injustice!"

"Are you questioning my authority," I demanded an immediate answer from Ben Azzai. From the tone of my voice, he knew he had just crossed a very thin line.

"Of course not, Excellency," he knew better than to keep pressing me on the matter. "There is no question you have the authority, as it is empowered to you by the Exilarch, but you should still recognize that this is Judea and not Mesopotamia. We have a different way of doing things here. Do you really think this is necessary? That is all I was trying to say. If he asks why he is being summonsed, how are your sons going to respond to such a simple question?"

"With these!" I reached into the inner pocket of my robe, grabbing the items in my right hand and slamming them down upon the table. Yehonatan, who was sitting to my right used his index finger to move them about on the table as he looked carefully at each item. "It would appear that Rabbi Akiva is selling these to the people of the city."

Ben Zoma shook his head, rolling his eyes as he did so, as if dismissing the items as being insignificant and not worthy of attention. "It is not uncommon to sell a few religious tokens that have been blessed. We Rabbis do it all the time."

"Do you?" I stared penetratingly into Ben Zoma's eyes which forced him to withdraw into his seat squeamishly. "Do you bless these as well?" I asked, separating out the zodiac carvings, so they could be clearly distinguished from the parchment bags and the strings of beads.

"They look like zodiac signs," Ben Zoma replied, Ben Azzai nodding in agreement with his colleague.

"I agree with Rabbi Simon. There is no law against possessing these zodiac trinkets either," Ben Azzai provided his professional religious opinion.

"What if I was to tell you they were more than Zodiac signs?" I posed the issue to them. "What if I was to tell you they had been blessed as fertility idols, designed to guarantee the birth of the child in that particular month the symbol represents."

"Heresy," the old priest, Yehonatan shouted out loud, disturbed by what I had just revealed.

"I might go as far as witchcraft," Abba Saul added his respected opinion. "This is not permitted to endow a graven image with specific powers. Especially in matters of creation and the birth of a child is very much an act of creation!"

"Now do you understand?" There was no further questioning of my motives by the two Simons. They had heard enough.

Chapter Four

The Encounter:

"I demand to know the meaning of this...this...interrogation," the elderly rabbi, known as Akiva ben Joseph, hammered his large meaty fist against the small wooden table that had been moved to the synagogue's central courtyard. His hair was gray with age, but there were still a few reddish blonde strands that immediately suggested he was very different from most of his peers.

It was mid-morning, and as promised, Jacob had escorted the Rabbi to the synagogue where the members of the city's Jewish elite had gathered in anticipation of something major about to happen. I sat there patiently, along with my travelling companions while Akiva ranted, knowing eventually he would tire and sit down as I had requested. It was already a miserably hot Spring morning, but despite the humidity and searing temperature, I sat in my woolen robe, draped over my inner white linen tunic. A chair had been placed directly across from me for Akiva to sit, but as yet he still refused, choosing instead to pace about the courtyard while shouting out his displeasure of having been summoned to appear before me.

He was clearly agitated, probably thinking I had exceeded my authority, and definitely not happy to have been forcibly brought into my presence. That was the reason why I had asked the city officials to be present because I knew how easy it would be for any of his supporters to accuse me of holding an illegal hearing, which would be reported to the Romans as being something entirely different from its intended purpose. It would not be the first time that those in support of the Rabbanite party tried to have me incarcerated in a Roman prison by making a false accusation, suggesting that as the leading Zadokite among our people that I was rallying the nation to oppose the Emperor. Religion and politics; never a good mix. We have borne this antagonism for three hundred years and I'm certain we will keep feeding the animosity for the next three hundred. All it would take is one twisted report of my setting up a court intending to defy Roman restrictions and even my diplomatic immunity would not be enough to protect myself and my family. And if I was right about Akiva, he would have no qualms in filing such a report if he was given the opportunity. That's why I had to make certain he didn't walk away today from this synagogue as a free man.

"Akiva, why don't you so us all a favour and just sit down?" I urged him once again. "You're making us all nervous watching you pace back and forth. I invited you here for a friendly discussion, but you're acting as if it is going to be an interrogation before even the first question has even been proposed."

Still standing with his fists shaking, Akiva stared at everyone that had been gathered to hear our 'friendly' conversation. "You have no right to treat me this way," his voice quivered with rage. "I have taken note of all of you that are seated here. There will be retribution for this. Mark my word, you will pay!"

Yes, there was the Akiva I had come to know. Arrogant, belligerent and abusive as soon as he felt threatened. I had not seen him in years, but it was clear that he had not changed even one iota. "Akiva, just have a seat," I repeated my demand. "All I want to do is talk with you and ask a few questions. Can that be so bad?"

"We all know that is not what you intend though you may fool some of these fools. I want everyone to know that you do not have the authority to summons me to what is tantamount to a hearing," Akiva argued his point but almost everyone knew the legal arrangements between the Exilarchate and the provinces that had been established almost sixty years ago, so they knew what he was saying was not true.

"It would be more correct to say, 'you have no authority to summon me to a hearing, Excellency.' I'd probably even settle for a 'My Lord' now and then. Why don't we try to have at least a little decorum between us, if possible," I knew that that would never happen as having to address me properly would only leave a bitter taste in his mouth. "But as you obviously seem to have forgotten, after the destruction of the Temple there was the Roman prohibition against the Sanhedrin conducting any courtly matters, so we adopted the Lex Judaica, where the authority was transferred to Babylon where we could still operate a Jewish court under the jurisdiction of the invested households of the royal and priestly families which reside there. Therefore, as that priestly representative, this is entirely within my rights."

"Eleazar ben Azariah is High Priest and he is the only one I will address so accordingly." His comment was met with the sounds of shock and alarm from those gathered in the courtyard, but I waved my hands slowly to tell everyone to calm down and ignore what he had intended as a grave insult towards me.

"Last time I looked, I am still High Priest of Israel, despite your naming someone else to that position. Unless you have evidence of my being proclaimed dead,

I don't know where you even think you obtained the authority to name anyone as the High Priest. Presuming, even if I did have the misfortune of being pronounced as dead, then it is the Exilarch's right to name the next High Priest, only his and certainly not yours. Or are you now suggesting that you are of the royal blood of the House of David? Did I miss that announcement?"

A few of those gathered to hear our debate laughed at my little jest but stopped almost immediately when Akiva turned to glare at them.

"If it truly offends you to address me as such, then so be it. Whether you do or do not think of me as your High Priest matters little as it does not in any way reduce my authority to ask whomever I please to come and sit for a serious discussion concerning a violation of our laws. I have requested your presence and you are legally bound to come. Surely you cannot argue against a simple discourse revolving around an element of the law. That is what you consider yourself to be an expert in I believe, or so you apparently tell your students, is it not?"

"Excuse me if I don't find myself being surrounded by community leaders and some of my colleagues from the Council to be a friendly little meeting to discuss the law as you describe it," Akiva raised his objection.

"I thought you rabbis were overjoyed to be surrounded by hundreds of students and on-lookers when you held your debates. Isn't it about which one of you can draw that largest audience that makes your reputation and provides you with bragging rights? I'm sorry if I haven't managed to arrange a large enough audience to be here today to meet your satisfaction. But I did think that it was a venue like this by which you rabbis hold your discourses on the law naturally, is it not? Why should you view this gathering as being any different from your usual way of doing things?"

"When you send armed men to escort me from my own home, you render the situation very different. You cannot deny that this hearing is nothing more than an attempt to condemn me for some offense that you have contrived and fabricated against me." Akiva was clearly into his old form where he would attempt to turn the tables, making myself appear to be guilty party and he the innocent victim. I had heard him talk numerous times before and I knew how he could play to the emotions of an assembled audience. That was his charm and special talent that he had exercised all his life and been rewarded well for it, if the rumors of his wealth are correct.

"I apologize if my escort alarmed you," I announced graciously and sincerely which caught most of those assembled by surprise. They probably never heard a High Priest apologize for anything in their lives and probably never will again. "I did not anticipate that you would misconstrue my offer to keep you safe from those that may have misinterpreted my good and sincere intentions for inviting you here as an attempt to cause you bodily harm. Your welfare was of paramount importance to me. So yes, I am sorry if you misinterpreted my intentions. But as you can clearly see, my guard is no longer holding you a prisoner here. There are no ropes or chains that bind you here. All of my men have left the courtyard, so there is no threat of which you presently speak."

"Then I have no reason to stay here any longer," Akiva acknowledged that if there were no armed men present to prevent him from leaving, then he would seize the opportunity to go.

"No reason other than the High Priest of Israel has summoned you for a matter of great importance to be discussed. How would your leaving be interpreted? As Akiva, the man who feared the truth? Or would they name you Akiva, the man who had something serious to hide? Or perhaps see you as Akiva the man that was petrified to face Elioneai ben Yosef?"

Akiva looked around the courtyard to verify that what I had just said had already registered with the officials from the community. They would regard him with suspicion from now on and the accusations of what they believed he might be guilty of would be whispered behind his back wherever he went. By now, it must have certainly become obvious to Akiva was that he was not dealing with some pompous fool like my cousin, Eleazar ben Azariah. If he thought he was going to take control of this meeting, my meeting, then he was sadly mistaken.

"I suggest you relax Akiva, and we can talk. I want to hear about your amazing escape from Beithar. I think everyone would like to hear about this fabulous miracle. Am I correct?" I raised the question to everyone that had assembled for the meeting.

The response was a resounding yes.

"It was not that spectacular," Akiva tried to dismiss the question so that the conversation would move to another topic.

"Don't be so modest," I urged him to continue. "I must admit, I have already heard about the extraordinary angelic intervention. Clearly it was a miracle. How else can you explain it? Over fifty thousand people were trapped in the city. General Julius Severus had completely walled off Beithar; a barricade that encompassed the entire city. Legions V Macedonia and XI Claudia sealing off every avenue of escape. There was no way to get beyond the Roman walls unless you could fly. Everyone here is so eager to hear about your salvation. We beg you please to tell us, in order to raise up our spirits so that we can appreciate that God is still watching over us and protecting us, even in desperate times like these."

Akiva finally sat down in the chair that had been provided, following all my urging. "I will not permit myself to be mocked," he snarled in response as he crossed his arms over his broad, muscular chest.

"How can I be mocking you. The townspeople told me that these were your very own words. You told them that a miracle occurred. Are you now retracting what you said? We are all listening, so tell us Akiva, how did you escape from the city?"

"I don't exactly recall," he said defiantly, refusing to provide any details as all of us gazed upon him with baited breath.

"Please, don't be so modest Akiva. If God intervened on your behalf, it is a great reason to celebrate," Ben Zoma urged him to respond, still confident that Akiva would prove to all of us that he was blessed and special in the eyes of the Creator. Clearly, he had pulled the wool over Simon ben Zoma's eyes a long time ago.

"Yes, brother Akiva," Ben Azzai now spoke up. "We are eager to hear of your salvation brother. I believe in you. Let the others believe in you too, so please tell us."

Abba Saul was not so gullible as Akiva's compatriots on the Council. Whereas they were so desperately eager to hear of his miraculous adventure, those like Abba Saul and myself know there is no miracle when one man survives and fifty thousand die. Though Akiva ben Joseph may think his life is worth so incredibly high a price, those that truly know God know that the Almighty would never pay so dear a price for the sake of one man.

Akiva lowered his head, only to slowly raise it up again with a sorrowful and pained expression upon his face. Even through his heavy gray beard, one could discern the stress lines etched cleanly across his brow and along his cheeks. 'He's good', I thought to myself, 'he's very good.' This man knew how to play to an audience. Every move he made, every expression he donned, it was as if he was conducting a performance. No wonder he had risen so quickly among the congress of the rabbis.

"I can't tell you exactly what happened," he began, "Because even now it is not clear in my mind. It was time for us to retire and I went to bed in my room, which I shared with Rabbi Eleazar Ha'Modai. I could not have been sleeping very long before I saw a bright light above my bed and in that light was an indistinct shape. It was so bright that I could barely keep my eyes open but slowly as I watched, the shape began to take form, until it was almost that of a man but obviously not of any kind of man known to us."

Those listening to his description were stricken with awe. How could such an apparition be anything less than an angel? Though none of them had ever seen an angel of the Lord themselves, they were desperately eager to believe that Akiva had, for in their minds they were convinced that if anyone was worthy of such a visitation it would be the famed Rabbi Akiva. How did we become so naive over the centuries, even after the Torah that God had given us warned against putting any faith in soothsayers and witches, I do not know. Perhaps out of our own desperation we needed to grasp on to something supernatural, but I am convinced that Akiva ben Joseph is neither that something or someone, who can provide that semblance of legitimacy to verify the visitations by heavenly beings. These people obviously yearn for such tales, but it was time for me to shock them out of their stupor.

I rose from my seat to address everyone that had assembled in the courtyard. "Woe is to Israel" I wailed, "For I was in Caesarea at the time that Severus came to report that the war had ended with the fall of Beithar. The Emperor Hadrian made it a point that I had to be there during the pronouncement as a member of his domestic debutante audience. In other words, he wanted to salt the wounds of those that he could not directly make suffer because of our diplomatic immunity. He was well aware that he could do nothing to me because I was a representative of the King of Parthia, but nevertheless, he still knew that even an ambassador's heart could be crushed beneath a millstone of sorrow. The knives he jabbed into our chests that day caused far more damage than any steel blade could ever have managed.

So, listen carefully because here are the words the Roman general passed on to us that day, so that we would return to our residences in distant lands and spread the word of how our people were made to suffer: "We built an earthen and wooden wall all around the town that was eight feet in height. No one could scale the wall without ladders and there was no breach anywhere that they could pass through. The top of the barricade was manned by archers in regularly spaced towers so that no one could even exit the city and not be taken down by my forces. After months of waiting, we knew they were running low on food and water. The spring that fed the city was sourced way up in the hills and it was an abnormally dry season. We knew that they were still managing to get a small number of supplies through their nightly excursions outside the city walls, but we had a spy in the city that drew the layout to their under-ground tunnels. He also knew their passwords. He even pointed out to us where some of these tunnels exited beyond our barrier wall. With that information we were able to effectively shut these down. When I considered the time was right, I sent my men into their own tunnels and then we emerged inside the city. My orders were quite simple; once inside, slaughter everyone they encountered. At the same time, one squadron's sole responsibility was to open the city gates to the main body of my forces waiting outside. Anyone my soldiers met with a sword in their hands was an enemy and killed on the spot. Woman and children, if they had obvious value were captured for the slave markets. All others deemed too young or too old were eliminated. By the time my cavalry entered the city their horses could barely move, the ground was so thick with blood, that their hooves sunk deep into a red river of mud. By the next morning the head of Simon bar Kochba was laid at my feet. In all, there were over fifty thousand dead and over two thousand preserved for the slave markets. Excellency, I can now say without hesitation, the war is over!" As all of Hadrian's courtesans applauded, there was only one thought that filled my mind: How could there have been a spy in the city that knew all the tunnels and all the passwords? I could not shake the anger that infused my entire being thinking of such a despicable and loathsome being. We had been betrayed. Not once, but over and over again by someone that had been close enough to Bar Kochba to know all his secrets. Who was willing to sacrifice the lives of our people, our nation and our God. What kind of person could this be, I wondered. I gathered that this person had to be the sliest of foxes, able to convince our leaders of his being trustworthy, assuring beyond doubt his allegiance, but all the while working towards our destruction. Not a person I reckoned but a demon?"

At that moment Akiva thew himself out of his chair and charged towards me as if he was prepared to strike. For someone rumored to be in his eighties, he moved quite spryly as he covered the distance in seconds. Not too surprising since there was always a doubt to his real age, for that too was one of the many secrets Akiva kept. I stepped backwards quickly, dodging his approach while turning to the assembly and forcing a smile to my face as I spoke distinctly, "It would appear that I have touched a nerve. Though I said nothing of Akiva's complicity in this matter, I must admit his reaction has taken me by surprise. Why would my talk of a traitor disturb him so? Unless…"

My words were enough to stop any further attempt by Akiva to land a blow, as he took a deep breath and regained control of his demeanor. He adjusted the turban he wore to cover his balding scalp then began circling the area so that he could address everyone gathered while staring directly into their eyes. "As I was saying, there was a bright light hovering above me while I lay in my bed. The next moment I recall I was laying in the middle of the road to B'nai Brak being roughly shaken to consciousness by strangers. I have no other recollection of that night. I must have passed out from the shock of the apparition. I was saved and I can only guess it was because the Lord Almighty still had a purpose for me." Those in the courtyard mulled over his explanation and appeared generally receptive to it. As far as they were concerned, Akiva was one of their own. I was still the foreigner that had come to their town and was casting accusations against their beloved Sage. Far easier for them to accept his tale of angels than my story suggesting his being a traitor.

"Why you?" I asked directly.

"What do you mean," he responded coldly, as if I had called him a liar, which essentially, I guess I did.

"Exactly what I said. Why you?"

"Because as I said, the Lord had another purpose for me."

"Just you," I scoffed at his reasoning. "The same Lord that parted the Red Sea with a blast from his nostrils, that tossed our enemies into the swirling waters with a sweep of his arm and tore down walls to defeat our enemies. Is that the Lord you are referring to? The worker of great miracles but that night He took no other action but to rescue you while sacrificing everyone else in the city, subjecting them to the horrors of torture and ignoble deaths. Really? Does that sound like our God to you? Does anyone here think that is what our God would do?"

"Who are we to judge the ways of the Lord?" Akiva responded defensively.

"Don't bother serving up your daily platitudes to me," I warned him, "For I do know the ways of God and what you have described is not the God of our forefathers. What you have described is the god of Akiva ben Joseph, and if that is the way your god behaves then he is certainly not my God. He is not the God of the Jews. So, I ask you once more, Akiva, how did you escape from the city?"

"And I already told you how," Akiva refused to change his story. "If you don't like the way our Lord works then why don't you take it up directly with Him?"

No point in concealing my words any longer as Akiva was not straying from his story. "Did you betray Simon bar Kochba?" I demanded to know. My voice trembled with anger and my hands were shaking. "Did so many of our young men die because you have been stabbing them in the back from the day 'you' began this war."

It was Akiva's time to shout back. "First you accuse me of being a traitor and now you insist that I started the war itself. Why don't you accuse me of being a Roman in disguise if you are going to make such absurd claims?"

"I don't need to accuse you of being such. If you are a wolf dressed in sheepskin, then I will find out sooner than later and I will make you pay for it."

Calming himself once more by taking several deep breaths, Akiva knew it was time to play to the audience once more. "Friends, colleagues, students, you have known me for years, yet you know nothing of my accuser. Who is this man that comes into our town and makes all these false and wild accusations? Where has he been over the past few years in our time of need? Did I take it upon myself to appoint another to be High Priest in his stead? Of course, I did! Why would I continue to support someone to hold that position who has spent the last four years wining and dining with his friends and allies, the Romans? Yes, that is where your High Priest has been. Whispering into Hadrian's ears while in Alexandria and kissing the hands of Tinnius Rufus when in Caesarea. This man dares to accuse me of betraying my fellow countrymen, while he spends all his time embracing his Roman friends. You need not look far to identify a traitor if you need to find one?"

My sons Joseph and Azariah were about to leap from of their chairs and beat Akiva mercilessly, but I was able to force them back down with a stern look, I had a better way to deal with Akiva. "You're right, I did spend all my time whispering into the ears of every Roman official I could find." My confession raised a few grunts of discontent and open-mouthed gasps of concern. "I do not deny I am a man of peace and if I could have found a way to end the war and save all our sons from death, I would have done whatever it took to do so. That is who I am, the Lord's messenger of peace but who are you, Akiva? That is the answer we all wish to hear. Are you the Akiva that told everyone that Bar Kosba was the messiah and we must follow him into the heat of battle, because you renamed him Bar Kochba, 'the Son of a Star'? Or perhaps you are the Akiva that sent his twenty-four thousand students to enlist under this rebel King of your making, even though most had never lifted a sword in their lives, telling them to die as a soldier of God was the highest tribute they could ever pay to the Lord. Where has the Akiva that said he would never leave Bar Kochba's side until such time that either the war was won or they died together on the point of the same spear? Is that Akiva anywhere to be found or are you merely the husk of a man that chose to preserve his own life no matter what the cost to the others? There were those far more worthy for God to rescue from the city than you. So, I ask you once again, how did you escape?"

"And I will tell you and everyone gathered here, once again; I do not know! One moment I was in my room and the next I was waking up on the road outside this city. That is all I know and all I can say!"

"Then let me ask another question that you can answer directly. If a man did not have a miraculous intervention as in your case, how else could he have escaped from the city?"

"You are trying to trick me," Akiva responded, refusing to answer the question.

"It is no trick," I reassured him. "You have already indicted that you are here because of some miracle. I'm asking about the others; how would they have escaped during those final hours before the Romans flooded into the city?"

"The only escape was through the tunnels," he finally answered.

"But they couldn't," I reminded him. "As General Severus stated in his report, the tunnels were no longer available. His men had sealed them off. So, was there any other means of escape?"

"If they could not use the tunnels then they had no other options. They were either captured or killed," he spoke without even the smallest trace of emotion in his deep voice.

"So, it truly was a miracle then that the Lord removed you from harm's way and delivered you safely to us. As the only survivor neither dead nor captured for the slave market, such a tragedy of loss must weigh heavy upon your soul. Oh wait! There was another to escape the Romans; the traitor that informed the enemy of the tunnels' existence and the passwords. He is the only other person that would be alive and free. What a pity we cannot find him."

"Your sarcasm will not blind these good people gathered here to the truth. I am not that man, and you should be ashamed to even infer that I could be him. God did not intend for me to die with the others, and it is by His will that I stand here."

I laughed at his insinuation. "No, that's where you are wrong. You may be very right that it is his will you are standing here before me, but perhaps for all the wrong reasons that you are thinking." My answer confused him as it did with many that had gathered in the courtyard. "I have a story of God's intervention too to tell. My story in many ways relates directly to yours. Except I don't deal with angels; I deal directly with God." The crowd was up on their toes, eager to hear this new story. "As I admitted, I have spent years appealing to the Romans, trying to convince them to be merciful and resolve the war through a peaceful means that saved face for both sides and still delivered gains that both Roman and Jew could claim at least a partial victory. I was succeeding in the first two years of the war, primarily because Bar Kochba, as I will refer to him, was winning on the battlefield, and the Roman Legions were suffering terrible losses. But the tide suddenly changed and the Jewish army was finding itself trapped in city after city, barely able to escape each time only to go to the next city and it too would be laid under siege. Julius Severus had changed his entire battle strategy from engaging in battle in the open field to one of siege containment. It was as if he could predict Bar Kochba's every move and he had knowledge of where the underground tunnels would lead. In my mind I figured it had to be the work of one man. Someone who could move about freely, without raising suspicions of his activities. Someone who could show up at each site where the Jewish army relocated without any question as to where he's been and why he would be leaving again. There would be very few people with that level of authority, but I could think of a few that it might be.

It became obvious that the Romans would sooner listen to him than they would to me, and I no longer had their ear. I grew despondent, blaming myself for every loss we suffered due to my failure to stop the war. Every death of a young man, rape of a Jewish woman, and slaughter of an innocent child was my fault because I failed in my mission."

"No, it was not so," someone gathered in the courtyard shouted. "It was not your fault Excellency."

"But it was," I countered their opinion. "If God had advised me to come to Judea to stop the war, then surely, he expected me to find my arch nemesis, the one responsible for delivering our people into the hands of the Romans. The first mission could not succeed unless the second proved successful. And then Beithar fell, and I still had not identified this Dathan of our time. Had Moses not found his nemesis, would we even have been here as a nation today? But I was not Moses, and this unknown enemy still tormented me through the night for the faces of the dead would flash before my eyes. I prayed to the Almighty with all my heart and all my soul. Lord, if it is the last act I do on this Earth, let me find the man that has caused us such suffering. Let me be your sword of vengeance. And do you know what happened?" I asked.

The crowd murmured in anticipation, "What? What, Excellency," I could hear them saying repeatedly. Over and over again until the words were building into a crescendo.

"Absolutely nothing," I deflated the moment much to their surprise. I heard nothing. I saw nothing. No angel to come in my moment of need to provide an answer. I was lost and I made the decision to return with my entourage in tow, back to Babylon, crushed and defeated."

"Then why are you still here?" Akiva challenged my lack of acting on my decision immediately and probably wishing afterwards that he had not said anything because he realized he had just provided me with an opening to respond.

"Exactly," I answered. "Why am I still here? The heart of Jerusalem had been closed off to me. The Temple mount is now forbidden territory. All of our intellectuals have already packed and left the city. I was watching a new exodus from our beloved Jerusalem, and I realized I could not leave without first visiting the tombs of my ancestors. While on my way there I overheard a couple of rabbinical students discussing their future, as if we actually had a future to aspire to, and I found their hope and confidence fascinating. I took it as a sign from God suggesting that our inexhaustible spirit will never be broken. So, I decided to follow along, listening as they spoke, so that my own spirits would be raised because surely that is what the Lord wanted me to hear at that time. And then the strangest thing happened, which changed my attitude completely. Do you want to know what it was, Akiva?"

"Do I really have a choice," the rabbi asked sarcastically.

"No, none at all. So, this one student said to the other that he was going to go to B'nai Brak. The other was surprised, asking what was left in B'nai Brak that would still be of interest to him. And he gave the most implausible, incredible, unimaginable answer I could never have guessed in a thousand years. In a low voice, as if he was trying not to be overheard, he said 'Akiva is back'. 'Impossible' the other boy said. 'Not only is he back but he is setting up a new Yeshiva.' Now it was my turn to say impossible though I did not say it out loud. Hadrian had forbidden setting up any new Jewish schools in what was formerly Judea and now being called Palestina by Imperial edict. Forbidden by the penalty of death. It would take a dispensation directly from the Emperor in order to defy this ruling. A dispensation he surely would not provide to the one Jew that caused this war in the first place and practically toppled him from his throne. Unless…."

I left the sentence dangling once again, so that everyone watching from the gallery could fill in the rest of the words themselves.

Akiva circled about the room like an angry crow. "This is ridiculous!" he exclaimed. "None of this is even remotely true. He has made up this story. Can't you tell. The House of Phiabi are nothing but liars and deceivers. Don't ever trust a word that comes from their mouths. Everyone knows there is a curse upon their house."

By this time Abba Saul had risen from his seat and was now practically standing on top of Akiva. Everyone was bemused by the incongruity of the spectacle; this giant of a man standing beside the muscular frame of the rabbi but making him look diminutive by comparison. As soon as Abba Saul spoke. it was very clear that he was not in an amiable mood. "How did you get permission to start your school, Akiva?"

"I have a letter from the Procurator. Tinnius Rufus granted me permission. It is all very legal."

"All very legal and all very suspicious," Abba Saul added. "Why would the Governor of Judea grant you anything? Especially when it is as Elioneai has said; only a dispensation from the Emperor can overrule an Imperial edict. So why would Rufus go out of his way to get you a letter from the Emperor."

"You know I was always kind to his wife," Akiva began to stutter as he watched Abba Saul ball up his huge fists until they looked like two sledge hammers. "She was always very interested in Judaism, and I went out of my way to teach her about our religion."

"The man hates us Jews and you want me to believe he rewarded you, the one responsible for electing a messiah to crush the Romans in a bloody war, because you were kind enough to teach his wife about Judaism. Do you really think I will accept that reasoning?"

"It is the truth, I swear it," Akiva claimed in his defense.

Others began to crowd around the revered Rabbi but it was not reverence that could be seen in their eyes but an element of doubt that was rapidly increasing the exchanges that were taking place in the courtyard. I knew it was in my own best interest to keep the situation under control. "Everyone, calm down. Akiva says he is innocent and that his being awarded a dispensation from the Emperor is all a misunderstanding on our part. If so, then let him have his day in court."

"What court?" Akiva ridiculed me as if he thought he could gain the upper hand in this situation. "There is no court any longer. The Sanhedrin was disbanded long ago. Even if it wasn't, where do you think you would find seventy rabbis and priests to sit upon it. That's the legal requirement and you don't nearly have that many judges available. Notwithstanding, any case that you could present would only be circumstantial. You have no direct evidence for any of your outlandish claims. This entire rush to judgement is ludicrous and based on nothing but lies and innuendo."

"He is right. It is true," Abba Saul announced to me seemingly disappointed. "We have not the number to set up the Sanhedrin."

"What is true," I corrected him, "Is that this is no longer Judea. This is Palestina according to the Romans. And as an entirely Roman province its court system is based on the Lex Acilia now. It only requires a minimum number of jurors under the auspices of the praetor repstundis. I believe setting up a Beth Din under these requirements will be well within our authority."

"You still have no case against me. Just your hearsay and we know from our own laws that *a person is to be considered more credible about himself than a hundred witnesses that testify against him*," Akiva preached.

"That is the statement proposed for our new book of laws," Abba Saul commented.

"It is, to put it politely, an ignorant statement," I provided my own assessment of the law, "Who was the one that proposed such a ruling to your Council," I questioned as if I didn't know.

"It was Akiva," Abba Saul answered.

"Why am I not surprised," I said sarcastically. "But nevertheless, it is a ruling that I have taken into consideration."

"What do you mean?" Akiva sounded concerned.

"You will see soon," I assured him.

"So, what crime will you accuse me of?" Akiva still considered himself to be in a situation where he could mock me. "You will never be able to prove your accusation that I betrayed Bar Kochba because it simply is not true. I tell you now, your proving any misdeed on my part will never happen and there are no witnesses that will ever confirm your fictional version of events."

"You're right," I agreed, "That is because they're all dead. But we have a saying in my family that if you listen carefully and long enough you will be able to hear the dead speak. They will have their day in court."

"Do you hear that," Akiva shouted to catch the attention of everyone that was now milling about the courtyard nervously. Your so-called High Priest accuses me of crimes but now claims he will have the dead speak at my trial. Necromancy, I say. Do you hear me, he practices necromancy. A crime punishable by death. He is the one that should be put on trial. He is the one that has spent the past four years enjoying the company of the Romans. I say he is the traitor!"

Akiva's wild accusations were enough to stir talk among his most ardent supporters. There would always be those eager to rush to his defense, but I had no idea of how many that might be. But more importantly I could not afford to let this gathering disintegrate into a battle between two camps. I called over to my eldest son Joseph and told him to go and find Jacob immediately and have him bring what he found as quickly as possible.

Jacob and his men must have already been outside the synagogue because he entered along with Joseph in what was only a matter of minutes. "Did you find it?" I shouted in his direction to which he nodded.

"Everyone!" I shouted, "Listen to me. A thief that steals from his host is a man without honour. And a man without honour is capable of performing the most heinous of crimes because he has no restraints. We have ten supreme commandments by which we are all bound to adhere. Everything else is just commentary. If we break even one of those ten commandments, we have committed an offense against the Almighty that we must be punished for. If we break two or more our punishment is to be severe. So let me show you the first of Akiva's sins. Jacob, bring it here."

Stepping towards the middle of the room, the Captain of the Guard carried the medium sized object concealed beneath a canvas drape. Setting it carefully down on the floor he removed the drape to reveal what appeared to be a *solid gold step stool*. Those assembled in the courtyard gasped upon seeing it, shocked not only by the sheer weight of the precious metal but none had ever seen something so ostentatious before.

"How dare you go into my house without my permission," Akiva screamed, before realizing he had just admitted the item belonged to him.

"You have no one to blame but yourself," I advised. "You have always been one to brag about your wealth and how over the years you have accumulated many treasures, so you did bring this upon yourself."

"A gold step stool proves nothing," Akiva defended himself. "So, I like to collect odd and expensive items. What does it prove other than I am rich and perhaps a little eccentric?"

"So, Jacob, what kind of bed does Akiva sleep on. A Roman one or a typical Judean straw mattress on the floor."

"A typical Judean one, Excellency," the Captain replied.

"This is a step stool for a Roman bed Akiva. They're raised off the ground, so some people need it to get into their bed. What do you do with it? Ascend the step and then dive off the top?" My joke managed to make most of those in attendance laugh, reducing some of the anger that had been festering.

"I like odd items with no purpose, what of it," Akiva's defense of the item was sounding weak, and everyone knew it.

"What if I was to tell you that this particular item already cost a couple of slaves their lives when its true owner found it missing?" I waved my finger in front of Akiva's face as a warning.

"That's ridiculous. My step stool is not responsible for any such thing," Akiva refused to acknowledge anything about slaves being executed.

"Except that it is not your step stool," I informed all the others gathered around. "This particular step stool belongs to Quintus Tinnius Rufus and when he found it missing, he accused two of his servants of stealing it and selling it. Sadly, he executed them when they would not confess. Something like this is unique and you really should have melted it down if you didn't want to be caught. It's not as if everyone has a gold step stool that you could hide it among others. Do you still want to insist it is yours or should I send you and it along to Caesarea to plead your ownership before the governor."

"I did not steal it," Akiva began to reveal the truth behind the object. "It was given to me as a gift."

"But obviously not by the Governor," I added. "It still makes it a stolen item and you just happen to be in possession of it. So, you lied, whether you stole it or were given it, and indirectly you are responsible for the murder of those two slaves. Therefore, there must be a trial to decide your guilt or innocence on this matter."

"You intend to put me on trial for a step stool," Akiva ridiculed my decision.

"I intend to put you on trial for being in possession of an item belonging to the Procurator of Palestina, which may have directly or indirectly influenced a decision by the Roman authorities to go to war."

"Over a step stool!" Akiva still could not get past the fact that he was being charged for a crime that he considered to be insignificant.

"Rabbis Zoma and Azzai, what is the ruling of your council regarding having stolen property in your possession and not making restitution to the owner?" I asked.

"*Failure to make restitution requires that the settlement be resolved through a court of law,*" Ben Zoma replied, only to have Ben Azzai agree concurrently.

"So, as you see," I pointed out to Akiva, "I am entirely in my rights to hold a tribunal in order to see how we can resolve this matter. And at the same time, we will see what other commandments you are guilty of breaking."

"In other words, you are on a fishing expedition because no one here will fault me for taking an item from Rufus. He is a tyrant and has made our people suffer for years. Most would probably congratulate me for managing to take anything from him and the majority will say that it was not enough."

"And they might, but I don't believe that this theft from Rufus is all you have done. I don't think it is even a fraction of your wrong doings."

"That is nonsense," Akiva still clung to his innocence. "You have no proof, and no man can be tried on hearsay."

"That is true, but as you said, your own direct testimony outweighs that of a hundred witnesses according to this ridiculous law you managed to push through the

Sanhedrin. If that is the case, then I will use your own words against you. Jacob, did you manage to find the book I asked you to look for?"

Pointing towards Joseph, Jacob indicated that he had given it to my son when they first met outside.

Upon seeing the thick leather-bound book with its hundreds of sheets of paper loosely tied inside, Akiva became infuriated. "That is my book," he screamed. "You have no right to take it. It's mine. I demand you return it immediately!"

"My understanding from what I've been told is that it is the official log of events as they transpired, as well as all of the discussions by both the Sanhedrin and the Rabbinical Council that you participated in. For that reason, I requested my Captain to search for it since I do have a final say when it comes to the approval of religious matters. Anything written in this book is to be considered being of a public religious nature. Should it just so happen to contain other material that can be used as evidence to prove corruption or a crime, then it also becomes the property of the tribunal. Is that not so, Abba Saul?"

"That is the book," he confirmed. "And Akiva has often said it will provide the basis for the Talmud he intends to author as the new guidance for the Children of Israel."

"So, it is definitely to be considered a religious document then," I qualified it further. "Therefore, it is well within my domain to adjudicate its contents."

"It is intended only for the members of the Rabbinical Council," Akiva objected to my taking possession of it.

"I have as much right to read through it as you do or anyone else that sits on your council. I am now exercising that right. Since I know that the voice you love to hear above all others is your own, I expect to find it filled with many of your own quotes. I'm looking forward to assessing your religious viewpoints. But of course, should I find any other material that happens to relate to the other matters that may have affected our war efforts, then we shall permit the tribunal to evaluate them."

"Any court you hold would be a sham," Akiva argued. "I have the right to defend myself against anything you think you might find and since there are so few of my peers available, it is already prejudiced against me."

"You talk of a court, and I simply spoke of a tribunal. But if you insist on elevating this to a court of law, then I will see to it that it favours your position," I offered him a solution. "I will stack the jurors of my tribunal in your favour if that pleases you. Doing so, there can never be an accusation that the hearing was prejudicial against the defendant. In fact, it will be the opposite, suggesting from the onset to all that examine it, that it was prejudicial against the prosecution."

"And how do you intend to do that," Akiva wanted to know.

"From what I have been told you have five new students, is that correct?"

Akiva nodded his head but still suspected I was guilty of some sleight of hand about to be revealed. "They are not ordained, and by our laws that means they cannot sit as judges."

"None of them are ordained as you have said," I agreed, "Which means none of them would be able to sit on the Sanhedrin. But there is no longer a Jewish court and as I have stated, this is only a tribunal to investigate if a crime has been committed. I have no issues with them sitting as judges. Do you?"

"They will be free to vote as they please," Akiva wanted to ensure I could not influence or force them to vote as I wanted.

"They are free to vote as they please. So having been trained by you, they are about as close to being your peers as possible. Simon ben Azzai and Simon ben Zoma will also serve as jurors. These two are definitely your peers, which you cannot deny. Clearly the judges are stacked in your favour," I emphasized.

Akiva appeared bemused, thinking I must be a fool to do so.

"The three remaining jurors will consist of Abba Saul and my two sons. So, as you can see, I am the one totally at a disadvantage to prove my case. As the Praetor to guide the trial, I nominate that it be Yehonatan ben Matthias, the Levite Priest of this synagogue. A man you are also very familiar with after all your years in this town. So, are you still going to object to my holding of a tribunal? Yes, or no?"

"You won't let me escape the fact that you found the golden step stool, so I have no other choice but to let you hold your little legal show for the benefit of your Roman masters."

"I take that as a 'yes' then," I wanted him to say it exactly.

"Yes," he declared loudly. "Have your sham of a tribunal and let's be done with it as quickly as possible." Akiva was confident that the trail would be over almost as soon as it had begun. No student had ever accused his Master of any wrongdoing in all of our history, even when their Master was known to be guilty. To do so was practically considered to be a greater sin than the crime itself.

"Then it is agreed. We will conduct a tribunal in regard to the stolen goods and see if there are any other related issues. If one shakes the tree long and hard, who knows what might fall out."

"Now who is the fool," Akiva practically whispered to me, ensuring that no one else could hear. "You will never get a conviction with a jury split before it even begins to hear the first statement." I could tell he was laughing behind that thick beard of his.

"That may be true, but I don't want it said that Elioneai the High Priest falsely accused and sentenced a man to death," I whispered in return with an emphasis on my last word.

"The death penalty for a stolen stool," Akiva scoffed at my expectation. "Have you gone utterly mad? No one receives a death penalty for thievery!"

"Actually," I corrected his presumption. "The death penalty is for treason. The stool was just my way of getting the town officials to recognize I had justification for a tribunal and now that you have agreed to let it proceed, I will do my utmost to unveil the truth regarding the traitor I mentioned."

Raising my eyes towards the crowd, I addressed everyone standing in the courtyard. "As the prosecutor I will provide Yehonatan with a list of witnesses that I want to appear. Some of you may be requested, so please do not leave the town. Similarly, Akiva will be given the opportunity to present a list of those he wishes to appear on behalf of his defense. The trial date will be set to begin after the second Sabbath. It shall be held in this synagogue's courtyard, and may God protect us all from the evil that men do."

Chapter Five

Pretrial; 6th of Adar 3896

As the evening wound down and we relaxed as a family following our dinner, my wife felt compelled to ask me a question that obviously had been plaguing her since we arrived at B'nai Brak and especially after she witnessed the scene earlier with Rabbi Akiva at the synagogue. "What do you think the future holds for our people? Will we survive? Be honest with me Eli."

I rested my arms across my full stomach and inhaled a deep breath, as I patted the steadily increasing girth of my belly. "That was an excellent meal my dear," I complimented her.

"And you're evading the question," she responded having grown use to my tricks over the many years together. "So, stop trying to change the topic."

"You're not going to let me get away without answering, are you?" I asked her.

"Of course not," she laughed, knowing that she'd always get her way with me.

"I'm probably a much in the dark as everyone else," I informed her. "Several years ago, I thought we would never see the day when we would ever battle Rome again. In fact, it was the reason I considered it necessary that we returned to Judea, even though my father was totally against our leaving, as you probably remember. I presumed he was only being selfish, wanting to keep us and his grandsons nearby but now I have slowly come to realize that was not his reasoning at all. He feared for our safety. He obviously saw things here that I was unable to see. Our lives and civilization are different in Babylon. We have our Exilarch, our High Priesthood and the learned council of advisors making up the Beth Din. But here they have none of that over-structure any longer. Only these rabbis, that do nothing but squabble and argue and try to find unwritten laws and mystic oracles by which they can arbitrate and adjudicate. It doesn't matter what it might say in the Torah, our sacred book of laws, they still want to make their own laws. And since it is a rare event that they can ever achieve a unanimous decision, they do nothing but continue to argue until one side throws up their arms and concedes, even if they were in possession of the right and proper decision. It is chaotic, destructive and most of all it is a pathway to our destruction. If we no longer have a unifying force that governs us like our Torah, then how can we possibly survive. The more they dissect it like it was a dead and decaying body, the more they divide and fractionate us."

"Surely we can do something about imposing the laws from Babylon on the diaspora so that we all behave accordingly in the same manner," she sensed my frustration. "After all, we do have the Exilarch, and he is our rightful king!"

"I wish it was that simple, my Dear but those in power in the diaspora have absolutely no intention of giving up any of their power." I rubbed eyes which had grown tired from reading Akiva's book all day. "Whereas, we have an Exilarch to rule over us, and head up our courts and legal system, who most definitely is a descendant of King David through his paternal line, they have said their Nasi or Prince is the equal of our Davidic King. But Hillel, himself admitted that he was no more of being prince or king than the commoner that lays drunk in the street. His father was nothing more than a simple Benjaminite, and it was only through his mother that he was able to trace himself back to any member of the royal family. So, what did these Judean rabbis do in that situation? They make up a law that maternal blood outweighs paternal blood lines and therefore they have claimed that Jewish inheritance of prestige and authority only comes through the mother. Thus, this line of Benjaminites that has been preserved for a hundred years lays claim to the throne of David, as absurd as that sounds!"

Deborah was shocked to hear my explanation. "They have no authority to do that," she protested. You can't make a donkey into a horse," she always had a quaint way of expressing herself.

"Go ahead and tell them then, and see how far you will get," I challenged her. "Not that they would ever let you argue a case because they also went as far as declaring women unfit to study the Torah. Anything you had to say would be considered worthless!"

Now her expression went from shock to being infuriated. "What manner of heathens are they?" she shouted. "Why did you even think it was worthwhile to return here and restore the priesthood? Women have been equal in our culture since Moses granted the daughters of Zelophedad their own land parcels."

"You know why I brought us all back here. We discussed it many times and we were all in agreement that the time seemed right for the Temple to be rebuilt. As for the rest, you certainly don't have to win me over," I let her know she wasn't going to get any argument from me on the subject. "Just like your namesake who was a judge over Israel, God has pushed for the equality of the sexes, but these so-called learned men of Judea have made a travesty of our laws and traditions. Where I once feared Rome would be the end of our people, I now fear it will be these men who pat themselves on the back as being scholars, but it is clear in some cases they know nothing, and like many of their members are nothing more than sandal makers, shepherds and butchers that have overly exaggerated images of themselves."

"What are you going to do about it, Eli?" My wife always had this ability to place the weight of the world upon my shoulders and the equal expectation that I would succeed. I love her for her faith in me but this time the load seems too great to bear.

"I was convinced when I first came back to this land that any war with Rome would be genocide. We wouldn't survive. That is why I always believed we would find another solution and God would reveal His plan to me. Perhaps a better governor or a new Emperor, but no matter which alternative came to mind, it seemed as if I was always being thwarted. I had always considered that my adversary had to be Roman in origin but I must confess, after reading through Akiva's notes I believe the real enemy always resided right here in Judea."

"What do you mean Dear?" she inquired, though I suspect she knew my meaning very well. We had grown up as children together, our families extremely close and by the time she was twelve we were engaged to be married. After so many years, she completes my sentences and knows exactly what is on my mind.

"I think you know what I mean," I smiled at her. "If you want a war badly enough, you can find a way to make it happen and then blame its genesis on the other side. Meanwhile, that person was the one to light the fire and stir the flames into an inferno but by the time it is all over, no one remembers how it even started."

"You're suggesting one of our own was responsible for deliberately forcing us into war. But why do that if there was an opportunity for peace?"

"Why do that indeed?" I responded leaving the question open ended for my wife to answer. "Why do men do anything?"

"Such a person would have had to have been very confident that he could win," she suggested.

"One might think so," I answered. "But that all depends on what he might consider winning?" After so many hours of analyzing that very question, my head hurt.

"I don't fully understand, Eli," my wife admitted.

"Whatever the reason, the instigator would know that once they crossed the line there would be no turning back. But defeating a legion or two in Judea would be no different than swatting a few ants on the crest of an anthill. It's not those ants you see exposed on top of the hill that should be your concern but the millions that lie below it. Even Bar Kochba would have known that beginning such a war was suicide unless a peace treaty could be arranged when both parties finally grew tired of the slaughter. If the Carthaginians could not do it, and the Parthians don't even bother to try, then it is obvious that we are far too small to bring down the might of Rome. I have seen Rome, and I realize that we are nothing more than the fleas on the back of a dog to them. So, eliminating the presence of Rome was never an option, I'm guessing as this individual's actual intention. Something else was his motivation."

"If not to win, what then?" she asked, grasping the hopelessness of the war.

"What then indeed," I tapped my forefinger against my right temple. "The only feasible answer I can arrive it is to lose," I answered in a stoical voice.

"What? That is ridiculous. Why would anyone do that? I think you're wrong dear. I just can't believe there would be a Jew, any Jew that would want to see his own race obliterated from the face of the Earth. That makes no sense at all."

"Actually, no that I think of it, it makes perfect sense," I advised her, "Especially after you read what Akiva has written in this book of his."

"You're not serious!" Deborah stared into my eyes and then rocked back in horror, her hand rushing to conceal her open mouth. "You are serious!" The normally soft violet of her irises became shaded by an infusion of fear, turning them a deep vibrant mauve.

"It was no accident I overheard those students talking and then God led me to this town. What do I always tell you?"

"There are no coincidences," she repeated, having memorized that phrase after so many strange episodes involving our family that she knew it was true.

Deborah picked up one of my hands from on top of my full stomach and held it to her face. "I have never doubted you in all the years we have shared together. If you believe there could be such a thing as a Jew that would wish to destroy all of us then I will not doubt you. I only wonder how you will be able to prove it."

"Akiva's book is certainly going to help," I assured her. "I actually must commend him for his note taking. He is very thorough and loves to write his own commentary on practically everything. Almost in every story he has made himself the centre of attention. That will prove to be his downfall."

"I still don't understand how you can be so convinced that he could be this consolidation of evil that you propose. Everyone in this town loves him as a great sage. Even the other Rabbis talk about his incredible insight and intelligence and his expressed love for the Torah. Are you sure about this Eli? To everyone else he is a paragon of virtue and honesty, and you are accusing him of being a vile and loathsome creature bent upon the murder of everyone that practically worships him."

"Exactly my Dear," I smiled knowing she had hit upon the point I was making. "No one would ever suspect him of being anything other than what they see him as being. That is the nature of the chameleon and if you had read what I have over the past couple of days you would recognize him for the poisonous lizard he truly is."

"How could any man hide his true nature that easily or that carefully that no one would have ever seen it? I can tell you as a woman, no man is that clever."

"No one?" I took up her challenge.

"She knew that I already had my argument prepared but nonetheless she took the bait and accepted the challenge. "Unh-uhn," she shook her head. "Not one."

"So, Abel, who loved his brother Cain dearly, knew all along that his brother inwardly hated him enough that he would kill him over a small offering of grain on the altar?"

"That was different," she tried to explain.

"How so?"

"It was an impulsive reaction. I'm certain that Cain felt remorse for the rest of his life for what he had done. We all have impulsive moments we regret. They aren't planned well in advance as you're suggesting," she argued.

"A good argument," I conceded. "Not a great one but good enough to suggest it might be different. What about Ishmael and Isaac? Nothing impulsive there, but as much as the two brothers loved one another, until this day, the descendants of Ishmael still harbour a resentment towards the offspring of Isaac. Yet there we are, living side by side in Babylon, pretending all is well with the world and that we still love and respect one another but you know any day they could throw us off the side of a cliff and we would probably do the same to them."

"What Sarah did to Hagar was unforgivable. As you know, had it not been for God's intercession, both of them may have died in the desert."

"True, I acknowledged, but the animosity between the two mothers should not have become a barrier between the two brothers. Yet it still stirs as a primary bone of contention between our peoples. It is truly a love-hate relationship where either side could easily partake in the genocide of the other."

"But you're still talking about two different races even though closely related," Deborah defended her opinion.

"Then look no further than Joseph and his brothers," I advised her. "That is one people, one family, and they so easily would have wiped out entirely one part of the Children of Israel. If there had been no Joseph, then we would have died out as a people a long time ago. We have always been a people plagued by our own inner demons. David against Saul, Reheboam against Jereboam, Northern Israel against Judea, Jews against Samaritans. We don't have to look very far to find those within our own race that would have annihilated a large segment of our population without giving it a second thought. So why should we believe this time should be any different?"

This time Deborah conceded to my point. "You may be right," she confessed, "But it is still hard to believe that one man would think that he had the capability to destroy an entire race of people. Not only that, but to be able to conceal his intense hatred so well that everyone would think the very opposite of him. That is almost too hard to believe. I still don't know if you are completely correct, my Love."

I sat up straight at the table. "I admit, it appears inconceivable but that is the only way something like this can actually take place. It has to be so unbelievable, so preposterous, so inconceivable, that even when it is happening, no one is prepared to acknowledge what their eyes are seeing and their ears hearing. But most importantly, the victims must be kept in a state of disbelief right until the last minute when it is too late to do anything once you have seen the truth. A man capable of performing such a thing is far from being an ordinary man. When you look at him, he has to appear charming and have a way with flourishing words, his tongue dripping with honey. Of course, charisma and a good appearance is necessary. He also needs something which provides immediate respect, either from wealth or power or even better, having both. He has to be able to lie so well that he makes the truth sound like it is fabricated. He has to be both a storyteller and a revisionist, capable to smoothly transition from one tale to the next until he finds the one most acceptable without anyone recognizing that he has presented to them conflicting stories."

"No one has such ability," Deborah met my explanation with a wave of her hand and a dismissive laugh because as I said right from the start, it sounded far too incredible to accept. My wife is a rational, logical woman but even so, what she fails to appreciate is that does not mean everyone else is. Most people will let their emotions control their thinking and reactions. So, if you know how to exploit those emotions then you could even control an entire nation.

"Akiva has," I corrected her. "Even now, you see only the false face he presents to the public and cannot see past the mask he permanently wears. I now understand why God has led me to this town. If I am unable to tear the mask away and expose Akiva's true self, then we will be destroyed as a nation. Our belief systems will be abandoned, our faith in God lost, and our families turned against one another."

"Surely Eli, you are being overly dramatic, don't you think?"

"I have not been dramatic enough," I warned her. "If I fail to convince the tribunal of his guilt, then all that we hold dear will be lost. This man will use the rest of his life to tear down our structures, to reduce the Torah to nothing more than a commentary on his own book that he is intending to write. Once you smash the cornerstone of our faith, then over time its remains crumble to dust and eventually blow away in the wind."

"Now I know you are being overly dramatic Elioneai ben Yosef. "Everyone knows he has been gathering and organizing all of the interpretations from the learned men of the Rabbinic Council and then he intends to publish their sayings as a guide to understanding the Torah. I really think you need to settle down and take another good look at the situation," she suggested. "Don't find monsters where ones don't exist."

"No! You aren't listening!" I realized that I had raised my voice harshly which I shouldn't have done. It wasn't Deborah's fault that she was taken in like everyone else. "Forgive me, Dear. I don't mean to yell. All anyone knows about him is what he repeatedly tells them he is doing but if you were to read what he has written in his book, then you would see that this is not his true intent at all. He is calling what he is producing, the Oral Law, those laws which Moses never bothered to write down because God had already written it upon our minds and our hearts. Actual laws that supersede those written down in the Torah. He's advocating a set of laws that never existed because as we all know, at separate times both Joshua and Ezra read out the Torah to the people, seven hundred years between their readings, and neither of them ever read anything different, nor did they mention there being this other set of laws that we should know of. This Talmud as he refers to it, will be the new 'Word of God', even though all it contains is the conflicting words of squabbling sandal makers, butchers and shepherds. He says it will explain God's true intent and not the literal interpretation of the Torah. How can anyone even suggest that what God has given to us should be considered fallible and not to be taken literally? Only the words of men are fallible. Men that have absolutely no right to express their views on God's laws. And once the Torah is displaced, there will be nothing left to bind our people together because everything becomes debatable. Only dissenting opinions designed to render fragmentation and the disintegration of a nation."

Deborah walked behind my chair and placed her hands across the back of my neck, massaging the obvious knots that rose from the tension as I spoke.

"Thank you, my dear," I acknowledged that I really appreciated her touch.

"I understand now Eli and I should not have doubted you," she said apologetically.

"And I should have not raised my voice to you. I am sorry, my Dear."

"There is nothing to apologize for," she reassured me but something in her voice was not comforted.

"You seem worried." I knew it from her silence that followed her comment.

"You know me too well, Eli," she gave her little laugh that I fell in love with when we were still children. It still sounded girlish and took me back all those years to a simpler time.

"Of course I'm worried Eli. If he happens to be as deceptive as you described him to be, then I'm afraid that he may be well beyond even your skills to handle. You have never had to argue in court against anyone like him before. I have always considered you to be the smartest man I have ever known but from what you have said, he possesses far more feral intelligence, a cunning and wiliness that you have never faced. To do what you say he has done requires a base wickedness beyond any you have encountered. You must be careful because he could just as easily turn those at the trial against you."

"Yes, he can," I acknowledged. "And I would be very surprised if he doesn't try. He has been playing with the hearts and minds of people for half a century and he has always gotten his way. In almost every case, I doubt those people even knew they were being played. He has talents and skills that most of us as public figures can only dream of possessing."

"Then how can you win against an opponent that can out-maneuver any charge you try to make against him. Surely, he will turn it against you and as much as I love and appreciate all you can do, you do not have the support of all the people; certainly not in this land. There are many that still curse your family because of the House you have descended from."

Deborah's concern was well placed. I know my limitations and one of those is that the people have already begun to turn against the high priesthood. They cast blame on the houses of Phiabi, See, Anan and Kamithos for pursuing peace with the Romans in the first war rather than siding with the rebels. Now they will see me attacking one of their own. A man that rose from the simple life of a shepherd to become one of their greatest religious sages and became the spark that ignited this latest war. He will still have the hearts and souls of many, even though indirectly he caused the deaths of over half a million of our people.

"Because I have faith," I answered.

"Faith! Faith!" I could hear the anger rising by an octave in her voice as well as feel the increased tension of her fingers as they gripped tightly into the muscles of my neck. "How do you expect faith to save you. What good did faith do for your grandfather as his own people lopped off his head? What good did faith do all those young boys that followed Bar Kochba? What good did their faith do when the Romans raped our young women and killed their children? How did faith stop the ground from being drenched with Jewish blood until it flowed like a river?"

I found myself suddenly looking around the room for anything I could write on. All that was in reach was clay plate and a knife. It would have to do, as I reached over the table to retrieve them.

"Eli, have you lost your mind," Deborah asked as I began scratching letters into the plate.

"I love you," I told her excitedly. "Even when you don't know it, you are my guiding light. You have given me the answer as to how I can win even Akiva's staunch supporters over.

"By destroying one of the plates belonging to the synagogue?" she sounded confused and possibly a little concerned about my sanity.

"I'm certain someone can donate another plate to Yehonatan to replace this one," I reassured her. "You know I love you. I can always depend on you to say the right thing at the right time."

Deborah still looked confused, having no idea what I was talking about. "So, what did I say?"

"It's all about the faith. It was faith that permitted Bar Kochba's army take fifty cities. It was faith that liberated Jerusalem in the third year of the war. That faith permitted them to do something no other country could do; they drove the Romans from our land. They wiped out legion after legion, all because of faith. As much as I would not have believed it, that faith may have been enough to win the war."

"But they lost," Deborah felt it necessary to remind me of the outcome.

"Yes, they lost. But how why did they lose. They lost because that faith was undermined, and they lost hope. We know that Akiva abandoned Bar Kochba at the end of the war. I just need to prove that he was undermining that faith long before Beithar."

Deborah could appreciate the point I was making but she still looked somewhat bewildered. "Well, how are you going to do that?"

"I already have a plan."

Chapter Six

The Trial: Day One 10th Adar 3896

In the center of the synagogue courtyard, the leaders of the city of B'nai Brak, upon Elioneai's request, assembled and listened as I explained how the trial was to be conducted. As the prosecutor, I would not have a say in the final judgment, which took many of them by surprise since I was the one that laid the initial charge against Akiva ben Joseph. But I explained it very simply to them, that since I was already convinced of his guilt, it would not be fair of me to have a deciding vote. It was necessary that impartial judges, those having no opinion one way or the other at the start of the trial be the ones to make the final decision solely on the evidence provided during the trial. This novel concept of proving guilt rather than having to establish one's innocence was unique to some of them, and they were quite curious how this experiment in jurisprudence would succeed. It had the immediate effect I desired, because in turn they explained it to everyone else from B'nai Brak that had come to attend the trial, and it convinced the general populace that I could be a fair and generous man, terms which recently were not associated with those of the high priesthood.

I was surprised to see how many people could squeeze into the synagogue's courtyard. By best estimate, I calculated there must be at least a couple of hundred. It was obvious that many of them were there merely for the entertainment value. But there was also a young crowd of rabbinical students that I had no doubt were there to express support for Akiva and demand his release should the case start to turn against him. For whatever reason, which I will never understand, the young were attracted to Akiva, more so than any of the other sages. Perhaps the more radical one's thinking, the more it appeals to the youth of today.

Then there were the older townspeople. I could tell from the expression on their faces that they only sought some form of closure for the loss of their children that fought and died in the war. In their parental minds, blood demanded blood. Someone had to pay for their loss, and it really didn't matter who that might be.

And finally, there were groups of scholars from other towns, having heard about the trial and were obviously curious as to its outcome, since it would ultimately impact on their own lives. For every one of those scholars that loved Akiva, I knew there would be another that absolutely despised him. In his lifetime he had managed to insult and disparage many of their masters and the students never forget what had been done to their teachers. They would be seeking retribution and I knew if I could engage them by having them vocalize their angst throughout the trial, then it would influence others, including the judges.

At last, it was time to introduce the judges and set out the parameters of the trial. I signaled for all those gathered to quiet down so I could speak. "This trial will be held according to the laws of the Roman Lex Acilia. Therefore, there is no need for seventy judges as was the case of the Sanhedrin. There will be ten judges, all to be considered peers of the accused. Conducting and managing the courtroom, Yehonatan ben Matthias, priest of this synagogue of B'nai Brak will serve as Praetor. He will have the final say in all matters and if there is a split vote of five and five, then he will have the deciding vote." Thus far everyone appeared satisfied with my explanation as I scanned the faces of those assembled in the gallery.

Pointing to the table directly behind me, I spoke, "The ten judges will remain seated behind this long table and will be permitted to ask questions only for clarification purposes only. They will not be permitted to interrogate the witness of their own accord." The table was covered with a plain white cloth and on the table were several pitchers containing water, ten red clay cups and several writing tablets for the judges to take notes. "I will now summon the judges to enter one by one to take their seats at the table. I call upon Abba Saul Ben Nash." As he entered the courtyard, those that had never seen Abba Saul before let out a loud gasp that sounded like all of the air was being sucked from the room. Some may have heard about his excessive height but until you see someone almost eight feet tall in person, you have no real perspective by which to assess the true magnitude of those stories.

"Travelling with me from Jerusalem to Galilee, Rabbi Simon ben Zoma." Compared to Abba Saul, Ben Zoma didn't seem to get any reaction at all. Even the rabbinical students didn't show any excitement by his presence.

"And also travelling with us to Galilee, Rabbi Simon ben Azzai." Once again there was no reaction. Never seeking the limelight, neither of these two rabbis had much to do with interacting with the common people. It struck me that here were two men on the Council, deciding the future of the community in Judea, and yet they had very little contact with the people they ruled over. They intended to impose rules as they saw fit without ever assessing the impact on the common people.

"I'm about to introduce five rabbinical students, all of them students of Rabbi Akiva." I wanted that fact clearly stated at the beginning so that any objections could be dealt with immediately.

"You've already fixed the verdict," someone shouted from the back of the crowd. "The trial is a sham!" Others in the crowd started buzzing, taking up the criticism and sharing the same sentiment.

"I assure you; this trial is no sham," I attempted to quell any such thoughts. "I have spoken with these students and so has Yehonatan ben Matthias. It is both our opinions that none of these five students will let any loyalty they harbour towards their master influence their decisions."

"Then you both must be fools if you think that," someone shouted from the crowd.

"I have no illusions as to how these student feel," I responded in the direction of the incorporeal voice. "There is no doubt that they love their master. But I can assure you that even more than Akiva, they love God, they love the truth, and they love their people. Their moral convictions far outweigh any loyalty they might have for Akiva ben Joseph. I have no doubts many of you standing before me also love Akiva ben Joseph. But if I am to perform in my role effectively, then it is my responsibility to convince you that he is not the man you believe him to be."

I could see some nodding, fully understanding my intentions.

"There are those of you that respect him and I will not consider myself to have been successful unless I can sever those bonds between you by showing you the truth. There are those of you who do not know him at all, and I will not be satisfied until I am certain that you know him very well by the time I am finished."

"God bless Akiva," someone shouted in his defense.

"No!" I shouted in response. "God bless the Jewish people. God bless the children of Israel. God bless all those young men that died in an effort to preserve our race. And any man out there that believes one man should be blessed above the rest of us has no understanding of the true essence of the Torah." It was enough to silence whomever it may have been shouting because he would not dare offend the majority that favoured and comprehended what I had just said. "Our religion will not tolerate demagoguery and any man that believes he can be promoted and elevated above all others has learned the hard way that we, God's Chosen People, will not tolerate such behavior. Only those that are anointed by God will ever serve in a position above other men and until you show me otherwise, there is no proof that anyone has ever anointed Akiva for any purpose. He is not God's anointed!"

"A blessing upon you Akiva," some others shouted only to be quickly silenced by others in the gallery that wanted no further interruptions.

"Now, I will introduce these next five judges. As I mentioned, all are students of Akiva and familiar to the people of this town. All should be considered to be trustworthy and honorable. They are not ordained but all have a good grasp of the law and the lack of ordination should not be held against them. I call upon Shimon bar Yochai, Yehudah, Yossi, Meir and Eleazar ben Shamoa to take their sets at the table. The young men all took up their designated positions at the judges' table. "The last two judges I summon are my sons, Joseph and Azariah." Following the announcement, my sons separated themselves from the assembled crowd, making their way to the side of the room where they took their seats. "To those assembled here, this tenth day of

Adar, I present to you the ten judges for the trial. I know that the Lord will guide them with His wisdom and impart to each of them the integrity and morality to conduct themselves well in His name. If any man has objections to the selection of judges, let him speak up now."

I waited for approximately twenty seconds but not a single voice broke the silence. "There are no objections," I announced. At that moment Yehonatan appeared and took his seat behind the small table set apart on a raised dais in the northwest corner of the room. From this location he would preside over the courtroom.

"I now ask everyone to clear a path through the center of the room so that the accused may be led in." This was the moment they all had been waiting for. No matter if guilty or innocent, the marching of the accused into the courtroom always stirred the crowd. Some would meet it jubilantly, others sadly, depending on which side of the charges their opinion stood. The defendant is also aware that the thirty second walk through the courtroom was one of their best opportunities to sway opinion based on how penitent and remorseful they could appear. Unfortunately, criminal trials had recently taken on the connotation of entertainment, and rather than appreciating the performance of justice, the people were only concerned if they were entertained. This callousness is what permits men similar to the accused to take advantage of mood in the courtyard. If they can manage to win over the support of the crowd by providing entertainment, then it was possible that they could alter the outcome of the trial as well by influencing the judges' opinion. It was no secret that they expected to be greatly entertained from this trial, the same way I had no doubt that Akiva would attempt to provide them with exactly what they wanted.

No bonds, no cord ties, Akiva ben Joseph marched into the courtyard, shoulder to shoulder with the captain of my guard, his head held high as if he didn't have a worry in the world. Perhaps he didn't. This time he wore a high peaked blue turban, reminiscent of the one worn by the High Priest when the Temple was still standing. It was an obvious direct challenge to my own authority. Across his shoulders he had draped a beautifully designed prayer shawl. I looked down at my own robe, the one I had been wearing during my travels. It was beginning to look tattered and well-worn. I should have listened to my wife who tried to make me dress better for the occasion. Unfortunately, I refused, thinking that a more common and plebeian appearance would provide myself with greater acceptance by the townspeople assembled within the courtyard. From their reaction, it appeared that the people preferred a better first impression as Akiva had provided. I still attribute his peacock like attire to his arrogant nature, and Akiva's arrogance was constantly described as his greatest flaw by others. Repeatedly rebuked by his teachers and superiors for his constant airs of self-importance, even beneath the pain of the lash they could not beat his smugness from his body, according to his own personal notes that he kept in the book I obtained from his house. I was counting on the fact that they never succeeded in beating it from him.

Akiva flashed a friendly smile to all those he recognized among the crowd, waving to some of them as if the trial was over and he had already won. Let him wave, I thought. His over-confidence would be to his undoing. Not even waiting for me to announce his presence to the assembled people, Akiva walked over to the raised platform and promptly sat himself down in the chair that had been made available for the defendant. He crossed his arms, creating an image that he was impatient, having more important and better things to do.

"Surely you cannot be that eager Akiva ben Joseph to get this trial underway?" I joked, raising a laugh from some of the people.

"No, I'm that eager to get this trial over with so I can go home and drink some wine," he quipped, which received a far bigger laugh.

So far, I had to concede he had scored the early points but the day was long from over. "Praetor, if you would be so kind to read the charges."

Rising to his feet, Yehonatan ben Matthias began to read from the notes on the table that I had provided, laying in front of him. He cleared his throat and began. "Let it be known, on this day, the tenth of Adar in the year of three thousand eight hundred and ninety-six, this court has been assembled in the sight of God to hear the charges on several accounts against the rabbinical Sage known as Akiva ben Joseph, which include the theft of worldly goods, causing the abandonment of the faith by thousands of our people, and the high crime of acting against the will of God. As the Lord is the King of the universe, we consider this last charge to be no less than treason."

As soon as the word treason was mentioned, the shock wave ricocheted through the stunned audience in the synagogue's courtyard, only to be followed by a growing murmur of discontent from that portion of the gathering that were supporters of Akiva. The annoying hum began to increase rapidly in intensity.

"Order!" Yehonatan banged on top of his table, and surprisingly the dissenters responded. Obviously, the old Levite priest had more authority in his town than I had given him credit for. "In addition, other crimes may be revealed either through accident or intentionally during the course of this trial and they will be dealt with accordingly should they warrant our attention." That line I had not written down for him and I suddenly realized that Yehonatan may be aware of something regarding Akiva that the rest of us were clearly not knowledgeable of; something that he hoped would be exposed during the trial. "The prosecutor, out of a sense of virtuosity has submitted a motion that there be three possible out- comes to this trial, rather than the customary two. The first being, a unanimous vote to convict on all charges, resulting in the applied penalty of death, to be carried out immediately. The second being the case where the majority of the judges vote for conviction but it is not a unanimous decision. If that should be the case, then the accused shall be turned over to the Roman authorities to administer punishment. And lastly, the third outcome being a majority in favour of acquittal, resulting in a dismissal of all charges. In respect that the defendant had to endure a trial that did not find him conclusively guilty of any crime, then Elioneai ben Yosef, High Priest of Israel has promised to this court, as compensation, that he will fund the construction and establishment of Akiva ben Joseph's school in its entirety."

It was a more than generous offer that did not go unnoticed by those present to witness the trial. It also did not go unnoticed by Akiva who recognized it was a strategic maneuver on my part to demonstrate my intent to be fair and non-judgmental, thereby lending credence to the accusations I had brought against the Rabbi. After all, who would be willing to spend that amount of money in building a school unless they were almost certain they wouldn't have to. He under- stood very well what had just happened. But as far as everyone else was concerned, the trial would be conducted fairly and any evidence I presented would be unbiased and unquestionable since I now had a considerable stake in the outcome as well.

"The trial will be conducted over the next several days but must terminate by the time of the Sabbath eve on the fifteenth day of the month. I also remind everyone we will not hold a trial day on the fourteenth as that will be the Purim holiday. Both the Prosecutor and the Defendant can call upon five witnesses to present evidence on their behalf. Letters of request to some of those that have been already identified were delivered last week. As the witnesses arrive, they will make themselves known to me and we will bring them forward to testify. As of this time, only one witness for the prosecution has arrived, so we will be hearing from him today. If neither side has no further questions at this time, then we will begin with the prosecution's case."

"I have no questions, Praetor," I answered.

"My only question your Honour," Akiva raised his voice so everyone could hear, "Is why have you placed an innocent man on trial?" As soon as he declared his innocence, his supporters in the crowd cheered loudly, showing their support was not about to wane through the trial.

Banging his fist on the table, Yehonatan was not willing to permit any disorder in his court. "Should there be another outburst like that and I will have all that were responsible removed from the courtyard. Is that clear?" There was immediate silence confirming that they all understood. "As for your guilt or innocence Akiva, let me remind you that is for this court to decide, not you. Let the prosecution begin!"

I rose from the high-backed wooden chair situated strategically in front of the judges' elongated table but directly facing the small platform on which the defendant sat, I walked towards the rope barrier dividing the courtroom area and addressed those that would remain standing all day as spectators on the other side in the gallery. "This is a sad day," I began. "A very, very sad day when we find it necessary to investigate whether or not we have been betrayed by someone we had assumed was one of our own. And I select the word betrayed because that is exactly what has occurred beneath our very noses and we have either not noticed or we have been so completely deceived that we failed to even ask the simplest of questions, such as 'Who are You'. So that is exactly what I intend to do now to correct the oversights we have made in the past, with the hope that we will never make them again." Turning on my heels, I spun around so that I faced Akiva, my right index finger pointing directly at him. "Who are you?" The question was direct but intentionally without context to make him wonder what was its true significance.

Akiva momentarily hesitated, obviously wondering was this in some way a trap, but then finally answered. "I am Rabbi Akiva ben Joseph. Who do you think I am?" His question back to me raised a few titters of laughter but it was exactly what I hoped he would say because I wanted to answer the question for him.

"I'm not exactly certain," I answered. "To be precise, they actually refer to you as Rabbi Akiva ben Joseph Ha Ger. That is correct?" Akiva nodded. "So, who is the convert. Is it you, or was it your father? I can't tell from that reference."

"It was my father," Akiva responded.

"And exactly where did this conversion take place?"

"Why is that important?" Akiva was indignant in his tone. Either he did think the question was irrelevant or he was attempting to deflect away from the question without answering.

"Surely you can appreciate that an event such as a conversion would be a big moment in one's life. It doesn't happen that often, and when it does, there is usually a celebration of the event. I just want to know where it took place because when I was making my inquiries, no one could provide me with an answer."

"It was in Lydda," he replied brusquely.

"Lydda certainly had a lot of Rabbis residing there following the first war with

Rome. I don't know how many would have been eager to perform a conversion considering the Romans prohibited it, but I'm certain there would have been at least one. I guess that is why no one recalls there being any celebration or registration of the conversion. It would have been too dangerous for the Rabbi involved. I'm certain you would agree."

"Of course, it was too dangerous," Akiva confirmed my statement. "Everything had to be performed covertly. So there never was a formal record!"

"I agree. It is obvious why there is no record of the conversion but why would someone like Rabbi Tarfon, who came from Lydda, not even know of your origins." I watched to see if that raised a reaction, but I couldn't notice any sign of discomfort on his part.

"As I said, it was private and performed covertly. Those were bad times after the first war."

"Yes, they were," I agreed. "Terrible times but fortunately Lydda continued to prosper. Shame though that the city seems to have been taken over by the Mineans now and almost every Jewish religious teacher has left. But your father wasn't from Lydda originally, was he? My understanding is that he came from Gaza. Is that not, correct?"

"It was possible," Akiva replied.

"You don't know! I find that a little odd. I mean, if I was growing up in Lydda and I had blonde hair and blue-green eyes, whereas all my friends were dark in complexion with brown or black hair and brown eyes, I'd be a little curious about my origins. Why weren't you? I think I would have asked my father at some point why I looked different from everyone else."

The crowd was hushed, awaiting Akiva's response.

"He may have told me we were Northern Greek in origin," the Rabbi explained.

"Well then, that would certainly explain it," I agreed. "And since Gaza is the nearest city with a large Greek population, then the rumor that he originated from there is most likely correct. The probability speaks for itself."

"What has any of this to do with the charges?" Akiva demanded to know.

"I believe it is necessary to establish who exactly I am dealing with. After all, we are merely products of our ancestors. We can't escape the fact that our past does influence our future. Knowing your past provides me with a better insight to understand you."

"Well, I believe you are just wasting time and we should move on."

"Not quite yet," I informed him. "Still a few more facts we have to establish. So, your father travels from Gaza to Lydda, where he converts and later where you are born. But his name wouldn't have been Joseph. That would be his adopted Jewish name. So, you really aren't Akiba the son of Joseph. You are the son of someone else. Do you happen to know your father's real name?"

"If you must know, it was Alexander."

"Alright then," I clapped my hands. "So, we have established that you are Akiva the son of Alexander. And that you father was a convert, but we know nothing about your mother. Was she from Lydda? Was she the reason your father moved from Gaza?"

"You are asking questions I don't know the answer to," Akiva objected. "Once again, I protest. This line of question is immaterial."

"And I insist this line of questioning is crucial. The fact is, we know nothing about you, other than you were an illiterate shepherd that one day decided to become a religious scholar. It's an amazing story that one should be proud to announce to the world, but instead you have kept your past hidden beneath a basket. Now is the opportunity to share that history with your friends, your colleagues and the community you are asking to trust you." I made it evident that my request was actually quite reasonable and from the sound emanating behind me, it was evident that the people thought so too.

"I don't know why my father moved to Lydda. Perhaps it was the easiest and most convenient place for him to convert. If my mother was part of that reason, he never told me."

"I presume your mother was a Jewess," I prompted him for a response.

"Of course," Akiva responded clearly irritated. "How else could I be considered a Jew if my mother was not Jewish?"

"How else indeed," I repeated somewhat snidely. "So, let's see if I have this clear in my mind. Your father was a descendant of the Philistine Greeks that inhabited Gaza. So, we're talking perhaps of twelve hundred years of continuous pagan ancestors and one day your father decides he wants to be a Jew. Therefore, he travels to Lydda where he converts but unfortunately, we have no record of his conversion, which is understandable considering the Roman oppression, but neither do we have anyone still alive in Lydda that can confirm the   conversion.   He marries a Jewish girl in Lydda and you are born.   But none of this can be confirmed because both parents are apparently dead.   I even tried to find siblings but that proved to be a dead end as well since apparently you have no brothers or sisters.   It is as if your past never existed and there is no one that can tell us even a dust particle of your past.   I find that strange. Do you not find that strange?"

"My parents are dead," Akiva responded.   "When did that become a crime?"

"It's not but it is so unusual. Especially for parents to have only a single child. That is not our custom. That is not even the Greek custom. You're here, so obviously your mother was not barren.   Not having other children cannot be identified as a crime but it certainly can be considered unusual.   Your past, if one looks from my perspective, has been completely erased.   So, what am I to think?   Was it intentional or was it purely coincidental."

Akiva rose from behind his desk and started yelling.   "I resent what you're implying.   There is no crime for a convert marrying a Jewess.   There is no crime to come from a single child family. You are pulling on straws hanging in the air.   You have no evidence to the contrary, and your attempt to present my past as a crime is reprehensible."

"You are right," I agreed.   "I have no evidence.   But neither do you. Maybe that's why you insisted that the Sanhedrin record as law that *the word of a single sage is worth more than a thousand witnesses to the contrary.*   It was as if you knew this day would come and you were already preparing for it."

"Praetor," Akiva turned to Yehonatan.   "This line of questioning is all conjecture.   The prosecution has no evidence but continues to pursue this misguided direction. I object to this line of questioning as a personal insult."

Yehonatan acknowledged the objection.   Turning to me he asked, "Do you have any specific evidence you can present because if not, I must agree that this line of questioning is unwarranted."

"My apologies Praetor for what may appear to be circumstantial and unwarranted. I will proceed with the actual context of my question and get to the point for the sake of immediacy. Deuteronomy, Chapter 23, sentence nine.   I presume you are aware of what it says Akiva?"

"It does not apply to me," he insisted.

"For those of you not aware of what is written in our holy book, it says that the convert who is an Egyptian or an Edomite, we will accept into our community and can join our congregation but only after the children of the third generation from the time of the conversion. Why Egyptians and Edomites you might ask? Because we are the same people. When we left Egypt under Moses, we were a mixed multitude, consisting of Hebrews and Egyptians and Edomites. They are us and we are them historically, but not until they prove themselves worthy after three generations may they enter into our religious services. That is the law as handed down to us from God. It is undeniable. It is irrefutable. It is indisputable. It is not even debatable. But what of other nations. As written in Deuteronomy, if they are Ammonite or Moabites, their sons will never be permitted to join our congregations. Those are the two extremes by which we govern our laws. Every other nation will fall between those two parameters. Either three or more generations before they are accepted or never to be accepted at all. Is that not true Akiva?"

"So, it is written," he replied, "But that does not mean it is correct." No sooner had he said that, it sent shock waves through the crowd. They could not believe the Rabbi that so many of them adored could make such a statement as to challenge the word of the Almighty.

"What," I practically screeched my state of alarm. His comment bordered on blasphemy, but I was not prepared to go there. Not yet. "You have the audacity to say that the Lord, our God was not correct! You, Akiva ben Joseph claim that the law as given to Moses by God is in error and you know better. Or is it that your acceptance into the Jewish congregation was incorrect and out of necessity you have pressed the Sanhedrin to believe the law was incorrect? That your entire career will be, is, and has been in defiance of God's own edict!"

Akiva stood up again and waved his arms in an attempt to calm the emotions emanating from those in the crowd that were actually shocked by his statement. "Listen to me," he pleaded for their cooperation. "Listen to me," he tried to silence them a second time and this time he was successful. "The Torah is the book of law as given to us by God through his servant Moses. I do not dispute any of that. But it is simply a guideline. A guideline to provide us with the basic knowledge by which we can make our own decisions. That is why God has given us free will, encouraging all of us to take His foundational laws and improve them. For example, *God gives us rocks that are scattered across the earth, but it is us that with hammer and chisel can transform those same rocks into beautiful works of art. The Torah is no different.* He expects us to transform its words into words of poetry that make all our lives better. So yes, it states the convert must remain outside the Jewish religious services for at least three generations, but the number three was merely a guidance and nothing more."

"That is where you are wrong," I interjected. "Three generations were literally engraved in stone. God gave you the best-case scenario and the worst-case scenario and then said use your own judgment to regulate all the other nations that may fall in between. But your crime is not that you are only second generation, if that is even true, or that you joined into worshiping with the community on a regular basis, but the most grievous is that you actually sought to take over the community and dictate how it should function. And from what I have read in your book, you most certainly have done that. You are the very reason that God specifically dictated that at least three generations must pass. The first generation He assumed might have regrets, and therefore brings that sourness into the congregation; The second might despise what has been thrust upon them without choice and therefore brings that hate into the congregation; But the third would be true to their faith and would only bring love into the congregation. I believe you brought your hate into the House of Israel Akiva ben Joseph, and I am here to prove it!"

Banging his fist on the small table in front of him, Akiva's response was highly explosive. "This is not true!" he exclaimed. "Elioneai ben Yosef is twisting our religious beliefs into something hideous, attempting to have you reject converts as if we are less than human. This is not God's way. Do not be deceived! Don't let his hate of a Ger blind you to the wickedness in his heart!"

Obviously, I had hit a raw nerve and Akiva felt it necessary to try and defend himself to those in attendance by saying I was racist. When all else fails, call your opponent a racist. It is a tactic as old as time itself. I needed to decide on how best to press my advantage. "Is that what you said to Rav Joshua ben Hananiah?" Announcing the name of his deceased master was enough to throw him off stride. He stopped his rant and stared at me with what I could only describe a pure and intense hate. "Perhaps that is exactly how you managed to manipulate Joshua ben Hananiah to take you on as a student? I know Rav Hananiah had a big heart. He bent over backwards to help every lost cause that existed in the world. I bet you presented yourself as an orphan that never had the opportunity to study his Jewish heritage and Torah. Not that you had any Jewish heritage being the son of a convert. That is not my being 'wicked', as you call it, it's just a simple fact. But I need to ask you about that simple fact. In order to convert, one has to learn how to read and write Hebrew because you have to read out of the Torah as part of the conversion process. Which, assuming that your father did convert meant he had to learn to read and write. And since it is every Jewish father's responsibility and obligation to teach his sons to read and write as well, how is it that you were illiterate? Rav Ben Hananiah actually had to teach you to read and write, if I am not mistaken. Is that not true?"

I tried hard not to make it sound as if I was ridiculing him. Akiva remained silent, but that didn't matter. Everyone already knew the story of how Akiva had to sit in a classroom alongside seven and eight-year-old children, learning how to write and read. That was one of the reasons he had so many admirers. To be well into his adulthood, learning the basics of writing and then emerge as a Torah scholar was quite an achievement. There certainly is no denying that, not even on my part. One had to be driven to accomplish such a difficult task. Well in Akiva's case, we also knew what it was that had driven him. That story would also be essential for this trial as I would elaborate soon.

"Or maybe Ben Hananiah took you on simply because you gave him a large sum of money to do so. I'm guessing that's the real reason, isn't it."

"That is a lie," Akiva bellowed. "I had no money. I was nothing but a poor shepherd at the time. You have no right to delve into my past and spread these lies against me," he protested but it was obvious those attending the trial wanted to hear more. It was apparent that not everyone knew his story as well as they thought.

"You can't actually call the truth to be lies," I advised him. "The simple fact was that if you completed your studies and became a religious scholar, you would inherit a tremendous amount of money. No, that's not exactly correct. Your wife would inherit a tremendous amount of money and you would simply be a beneficiary in control of the funds. But that is a powerful incentive to learn, wouldn't you agree?" I walked over to the rope barrier that held back the people in the courtyard. "No need to answer that question," I said as I turned back to face Akiva. "It's merely rhetorical. That was the condition placed on your marriage by Kalba Savuah, was it not. If he was to approve of your marriage to his daughter Rachel, then you had to prove yourself worthy by becoming a Torah Scholar. After all, if you marry the daughter of the third richest man in Jerusalem, there must be a price. He wasn't exactly happy with what his daughter had done but he still loved her enough to make her inheritance conditional. Do you want to tell the story, or would you prefer that I do?"

"There is no story. I was a shepherd working on her father's farm. We saw one another and we fell in love."

"Love at first sight," I interrupted. "How sweet. Of course, you knew she was worth a fortune, so loving her would come easily to most men."

"I knew her father intended to disown her if she didn't marry whom he chose. But that didn't stop me from loving her. And she knew her father would never approve of her marrying a lowly shepherd, but still we ran away together and found a rabbi to marry us. When her father found out he disowned her, just as he said he would, and he refused to give us even one zuz to survive on. We lived in poverty, so your story that Rav Hananiah was paid to take me on as a student is false."

"Or so you would like everyone to believe. Isn't that part of your pity me story that you have played upon very well for the past forty or fifty years," I challenged him. "One thing you fail to understand, Kalba Savuah was the third richest man in Jerusalem, meaning that there are two families which are even richer. One of those in case you have forgotten is my family, the House of Phiabi. Between my cousins Eleazar ben Azariah and Reb Ishmael, I'd think we were probably number one in Jerusalem. Not that I would have much to do with Eleazar, but Reb Ishmael and I were like brothers and we spent a lot of time together whenever I visited Jerusalem. And being one of the richest families, it was customary to have guests over to the house all the time. The interesting thing about the guests attending dinners at a rich man's house is that they all tend to be other rich people. It's what happens when people are from a certain social status. So, I got to know your father-in-law very well as a frequent guest of my cousin's family. And here is what Kalba Savuah told me about his daughter and her husband. And so, everyone here knows that what I say it the truth, I swear an oath to the Almighty God, that every word I am about to say is exactly what was said to me by Kalba Savuah. May Yahvu cast me down if I deviate in any way."

I had definitely caught everyone's attention by swearing an oath in the Lord's name. They all knew that to use God's name and failing to honour the oath by even the slightest deviation from the truth would result in divine punishment. It is why hardly anyone will pronounce the Lord's name now for fear of retribution. By doing so, it also prevented Akiva from raising any objections.

"Kalba Savuah loved his daughter more than any of his worldly possessions. She was young and beautiful, but she also tended to be impetuous and impulsive. He knew that he spoiled her, but he could not help himself as she was his only child, his wife dying in childbirth when they tried to have a second. There were many suitors for his daughter but when you are one of the richest men in the city, your circle of friends tends to be limited to those that are like you or those that have power, as I have mentioned. But as you all are aware, those in power happen to be the Romans and there was no way that Kalba would permit his daughter to marry a Gentile. But when you're constantly surrounded by Gentiles, your judgments as to what is handsome and what is desirable becomes based upon your exposure. In this case, Rachel bat Kalba, was attracted to men that weren't from among our people. I think any of us that are parents can appreciate how a young girl's mind might work but this was a real concern for her father. We all know the stories of how Kalba Savuah would invite the students from the yeshiva in Jamnia to dine at his house in the hope that his daughter might find even one that she found to be a little attractive. But poor Kalba, his daughter refused them all. None were suitable."

I paused to look at some of the older men in the assemble crowd. "In fact, I'm probably not wrong in thinking that some of you may have received one of those invitations to come to dinner and meet his darling Rachel. Had I been born at the time, I expect one of those invitations would have made its way to Babylon," I jested, and the audience responded with a round of laughter. It was common knowledge throughout the land that Kalba Savuah was in search of a husband for his daughter and no one from the Jewish community could meet her requirements. I would not be surprised that many a young enterprising man thought to himself, if only I could find a way to meet her, I'm certain I could win over her heart. Especially if that man didn't happen to look like your typical Jew. All that money that would come with her as a dowry certainly would attract those with a more creative mindset. Suddenly, there is a young man tending sheep at one of Kalba's farms outside the city that catches her attention. As her father said to me, he wondered how it was that they even managed to encounter one another since it was only rarely that his daughter ever visited the farm. He assumed it was coincidence, perhaps even providence, but I believe it may have been more of determination on the young man's part. If you want to make something happen, then you will find a way to make it happen. So here was this handsome shepherd with his blond hair and his blue-green eyes, athletically built, practically looking like a Roman god, and most amazingly of all, he is a Jew. Kalba was certain his daughter must have been saying to herself, that he was the answer to her prayers. There was only one problem, he was a shepherd, and therefore he had no money. As far as Kalba Savuah was concerned, he was the last man on earth he would ever let his daughter marry."

I could ascertain that the story was already influencing the women that were present in the audience. They would see it as a love story that had become shamelessly twisted, which in turn would make them angry. I knew if I was to win this trial, I had to severe the bonds the people still had with their Sage. If I could create just a tinge of anger and resentment, then I could gain the upper hand.

"I don't know how many years Akiva ben Joseph worked on that farm or how many times he met with Rachel before they ran off and eloped, but I am suggesting what took a young man from Lydda to Jerusalem, to work as a shepherd was more than mere coincidence and certainly wasn't providence. If I want to find employment as a shepherd I'll go to the countryside, or even better I'll go to Galilee where the grass is always greener, but going to a city like Jerusalem would not have been the first place I would have looked for such a job."

I could see that most people were nodding in agreement. That was good. If I could prove that Akiva had motives that were not considered pure, then everything else would begin to fall into place. But it was Akiva's lack of emotion that had me confused. He continued to sit quietly at his table, as if he didn't care about what I was saying. I couldn't even see him sweating and the day was already getting hot. What could he possibly be thinking?

"Her father was not one to be trifled with, and being very protective of his daughter he began to investigate the background of the shepherd that she was continuing to visit despite his objections. The more he objected, the more she persisted and insisted that Akiva was the only one for her. He admitted to me that he was the cause of the elopement. When Rachel found out her father was investigating her lover's background, she insisted they run away and get married in secret. He was furious but he knew it was his fault. But his investigators did find out a very interesting item about Akiva and his life in Lydda."

"May I tell them," Akiva interrupted. "After all, this is my life you are exposing and I should have the respect to be the one to tell everyone."

He caught me by surprise. I had not anticipated that he would actually wish to reveal the truth of his own accord. But if I denied him the opportunity then the judges might think I was trying to hide some exculpatory evidence. "If you would like, but if I should find you straying even a hair's breadth from the truth, I will stop you immediately."

"Have no worries, I have no intention to change the story from what you already told. But if I am correct about what you were going to say next, then I think it must be said in its proper context. So, if you don't mind." I bowed my head for him to continue. "Everything you heard thus far is true. It is no shame for a young man to set his sights on a rich girl if the opportunity presents itself. And believe it or not, I was a young man at one time." Akiva's comment received a loud round of laughter and applause. "And I was a handsome man too, there was no doubt about that. But I was like a rough gem, uncut and unpolished. I was undisciplined and ignorant, all the things you already know and why it wasn't until my study of the Torah that I finally discovered who I truly was. Now I look back and see that I was a terrible person, capable of doing terrible things but I think we all know that God has forgiven me for my sins and I have devoted my life to giving far more back to the community than I have ever taken. So, if the Lord has found it in his heart of hearts to forgive me, then I pray that you can do likewise."

This was a mistake I realized. No wonder he was sitting so calmly. He was looking for the right opportunity to take over the presentation of the facts and I handed it to him on a platter. I should have known better, since he was famous for his oratory skills. If I tried to take the story's disclosure back under my control, it would definitely suggest that I'm trying to hide evidence and suppress him from providing what might be the truth. Best I wait for him to make an error that I can object to and then seize back control of the storyline.

"But I loved Rachel and I told her everything about my life before I met her. I revealed to her that I was already married and that I had a son back in Lydda. It was a marriage of youth, when you don't know exactly what you want in life or what it is you really want in a wife, but you go ahead and get married anyway. It was a mistake, a mistake we all too often make, and I had already walked out on that life and was looking to rebuild a new life."

"But you didn't divorce your first wife," I interjected quickly, seeing the chance to shift the storyline back towards the right direction.

"You're right, I never divorced but I never lay with my first wife again either. That is what her father found out about my past and Rachel knew all about it before her father confronted her with that information. But show me where it is forbidden for a man to have more than one wife. As long as the wives consent to the arrangement then it is condoned by God. There is no sin. And I loved Rachel very much as you all know, and she loved me."

There was my opportunity. He provided me with an opening because he was unaware of exactly how much information I knew. He may have convinced the judges he had done nothing wrong, but it was what he didn't do that I could use to condemn him.

"And which Rachel did you love more? Rachel bat Esh or Rachel bat Kalba?"

He was speechless as soon as I asked that question. "Did you think I would not find out the name of your first wife. Every synagogue in Lydda records the marriages that take place in their halls. Even the marriage between two poor children that had nothing to offer but love at one time to one another. Don't look so shocked. Of course, the marriage was recorded as one Agrippa ben Joseph and Rachel bat Esh, because you had not gone through the ceremony of officially adopting a Hebrew name yet. But it looks like the priest at the time must have asked you if you had such a name in mind because he wrote another name underneath in smaller lettering. What he wrote was Akiva. You intentionally chose a name that would sound like Agrippa. You might ask, how do I know all this, well that's because Judah ben Tarfon has come to B'nai Brak at my request as a witness. Shall I summon him to come up to testify that what I have said is the truth."

"Best to let him stay where he is," Akiva advised. "There is no love between Judah ben Tarfon and me. Any words by which he testifies are tinged with hate and therefore prejudicial and should not be considered. Praetor Yehonatan, I object to the presentation of any testimony from this named witness!"

"On what grounds do you deny this witness the opportunity to speak?" Yehonatan ben Matthias questioned the Defendant.

"On the grounds that he is hostile towards me and therefore anything he says cannot be construed as the truth but in fact is a construct of the animosity he bears towards me."

"Praetor," I began my defense of my witness. "I ask that you take into your consideration that he is of a high priestly family, the son of one of the great Sages, and no matter what his feelings towards the defendant, you cannot cast dispersion upon his integrity. How can Akiva ben Joseph even dare to say such a thing? Yes, Judah ben Tarfon bears a grievance with him but perhaps that complaint is more evidence to this case as well. Praetor, if I may, I would like to call upon my first witness to come forward, Judah ben Tarfon, the priest of the synagogue of Lyddah. I request your permission to do so."

"Call upon you witness prosecutor."
"I still object," Akiva made his position known once again.

"Your objection has been overruled," Yehonatan dismissed him with a wave of his hand.

"Judah ben Tarfon, please step forward," I announced. Everyone in the courtyard looked around to see the man in question. Finally, a man, approximately my own age made his way through the crowded gallery and crossed over the thick rope barrier.   I directed him to take the chair that was situated beside the praetor.

"You are Judah ben Tarfon?" I asked.

"Yes, I am," came his reply rather monotone.

"In the presence of God do you swear to tell the truth?"

"I do."

"How is it that you know the defendant?" I needed to establish the background between Akiva and Judah.   Yes, it was true that Judah hated him passionately but if I could convince the judges that it was warranted then his testimony would not be tainted by his animosity.

"He would visit our home frequently," he responded. "Pretending to be a friend of my father but all the time he was merely playing him, just like he used so many other people." The response raised a hissing sound of displeasure from a few in the courtyard.

"And this home you speak of, that was in Lydda, correct?"

"Yes, my family has lived in Lydda for several generations.   We serve as the priests in the main synagogue of the city."

"So, in that position," I continued my line of questioning, "You would have access to all the records stored at the synagogue.   "Records of those reaching the age to joining the congregation and going through the ceremony, plus all of the marriages conducted there, and anything else of a similar nature. Is that true and if so, what can you tell me about this first marriage of Akiva ben Joseph that I mentioned?"

"It was when my great uncle served as the synagogue's priest; he was from my mother's side.   He was very meticulous in his record keeping."

"Now if I understand correctly, your uncle was also a Kohen, your father maintaining the tradition that a High Priest should only marry a daughter who was also from a High Priest's family.   Is that correct?"

"Yes, it is," Judah replied proudly.

"I am impressed," I admitted. "It certainly is not a tradition that my family has been able to sustain over the years.   But it tells us all something about your family. That the offspring from a double lineage of Kohenim is to be considered born without flaws or blemishes. I won't embarrass you by asking if the story is true, but I just wanted everyone gathered here to understand your family background. It at least suggests to me that I should believe what you will tell us about this record. As the record is kept in a large tome that is not easily transported, it was not possible to bring it with you, but I don't want anyone to question your word. You have sworn before God to tell the truth, and you are the son of a Kohen marrying the daughter of a Kohen, and thus your word is sacred. But I am curious as to why you searched for the record in the first place."

"Because of my resentment for Akiva ben Joseph," Judah freely admitted. "When my great uncle died, those that knew him or appreciated him came from all over the country and even beyond to attend his funeral service. One by one they stood up and heaped their praises upon him, recounting stories of how great and generous a man he was. One man in attendance, took his turn to talk about my great uncle and related how no one, not even your family in the Temple of Jerusalem could blow the shofar like he could. He said that when my great uncle blew on the shofar, the heavens wept and even the angels would put aside their lyres to listen. It was true because I could recall all the times I heard him sound the shofar and it would make my skin shiver in excitement. And after that man sat down, Akiva stood and made his comment about this most holy man, my uncle, that had passed away. He began by saying *it was a sin to praise my great uncle in such a manner. That because he was lame in his one foot, he should have never been permitted to put his lips to a shofar, let alone blow it in the synagogue on our holiest of days.* Those attending the funeral became angry and had it not been for the intercession of my father, I think they would have beaten Akiva to death with their bare hands, so great was their anger. But Akiva would not stop his baiting of those in attendance. He called them all sinners because they all knew what the law permitted and forbade. He said *perhaps if it was a Jubilee year, then God may have forgiven my great uncle for sounding the shofar* but now his soul would be denied its place in the Shekinah. As you know, as High Priests, that is the cornerstone of our beliefs. That all things come from the Shekinah and at death return to the Shekinah. To be denied that basic tenant of life meant our souls would be cursed to endless wandering. My father tried to smooth things over by announcing that any time his wife's uncle blew the shofar, God considered it to be a Jubilee year, but the anger had boiled over, and I knew that those in attendance would have killed Akiva for his cruel words. My father Rav Tarfon was a kind and gentle man, too gentle sometimes and he made the choice to rush Akiva away from them and hide him safely until everyone went home following the service. I knew that Akiva remained hidden even while we sat for the week to honour the dead because my father would disappear from the house every now and then with a plate of food and a jug of water. It was the only time I felt disrespect for my father, and I am still ashamed of myself for feeling that way."

"But as for your searching for the marriage record, how did that come about?

"Following the death of my great uncle, I was appointed to the position of the synagogue priest. I thought my father would be pleased for me, but all he could talk about was Akiva said this or Akiva said that. They rarely agreed on any subject and in most cases my father's interpretation was correct, but he would always say that Akiva defended himself well and created doubt in my father's mind. I realized that was Akiva's purpose, to make all the great Sages begin to doubt themselves. If they could no longer believe in what they were saying, then how could there be a future for our people? And then one day my father looked despondent, his eyes glazed over as if he had been crying for a long time. When I asked him why, he said Akiva had asked him a question that he failed to defend properly and now he had serious doubts about his entire life. I asked what had been the question and he replied, *"What is more important, studying the Torah or living your life according to the Torah."* In my mind there was no doubt to the correct answer. It was far more important to live your life according to the Torah. He said that was what he thought too, but Akiva had convinced him otherwise. I could not believe what my father had admitted. We all know that God praises us for action rather than inaction. It is the act of charity that we are rewarded for, not thinking about who we should be charitable to. It is the act of preparing for the holy days and festivals which God delights in, not our sitting around while others make all the preparations for us. It is our living and following the commandments by which we will be judged at the end of days, not by our debating endlessly what the true meaning of those laws might be. My father knew all that and yet he failed to defend the truth against the lies presented by that demon, sitting there in disguise." Judah pointed directly at Akiva as he lips spat out his words. I tried to console my father and tell him everything would be all right but then he confessed to me that after he lost in his defense of the question, he leaned over and kissed Akiva saying, *"You are my true son and you have proven yourself to be far more worthy and smarter than me."* As soon as he did that, he heard the voice of the Almighty whisper in his ear, *"You have failed me Tarfon. No longer will your bloodline sing my praises. When your grandson is of age he will be like an animal, devoid of knowledge, carnal in his lusts, feral in his desires, and no matter how many of the great men of the Council attempt to rescue him they will fail. So shall it be!"*

That is my son that was cursed and for what reason? What did my boy do to ever deserve to be punished in this manner. The day we let that devil into our house was the day we became cursed. My father always favoured him for some reason that I could never understand. It was not as if my father did not know what kind of man he was. After the incident at the funeral my father said to him, *"How long will you rake words together and use them against us Akiva? I cannot bear it"*, yet he would not say a bad word other than this against him. It was as if Akiva had cast a spell upon him. How else can you explain Akiva *telling my father that he would like to make a major investment on our behalf and then taking four thousand gold aureus from my father.* Yes, we are a rich family, but so is Akiva. Why take our money? And why ask for such an incredible amount. Why would my father even agree unless he was compelled under some form of witchraft?"

My jaw dropped upon hearing the amount disclosed. It was an incredible amount of money to just hand someone. I did some quick calculations in my head to determine exactly how much. "Let me stop you there Judah." I held up my hand to pause him from talking further and turned to face the crowd. "Does everyone understand the amount of money we are talking about." I knew they would be confused because most of them wouldn't even be able to fathom that amount of money. Even a single gold aureus was probably more than many had seen.

"A lot!" someone shouted, causing everyone to laugh.

"More than a lot, my friends. Let me tell you how much more. Four thousand aureus is the same a one hundred thousand denarii or zuz. Imagine a pile of one hundred thousand zuz in front of you. Now imagine what you could buy. Each aureus would get you a hundred gallons of wine. And if it's not wine you want, then think of it as two hundred pounds of flour. For most of you, that one aureus represents a month's wages. The total amount would pay a hundred people for over three years in wages."

"Is there a point to all this?" Yehonatan interceded.

"Yes, Praetor. I need the people to appreciate how much money we are talking about so they can better understand what happened to it." Yehonatan nodded his consent for me to proceed. "No matter which way I describe it, we are talking about an incredible amount of money. So, Judah ben Tarfon, how well was the money invested on your father's behalf?"

"I don't know," came the reply.

"I didn't quite hear you. What did you say?" I heard him perfectly well, but I wanted the point he was about to make to be as dramatic as it could be.

"I don't know. *When my father finally asked about his investment a year later, Akiva said he gave it all away.*"

"He gave it to whom?" I inquired.

"He said he gave it all to students in need so that they could study the Torah."

"We must be talking hundreds if not thousands of students that were able to study the Torah as a result of this money. With that amount of money every student could have his own Torah scroll. I bet some of those students that received some of this money must be gathered here today." Turning once again to the people standing in the courtyard, I asked all those that had received some of this money to raise their hands. Not a single hand was raised. The outcome even stunned those within the peristyles as they looked around the courtyard only to see that no one had gained from this incredible act of generosity.

"I'm guessing you are not surprised," I said to Judah.

He shook his head. "Not surprised at all. I knew that Akiva considered my father to be a fool and easy to take advantage of, covering his true feelings with constant praise, referring to my father as the Elder. But by Elder I think he only meant the 'old fool'. I even told my father that he had been taken advantage and lied to, but he would not hear of it. He said that Akiva may be many things, but a thief was not one of them. He was blind when it came to this man that he considered a friend. I don't truly believe in spells or witchcraft but I have no other way to describe it."

"Ahh...but Akiva believes in witchcraft." At that moment I withdrew a selection of the trinkets I had purchased off the old woman from the pocket in my robe. This one here is a blessing for making money, signed and blessed by the defendant himself. And this one, is a string of beads to provide good health. But this one I find very interesting. It is in the shape of a scorpion. It is designed to ensure your baby is born in the corresponding month when the constellation of the scorpion crosses during the night sky. I'm guessing you pray to it and Akiva ensures it will happen. Idolatry! The curse of Moab still exists. The bane of our entire Jewish existence for over two thousand years and here is this rabbi disseminating his little idols throughout the land."

"They are not idols, merely charms," Akiva finally broke his silence.

"As soon as you pray over a charm bearing an image then it becomes a graven image and a graven image is nothing other than an idol. One that you made and provided to the populace. This is an unforgivable sin!"

"If that is true then Terah was a sinner and not loved in the eyes of God," Akiva argued. "We held this debate within the Council, and I won. *If a non-Jew carves an image, then he does so in order to pray to it and that is idolatry, but if a Jew carves an image and has no intention to pray to it, then he is not an idolater.* Only the person that actually uses it for their prayers commits a sin. This was agreed to by the Council and therefore I have committed no such sin."

"But everyone that buys one of your little charms and prays to have a child in the month of the sign, they would be the ones committing the sins. Is that what you are saying?"

"I cannot be held responsible if they use the charms in a manner that resembles idolatry. That is a decision they made of their own accord," Akiva explained his innocence.

"Do you actually believe that? I cannot believe the sheer arrogance of your statement. You lead them astray and then you say it is their fault. How can you even refer to yourself as a man of God? When I read it in your book, I could not believe it myself but now upon hearing you actually speak these words it become even more profane!" I walked over to the judges' table where the book had been placed and opened it to the designated page where Akiva had made these comments. I pointed to the paragraph where he wrote not only this but the statement that *when Rabbis perform magic it is not considered witchcraft.* When the judges saw that, even his own students looked shocked. "We will deal with these abominations at a later time," I suggested. "Right now, we must get to the topic at hand. So, tell me Judah, why did you search the registry in the synagogue?"

"I knew from my father that Akiva had grown up in Lydda and I was desperate to find anything I could use to make my father understand what Akiva was doing to him. The great sage that Rabbi Tarfon had been, was slowly being destroyed bit by bit by this idolater."

"Like a rock being worn away by water," I interjected.

"What?" Judah did not understand why I said that.

"My apologies for interrupting. Something I will comment upon later. Continue." It was my way of making a mental note to myself not to forget what had been said.

"I thought maybe my great uncle had written something in the synagogue's diary. For Akiva to show such contempt for a great man at his funeral, there must have been something that occurred between them in the past. I was desperate to find something, so I started with the log of events. I almost missed finding it because it occurred so long ago. Practically when my great uncle first became the priest of the

Lydda synagogue. This entry stood out because below the written names, he made several comments, which was unusual because he rarely did so. The names written were Agrippa ben Joseph as the groom and Rachel bat Esh as the bride. It wasn't until I read his notes that I realized I had found Akiva's entry. At first, I was confused by the timing of the event. We knew approximately when his marriage to Rachel bat Kalba took place, but this wedding was dated almost ten years earlier. And I doubted very much if my great uncle would ever marry two young people without the proper witnesses to sign the ketubah. It just isn't permitted. Especially when the father of the bride is one of the most important men in the Judean community. Something else was at play here to have my great uncle commit to what is a most unusual behaviour on his part. I have no idea how they persuaded him to go ahead with the marriage. Then I saw that he had requested the groom to provide a Hebrew name along with his common name. I guess they must have argued about the name selected, because my great uncle wrote that he considered the name chosen to be offensive, but the groom refused to change his mind, insisting that it be recorded as Akiva."

"And in light of all that has happened recently, not to overlook why we are holding this trial, then the name probably is just as offensive now as when your great uncle took it to be, long ago," I commented. "How else can you describe a name that means 'the Supplanter'. One who's entire purpose is to throw out the old and bring in a new order. To discard everything from the past and to embrace a new age where he is the one in charge. The name selected was a forbearance of things to come and we failed to recognize the warning signs that were provided to us by the offender, himself! So through your investigation, not only did you find that Akiva had been married ten years earlier to another woman but that the seeds of discord were planted between your uncle and him at the time of this wedding. A grudge that defendant may have borne against your entire family for decades because of an ideology he declared upon naming himself. An ideology directly opposed to everything your family stood for."

"There is more," Jonathan wanted to add another point. "When Akiva insisted that Bar Kochba was the messiah and we had no alternative to war, my father and all his students stood against him. They were men of peace and united in their efforts to stop the revolt. I remember my father's student Yose ha Gelili saying to Akiva, *"Akiva, even if you carry on all day, I shall not heed you."* Unfortunately, he was executed by the Romans just as the war was starting so he never really had the opportunity to try and prevent the bloodshed."

"The same pacifist beliefs as your father," I commented. "Against the war, yet the Romans executed him." I could see Judah ben Tarfon was thinking about something else as soon as I reflected upon his father. It was as if a light had suddenly turned on and he was analyzing what it meant.

"And my father's other student, Judah ben Ilai. He heard that the Romans were coming for him at the beginning of the war and narrowly escaped being caught. He went into hiding for four years, only to come out recently."

"Who else was a student of your father?" I inquired.

"Eleazar Ha'Modai."

"Who happened to die at Beithar at the hands of Bar Kochba," I commented. Another rabbi closely associated with Akiva but a pacifist as well. I was beginning to see a pattern here that I didn't like. The Romans were eliminating anyone that had significant authority over the people and might have intervened by stopping the people from joining Bar Kochba. This was too much of a coincidence and as I said before, I don't believe much in coincidences. Of course, Ha'Modai's only crime seems to be that he said nothing after Akiva fled the city, so I have no doubt that Bar Kochba kicked him to death as a substitute for the disappeared Rabbi whom he realized had betrayed him. The real question is how could the Romans even know which rabbis were the pacifists unless they were being told? I made a mental note of all these men because I realized that over the next few days of this trial, I would need to give this question some very serious thought. Perhaps the answer underlies the entire issue of guilt or innocence and whether or not we had a traitor in our midst.

"Praetor, I have no further questions for the witness," I announced. "I think it has been clearly established that the man we know as Akiva ben Joseph is simply one Agrippa son of Alexander, a descendant of Greek Philistines, who from the testimony we have heard today, may still harbour deep resentments against the Jewish people even though he disguises himself well, just like a wolf in sheep's clothing. I would like the judges and the people to take the time to reflect well on what they have heard. I believe if they review the facts, they will see a very different portrait from the man they thought they knew. A man who in fact may have lied about much of his life, as to who he was, what he has done and what he intends to do. A man that was obsessed with money and used both marriage and friendship to obtain more than he had a right to. At this time, I submit the floor to the defendant for the remainder of today's session." Upon the completion of my statement, I returned to my chair and little table, falling back into my seat in near exhaustion.

Yehonatan stood up and cleared his throat. "Does the defendant wish to pose any questions to this witness?"

"No Praetor," Akiva responded. "I believe we have heard enough from the poor boy whose father preferred to be with me than his own son. How sad that one's own father preferred to call me his son rather than his natural born offspring. What does it say about his attitude towards his own first-born? If one's own father cannot place the trust that a son deserves in his child, preferring to choose another, are we able to overlook that clear signal from his dead father and accept anything the son has said today as being the truth. I don't think so but I wish not to disparage the good name of Rabbi Tarfon and open this to debate."

Akiva certainly said a mouthful and did so succinctly with even a touch of humility on his part so that he appeared merciful by not performing any cross-examination. The strategy was very clever I had to admit and may have negated much of what I had gained from Judah's testimony. I realized that any underestimation of my opponent could prove fatal to my case. I could see Judah ben Tarfon, balling his fists and preparing to launch an attack against his tormentor. 'Don't do it. Don't do it,' I repeated silently to myself, praying that he didn't do anything so foolish. Attacking Akiva would cause him to lose all credibility that remained after having presented the facts so well. I knew I had to do something quickly. "Judah," I called out. "Since the defendant has no further questions, I would like to thank you on behalf of the court for your excellent testimony and assure you that the truth will prevail."

Yehonatan saw what I was doing and immediately asked the witness to step down and return to the other side of the rope. "Does the Defendant have any of his own witnesses that he would like to call upon today?" Yehonatan quickly turned the conversation away from the son of Tarfon and moved the trial forward.

"None at this time Praetor."

It became clear to me that Akiva was going to stack all his witnesses to appear the last couple of days of the trial. It was an old legal trick. Monopolize all the time at the end of the trial and the only thing the judges can remember is what they heard closer to the end and forgetting most of what they heard at the beginning.

"If there are no further witnesses, then I declare this trial be closed for the day and we will continue tomorrow at the same time. May the Lord keep you from harm." Yehonatan banged the top of his table to signal the day was done.

It was time to return to my room at the Annex. Reflecting on the day's events, it was hard to say where the case against Akiva stood. For every point I had made, Akiva managed to generate some doubt. And as long as doubt remained, it would be impossible to win this case.

Chapter Seven

Evening; 10ᵗʰ Day of Adar, 3896

"Looks like that went pretty well, today," my son, Joseph, provided his own summary of the day's events.

"Are you trying to get me to discuss the trial?" I asked sternly.

"Maybe...yes," he responded.

I addressed both of my sons at the table. "As judges, you must remain impartial right until the end.   If I influence you in any way, and the defendant finds out about it, don't ask me how, I don't know how, but if he does, he can claim the trial was conducted improperly and call for a mistrial.   Do you understand?"

"Yes, father," they both replied simultaneously burying their chins onto their chests.

"Well, then," Azariah was now thinking of something to say that could in some way circumvent my refusal to talk.   I know my sons well and they think like I do, so it's no surprise he was going to probably surprise me with a very difficult question. "Why is it that the greatest enemies to our people always seem to arise from within our people?"

I couldn't help but laugh. My youngest son is quite the sly fox.   "So is that a general question or are you asking specific to this case."

"General of course."

"Of course," I accepted his response.   "As God has consistently described us, we have always been a stiff-necked people. Most often we agree in order to disagree. We laugh at our own joke that if there are two Jews in a room you will get three very different opinions.   Sadly, that is the truth and not merely a joke."

Deborah entered the room at that time and sat down at the table with us.   She smiled gently, knowing the story I was about to tell very well because it was one my family played a significant role in, and she had heard it many times before.

"The story I'm about to tell you is the epitome of our own ability to destroy ourselves by our own behaviour. The Mineans are no different from those that decided to call Bar Kochba the Messiah, except that they chose a Jew that had no intention to fight a war and that did not agree with those holding the opinion that in order to be the Messiah you must physically defeat your enemies. Instead, these Mineans chose a man that they said could perform miracles. So, in some way, they were no different from what Rabbi Yochanan ben Torta said, when asked if he supported Bar Kochba. He said, '*No, because Bar Kochba couldn't perform miracles and therefore he could not be the Messiah.*' As for Yeshua ben Yosef, the one the Mineans called their Messiah, most of the Rabbis said, he can't be the one because he won't fight a war and defeat the Romans. If we can't even agree on the definition of the Messiah in the first place, then how would it even be possible to live together as one people with a single mindset."

"So, you're saying that we were wrong to reject the Mineans and refuse to accept them into our congregations any longer?" Azariah had the makings for a good legislator. He was already showing an excellent capacity to twist my words.

"What I'm saying is, if we had been smarter, we would have known how to use our differences to our advantage rather than reject each other because of those perceived differences. Now that the Mineans are expounding the false believe that we, meaning us traditional Jews, were responsible for the death of Yeshua, as a result, I'm afraid they will never return to the fold."

"But why would they think that?" Joseph's turn to ask a question. "Everyone knows it was the Romans that sentenced and killed him. The same way they've slaughtered us for the past four years."

"You would think that was common knowledge, but mankind's memory tends to be short term at best, which is why history can always be altered by those in power. And trust me, power is behind every bad decision that Jews have made that landed ourselves in trouble. We were making bad decisions from our first days of existence. Remember, Moses went up the mountain and it was your ancestor, Aaron, that decided to construct a golden calf while he was gone. Now that was a bad decision!"

"But what's that got do to with Yeshua ben Yosef?" Azariah was eager for me to get back to the storyline.

"What if I was to say that it wasn't really the Minean's fault for fostering this belief that we killed their Messiah? What if I was to say that our great Sages of

Judaism, these so-called Rabbanites, who sometimes I think share less than half a brain between them in total, were responsible for the libel! That in a foolish effort to demonstrate how strict they were as true enforcers of God's will, they decided through their arrogance to willingly spread a lie. Trust me, these are not the wisest of men. As you have seen, they are shepherds and sandal makers, bakers and merchants. Men that for some reason have so much idle time on their hands that they can sit around and do nothing but engage in idle chatter. They are worse than women."

No sooner had said that, when one of the hand towels on the table came flying through the air, hitting me squarely across my face. My wife did not appreciate that last comment. "Keep making foolish comments like that and you will be sleeping with the shepherds and sandal makers from now on." Both of my sons thought that was hilarious as they laughed uproariously. It wasn't that funny.

"Yes, my Dear," I responded somewhat sheepishly. "My apologies. You know I only said that for story enhancement. And there's another lesson for you boys," I wagged a finger at my sons, "Always respect you wives." They continued to laugh. "Any way, as I was saying, they made up a story that was so wrong in so many ways but thought at the same time they were so smart. *They said that they lit a lamp for him in the inner chamber and placed a witness in the outer chamber so that they can see and hear him but at the same time he could not see nor hear them. Then one of the members of the Sanhedrin said to him, "Tell me again what you said to me in private." Apparently, he claimed to be the Son of God but he denied saying so. They then wrote that if the prisoner had repented, then they would have released him, but instead he says, 'It is your obligation to do what you must do.' Even though he did not admit to any crime, since he didn't repent, they wrote that they brought him into the center of the courtroom and they stoned him. And then they hung him on a tree on the eve of the Passover.*"

"That doesn't make any sense," Joseph muttered somewhat dismayed, totally confused by the passage I had quoted.

"That is straight out of that book that we took from Akiva. Obviously, the Council of Rabbis were trying to recall a very special meeting of the Sanhedrin, except none of them was ever there to ensure it was accurate. They fabricated the entire story. They all were born well after the event. So, you tell me exactly where they went wrong. It was your question Azariah, so you get to go first."

"It was a night meeting, hence the need for the lamp. But they got it wrong. The Sanhedrin was prohibited to meet at night."

"Correct. It couldn't have been the Sanhedrin that they're describing but some other clandestine group taking the law into their own hands. Continue Azariah."

"The witnesses were placed outside in order to come in and defend the accused if they heard something inaccurate. You needed two witnesses to deny or uphold the accusation, otherwise the prisoner would be freed."

"Very good," I commended him. "You remember the history your grandfather taught you. So, the hidden witnesses were there for the benefit of the prisoner, expecting to declare his innocence if they think him falsely accused. A single witness was insufficient to do so. Alright Joseph, your turn to comment again."

"But how do you know the notes are not talking about another case? Why did it have to be about Yeshua ben Yosef?"

"Because in their notes they refer to this section as the *trial of Ben Stada.*"

"So, who's Ben Stada?" Joseph asked completely confused as to how this could be related to the Messiah of the Mineans.

"Another good question. You're going straight to the heart of the issue. Ben Stada is not a who, it's a what. These Rabbis love to play with words. Look what they've done with Bar Kochba. When he first arrived in Judea, they knew him by his real name which was Simon bar Kosba. Then Akiva decided he was the Messiah and started calling him Simon bar Kochba or the 'Son of a Star'. Amazing how Akiva seems to figure into everything, but we can't talk about that now. And now that Bar Kochba has lost the war, look at how they are referring to him; Simon Bar Koziba, or the 'Son of Deceit'. So quick to tear down their messiahs and ridicule them with names. So, they did the same thing to Yeshua as well. When he was alive, Yeshua was referred to as Ha Stadlan; The intercessor. Because that was the only claim he made as to whom he was. He proclaimed himself as the intercessor for the people to reach God. He said, 'Everyone seeking God must come through me."

Both my sons nodded their understanding.

"So instead of referring to him as an intercessor for God, they call him Ha Stotah or Stada in the Aramaic," I commented.

"The son of gibberish' or as my generation would say, the son of bull shit," Joseph responded.

"Watch your language, young man," my wife warned him. "You may be a man now but I'm still your mother and I can still tan your backside."

"Mom, I'm almost twenty-one years old," Joseph pleaded.

"I don't care," Deborah answered.

"Can we get back to what they wrote," I attempted to steer my sons back to the matter at hand. Joseph, what else is wrong with their story?"

"They said he was taken into the court and stoned and then hung from a tree on the eve of Passover. Firstly, you don't stone someone inside the courtroom. Stoning was for a religious crime, in an outside area and if you're stoned, it is until your dead."

"Keep going," I encouraged him.

"So, if he was stoned to death, then why would you hang him on a cross? You can only be dead once. And it was the Romans that crucified criminals, not us. And they said it was the eve of the Passover. The eve of the Passover is considered equivalent to the Sabbath evening. It would have been forbidden to punish anyone on that particular evening. At best it would be afternoon and they would have to take him down by sunset."

"So, was there anything else unusual they wrote?" Azariah wanted to know.

"There was. In another book entitled Toldoth Yeshua that they're currently composing, they say that he was being helped by the High Priest. So, it paints a difficult picture of the Sanhedrin under the control of the High Priest, who in one story is condemning him to death while at the same time being accused of helping him in another."

"You're talking about our third great grandfather Caiaphas, right?" Joseph asked.

"That's right. The rabbis still can't resist making our family out to be the bad ones, even in a story like this, which is completely fabricated. Their entire purpose was to say to any Jews considering the temptation to become Mineans, that Yeshua was bad, Yeshua had to be punished, and they want to take credit for carrying out that punishment. But at the same time, they are saying that the High Priests are bad too. So don't blame them, blame our family instead."

"I'm confused," Azariah admitted. "How could they accuse Caiaphas for his death while at the same time condemning Caiaphas for trying to save him?"

"Exactly," I answered. "Put two Jews in a room and get three opinions. Just like I told you!"

"And that's why you use this story to illustrate how we are our own worst enemies, Father," Azariah summarized the points. "Not only have they driven a wedge between us and the Mineans, so that we can never be united again as one people, they are also dividing us into being either Zadokites or Rabbanites."

"Remember, it is not they, but We. It is what we have always done, from the time we had our origins as a nation. Years of tribal warfare where we slaughtered each other like the tribe of Judah against Benjamin. Then we fought as Northern Israel against Judea. Then the Samaritans against the Judeans. Now Jews against Minean Jews or the Rabbanites against Zadokites. We will continue like this either until the end of time or until we destroy ourselves. Of that I am certain."

"I guess then you're not surprised that someone would actually try to destroy our nation, our people from the inside," Joseph floated a comment seeing if I would take the bait.

"In relation to this case, I cannot say anything to you privately. You both must make your own decisions based on what you hear in the courtroom. But if you are asking me in general, then I can tell you exactly what your grandfather said to me, "We tend to be a people that every generation produce men who do evil things because they honestly believe they have some divine authority to do so. They are filled with venom that they spit it out as ridicule and scorn, not so much because they hate the people that they have targeted but because they hate that part inside them that separates themselves from the very people they want to be part of."

"Now we're both confused," Joseph and Azariah admitted.

"If you're confused, imagine the person I just described. Two halves that can't unite properly, so each half wishes it can do away with the other in order to find some semblance of peace. It reminds me of something that Yeshua ben Yosef said. He held up a denarius from Tiberius Caesar. On one side was the portrait of the Emperor. On the other side was the picture of a temple. So, he tells the Pharisees, "Give unto Caesar what is Caesar's, give unto God what is God's.""

"But that's impossible," Joseph expressed his opinion. "Depending on what side of the coin you are looking at, it can go to either because you can't split it in half."

"Exactly," I emphasized. "Yeshua was saying you must make a choice. One or the other but not both. So, in the case of these people having two distinct sides to their heritage, they can't cut themselves in half either. So, they try to be both at the same time, thinking of themselves as intellectually superior to everyone else but never permitted to be in a position of authority because the others can't see past what they consider as the half to be a fault or blemish. Love and hate, interchangeable at any moment. Good and evil. Two sides of the coin that can't be split."

"Eli," my wife felt it time to end the discussion, "I think the boys have heard enough about this topic. What they need to know is that the world can be protected from these people. Our survival as a people, while other nations have disappeared from the face of the earth and civilizations have blown away in the wind, is because God has always protected us and always will."

"You are right Dear; the Lord has protected us. Our nation is like a garden and every now and then a weed appears and threatens to crowd out the beautiful flowers. Think of our family as the gardeners of God's garden. That has been and always will be our mission."

"And here I thought we were High Priests," my son Joseph turned and teased his younger brother. "Now we find out we are nothing but a bunch of gardeners."

"Very funny boys. Now get to bed," I instructed them. "We have another busy day tomorrow and I need you both clear headed."

Chapter Eight

The Trial: Day Two 11th Adar 3986

The morning was born with an uneasiness that did not go unnoticed by all those heading towards the synagogue. Many of the shops in the marketplace remained closed, as their owners rushed to find a standing space in the packed courtyard. The crowd nervously awaited the arrival of the judges. "They're coming!" someone shouted, and the throng of people jostled for position in order to attain the best view. Those that had not been there the previous day, heard from their neighbour and friends of the unexpected revelations and now everyone wanted to participate in what they anticipated would be a trial for the ages.

Not wishing to miss out, young lads were perched high up in the cedar rafters, while others managed to squeeze themselves into every available crevice between the peristyles. How they were going to extricate themselves from these highly precarious positions would be another matter. Surrounded by the ten judges and the prosecutor, Praetor Yehonatan marched with head bowed, past the dense mass of people, barely acknowledging their presence. It had not been his intent to turn the trial into a show, where the townspeople would come for their dose of daily entertainment, but it had come to that and he realized there was absolutely no way to avoid it. For the coming week, this is where everyone was going to be if they had the opportunity. The city's commerce would shut down, its schools and government house would close, and essential services would fail but no one would care because they would be able to say at some time in the future, 'they were there!' Those in attendance would immediately attain a higher social status, while those unable to attend would feel as if once again opportunity had passed them by.

I knew that for years to come this trial would be all that the people would talk about. And then the strangest thing would happen. Like all things in life, it will have its moment and then be gone. The event would completely disappear from everyone's memory as if it never occurred. There would be far more exciting matters to discuss, new events to ponder, and just dealing with life's constant twists and turns would suddenly be the only concern for most. That strangely is the way the world turns and sometime, long in the future, some old man sitting in a chair, with one foot already in the grave will say, 'I remember that day in the courtyard of B'nai Brak.' And when his grandson says, 'What day was that grandpa?' he'll have to think hard about it and finally will say, 'I forget.' Because life is nothing more than the sand on the beach beneath the ebbing tide of an ocean. What I do this week will only have an impact for a short time and that was why it was so important that I do whatever it takes to prove my case. With that thought in mind I had prepared myself for the day's events. I would not permit myself to lose focus.

"How long do you think these proceedings today are going to take," Yehonatan asked me.

"As long as is necessary," I answered. "Either long enough to get all my points across or until I have nothing left to say."

"It is not safe to have all these people gathered in one place for a long time," the Levite's face showed him to be extremely concerned. "The Romans might interpret it as a sign of further insurrection. We have close to a hundred and fifty trying to squeeze themselves into the courtyard and I'm guessing three times that number sitting in the field just beyond our gates. It violates their edict on public mass gatherings."

"I'd only worry if someone from the town was to ride off to Caesarea in order to tell them," I attempted to allay his fears. "But if my suspicions are right, and I think they are, then the only person that might try to contact the Romans is safely under house arrest and being watched closely by my own guard. Everything will be fine, Yehonatan. You have this under control."

"I sincerely hope so Excellency."

"What did I tell you about calling me that," I reminded him. "Elioneai will do."

"I will try my best to remember," he smiled. "So, are we going to stay on course today or am I going to have to restrain some of your questioning?"

"Today should prove quite interesting," I promised him. "If you think anything I do may be out of line, then you do what you have to do to ensure this trial remains free of misconduct. I don't want the Defendant freed on a technicality."

Yehonatan called the court to order advising all the judges and myself to take our seats and then inviting the Defendant to be escorted into the courtyard and over to his small table where he was sitting yesterday. Everyone remained silent in the courtyard as Yehonatan spoke.

"I welcome back those that were in attendance the previous day," the old Levite Priest greeted those assembled in the courtyard gallery, "And I see from the size of the crowd today, you may have an urgency to build me a bigger synagogue." The comment was received with a round of laughter and a bit of clapping. "As you know, this is the second day of the trial against Rabbi Akiva ben Joseph, who has been accused of several crimes. On this, the eleventh day of Adar in the year of three thousand eight hundred and ninety-six, we are once again assembled in the sight of God to weigh the charges concerning theft, abandonment of the faith, and the high crime of acting against the will of God. By the power invested in me, I hereby declare this second session of the court to be open. Prosecutor, you may take the floor."

This day, I let my wife select the clothing I would wear to court. I told her how Akiva had attired himself rather impressively the day before, and how that made me feel awkward, standing there in my traditional robe that I had worn for years, as if I was an old coat of paint peeling off the side of a building. She knew exactly what to do. Rather than dress traditionally in what would be considered standard Judean garb, she pulled out one of the Persian outfits from my bags. She selected a long silk tunic trimmed in silver and gold embroidered designs, tied with a golden rope belt around my waist. The blue half jacket with golden tassels along the fringes created quite the impression. She found a matching blue cap that had neither peak nor brim but sat neatly on top of my head almost like a crown. "Bring in the accused," I announced.

I think Akiva was surprised to see me dressed in all my finery. The look he gave me I could only interpreted as victory on my part. He knew, just like I did, that impressions are important when it comes to influencing people. The slight nod he gave me was saying, 'Well done.' But that first impression can be fleeting, and I knew the real challenge was getting the crowd and the judges onto my side of the argument as quickly as I could.

"Akiva ben Joseph, are you prepared to swear an oath before God that the answers and responses you provide today will be truthful as to the best of your knowledge?"

"I will swear an oath, but will you," he challenged me as to the worthiness of any testimony I might provide. "I so swear," he bellowed loud enough that they could hear him way at the back of the crowd.

"I am obligated to swear as well," I reminded him. "But if it makes you feel better, then I will swear an oath now before God that any testimony I provide today and every day of this trial afterwards will be the truth and done without malice."

"Without malice.   That is such an interesting turn of phrase," Akiva commented. "But I don't think that is possible for you. You resent every aspect of my life. Everything that I have done as part of the Council of Rabbis. You are full of malice and that is the very reason you have laid these false charges against me."

"I agree, it is an interesting turn of phrase but before you go off on a path of trying to convince the judges that I am prejudicial and therefore the trial is not and cannot be impartial, I think it would be best to let the people know the actual meaning of malice.   It is the desire to harm others. It is wanting to see another person suffer out of spite.   I can reassure you that I have no desire to harm you.   And that is why I will accept your acquittal if the judges so declare it with the most gracious of offers as I made yesterday.   As for conducting this trial out of spite, you would have had to do something to me personally in order that I become spiteful. As you have not done anything against me personally, how then can I be spiteful.   Therefore, I declare to the judges of this court, malice is not an appropriate counter charge and the Defendant's effort to malign the prosecution is not only negated but dismissed."

Yehonatan made his declaration. "The oath of both parties stands and there is no intention of the prosecution to malign the Defendant because of personal animosities. Let the trial begin."   He struck his hand against the table in front of him to indicate court was in session.

"To the judges that will decide this case, it is my intention to carry on from yesterday. In our testimony from the previous day, we tried to investigate who exactly is this man we know as Akiva ben Joseph.   What we found instead is that he is truly a mystery. What we discovered is that we know so very little about him. And yet, here is a man that has risen rapidly to a position of power without ever disclosing even the smallest details of his past. How is that even possible? He is truly an enigma. A being of unknown origin that now chooses to make his sole purpose in life the determined effort to do away with the Torah, our foundational cornerstone of all that we truly believe, and replace it with his own interpretations of what he thinks God meant to say. Yes, you heard me correctly.   The words of Akiva ben Joseph shoved between God's lips. How do I know this?"   I walked over to the dais where Yehonatan sat and raised Akiva's book from the table in my left hand, holding it high above my head so that everyone could see.   "Because of this!   As I explained yesterday, it is his own record of the details of every meeting he ever attended with the Council of Rabbis and the Bet Din in Yavneh, from what they said, all the way to what they decided. And he writes clearly in this book that it is his primary   desire to ensure that the Oral Law becomes the defining text by which all judgments will be made and essentially replaces the Torah. The oral law, which he insists existed for over a thousand years without any attempt to write it down until now. There was never an attempt because it never existed.

When Moses came down the mountain side after seven weeks communicating with God, he did not say to the people, 'I have brought you two Torahs, one written and one not. No! He says I bring you 'the' Torah, written by the hand of God. A singular Torah that contains everything we needed to know on how to live our lives righteously. And when Joshua finally conquered Canaan, he assembled all the tribes and read the Torah from beginning to end to the people so that they all might hear the word of God. He never mentioned that God had provided an oral law that was on equal standing to the written word. And when Ezra wished to commemorate the rebuilding of the Temple after the return from exile in Persia, not even he mentioned there was such a thing as an oral law that needed to be disclosed as well. None of our great lawgivers of the past ever mentioned it because it did not exist six hundred years ago. It only exists now because Akiva ben Joseph believes it necessary to break the very cornerstone of our faith.

Even if he was correct and the Torah needed to change, even if such a thing was remotely true, which I can attest to you that it is not, who appointed him as the arbiter of what is right and what is wrong? Only a man like Moses could ever make those decisions and this man," I pointed towards Akiva, "He is certainly no Moses!

Our Torah contains nothing but truths. It is the one and only word of God. But there are certain things in the Torah that if I was Akiva ben Joseph, I would want expunged from existence. Therefore, what better way to do away with our Torah than by creating an alternative set of laws that are not necessarily reflective of what is actually said in the Torah. *Building a fence around the Torah* as he states several times in his notes, making the other Rabbis falsely think that he is protecting the Torah, when in reality his focus is for that fence to keep everyone away from the Torah. This set of oral laws that he intends to call the Talmud, once it is written down becomes that fence. As soon as he has everyone searching through his Talmud for answers on the laws, or on the procedures for the Holy Days, or on the conduct of services for normal life events such as weddings or funerals, then on that day he will have succeeded in eliminating the cornerstone of our faith and we will cease to be God's children as we were intended to be. It is all in his notes, contained in this very book, and it is as clear as night is from day that he will find a way to impose this Talmud into our lives and drive us far from the true faith in our God. But don't take my word for it; let Akiva's own words speak for themselves!"

"Why don't you let me speak for myself, and not some misguided misinterpretations you derive from my writing?" Akiva demanded his turn to speak. "You have accused me of trying to replace the Torah. Yesterday you attempted to trick the people into believing that my Hebrew name was chosen specifically because I wanted to supplant or replace the Torah and I can assure every one that is a lie. What I wish to supplant is the ignorance of the Torah that our people display after they have read it and think they understand it, but in reality, they do not know God's words at all."

"And you do," I challenged him. "Their understanding is wrong, but yours is right. You are the judge of who is right and who is wrong, is that what you are telling us? No one but you!"

"In their ignorance, they see and hear what they want from reading the Torah, thereby falling into sin because they do not know better; because they are not aligned with God's point of view."

"Which you just happen to be aligned with," I taunted him, "Even though you were worse than ignorant, since you couldn't even read the Torah until you were almost middle aged. So how can you even dare to say that you are the one to lead them away from the path of sinning?"

"Because the light of God is within me," he voiced his response angrily as if no one should dare challenge his opinion.

"I see no light. Does anyone here see a light?" I turned to raise the question to all those in the gallery. "Make me a believer Akiva! Show me this light. It is said the light shone from Moses like two horns. Why don't you even show me one horn and perhaps I will believe you! Show me your light now, I demand it!"

"The light is inside me," Akiva waved me away with a dismissive hand motion. "And you are a fool."

"Rather a fool that wishes to see proof, than a liar that leads people to their destruction. So tell me, when you called Bar Kosba, as Bar Kochba the King Messiah, were you absolutely right then? And now when you refer to him as Bar Koziba, the Son of Lies and Deceit, you are also right. How fortunate it is for you to be right no matter what you say."

That statement finally provoked the townspeople to finally react. They could practically taste the hypocrisy that dripped as drool from Akiva's mouth. Angry shouts filled the courtyard, especially those that had lost sons or fathers because they believed so enthusiastically in Akiva's initial approval of Bar Kochba. So much so, that they marched off to war without a single concern as to the outcome.

What is this strange power you have," I posed the question, "That you can speak out of both sides of your mouth and you still can get people to listen to you? If anyone else, they would have lost their following a long time ago. But you…not you…they hang on to your every word as if you were the Messiah, yourself."

"Bar Kochba became obsessed with his own power. Like Saul, he was God's choice to be King and Samuel anointed him with the sacred oil. But in time, Saul's true nature became evident and God turned away from Saul and Samuel anointed another in his stead." Using the story from the Tanach, Akiva explained away his abandonment of Bar Kochba.

"So that is your explanation for your betrayal of your hand-picked messiah. You consider yourself to be another Samuel. But Samuel never removed his blessing from Saul in the middle of a battle. Samuel never caused our valiant sons to lose heart when they needed it most. Samuel never turned his back on the Children of Israel and condemned them to death in the middle of a war!"

My guard had to immediately space themselves the length of the rope that separated the crowd in the courtyard from the area of the tribunal. It was obvious that my last few statements had finally fueled those in the crowd that shared similar sentiments regarding the perceived betrayal. My only question was what had taken them so long to display that anger. Could they not have seen earlier that their family members died as a direct result of Akiva's game playing when he withdrew his support of Simon bar Kochba.

"That is not how it happened!" Akiva shouted, trying to win back the people, his people, but to no avail. "Bar Kochba turned his back on God. I had no choice but to leave him."

"Why should they believe you?" I shouted in condemnation. "Why should they believe anything that you say? How many times Akiva does the Torah tell us to welcome the convert among us but never to trust the convert? Can you tell me, you self-righteous and self-appointed scholar of the Torah, who claims to have all the answers, how many times?"

Akiva refused to answer the question.

"Lost your voice? Then I will tell you. Thirty-six times. God knew about your kind and he was warning us that the day would come when you or someone like you would lead us astray and thus cause the death of over half a million of our brave sons."

The anger in the crowd was fueled to such a high degree that I now feared my _{guards} would not be able to hold them back any longer. Perhaps I had stoked the flames a little too hot this early in the trial. That which burns hot tends to run ice cold later and I could not afford to lose the momentum before the time I really needed it.

"Enough!" the old Levite Yehonatan shouted, taking off his shoe and banging it loudly against the table top, so that the sound thundered between the columns of the peristyle. Surprisingly, it worked effectively, being enough to restore order to the crowd. I had certainly underestimated this synagogue priest. He obviously commanded much more respect and loyalty from the people of B'nai Brak than I had given him credit for. Perhaps even more than Akiva at this moment. "You may continue now, Prosecutor," he instructed me.

"Perhaps that is why you are so eager to replace the Torah?" I proposed my hypothesis to Akiva. "I'd probably want to do away with a book that held me in contempt three dozen times as well. "How can you possibly say to the people you are loved by God when it is so obvious that he is wary of you and your kind. Thirty-six times," I repeated, drawing the words out slowly. "Do you even know why it is thirty-six times, not thirty-five or even thirty-seven? Don't worry, I will tell you why that is. The answer is simple; Because thirty-six is twice the number eighteen. And the letters that make up the number eighteen are the same as those that make up the word life. So, thirty-six is two lives and that is exactly what the convert is. Two lives wrestling for the control of one soul. We never know with which life at any time his heart may be residing, so we are warned not to trust him but to still welcome him in order to be a beacon of light to show him the right path. I think you are afraid that when people rely solely on the Torah, they will see the truth and they will see what the nature of people like you truly is. As a result, you made up this fable about an oral law that is as old as the Torah itself but supplants the Torah because it explains the messages that our Lord was trying to say to us. We don't need a messenger to explain the messages. God does not need an interpreter. The Almighty has given us the ability to see the truth of his words all on our own!"

Ben Zoma and Ben Azzai knew that my statement wasn't directed at Akiva only. It was a warning to all these rabbis, that if they continued in their pursuit of being God's appointed messengers it would only serve to fractionate our people in the future. The Torah was provided so that God could communicate directly with His children and He had no intention that an intermediary would be necessary other than to read the words as had been written. But now I had to pull back and restrain my comments as I couldn't afford to have two of the judges that I had brought to B'nai Brak alienated from me. As for Akiva's students, they were still young enough to appreciate what I was saying and perhaps they would pull back from this plan to produce this thing called a Talmud.

"Except you make the mistake Elioneai," Akiva addressed me by my personal name, "I am not the convert, my father was." By not referring to me as High Priest or Prosecutor he hoped to diminish me in the eyes of everyone listening.

"Or so you say," I responded. "We still have no proof of that. "But we do have proof of how you failed to respect the Torah in your younger days."

"None of those stories can be verified," Akiva challenged. "Until yesterday, hardly anyone even knew of my life when I was younger."

"Exactly what I was going to say," I congratulated Akiva, which took him by surprise. In your younger days, no one knew what was true or wasn't true about you and you used that lack of knowledge to perform some of the greatest of your sins."

"That's ridiculous," Akiva dismissed my claim. "If there are no witnesses to my youth, then how can anyone say what I did or I didn't do."

I laughed loudly so everyone could hear my disdain for the man. "That is where you are very wrong, I'm afraid. There were actually hundreds of witnesses, they just didn't know that they were witnesses at the time."

"That doesn't make any sense," Akiva attempted to ridicule me, pointing out what he took to be a mistake on my part to the judges and the crowd. "The prosecutor is now uttering nonsense. How could anyone be a witness to a sin or a crime and not know it? Obviously if they saw it and did not recognize it to be so, then it wasn't so."

"How indeed!" I exclaimed. "Only someone clever and devious could think of such a thing when trying to conceal the truth from the people around him. As I had mentioned yesterday both of your wives were named Rachel. Not an unusual occurrence these past couple of generations, since I think probably a quarter of all the girls born are name Rachel. But in your case, you had a poor Rachel and a rich Rachel, but none were the wiser because you never actually lived with your wives, as far as they could see. For twelve years you proudly proclaim in your own handwriting that you left your rich wife Rachel behind and pursued your studies. Your colleagues praised you as a true treasure, a man so devoted to his studies that he took no interest in the simple pleasures of life, such as a home, a wife, and being with those you love and whom love you in return. Those things which God tells us in the Torah are credited with the greatest blessing bestowed on mankind. A man and a woman, becoming joined as one, united in their support one another, family and faith, inseparable, right from the time we were in the Garden of Eden. You spat in the face of such a union and the Council had the utter gall to praise you for it. Shame on them, shame on you!"

"We had our children," Akiva announced. "I did not abandon her. I fulfilled my obligations as both husband and father."

"Are you certain about that Akiva? Are you prepared to swear before God that you fulfilled those obligations. Swear it in his name and let us find out."

That was already more than Akiva was prepared to do. He realized immediately that I had led him into a trap, and I was about to spring it closed. He knew better than to swear in God's name, that he was certain.

"So, while Rachel bat Kalba lived in her own home, with her finery and her jewelry, Rachel bat Esh lived in squalor and poverty. Two women, each at the opposite ends of the scale when measuring wealth. So, when one day Rachel bat Esh came to Jerusalem, begging to see you, hoping that the great scholar Akiva ben Joseph would remove her from the shackle of poverty he left her in, the crowd refused to let her pass, seeing nothing more than a beggar, so pathetic in her yearning that she was not even deserving of their charity and obviously insane as she claimed to be the wife of the great Sage. But you heard her cries and you said to the people, '*let her pass, for that is the woman that made me who I am?*' Hundreds heard it, perhaps even thousands, and they are the witnesses of which I speak. And then you bragged to the crowd that '*your wife has suffered much in order for you to become the man you were today. Soon you said she would be bedecked in the finest jewelry money could buy, and she'd wear dresses fit for a queen.*' And in time when those in the crowd who remembered this incident asked if you had fulfilled your promise to your wife, how did you respond? '*See for yourselves, all that question if I fulfilled my vow to my wife Rachel. Go to my home and call out my beautiful wife and see how I have provided her a life of luxury and plenty, just as I promised.*' When they did so, they had no idea that this was the other Rachel and not the one they had witnessed at an earlier time. How were they to know that the beautiful woman standing before them was not the transformation of the ugly haggard old lady that they saw in her filthy and tattered clothes and matted hair, her features covered and hidden with the dust of the earth? Yes, they were convinced that Akiva ben Joseph had kept his word, but if anyone truly merits the name of Bar Koziba it is you. You are the deceiver. You are the prince of lies."

"A nice story, Elioneai, but you cannot prove it? Bah, just a tale of nonsense. There are no witnesses that can verify your story. And as Jewish law proclaims, if there are no witnesses to verify the charge, then it must be dismissed."

"Why, Akiva. Because both Rachels are dead now and they will never get the opportunity to speak the truth about you. What do I need of them when God is my witness. As He stated to Moses in Exodus Chapter 21, verse ten, 'If a man takes for himself another wife, then he is not allowed to permit his first wife to be deficient in food, support or conjugal rights.' God has thus condemned you according to all three requirements. Or perhaps I should quote the Lord from Deuteronomy, chapter 21, starting with verse fifteen. 'If a man abandons his first wife with a child, then that child will receive a double portion over all the children he might have by his second wife.' Please tell the court where your child from Rachel bat Esh is now."

Akiva became sullen and quiet at the mention of his son from his first wife.

"What was his name again? Let me try to remember...oh, yes, Joshua." I did not intend to sound or be cruel, but his testimony in this regard was crucial to my case. Yesterday I was determined to broach the question as to 'Who truly is Akiva ben Joseph' but today my goal was to define what kind of man Akiva ben Joseph is. Discussing his dead son, Joshua, was critical if I was to prove my point.

"Yes, my son's name was Joshua," was the only response I could raise from the Defendant.

"I'm guessing you're not willing to talk much about Joshua right now." My comment was met with silence, which I took as a refusal on Akiva's part to speak any further at this subject. "Praetor, if I could make a request at this time to disclose such information I have on the Defendant's son. If necessary, I can show you in the book that Akiva has been keeping that is sitting on your table, exactly what I intend to say. Do I have your permission to proceed?"

Turning to Akiva, Yehonatan asked if the Defendant refused to have the story of his son made public and if so, on what grounds would he make his refusal. Akiva still sat like a stone wall, looking neither right nor left, nor uttering any sound at all.

"Proceed Prosecutor," Yehonatan consented to my request. "I can hear no objection from the defendant."

"Some of you who were students thirty or forty years ago of Reb Ben Hananiah may remember Joshua ben Akiva," I addressed the people standing in the courtyard. "I don't believe he was known as Akiva's son but the two were certainly seen together quite often. He was considered a fair to middling student, not to say that he wouldn't have been successful as a Rabbi, but he never displayed an aptitude to learning, much to the chagrin of his father. I'm certain that the money Akiva received from his wife's father for agreeing to become a Torah scholar seemed wasted. Not everyone is intended to be a great sage, but from what I understand, this lack of achievement did disappoint his father gravely because eventually the son was dismissed from the class. From my understanding, that meant someone stopped paying for his tuition.

Many of us view our immortality through our children, others see it as a family legacy. I can't say for certain how Akiva ben Joseph viewed his son's future, other than perhaps seeing him as someone that could carry on his unfinished business once he had departed from this world, but sadly, he realized that was not to be possible. So, the money for the studies disappears and the father began to distance himself from his son, speaking very little, if anything about him. So great did that distancing become, that after some time of his son failing to attend the school, it took others who were aware of their familial relationship to actually say, 'Akiva, where is Joshua'. In all that time Akiva never thought to check on the welfare of his own son or even to contact his first wife to ensure his son remained well.

It wasn't until sometime later that Rachel bat Esh, sent word to Akiva to come quickly to where they were sheltered because their son was very sick, and she feared he was dying." I could see tearing in the eyes of some of the people in the courtyard. I believe it is everyone's greatest fear as a parent that their child will die before them. Those feelings of fear, compassion and sorrow that the death of a child evokes, I think is common to all of us. Or should I say common to all but one.

Reb bar Hananiah said, 'Akiva, go to your son, he needs you." But Akiva acted *as if he did not hear his master.* Some of the other sages came to Akiva and said, 'Go to your son, he is dying.' But again, Akiva paid them no heed, responding only that *the study of the Torah supersedes all else, and God will determine whether my son lives or dies based on my devotion to my studies.'* And what did these wise- men of the Great Council say after that? They said, *'No one is holier in the eyes of God than Akiva ben Joseph because he places his study in God's law above family needs.'* Shame, shame on all these ignorant scholars that even think that the Lord Our God would even think such a thing. They had forgotten the fundamental principle of the Torah to care for family first and in so doing these men have proven themselves unworthy of your praise. For the Torah teaches us God loves Israel like a father loves his child. Whenever Israel is threatened, He rushes to save us from our enemies. When calamity befalls us, He is there to raise us above our suffering because He is our father. In so doing God has set the example of how we must behave. A child must respect his father and mother and in return a father and mother must give their child love. Joshua gave his father the required respect, but he received no love in return. One hundred-and thirty-one-times God speaks of his love for his child, Israel in the Torah, and could Akiva find it in his heart to show love even once; No! What Akiva did was show us that he is incapable of love and as a father he failed miserably. God will not forgive him. I will not forgive him, and all of you should not forgive him. There is no parental love in him, for Akiva loves only one person, himself."

Through all this time that I berated him, Akiva did not move, he did not say a word. A nervous twitch encumbered his left eye. His gaze fell upon several vines that hung from one of the columns that surrounded the courtyard. I couldn't tell if he could hear me or not. I thought perhaps the stress of the case had finally taken its toll, and he had suffered a stroke. I looked nervously at Yehonatan, signaling that I thought something was wrong with Akiva. Stepping down from the dais, the Levite approached the Defendant and stood before him, only to have Akiva finally speak up. "Do you mind moving Praetor; you are blocking my view of the beautiful white dove that has nested atop that column."

We all looked up to where Akiva was staring and realized all this time, he had been watching the bird and ignoring what had been said. As a result, now everyone's attention in the courtyard had been drawn towards the white dove sitting in its nest.

"So, tell me Elioneai, what do you see?" Akiva asked me.

"I see a white dove, sitting in its nest atop a column covered with vines."

"And that's where you and I differ. You see only what is directly in front of you. You don't see beyond the obvious. Whereas I see a message from the Lord. Here is His bird of peace that has settled into a holy house, at a time we are in discord, ignoring all the accusations and shouting that may arise from this trial, in order to lay her eggs and bring new life into this world. In spite of our terrible losses, the antagonism that exists between different factions of our people, the Lord's message is we will survive, we will rebuild, and life will ultimately be restored here in B'nai Brak."

Upon hearing Akiva's words, the people in the courtyard became excited about the good news that he had delivered. Some even left the synagogue to run into the streets to announce that God had sent a message to the people of the city, promising to restore Israel's greatness as it had been in the past.

It was hard for me to believe the reaction he had achieved by making just a few musings about a bird. How is it that they could ignore everything that I had been talking about and just focus on a bird? It made no sense to me at all. How can justice be delivered if people are so gullible to see miracles where there are none? "And your point is, Akiva?"

"You and I will never see eye to eye. You want to judge me by using the Torah as your guidance because you see it as the beginning and the end to everything. All you need to know is written in black ink on bleached parchment. But you fail to see what is written in between the lines."

"There is nothing between the lines," I informed him. "Nothing but blank spaces."

"So, you say, but I say different," he lectured. *"I see all the truths that God wanted to reveal to us written in those spaces between the lines* and I feel sorry for anyone that can't see what I see."

"But you are filling in those spaces with your own thoughts, your own words, not those of God," I warned him.

"True," he admitted, "But in order to fill in those spaces I am inspired by God and therefore, just like the dove, sitting above our heads, the message is His and I am merely the transmitter that is fortunate enough to understand what He says."

"And if I was to say to the people that the dove is a sign that this synagogue will be torn down and crumble into dust so that the forest engulfs B'nai Brak once again and wild animals will dwell where once we prayed, is that not as true as being a message from God as were your own words?"

"It depends," he whispered so those in the crowd could not overhear him.

"What do you mean it depends? Depends on what?"

"It depends on the circumstances of course," he laughed at my question. "Do I want to present the people with an optimistic message, or do I want to discourage them? I don't know until that actual situation arises," Akiva explained.

"That ridiculous," I chided him. "Just now we looked at the same dove in a nest. You gave your explanation and I gave mine. They are as opposite as opposite can be. The only reason people are running in the street saying it is good news is because you provided your vision before I had a chance to formulate mine."

"You're right," he agreed. "And even if you were to tell them now repeatedly what you think you saw when looking at the dove, they won't believe you. They wanted a message that would lift their spirits after you've taken the best part of a morning of describing how terrible a father and husband I was. All you did was make them question how terrible they must have been if they didn't stop their son from being conscripted into Bar Kochba's army. All you did was rub a festering wound that they all bear because of their own personal failures. I gave them a salve to rub into those wounds and ease their pain."

"I gave them the truth," I insisted.

"Who's truth?" Akiva challenged me. "Is your truth the same as my truth?"

"Truth must be based on facts," I insisted. "There is only one truth!"

"Truth has nothing to do with the facts," Akiva continued his rejection of my thinking. "Truth is only about making the facts fit with what you want to hear."

"That is so cynical," Ben Zoma finally entered the debate, having sat silently all this time beside Yehonatan, while Akiva spouted his philosophy. "So, all those arguments and sermons and parables you presented at our Council meetings were nothing more than your manipulation of its members into a position that we would approve your suggested changes to the law."

"I opened your eyes to see things that you couldn't see before," Akiva defended his actions that he had promoted within the council. "I never forced any of you to agree with me. That you did of your own choosing."

"So why tell us all this now?" I wanted to know.

"Because I want you to see how easy it will be for me to change the attitude of the people regarding my son's death. It doesn't matter if you presented evidence for days on how terrible a father I was, I will negate your arguments so swiftly that you'd wonder why you even bothered to try." Akiva was calm and reassured as he spoke but in a low enough voice that he could not be overheard by the crowd.

"I am not here to play your games," I warned him. "I am here only to see that justice and the law are properly served. If a crime has been perpetrated, then this court will pass judgement and the punishment will be meted out appropriately."

"You don't even realize that you are already playing my game," he responded with a broad gloating grin. "Look at the people. They're not even focused on our little conversation we are having. All they can see is the white dove sitting on her eggs and you must realize by now I can switch their focus as easily as that."

"Of that I have no doubt," I acknowledged. "But what you can't hide is the truth and it will come out."

"But as I have pointed out, not everything in this world is black or white, or for that matter written in the sacred text of the Torah. What are you going to do then when I convince the people that even when you accuse me of doing wrong, it might be right? Will you try to adjust the crime to fit the law, or will you try to make the law fit the crime? Then who will be the one playing games? Just remember, that as soon as you exercise either of those choices, then I will be able to show the world that the so-called High Priest of Israel is not averse to altering and violating the laws in order to serve his own purpose. Then who will they say is the hypocrite?"

"Maybe I won't need to violate any laws in order to prove you are guilty. What will you say then?"

"Oh, you will," he mocked me. "I guarantee that if you are desperate to win this court case then you definitely will violate your own ethical standards to do so!"

"Never," I refused to believe him.

"We shall see Elioneai, we shall see," he scoffed.

Chapter Nine

The Trial: Afternoon Day 2

Yehonatan thought it best to recess the court hearing until later that afternoon once everyone had rested. He assumed that would give everyone more than enough time to refocus on the case and forget about white doves and prophetic futures. Unfortunately, it would also give the people time to forget everything they heard in the morning and Akiva would be proven right about the fickleness of people. All that they would remember is what he wanted them to remember, not necessarily what was true or not.

As the afternoon session began, I saw that the people's attention being drawn automatically towards the dove sitting in her nest, as if they were expecting a miracle to occur immediately before their eyes. In truth, there is no requirement that the courtyard needed to be filled with the presence of people in order to conduct a trial, but the facts are that the judges needed the people so that accusations of holding secret trials to arrive at predetermined decisions could not be leveled against them. They needed to see the expression on the faces of the people in order to calibrate their own measurement scale of what is just and what is not. As long as they could arrive at a decision that seemed to be popular with the majority, then not only could they be satisfied that they most likely made the right decision but also one that they would not be harangued for. I knew that as far as Akiva's students were concerned, being able to defend their decisions would be especially important. Here they were in a situation where they will be passing judgment on their own master and that was probably currently sending shivers of fear up and down their spines. If they were to condemn their master, then what teacher would dare to accept them into his school afterwards for fear they would someday do the same to him. If they were to acquit their master, then they would always be stained by a portion of the people of having abdicated their commitment to the truth. If that occurred, who then would seek out a rabbi that was accused of lacking integrity. But with so many watching the bird, instead of paying attention to the court case, it meant the judges would be relying on their own instincts a good portion of the time and that was too great a risk for myself to accept. I knew I had to act immediately to put an end to the distraction of bird watching.

"Who knows a good story about a bird," I suddenly blurted out, catching the attention of those surrounded by the peristyle. "I just happen to have one," I announced. "There was this African parrot that had learned only two words. These were 'I did'. So, every day people would pass by the merchant's shop and would be chatting among themselves saying things like, 'Did you buy what we needed?' Immediately the bird would say 'I did, I did'. Or when other merchants would be hawking their goods saying, 'Who liked my fruit,' and the bird would shout out 'I did, I did.' All those working in the area thought it was very funny and they were very happy to play along with the bird that knew only these two words. But one day when the king's guards were moving through the shop area, someone threw a stone at the guards, hitting one in the head and seriously wounding him. The captain yelled, 'Who threw that stone?' and immediately the bird squawked, 'I did, I did.' Looking over to where the answer came from the captain only saw the merchant sitting immediately to the right of a bird and arrested him. That merchant was arrested and never seen again. The next day the king's guards were once again patrolling through the streets when someone threw a tomato, hitting the captain in the chest and staining his uniform 'Who threw that tomato?' he screamed to which the bird replied, 'I did, I did.' The captain saw the merchant in the next stall sitting to the left of the bird and arrested him. That man was never seen again. The next day when the guards were marching down the street, someone yelled out, 'Death to the King.' 'Who said that?' the captain shouted but there was no answer. Thinking he might know where it came from, the captain walked to where the parrot was perched on its stand and stared directly at the bird. The parrot turned to his right and saw that there was no one sitting there. Then it looked immediately to its left and saw that no one was sitting their either. Then the parrot looked at the captain and said, 'Not me, Not me.'"

No sooner had I finished the story, everyone was laughing, some of them I could even hear saying, 'Not me, Not me.'

I waited until the laughing subsided and then addressed the crowd again. "There is a moral and profound meaning to this story. It is about not necessarily believing everything you think you see or hear. We can be easily misled because we never bother to gather all the information. So, when you're looking at that dove, I don't expect it to talk like the parrot did in my story, but until you know the facts it is nothing more than a bird that decided to build its nest at the top of a column in a synagogue. Nothing more and nothing less." That was enough to break the trance that the dove had been holding them under since the morning.

"This afternoon, I will provide you with more facts, but they are only one small step towards drawing a conclusion. Until you have all the facts, and hear all the information, you really can't come to a decision. So, I ask you to listen carefully. As we build the story, brick upon brick, you cannot tell what the outcome will be until that last brick is laid. Is it a wall that is being built, a house, or perhaps even a dam. Only when we reach the end of this journey will you be able to tell me what the final outcome will be. Not even I can tell you what the decision of this tribunal will be. It all depends on how well the story is constructed. And believe me when I say, this story is only beginning."

Walking towards the ropes that divided those of the tribunal from the assembled crowd, I restated the introduction that I had made earlier in the day as to my next line of questioning. "We still have to decide upon what kind of man is Rabbi Akiva ben Joseph. Is he a good man? Is he a bad man? Or is he neither, just a man doing what he does with no actual motives pushing him in either direction. To discover that man, we still need to look into his past. We need to look at Akiva the student, who not only detested the Torah but hated his classmates as well. He told them that he wished *he was a wild ass and he would bite them all.* The other students laughed at him and said, *'You mean a wild dog!' thinking that Akiva didn't appreciate the difference between a donkey and a dog.* But Akiva spat at them saying, *'I definitely meant a wild ass because when a dog bites, you only suffer some broken skin, but when a donkey bites you, it will not only break your skin but it will crush all of your bones and muscle beneath it as well, rendering your limbs practically useless, and making you cripples for the rest of your life.* Do you really believe a man that says these things to other children and teenagers would wake up the next day and profess that he loves them all?

When challenged as to how does a man that says he hates hate the Torah suddenly love it one day and become an inspiration to others, Akiva tells you straight that he never developed a sudden love for the Torah. He says *his heart was like a stone, and the words of the Torah were like water dripping against it until it wore a hole through the rock.* But I say his story is far more nefarious than he wishes to make it sound. First, if the watery words of the Torah eroded the stone, then he is admitting he has no heart remaining, which we already established concerning his son Joshua. The teachings of the Torah left him bereft of any feeling, cold and heartless.

But we should all know better because we have all been taught what is the true symbolism of the rock in Judaism. We all know the allegory. The rock is the world stone, the foundation stone of the universe upon which the Holy of Holies once stood. The rock is the Ten Commandments that Moses brought down the mountain inscribed by the finger of God. The rock is the Torah upon which our entire existence rests. These are the rocks of Judaism, and these are the rocks that he intends to erode away because what he failed to tell you is that he is the actual water that will continually drip against these rocks until they exist no more. Let me remind you how he selected his Hebrew name. What is the difference between the 'supplanter' who discards the rocks of the past and the dripping water that eventually erodes away the rocks of the past. I am convinced there is no difference. I say they are the same. I have never met a cheetah that can change its spots, or a zebra that can changes its stripes. What we are, does not change, we merely adapt and learn how to conceal ourselves better. That young man that hated Torah is no different than this old man that wishes to have you only follow what is written in this Talmud he is writing. He has only learned how to achieve his purpose without exposing his true nature. Do not be deceived and listen closely, because I am about to tell you about the young Akiva that most of you don't know because he has deceived all of you over the years. As my second witness I would like to call upon my father in absentia, the High Priest of Israel, Yosef ben Jeshua. Although he cannot be here physically, he has sent this letter to me which has remained sealed and is signed by a notary that it is the identical copy of the original letter from Joseph ben Matthias, the man the Romans have called Flavius Josephus. A man that you are all familiar with." Upon mentioning that name, a shockwave passed through the courtyard, affecting both spectators as well as the judges.

"Praetor, if you could do me the favour of breaking the seal and confirming that it is as I have sworn; That this is an identical copy of the original." Yehonatan did as requested and after confirming the notary's statement, handed the parchment back to me.

"I would now like to read the letter from the man called Flavius Josephus."

My dearest cousin Yosef,

I hope this missive finds you well. I know I have been derelict in my promise to your father to check up on you and your mother often. It shames me to know that I have not even been to Babylon to visit you since we last said goodbye to each other twenty-six years ago in Jerusalem. Although I have kept you up to date with events as they have transpired in Rome, it is still not the same as sitting with you in person and seeing the man you have grown in to.

I have worked tirelessly to try to convince the Flavians to restore our country to us and much progress was being made, only to be voided by the

untimely deaths of both Vespasian and his son Titus. Even though many of my countrymen accuse me of being a traitor to my own people, I have ensured through my writing of the history of our people and about the war we fought with Rome, that they should know the truth of my loyalties. I would never abandon my God or my people. Everything I did was in order to preserve our existence so we could rise from the ashes once again.

More so with my efforts to convert Rome's aristocracy to our beliefs. As you know, the Flavians were already joined in marriage to the Hasmoneans when Vespasian's uncle married into the royal family of Judea. Their exposure made it easy for others in the family to adapt to our ways. So successful were my efforts that Flavius Clemens and his wife Flavia Domitilla embraced our religion fully which meant that if the Emperor Domitian should die without heir, then Flavius Clemens would become the next Emperor. Oh, what a glorious day that would have been, should it have happened.

But then this delegation arrived from Judea consisting of Rabbis Gamaliel, Jochanan ben Hananiah, Eleazar ben Azariah and the one called Akiva ben Joseph. I have no angst with Gamaliel and Ben Hananiah. They are good and honest men, even if I don't agree with their policies and interpretations. But those other two, they were the epitome of the ignorance I had faced during the war from the Pharisees. Young and arrogant, refusing to accept any opinion but their own, typical of all that had gone wrong with our people over the years that led to the destruction of our Temple. They were living proof that we had learned nothing from our failure.

My words may seem harsh, and I know that Eleazar is your first cousin, but beware of that young man Yosef, he is nothing but trouble. Money is his only god, and he makes certain everyone knows he is a byproduct of the spoilt rich.

Of course, the Emperor gravitated towards these two young rabbis because he felt a common kindred spirit with them. They were all about the pursuit of power and money and those are the kind of men that Domitian surrounds himself with. In his discussions he ignored Gamaliel and Ben Hananiah completely. Whereas the two old sages wished to discuss an alleviation of the Jew Tax that Domitian had enforced, and the physical punishments that the Jews of Rome were suffering at his hands, the Emperor preferred talking about the Mineans and the Nazoreans and how one could tell the difference between the two. The question was an obvious trap, designed to help Domitian's praetorians move through the city in the darkness of night and distinguish between the two groups, so that one could be tortured and brutalized, while the other would be permitted to go their own way unharmed.

The two older Rabbis immediately recognized the trap that had been laid. I was there as well, and it was obvious what Domitian intended to do. But the one called Akiva; he was more than happy to assist the Emperor to distinguish between the two. Gamaliel tried to silence him, but in so doing, Domitian had all of us except Akiva escorted from the audience chamber. I didn't have to be there to know what Akiva would suggest. It was obvious that he wanted to say how the Mineans were no different from the Jews. In fact, they were Jews that simply added another prophet to the already lengthy list of the Prophets of Israel. Whereas Nazoreans were merely people from other nations that wanted to believe in this new prophet but did not want to adopt the laws and customs of the Jews. As such, Akiva would have explained that it would be easy to tell the difference. Merely raise the hem of their tunic and see if they were circumcised or not. If yes, they were Mineans or simply Jews, and if not, then they were Nazoreans or Christians as they were now calling themselves in Rome. As for the women, Akiva noted, you could only tell from the men they were associated with. He must have been so proud of his private audience with the Emperor. Celebrating how clever he was to have resolved Domitian's dilemma so easily. Several days later when Domitian executed his cousin Flavius Clemens and exiled his wife Flavia Domitilla to the Island of Ventokne, I wonder if he considered himself so clever, now that he realized it was all a trick by the Emperor to know how to be a hundred percent certain his cousins had become Jews and provide him with an excuse to eliminate them,

Domitian knew his cousin Clemens was a threat to take the throne from him. I ask myself, was this Akiva that blind to the intentions of Domitian, that he would willingly become an accomplice to murder, or did he actually know what he was doing. I warn you cousin, beware of the one called Akiva, I certainly do not trust him.

I fear this will be the last time I will be writing to you. I cannot let the death of my close friend and fellow Jew, Flavius Clemens go without being avenged. Those and I in his household are plotting to assassinate his killer. I will likely die in the effort, when they find out my part, but I have no regrets. I do what I have always done for the good and safety of my people. Domitian must pay for the persecutions and killing of our people. I will not let him become another Caligula.

God let me succeed one last time in saving my people.

Farewell Cousin,

Joseph ben Matthias.

No sooner had I completed reading the copy of the letter that had been sent by my father to this hearing, when I heard the clapping from Akiva's hands breaking the solemnity of my recitation of the document.

"Bravo, well done," Akiva congratulated my reading of the letter. "Praetor, if I may have my time to cross examine the testimony; the testimony of a known traitor to our people, who rather than die along with his men at Yotapata, chose instead to persuade them all to commit suicide, while he surrendered himself to the Romans. I ask, what kind of man is this that we should be lectured by him in regard to the kind of man that I am? I am sincerely insulted that his words would be given any credence at all. And what has he actually said other than the Emperor wanted to know how to tell the difference between a Minean and a Nazorean. I provided him with a truthful answer. Should I have known that it was all a ruse and he instead wanted to know how to determine if a non-Jew had fully committed to convert to Judaism in order to put him to death? I don't think anyone could have possibly known that was his intent. Am I accused of being a mind reader too. Because I'm not. Nor was Rabbi Gamaliel or Rabbi Jochanan ben Hananiah. For Josephus to presume that I should have known better is like saying he should have known Titus would destroy the Temple even after all the promises that he would not do so. The mind of a Roman is so foreign to us that our normal codes of honour and integrity for making judgments are askew. We presume they have honour, but they have not!"

"Do you deny that both Gamaliel and Ben Hananiah recognized it was a trap from the onset, but you ignored their warnings, choosing instead to meet the Emperor privately to discuss this and other matters." The opinion on the matter by those two sages was already widely known.

"I do not deny it, but nor do I accept it to be factual as stated. I had many discussions with the Emperor Domitian, trying to persuade him to be more lenient with his Jewish subjects but I have no way to prove it, in the same manner that you cannot prove any of your assertions and accusations. I would suggest for your sake that you move on to your next line of questioning as this one is leading you nowhere. All my roads do not lead to Rome."

Akiva's sarcasm was not lost on those assembled. For the Defendant to tell me as the Prosecutor how to present my case by suggesting that I need a new line of questioning certainly did little to enhance my reputation today and win the crowd and judges over to my side.

"Praetor, I have another letter that I would like to present at this time," I pulled another missive from beneath my tunic and waved it in the air to catch everyone's attention.

Yehonatan did not appear too impressed. "If this is another letter from Flavius Josephus, then perhaps it might be best that you don't present it," he suggested. If the Praetor of the Court would suggest such a thing, I can imagine what the other judges were thinking at this point.

"No this is from someone completely different, Praetor" I assured him.

"Then the court will recognize this as your third witness," he informed me.

"But Praetor Yehonatan, it arrived with the other letter," I attempted to explain.

"These letters are not as if your father is sitting before us and testifying," he explained his ruling. If that was the case it would be a single witness but that is not the case, is it?"

"Actually, this letter came to me from the Exilarch in Babylon. It's not from my father.

"Then it is definitely a statement from another witness. Let us hear what your third witness has to say." Yehonatan had made his decision and he was not about to change his mind.

"I would like to read a letter that was received by the Exilarch in Babylon during the first year of Trajan as Emperor," I announced to everyone in the courtyard. Because of the nature of the accusation in this letter, it was given to my father to determine how the complaint should be dealt with. With the court's permission I would like to begin reading."

Hail to my Brother Mar Akkub who sits on the throne of Israel in Babylon, from his brother King Metwa Germa Asfar of Ethiopia.

As the lions of Judah, we pledge our allegiance to serve and protect each other in times of need. I need you brother, to see that justice is done in my name. I have been shamed and as we share the same blood descended from Solomon the Wise, the man that shames me, shames you as well my Brother. In the name of Yahvu, God of our ancestors, I ask that you do not turn me away in this hour of need but fulfill my request and see to it that justice is done.

It was over a year ago that the Sanhedrin in Yavneh sent to me a scholar upon my request to refresh our knowledge in all matters of the law as derived from the Torah as well as to replace the ancient Torah scroll that was now too fragile to be used any longer. Some say this may have been the original scroll that accompanied Prince Menelik when he departed with his mother from Jerusalem, presented to him by his father, Solomon. It certainly looks old enough to be the same and it would be another of God's great miracles that it has been preserved this long. This scholar looked unlike any of my other visitors from your homeland, his hair was gold like a field of wheat and his eyes blue like a settled pond. His presence warmed my heart for now I felt if one of his kind could become a scholar, then there was no reason why some of my own people with their swarthy complexions should not become Sages in the future either. This Akiva gave us even more reason to celebrate than just his arrival with a new Torah scroll.

So it was with great jubilation that we received the ambassador from the Sanhedrin and the beautiful scroll that he presented to us a gift from our brothers in Judea. My people were thirsty for knowledge and none more so than the members of my immediate family. We set up schools so this Great Sage from the land of Judea could reach out to as many of my people as was possible. As the cycle of the Torah is divided into fifty-two sections, so too were his lessons designed that they would be completed after he had been a year with us. He did great reverence to my family, privately tutoring my wives and children, ensuring that their education would be superior to any of my subjects. For this I was eternally grateful, showing this man with many gifts and many favors. I welcomed him into my home as a brother and he dined at my table. He broke bread with me and drank my wine. All this I had I made available to him but it would appear that was not enough.

My youngest wife, Nefra Gemma became pregnant with her first child and I said, 'Surely this is a sign from God that he is pleased with us for keeping his Torah and ensuring the Almighty enters into every home of my nation. I planned a great feast day for all of Kush the day my child was born. This child would be blessed above all others.

From outside the birthing room, I could hear his cries spring to life. I could tell immediately that I had a son, but for some reason the midwives did not bring him out for me to hold and welcome into our world. I waited, and when I could wait no longer, I burst into the room and demanded to know what was wrong with my son.

Suckling upon my wife's breasts was a child whose skin was pink like coral and I knew this could not be my son.

I called upon the Great Sage to explain to me how such a thing could be, and he said to me as recorded directly from lips, *"he was afraid such a thing might happen because my wife's room was all in white. From the white marble of the floors to the white plaster of the walls and ceiling. The white alabaster statues to the white linens that hung on the windows."* He then claimed, *"That he heard that it was proven that if an unborn child is exposed to a room without any colour then the child will be born without colour as well."* He then told me to have my advisors and scholars check this out for themselves, to prove that this was indeed the case.

No sooner had I finished reading that line, then the people began to laugh

139

mockingly at the Ethiopian King's gullibility. It was not the reaction that I had desired. I wanted them to be shocked and outraged by what most likely was an act of adultery on Akiva's part but instead they found the situation and predicament in the story humorous. Even the ten judges were smirking though they tried hard to hide it. I waited for the laughter to die down before completing the letter.

I immediately tasked my advisors to investigate this strange tale as to its validity and they came to me by the second day after the child's birth to say that there is no truth to what the Sage had said. But when I sent my men to find this Akiva and bring him before me, they discovered that he had sailed away during the night along the Red Sea back to his homeland.

Those in the courtyard apparently found this statement even more amusing than the previous one, laughing louder and longer than before. Perhaps, they were all envisioning Akiva standing at the rail of his ship as it sailed north, knowing that he had outsmarted an entire kingdom. Whatever their justification, I could only see the vile injustice and nothing more.

Therefore, I beg of you my brother, let me have my justice. Find this Akiva for me and have him returned to my Kingdom. I have written to the Sanhedrin but I have received no reply. I know that yours is the final word in all matters and they will listen to you if you say it must be done.

Please see that the Lord's Justice is done.

Your Brother Metwa Germa Asfar.

Rising to his feet, Akiva addressed his comments to those within the gallery. "Well, I'm still here, so obviously the illustrious Exilarch Akkub didn't feel there was any merit to this accusation. Surely, they did not believe that I was the only light skinned person living at that time in Ethiopia. There were ambassadors from almost every known country present in the palace on a regular basis. Queen Nefra Gemma was exceedingly beautiful. Anyone of those men would have jumped into her bed despite the consequences just for the opportunity to lay with her. But I knew that when he summoned me, he had only one person in mind that he wanted to accuse and blame for his wife's infidelity. Of course, I was going to give him a fable to chase after while I made my escape. I would have been an idiot not to do so, knowing that I was going to be blamed for the crime regardless of whether I was innocent or not?

But it is rewarding to see that the Exilarch saw through this false accusation and never bothered to act upon it. I don't understand why you even bothered to raise it here if it didn't even merit an investigation thirty-eight years ago when it happened. It was nonsense then and there is no factual basis to it now."

"Actually, there was an investigation," I corrected him. "As I first mentioned, the Exilarch gave the task to my father. He dispatched two of the best legal minds that worked in our self-government to the Kush Kingdom but by the time they reached the palace, the young queen had taken her own life and that of her infant child. They searched through her personal belongings, but they could not find anything unusual, other than a charm similar to the ones you had the people selling here in B'nai Brak. I don't suppose you were trying to help her with any issues of fertility, were you?"

"If I was guilty, your father would have laid charges against me. Everyone knows that Yosef ben Jeshua has a penchant for laying groundless religious charges against the Rabbis within the Parthian Empire."

Without testimony from the queen, there was no way to prove anything. Akiva knew I had no way to prove any of it. "As you said, it could have been any light skinned man in Ethiopia, even though there was only one man that had access to her personal quarters to train the young queen in the Torah."

"I don't like what you're implying," Akiva shouted, as he made a threatening motion with his hands as if somehow that would stop me.

"And I don't like what you're denying," I shouted back at him. "So why don't you tell everyone gathered here once and for all, are you or are you not guilty of sleeping with Queen Nefra Gemma?"

"I don't have to answer that question," Akiva refused. "It is irrelevant, and I am insulted that you would even accuse me of being capable of such an action."

"Whether you are insulted or not, let me be blunt, did you or did you not fornicate with the Queen of Ethiopia?"

"I'm not even going to dignify that question with an answer. Praetor, inform the Prosecutor that this line of questioning has nothing to do with the present case and therefore is totally irrelevant.

"Prosecutor Elioneai. You cannot bully the defendant into saying something he refuses to answer. If he answers no or yes, there is no way to corroborate either response. Therefore, unless he gives an answer freely, you cannot force him to do so. And no one ever confesses freely to a crime. Please move on to another line of questioning or if you are finished then close this section of the trial."

"Thank you, Praetor. I withdraw the question and I propose we draw the after-noon session to a close. In my summation I will be brief and to the point. There were a lot of accusations, perhaps some of them you might even consider wild, that you heard today, that were directed towards Rabbi Akiva ben Joseph. You would have to be blind and deaf not to realize that even though we cannot state emphatically that he is guilty of the events behind these accusations, the obvious fact remains that he is constantly present when they occur. His persistent presence goes far beyond coincidence. At some point one must admit there is more than enough circumstantial evidence pointing in one direction and therefore coincidence as an explanation is no longer an option. I began this afternoon telling a joke about a parrot. Rabbi Akiva is a lot like that parrot except he was trained to speak in the reverse manner. Whenever faced with an accusation, the Akiva parrot immediately says, "Not me, Not me" But I assure you, we will reach a point this week when you hear about some of the criminal activities the Defendant has been involved with, and the weight of the guilt will be so overwhelming that when you stare him straight in the eyes, after he's looked right and left to see there are no alibis there, he will have no choice other than to say, "I did, I did." Ladies and gentlemen of the B'nai Brak, as well as Praetor and Judges, I appreciate your attention today and I ask that we meet tomorrow on the twelfth day of Adar."

"Does the defendant have anything further he'd like to say in his defense?" Yehonatan asked.

"I certainly do, your Honor." Akiva paraded around the open space ahead of the dividing rope like a caged lion daring the spectators to put their hands through the bars. "So, what have you heard today? A lot of stories with no endings. The Prosecutor would like you to write those endings for him. He would like you to link my name with every potential criminal act he mentioned. Why? Because the people directly involved were never able to do it, and they could never make any formal charge against me for these alleged inappropriate actions. And they couldn't do it because none of it was true!"

The Prosecutor has spent the morning trying to prove that I am unworthy of my title. That as the son of a convert I have never truly adopted the Jewish faith and in fact have been working clandestinely against it in an effort to eradicate any trace of Judaism from the Earth. He says I have betrayed my family, my colleagues and my countrymen. Yet here I am, almost forty years after my ordination as a rabbi and I am respected on all matters of the Torah, like few other Rabbis ever have been because I am gifted in having the ability and foresight to unbind and unravel some of those laws which appear to be designed specifically for a time in the past which no longer exists today. I find the means by which to make them relevant for our modern world. But to disparage my character, he has brought forward comments and letters from people who are of questionable character themselves. What is their purpose if it is not to assassinate the character of Akiva? It is now two days into this trial and what has been proven? As far as I am concerned, absolutely nothing. Tomorrow will be Akiva's day as I bring forth my witnesses that will testify to the prejudice and dishonourable behavior set against me and we shall see how the shoe fits on the other foot! We will be shown how it is the despicable behaviour and dishonesty of the Prosecutor and his kind that have brought us to the edge of our elimination. I don't require that many witnesses to show you the truth. I don't need to parade out one person after another to prove my case. I just need to let a couple of honest and trustworthy men to speak for me and you will recognize what is the truth!"

It was time for me to interject. "Then let us see if tomorrow I cannot show the good people of B'nai Brak how men like you were not only responsible for instigating and initiating this brutal war we just lost, but also how they actually manipulated the outcome to satisfy their own bizarre and nefarious purpose." It was a wild boast I had just made. The problem was that I could not state at that time, what their actual purpose or motivation would be. In my own mind I couldn't even rationalize how someone could take pleasure and relish in disaster. I am told that some people just like to watch things burn to the ground and that is their satisfaction without any other motive. Was it possible that Akiva was one of those people. I wild boast indeed and now one that I desperately had to prove. Until I could find the motive, everything I had was merely speculative. At this moment, I had nothing at all.

Chapter Ten

Evening: 11th Day of Adar, 3896

Trying to sleep that night was proving impossible as I tossed and turned for what seemed hours, most of the time staring at the ceiling, while I kept telling myself, you must sleep, you must sleep. The more I said it, the more impossible it became. Finally, my wife could not tolerate my attack of insomnia any longer, as she tossed off the covers and found her sandals.

"I will make us an herbal tea," she said softly, as she shuffled from the bedroom towards the kitchen area.

"Be careful with the pot," I warned her, having wrestled with it earlier that evening when I was trying to ladle out another serving of soup for myself. It hung inside the fireplace from a metal bar that could swivel fully out from the hearth when it was time to ladle whatever might be the contents of the pot into a smaller vessel. But because the fire beneath the pot was burning continually, the cast iron pot was always hot and I found if you pulled on its handles too forcibly, it would swing out rather quickly and burn you as soon as it made contact with bare skin. Fortunately, I had on several layers of clothing when I learned that lesson. At night the pot was always filled with the anise seeds in order to make yansoon tea. As the water simmered over the slowly dying embers, it would brew a rich, sweet tasting tea in time for morning breakfast.

Before long Deborah had returned to the room with two cups of hot herbal tea. "Did you have a problem with the pot," I asked quite concerned.

"No," she answered somewhat bewildered. "Should I have?"

"It was just that earlier today I had a problem with it."

"That is because you are not a woman," she verbally stung me.

"I guess so," was the best I could respond. My mind refusing to think of anything witty to challenge with.

"So, what is the problem Eli," she went straight to the issue. "Why can't you sleep?"

"It's something that Akiva said today. He told me in order to win this trial I'm going to need to bend the rules. Either I will change the law to fit the crime, or I will change the crime to fit the law."

"What else would you expect him to say?" my wife remained calm.

"But the whole day was like that. I could identify numerous crimes, but I could not tie him definitively to any of them. Or I could identify numerous behaviors on his part that made him suspicious but nothing by which he could ever be charged for with a crime. It's like I can't make the fingers of my right hand interlock with those of my left hand. The truth is he made me look like a rambling and stumbling fool today and he did so while hardly saying a word. He just let me keep on talking and talking and in the end challenged it by simply saying, 'So What?' and I had no real argument to come back with."

"You are the next High Priest of Israel," she said to me while staring directly into my eyes. It was a bit unnerving. "Are you pursuing this man because you truly believe him to be guilty or because you want him to be guilty?"

"Why would you ask me that question after reminding me that I'm the Kohen Gadol?"

"Because you once told me that you have lived your life according to everything that has been written by God and by those faithful and true of heart that served him well. Do you remember telling me that?"

"That was the day I proposed to you," I remembered.

"Yes, our parents left us alone in the garden and it was only our second time alone together as adults."

"I don't really know if at that age we could actually be considered adults," I interrupted her.

"Shusshhh," she warned me to be quiet. "You had your turn to talk all day, so now it is my turn. We were old enough to be married, so we were old enough to be adults. You wanted to impress me with the kind of person you were and to let me know that you considered yourself to be special. So, you said, 'God selected those that would speak for him, not some council of old men that believe they have some special privilege.' Even then, at a young age, you were afraid that these men that ordained themselves a rabbis would somehow make your family irrelevant. You feared that the position of the High Priest would fade away under your watch. Do you remember?"

"And then you asked me, 'Why do we need a High Priest?' Not in a disparaging way but in an effort for me to state what my purpose was in life. So, I answered that, 'I feared we will lose the wisdom of our past if we do not let the Torah shine as a beacon of light for all future generations. The High Priest must always be that beacon.' I knew that no one else would be willing to carry that torch."

"You are that beacon of light Eli and God speaks through you. I have heard that voice emanate from your lips, and I know it is Yahvu's and not your own."

She smiled with the confidence of her conviction. "If the Lord, in His wisdom, is willing to designate you as his spokesperson, then I am certain He has the faith in you to determine when something is right or wrong. If you feel this man has betrayed our people, then I believe you because you are still that young man I fell in love with in the garden. You have never changed, and you never will. Back then you felt these rabbis were nothing more than narcissists grasping for those special privileges that didn't belong to them and there is no reason to think they changed either."

From the look in her eyes, he could tell that she was thinking about something profound. "You didn't doubt yourself then, so I don't expect you to doubt yourself now. So, think! What is it that troubles you most about him. What are the common factors that rise to the top every time that are creaming within your head? That is how you crack the veneer of his lies. Exploit his weakness!"

"Women or money," I responded. "Sometimes it is even both. Even in this book that he is writing, he is continuously keeping a record of all their Council discussions, but constantly focuses upon their arguments concerning the subjects of women or money. It is as if he is obsessed. Silly things he writes, like *a man should be able to instantly divorce his wife if he finds a woman that is better looking*. Or how *a woman must not be taught Torah as it is not their place to learn and be close to God*. He is constantly degrading womankind, and it appears as if he is trying to convince his colleagues to do the same.

"Now you're even making me mad, and I want to see him charged with a crime," Deborah responded both jokingly and seriously. "What else?"

"As in being derogatory about woman?" I questioned.

"Yes, particularly that," my wife wanted to know. "But other things as well."

"In his book he wrote that *a menstruating woman is the same as a man found with an idol.* I couldn't make out the comparison myself, so I don't know exactly what he was trying to say," I admitted.

"Then let us examine his statement together. A man with an idol is cut off from the people," Deborah tried to guess at the meaning. "The man is defiled, therefore he must be saying a woman is defiled as well. You are compelled to break down idols, smash them to pieces, and even kill the idol worshipper without suffering any penalty for doing so. Whatever his reasoning, it signifies he has a serious aversion to a woman during her flow. As much as he loves women, he despises that part about them."

"Hates them in what way?" I was curious as to her thinking. As a man, I could never understand from a woman's perspective what they thought of their monthly flow. Did they think it was a punishment from God? Or was it designed simply to give them a rest period where their husbands would not press them for sexual favours. Why would Akiva have such an adversity towards that time of month? I needed my wife's perspective more than ever.

"It's only a hunch but it is almost as if he thinks that women do it on purpose, to deny him partaking in his own sexual pleasures. An idol doesn't manifest itself naturally. It cannot create itself or any other idols. A man actually has to intend to create it with hammer and chisel. Therefore, there is an intent to sin. I think he is suggesting a woman does it on purpose too. Is responsible for creating her own monthly flow. It is as if he accuses women of intentionally creating this sin to stop his sexual advances. What he craves is a normal human desire which he considers good and godly. A woman menstruating prevents him from attaining that godliness, so she must be evil, an unclean beast that must be treated as such."

"That thinking is pretty convoluted. I'm not certain if I follow it."

"Because you, like most men, know it to be natural process and all part of God's creation. Before there can be conception, a woman's body must cleanse and prepare itself for the possible impregnation to follow. As such, a man must learn to restrain and control his urges. The reality is that the woman is exerting control or dominance over the man's behaviour and Akiva can't tolerate being controlled. He certainly can't accept the woman as dominant."

"I never saw it that way," I confessed.

"And why would you," she asked. "You're a man. You don't have to deal with such issues unless it interferes with your plans. What else does he say?"

"This was an interesting point he happened to write," I recalled one of his notations in the book. *'If semen escapes from the woman on the third day after copulation then she is to be considered unclean.'* I didn't know it was possible for a woman to store the semen after copulation. Yet, he seems convinced otherwise."

"We can't, but I'm guessing from his point of view it is a far better option than the woman being labeled as promiscuous or worse," Deborah replied.

"You are implying that it simply is an excuse," I guessed at her meaning.

"The real question is why he would bother providing a woman an excuse unless for some particular reason he feared that this unusual flow of semen could be traced back to himself. We know he doesn't respect women, so he certainly isn't going to make an effort to try and protect a woman's reputation." Sitting beside me, Deborah rested her hand on my shoulder and explained. "He's a womanizer, correct?"

"From what I presented in court today, there should be no doubt about that," I responded.

"Darling, think of it this way. If you were to come home one night and we you decided that we must engage in intercourse that night but as I undressed you saw semen leaking from my groin and flowing down the inside of my leg, what would be your first thought?"

"I would be devastated," I explained. "I would suspect that you had laid with a man earlier that day."

"Would you have even considered that perhaps it was the remnant from our intercourse three days earlier?" she questioned me.

I shook my head. "As much as I would want to believe that, I could never accept it as the truth. I would know it to be a lie."

"Because you know in your heart it could not be the truth and physically it would be impossible, There'd be no doubt about it unless there was a way to challenge the truth, such as by a religious dogma." Deborah was even more explicit. "Most husbands would be demanding to know who the other man was, and the woman would be lucky if all she received was a divorce decree and not punished for adultery by death. As for the fornicator, if the husband ever found out who he was, he'd probably kill him, himself."

I scratched my head, fathoming all that Deborah was explaining. "I still don't understand. Why would Akiva go out of his way to force the Council to pass such a ludicrous ruling? As you pointed out, it has nothing to do with being unclean or for that matter, even requiring a purification ritual. It is purely about adultery and being stoned to death. If he lacked respect for women as we surmise, then why bother to even create a ridiculous ruling in order to protect the woman complicit in adultery?"

Deborah gave me a playful slap across the back of my head as if to say 'wake up'.

"He didn't do it to protect the woman; he's protecting himself. Because it is clear Akiva was or is currently in a sexual relationship with a married woman," she explained. "He is creating legalities to escape any charges by incorporating these absurd anomalies into a revised book of our laws. Why, you ask? In order to protect himself from being discovered. If the husband of his lover should find her leaking Akiva's semen, he can be shown that the 'wisemen' of the Council have already taken it into consideration because it is not an unusual or abnormal event. An attempt to make the impossible plausible. A smart husband may still choose not to believe his wife and will most likely still choose to divorce her based upon his suspicions but there's no possible retribution against a lover because the religious law will now say it's merely a suspicion and nothing more. They will say that the wife is merely unclean under the law, not defiled and not cheating and the courts will no longer pursue it any further. Who can say it to be otherwise? The unfaithful wife has been given a small thread of hope by which to escape punishment but more importantly, as far as her lover is concerned, he will never be identified because it can be said he did not exist."

"So, if I understand this correctly, you're suggesting the only reason he would ever had proposed such a ruling as this, would be because of a personal need to protect himself."

"Yes!" she practically shouted. "Do I have to slap you on the back of your head again. Now do you understand?"

I nodded sheepishly while grinning foolishly at the same time. On my own I never could have imagined or considered such a thing. Whereas Deborah could see it almost instantly. "So, how exactly does this help my case?" I shrugged my shoulders waiting to be slapped again.

"Sometimes Elioneai ben Josef, you can be the smartest man in the world, and other times…" she never completed the sentence.

I remained silent, hoping she would tell me the answer but she just continued the conversation as if it didn't matter. "So what else has he written." Deborah pressed me for even more information.

"There is an episode where he was in debate with his student Rabbi Meir about accusations of having illicit sexual intercourse."

"And that didn't strike you as unusual either," my wife challenged me.

"Of course I found it unusual but I couldn't think of what I could do with such information. What he wanted to know from his student was *whether you can accept the word from two witnesses in court that swear you had intercourse with an espoused maidservant over your own sworn declaration that you did not have intercourse because you did not complete the action. Akiva insisted that if that was the case, then there is no guilt and no crime.*"

"What he is really asking, "my wife decided to rephrase Akiva's wording, "So if I spill my seed outside of her womb, does that make the act of the initial penetration count for less or in this case not count at all? Another ridiculous question. What he does, doesn't make her any less married than she was when they first engaged in the act of sex? I don't understand Eli how you can overlook all this pile of evidence he is placing right in your hands. He's giving you the noose by which you can hang him and you're obviously turning a blind I to it for some reason."

"I'm uncomfortable discussing these matters in court," I responded, my natural instinct to avoid such topics.

"Then you better get comfortable for my sake and the sake of countless other women in our society. What you fail to see is that the man who would make all these statements and try to incorporate them into law is a predator, a monster, legally finding ways to prey upon women without suffering any penalty. You must raise these issues in court," she argued, becoming highly emotional as she expressed her concern.

"There is another problem," I tried to explain to her. "The court case is and always has been about proving Akiva to be a traitor to our people, about betraying us to the Romans and there by extension being responsible for the murder of over half a million Jews. I can't suddenly say to the judges I want to alter the charges and talk about Akiva's vile sexual habits and misconduct. They would all look at the man sitting in the defendant's chair, who is probably in his early seventies and be nothing but impressed, wondering what his secret is. That is the way men think! We don't see it in the same way that a woman does. I must focus on treason and nothing else."

"Since when is a crime of treason only against other men. Do not women account for half of our population. If you persuade the women in attendance that he is evil, do you think any wife is going to let her husband get away with thinking how magnificent Akiva must be in bed. Anyway, why do the two crimes have to be necessarily in opposition?" Deborah came to the logical extension that they could be connected.

"Obviously I must be wrong but may I remind you, treason is treason and sex is sex," I challenged her reasoning. "Where do you see any possible connection?"

She had been waiting for me to ask that question, as she pounced upon me with her answer immediately. "And what was Paris and Helen of Troy, or Marc Antony and Cleopatra. Were they considered guilty according to acts of treason or were they guilty of having illicit sex? History is full of examples where the lines have blurred between the two and I'm certain that this time you won't find any difference. From what you have told me thus far, This Akiva is apparently arrogant enough to write about his sexual exploits but conceals them with the thinnest of veils. Penetrate the veil and you will find the treason. I just know it to be true. The implementation of these ridiculous laws and they are only ridiculous because you're not the one trying to hide a trail of evidence. See where the trail leads and you will likely find his act of treason."

I rubbed my chin, a habit I do when I'm always deep in thought. Deborah recognized the expression on my face as she had seen it many times before and she remained silent while I focused my memory to search page by page through Akiva's book. From the time I was young I had this ability to picture the page of any book and know exactly what was written on a particular page.

Coming into view was a picture of this one story that covered several paragraphs that I had glossed over earlier, considering it nothing more than a childlike fantasy. Truthfully, I should have known better. As my wife stated, everything in Akiva's book served a purpose. It was unlike him to include a useless fable with no intended purpose. I gently slapped my forehead, How was I unable to see that earlier?

"I can tell you are seeing something," she reacted excitedly.

"He writes about how *found money must be returned to its rightful owner by everyone else, even if the owner is not known.* They must do an exhaustive search to find an owner before they can declare the money truly lost. Yet, he has included a story in the book where *he claims to have found a fabulous treasure that was washed up from the sea and he decided to keep it for himself without attempting to return it.* The really strange part is that he claims to know for a fact that *the treasure was tossed into the sea by a foreign heartbroken princess kept prisoner in her palace.* He wants to keep all of this treasure *but one day he is approached by a man, another foreigner that he has known and whom he is in debt to. This man demands that the loan be paid back immediately. It is an exorbitant amount and Akiva admits he had to use some of the hidden treasure to repay the debt."*

"Find that trail of money and you will have the proof of your treason. I can practically guarantee it. In fact, find that princess and you will know exactly who he has been having his illicit intercourse with." Deborah stated so calmly that she practically convinced me that the treasure actually existed and how easy it would be to find.

"I admit that money does play a major role in Akiva's life," I commented. "Not very long ago I was in a discussion with Ben Azzai about Akiva's wealth after we exposed that golden step-stool. He told me that at some point in the past *he had confronted Akiva bout his flaunting of his wealth to make himself superior over the other rabbis.* Apparently, many of them resented his doing so, as well as the fact that he had become very friendly with certain members within the Roman government at Caesarea. His exact quote went something like, '*Do not make yourself prominent among the government officials and neither should you provide them with your neighbour's name.*' But Ben Azzai is one of the jurors."

"Is that a problem," she asked.

"Yes, because I can't ask him simultaneously to be both juror and witness. He can't be asked to testify. But now that I think about that story, they must have caught Akiva turning over those in resistance to the Romans. What else could the reference to neighbour's names mean?   Selling information?"

"From all that you have already said, Akiva certainly strikes me as a man that would easily compromise his integrity, if he had any, for money," Deborah was not too shocked by what Ben Azzai had said.

"Now that I think about it, money was the driving reason he left his first wife and pursued the daughter of Kalba Savuah, leaving the first Rachel and his son Joshua to both die alone in poverty.   I never even bothered to mention in court that when he started studying with his son, he wouldn't permit his son to register as one would expect for the son of such an esteemed rabbi, as Joshua ben Akiva."

"How was he registered?"

"As one *Joshua ben Karkhas*. I'm thinking that the name Karkhas may have been worth mentioning at the time."

Immediately covering her mouth with the palm of her left hand, my wife was astonished by the callousness of Akiva. "Oh my," she was dismayed to hear that he referred to his son in that manner. "What kind of father, even a horrible father, would register his son under such a foul name. It's like saying he was no better than the soil you wipe from your feet, by calling him the son of dirt."

"But if I was to confront him with it in court, he'd probably say it was for his son's personal benefit so that he wouldn't think himself better than anyone else. Akiva is very sharp in that way. So far, I can't seem to catch him off his guard."

"That is your mistake. You don't have to," Deborah expressed her enlightened reasoning. "You've already identified that he is a man obviously attracted to wealth.   In his case, this would mean rich and powerful women.   He's admitted as much in all that he has written.   That is a weakness and one that can be easily exploited by a woman if the men they select aren't aware of it."

"I don't understand," I admitted.   "What do you mean by not being aware of it.   How could a man not be aware of being exploited by a woman?   Is this some woman thing I should have known about?"

Deborah couldn't help herself but to laugh.   "Darling, whether you are willing to admit it or not, you men are so very naive when it comes to dealing with women. If a woman is beautiful, rich or powerful, she has the power to bend a man in every direction and he won't even know she is doing it to him. Now, it's possible everyone else may see it but even if they decide to tell the man, he will refuse to believe it. He will go against his own nature, if necessary, just to please her. Now if that woman should happen to be beautiful, rich and powerful, all at the same time, then that is the most dangerous combination because the man becomes little more than a puppet if the woman so desires to use him in that way. I believe these stories Akiva writes are his confession. Certainly, he disguises them in parables and metaphors, but he feels compelled to express his sins and get them off his chest. He knows he is compelled to do as she pleases, and he resents it, but he can't help himself. I can't tell if he actually wants to be caught or whether he is so arrogant in his belief of superiority that he doesn't believe any of you are smart enough to figure it out."

"So, you're suggesting, if I find the common thread in all these stories, I will find the proof I need to prove he was guilty of betraying his people and abandoning Bar Kochba."

"I believe you will find much more than that, my Darling," Deborah caressed my temples as she spoke. "I believe you will sleep much easier now."

I put the now cold cup of tea down and lay back on the bed, my head resting on the goose down filled pillows. "I just need to find that single thread that links all that we have discussed," I mulled over in my mind but spoke simultaneously.

"Just follow the money," Deborah suggested as she rolled over, while stealing all of the covers.

"Just follow the money," I repeated as a smile crept across my face. It sounded like a simple plan, and I already had an idea that would need looking into in the morning.

Chapter Eleven

The Trial: Day Three, 12th of Adar 3896

In the morning I dispatched Jacob with a couple of riders to Caesarea. He took with him a sealed letter that I had written, and which was only to be opened by the person I intended it for, whose name I whispered in his ear. It was imperative that he kept this mission a secret from everyone. He was not even to discuss it with the riders accompanying him. How he would deliver the letter I left for him to resolve as it would not be easy. But I had complete faith in Jacob. He always managed to succeed where others would fail. I instructed him to wait for an answer, knowing that it would only be delivered verbally. Jacob had never failed me and he swore he would not fail me this time either. He was a good man; better than most. I had no doubts in his succeeding to deliver it; I just hoped I was correct in my thinking and the answer he would receive in return would be the right one.

The first thing I noticed this morning was that there were fewer peopled packed within the peristyle of the courtyard today. Perhaps that was a good thing. It meant less distractions and certainly fewer emotions spinning out of control that could possibly interfere with the trial. Recognizing that the previous day had not exactly been one of my better performances in court since Akiva by my assessment was able to deflect practically everything I challenged him with, today had to be far more convincing, leaving no doubt in anyone's mind by the time court was dismissed. I certainly thought the letter from the King of Ethiopia would have been enough to keep the townspeople enthralled but obviously the events in far off Numidia meant little to the everyday lives here. Yet, who knew what unexpected surprises I might have for them today. I couldn't comprehend the waning interest, but it was obvious Akiva considered it to his advantage as he sat smiling smugly in his chair, another token in his favor.

Yehonatan moved rapidly through the daily swearing in procedures, wasting little time in asking that I present my opening remarks for what was now day three of the trial.

I took up my usual position a foot or two away in front of the rope and in line with the center of the courtyard. I had a clear view to the back columns, which let me estimate that we probably had perhaps two thirds of the usual number with us. Still a large enough crowd assembled to generate enough noise to stir the interest of those that might be outside. I cleared my throat and began my opening remarks. "How did we get into this war, I'm certain you all have your thoughts on that matter, but I doubt any of you know the actual story of how it all began. It's not well known outside a very small circle. It's probably not at all resembling the stories that have been told, emphasizing the fact that we had no choice but to fight as we were facing the total annihilation of our faith and culture, which in essence would have been our end as a particular race of people. So let me tell you the truth of how this all began on that one particular day in the thirteenth year of the reign of Emperor Publius Aelius Hadrianus. On my oath before God, I will tell you exactly what I experienced."

"Elioneai," the Praetor Yehonatan interrupted me. "Is this history lesson necessary. You placed a man on trial, not the history of the war which we have all experienced. This is neither the time nor place for a history lesson. Please confine your presentation of facts to the matter concerning the defendant."

"I beg the Praetor's indulgence, but the beginning of the war does directly impact on the Defendant's guilt or innocence. Most do not realize that he was there at the time the war began and may have had a role as a major influence as to the decision to attack Judea. I beg you to let me continue. If at any time what I have to say is deemed not to concern the Defendant and this trial, then order me to cease my prattling and I will obey. Otherwise, I beseech you to let me speak."

"Go ahead," Yehonatan agreed, "But do not take your time in revealing the connection. The patience of the tribunal is not endless."

"Of course, Praetor. I bet right now all of you assembled here are probably thinking, I have made a mistake. You are thinking, it was in the fifteenth year of Hadrian's rule that the war begun. You want to shout out, 'You are wrong' but the fact still remains that I am right because of knowledge that you do not possess. Perhaps, we could agree that the first swords clashed in the year you propose, but the war began two years earlier, on the Mediterranean shores of Egypt, just west of the Nile Delta in the city of Alexandria on a summer's day. You know this story and you know exactly who was there at the time, because everyone in the land was excited by the news. It was supposed to be a time of our rejoicing, of our rebirth, and rededication to the building of the Temple in the holy city of Jerusalem. The Emperor had just completed his tour of Judea and all the signs appeared favourable. Now, everyone that had a stake in the rebuilding of Jerusalem had been invited to spend the summer as guests of the Emperor, as again you well aware because it was well publicized. What better sign could there be than we were about to be given permission to rebuild? All the right people had arrived in Alexandria. There were government officials from Caesarea, including the Procurator and his wife, representatives of the Rabbinical Council from Yavneh and Lydda, and on behalf of the Exilarch and the High Priesthood, myself, having journeyed from Parthia to participate in this momentous occasion. One could not help but believe this was the miracle we had all been waiting for, that God Almighty had melted the Emperor's heart and he was prepared to restore to us everything that we had lost since the time of Vespasian. Oh, glorious days were ahead of us, Hallelujah! And the people of this land sang out in praise and celebration as you may recall. So what possibly happened that two years later our songs of praise became dirges of death and destruction?

Of course, the true miracle relied on the youth that Hadrian had fallen in love with. Aquilius Aelius Antinous was as handsome a young man as anyone could imagine. So handsome in fact that the pagans that saw him swore that he must be fathered by their gods. Some even said he was the manifestation of Apollo on Earth. Little did they suspect he was merely a young Jew from Claudiopolis in the province of Bithynia. But it was this young man's influence on Hadrian that finally convinced the Emperor, despite all the animosity he bore after we fought against Trajan, that he should overlook the past and restore that which rightfully belonged to the Jews. The young Antinous had become enthusiastic regarding the restoration of the city after their visit, and as a result the invitation to come to Alexandria where we would spend several months as guests of the Emperor was extended. It was said that Hadrian would do anything for his young lover, even tolerate the Jews and let them rebuild their capital city, if he must.

That toleration following prodding by Antinous would extend to our land, our country, our Temple, and even on the table for discussion was the topic of reinstating a Jewish King. But this time it would not be a Hasmonean nor a Herodian, but a proper scion of David, from the House of the Exilarch in Babylon. Imagine what our history over the past few years would have been, had the offer from Hadrian manifested itself into a reality. Close your eyes and imagine our lives at this moment if everything had come to fruition. It should have it would have, but sadly it didn't. How was it even possible we could fail in this mission with God aligning every circumstance and event to perfection. Throughout the months of August and September we negotiated, and we were so close to turning our dream into an official decree that you could practically envision the cornerstone being laid for the Temple. By the time October of that year arrived, we were already thinking that we'd be back with our families very soon to celebrate. Perhaps one more month, or possibly two at most. We were that close to succeeding that no one could even consider that we would fail. Yet fail we did.

I remember that day when all are dreams were ground into dust. First came the terrible news that morning of the eighth day of Cheshvan or what the Romans refer to as the twenty-eighth of October. Antinous had gone down to the Nile River the night before and drowned. No one knew why he would even think of going to the river at night and there was no one that came forward to be identified as having been with him. It could only mean that he chose to go alone. The Emperor was beyond consolation, weeping like a young child upon hearing this most grievous news. All he kept asking was 'Why, why? Why did Antinous have to die?" It was a fair question. With all the stars that had been aligned for our sake to see Jerusalem restored, why would God have allowed this to happen?

A wise man knows when it is best to keep one's distance from a grieving man because in their terrible time of anguish, even the simplest of words can be misconstrued and the best of friends become bitter enemies. Those of us that had come to Alexandria at Hadrian's request knew not what we should do at that time, other than to avoid Hadrian. One wrong word or wrong action could be our undoing. As much as we wanted to extend our sympathies to ease the Emperor's affliction, we feared even being in his presence. This was certainly not the time to discuss the future and many from the Council of Rabbis decided it best to return to Judea. There would always be another day they said, a far more suitable time arranged by the hand of God to talk. As more government officials from the Roman provinces began to gather in the city, including legates, procurators and ambassadors to offer their sympathies, I decided it was my duty to stay longer as well, since I would be the only diplomat there representing the Parthian Empire."

I bowed to the Praetor. "That is your history lesson, now comes the connection to this tribunal. I found it curious that one of the Rabbis from the council still remained behind as well. That Rabbi just happened to be Akiva ben Joseph. Yes, at that time Akiva was the president of the Council in Yavneh but it still made no sense why he decided to stay behind, especially since there were others more acutely aligned to Roman ideology and far more capable of being empathetic. Apparently, there was a meeting with the Emperor that I was not invited to. The local governors were invited, so too were administrators from the various public services scattered around the city, but the one invitation I had not anticipated would be made was the one extended to Akiva ben Joseph. Yes, this same man who now stands accused of treason, decided to say in Alexandria. For what purpose you might ask? What was so urgent that he felt it necessary to stay behind while the rest of the Council returned home? It was not until I overheard several of the administrators talking in the corridors that I became fully aware of what had transpired.

Apparently, the Emperor appealed for any explanation to the local astrologers and seers from all of the public administrators' offices for which Egypt is famous for to help him deal with his tragic loss. None of them could provide him with a credible answer as to why Antinous had to die. Perhaps they did know but no one dared say a word, that is until Akiva decided to speak up, making no effort to conceal his opinion. It did not take long for word to get back to the Emperor that there was someone with an explanation and as a result, that is why Akiva was extended an invitation to this high level meeting and the reason that he remained behind.

Some of you may know of what transpired as it has been public record of what Akiva said that day for many years. It has been debated often and many of you may even agree with what was said. But let me remind you anyway. "He had to die," Akiva ben Joseph proclaimed, "Because the God of Israel, the Lord of the Universe would not permit for the restoration of Judea and the rebuilding of the Temple to be seen or credited as the result of the efforts by a homosexual. As I said, some of you know this story but do you really understand it? Akiva insisted that even though Antinous lived in a completely Roman world, he was still born a Jew and therefore would be judged as a Jew. According to the Torah he explained, if a Jewish man lies with another man as he would with a woman then he must die. There could be no exceptions no matter how well intentioned or good natured that homosexual man might be. That was the law and punishment of God," Akiva reiterated. "There were no exceptions!"

Hadrian went wild, furious not with Akiva for providing such a cruel and despicable answer but with our God, vowing that he would do whatever was within his power to punish our God for what He had done. That is the story you may know, but what you most likely do not know is that the Emperor challenged Akiva with a riddle soon after he gave that response, disguising it as a metaphor but Akiva was either too slow to discern and recognize the threat behind the riddle or didn't actually care about the aftermath. I was there, I've seen the transcribed accounts. It is written that Hadrian said, *'You have been honest with me Rabbi, so I will seek your opinion on a medical matter that has vexed me sorely. There is an infection in my foot that is festering and if leave it unattended it will become gangrenous, and I will surely die from it. Should I do as one of my doctors suggests and have my foot removed and be done with it once and for all, or should I follow the advice of my other doctor who suggests we treat it with salves and ointments and give it time to see if it responds, meanwhile the infection may spread. What should I do?"*

You told him *to saw off his foot and be done with it.* How could you not have realized that he was talking about Judea and either eliminating us entirely as a race or perhaps giving us time to see if we could heal the wounds between our two peoples? I know you are not a stupid man, Akiva so we all need to know what your true motives were. From what I can see, you were bent on causing this war at any cost and you made certain that Hadrian would attack us religiously, to justify your own call to war. I think you intentionally created the spark that resulted in this war that practically wiped us from the face of the Earth. Considering what we already know about your advice to Domitian, almost forty years earlier, I wonder if declaring circumcision unlawful was Emperor Hadrian's decision or did you help draft that prohibition as well?"

Akiva stepped down from behind the table where he sat and approached me with a fire burning in his eyes. "I told the Emperor the truth! God despises those men that lie with another man and demands that they be put to death. I am God's servant and if He wishes me to be his messenger, I will do so without hesitation!"

Putting my hand against his chest I pushed him backwards. He had deliberately closed the space between us as a direct challenge and I could not tolerate his being that close.

"Praetor, did you see that?" he screamed. "He attacked me! I demand that Elioneai ben Yosef be censured immediately."

Yehonatan acknowledged that he had seen the contact. "The Prosecution will apologize for putting a hand on the Defendant and the Defendant will ensure that he provides at least three feet between himself and anyone else he might address during this hearing. Do all the parties understand?"

We both nodded and I stated my apology. "I ask the Defendant to accept my apology for deliberately brushing him back, but it was too much to ask me to tolerate that much ignorance violating my space. If the Defendant had any true knowledge of the Torah, then he would have known that is not what God demands. Perhaps if he actually studied the Torah rather than write commentaries on matters he knows nothing about, then and only then would I consider him a scholar. I apologize to the Defendant for pointing out to everyone gathered here that he is an ignorant fraud, a charlatan that has pulled the wool over the eyes of so many. The same way that I now apologize to the court that I have to take the time to explain what is actually written in the Torah because they have obviously been misled by this fool dressed as a scholar."

"Your Honour," Akiva protested. "This is in no way can be construed as an apology. The Prosecution has continued to demean and insult me repeatedly and such behaviour is unacceptable. His prejudice is obvious, and it undermines any possibility of having a fair trial."

"Of course, the Prosecutor is prejudiced against you," Yehonatan could barely stifle a laugh. "Why else do you think he leveled these charges against you in the first place? Because he likes you?" A good portion of the people in the gallery could not withhold their snickering as the Praetor stated the obvious. "But the Prosecutor has made a statement of fact that you have misinterpreted the Torah, either mistakenly or intentionally and I believe he needs to prove it, otherwise the court will object to his making unsubstantiated statements. So Elioneai, can you support what you have said?"

"There are two sets of rules in Leviticus, one for the common people as written in Chapter 18 verse twenty-two, and the other for the priesthood that serves in the Temple, Chapter 20 verse thirteen. In the first instance, God calls it an abhorrence and says that the offenders will be cut off from the rest of the people. Antinous was without any doubt, already cut off and cast away from his people. Therefore, he had already received his punishment. He had no place with us any longer and his life was from then on Roman as far as we were concerned. He certainly was no priest and he never served in the Temple so the sentencing in the latter instance did not apply. Either Akiva filled the Emperor's head with your nonsense because he is an idiot with no understanding of the Torah, or else he did it intentionally to deliberately force Hadrian to change his plans for Jerusalem that we had agreed upon prior to the death of Antinous."

Akiva was practically jumping up and down, stamping his feet angrily against the ground. "How dare you even suggest that I prodded Hadrian to declare his edicts against us. I provided him with the truth. I was the only one willing to be honest with him during his period of anguish. I did as God instructed me to."

"You did what your own demons demanded you do. How dare you point to God and say he instructed you to rile the Emperor to a point he wanted to destroy us. You played him against us," I yelled. "You wanted to undermine the agreement we had! You wanted him to declare Jews as the enemies of Rome! Just like when you told him to cut off his foot. You knew exactly what he was talking about, and you provoked him. I know you did all this intentionally because if God is speaking to anyone, it is to me and He's telling me it is so!"

The declaration that I was hearing the word of Our Almighty God in my ears ricocheted between the peristyle. Hearing it from the High Priest gave it far more credence than an unproven claim from a rabbi whose behavior was starting to be seriously questioned.

Turning to the crowd, Akiva attempted to explain his behavior directly to the people. "Don't you understand, Hadrian had already made up his mind as to what he intended for us," Akiva proclaimed. "Without Antinous present to calm and mollify his heart, Hadrian would have reverted to his original plans of dealing with Judea regardless of anything I said. 'If they right eye offends the, cut it out!' Is that not what the Torah says? I merely passed on God's own words to him, exactly as he had asked me to. What was the point in lying if it was obvious that he intended to impose his cruel sanctions against us. Better to stand up to him and say, 'we are not afraid of you'. That is what my defiance was all about. A clear message to him that we stand by God's laws and as a result God stands with us!"

"Who in all of Ghenna are you to pass on anything," I screamed at him, though in my heart I truly wanted to beat him soundly. "You are nothing more than a soulless man that brought death and destruction down upon hundreds of thousands because of your so-called defiance. You are not God's spokesperson, as much as you believe you are. Because of you, Hadrian declared his lover, Antinous, to be a god and threatened to put his statue into every holy place within the Empire. In fact, from what I've been told, he has done so already in many places. That is the direct result of your lying to him and saying Our God killed his lover. In what other way did you expect him to react other than to challenge our God directly, whom you made out to be his enemy? He banned circumcision, he forbade us from the Temple Mount, he banned the teaching of our religion and our laws, all these things he did because of you!"

The fury within my body was mounting steadily. I couldn't believe how much I desired to knock him down and beat him within an inch of his life. What was happening to me? I had to keep reminding myself that I was the High Priest, and this was a court of law in order to stay my right fist from dispensing justice. Was that what Akiva wanted all along? Was he trying to intimidate me, to provoke me to strike him so that he could call for a mistrial. I knew I had to resist the urge though at times the temptation was overwhelming. It took every ounce of my strength to hold back. I took a deep breath and settled myself down. I had to refocus and took several deep breaths to do so. "So tell us the truth, why did you stay behind in Alexandria after the rest of the Council left. Usually, Joshua ben Hananiah was the only one that the Emperor would speak to on a one to one basis. How did you know you would receive an audience? Who authorized or advised you to stay?"

"No one authorized me," Akiva could already sense where I was leading with this line of questioning and was preparing his answers craftily. "I made my own decision."

"So then, why did you stay?"

"I had business to tend to," he replied, an obvious effort to avoid answering the question.

"What kind of business?" I pressed on.

"Personal business," he said curtly. "And that is all I will say on that matter."

He had already provided me with enough of a clue. As my wife suggested, 'Follow the money.' The only personal business Akiva would have had was either a woman or money, or perhaps even both. It was just a matter of finding the connection and now more than ever I was determined to do so.

"So let me summarize exactly what the court has heard during this deliberation that we have partaken in," I began to paraphrase. "Whether you are willing to admit it or not to this tribunal, your responses to the Emperor resulted in Rome increasing its persecutions and suppression of our religion. We all went to Alexandria with hopes of returning with religious freedom and liberty, which was well within our grasp, and instead we came back to a war. That is the undeniable conclusion of your time with the Emperor!"

"That is not accurate," Akiva challenged my claim.

"You are right. Permit me to correct my statement," I apologized sarcastically. "We all went to Alexandria with hope and returned in despair. It took you another couple of years to turn that despair into an actual war. You needed time to select your Messiah, to teach your students that martyrdom was more precious than life itself, and to convince the people that unless they supported your cause then they were the traitors and not you who was the one that eliminated any chance of a peaceful solution while in Alexandria. That is the truth! Furthermore, that is an accurate assessment! Say what you want but the truth is obvious and inescapable!"

Copying my usual tactics of approaching the rope dividing us from the crowd, it was now Akiva's turn to present his own version of the facts to the public. "If you truly believe there was a legitimate chance of pursuing peace and restoration after all that we had lost in the earlier wars when we were in Alexandria, then do you also truly believe that God would have let that young man drown in the Nile, knowing that his death would destroy any opportunity to achieve those goals. Is that how you picture our God, a vindictive and merciless being that would steal away any chance we might have had of living in peace and religious freedom because He loathed and despised the lifestyle of this young man. That is not the God I believe in. Shame on any of you that believe that to be true. I advise that you should pray now for God to forgive you for having such depraved thoughts regarding Our Lord. If God did not consider that the death of Antinous would lead us to war, then it can only mean that in His omnipotence, He already knew that Hadrian had already considered and decided to impose his cruel laws upon us, and all the talk in Alexandria was simply nothing more than talk, without any real purpose. Nothing more than a cover for Hadrian's real intentions and everyone should be grateful that I was able to expose his true plans for us in time for us to take arms against him. I did not entice him to go to war, instead I merely exposed his true intentions to go to war! Had we not made the necessary preparations, he would have succeeded in annihilating all of us, not just a portion of our population. What I did during my time in Alexandria resulted in the saving of the Jewish race. Condemn me if you wish to believe the lie that the Prosecution has filled your heads with, but I know the truth because I was there, I was the one speaking with the Emperor, and I know what his intentions were regardless of anything I had to say."

I could see from their faces that Akiva's words had hit home. Pitting the people against God's omnipotence was a clever tactic. He was gifted, I had to admit that. It was rare to find someone that could take a statement and twist it in such a way that it could adopt a completely opposite meaning of what was intended. But now it was my turn to rebut, and I was equally prepared.

"Yes, we do expect God to intervene on our behalf, especially when we are innocent. But what if we were not truly innocent. What if providing someone like Antinous into the Emperor's life was God's true intention? What if softening Hadrian's heart against our people was the miracle being perpetrated by God. And what if another individual recognized this and was determined to undermine everything that God intended. This person not only understood how Our Lord operates but also knew from our history that if we nominated a Dathan, a Korah, an Ahab, or a Manasseh to rule over us, then the Lord would let the evil befall us because of our continued failure to identify the true evil among us."

Akiva swung around to face me directly. "This man would have you believe that I am that evil. That I have misdirected you and lied to you over the years. Me! The one that has made the Torah accessible to all of you by distilling its essence into a simple language that you could understand. Me! Who the other rabbis have declared to be a great Sage. Me! Who has donated to all worthy causes to safeguard our children's future and learning. How dare him even suggest such a thing. This priest that can't even be bothered to live among you and prefers to live in Mesopotamia, the land that God brought our father Abraham from and intended for us never to return to. What do you know of this man? Nothing! But you know me. I have been here for you for fifty years and I have not deserted you in all that time."

'Amazing' I thought to myself. 'He has managed to place me on trial without skipping a heartbeat. I could see some of the people already staring and thinking that I was nothing but an interloping stranger to them, a complete unknown. I had to stop this before their discontent grew out of control. "Don't accept my word," I exclaimed, as I walked over to Yehonatan to retrieve Akiva's book. Fortunately, I had folded the pages in advance where I had identified key information that I knew I would need for the trial. "Accept the words from Akiva's own lips to his hand. Listen to what he writes by his own hand. *'And Rabbi Yohanan ben Nuri approached me and confessed that it was he that had been reporting my sinning nature to Rabbi Simon ben Gamaliel. That he regrets all the lashes I have received in punishment from the President of the Council. He says he prays that I will stop in my sinning so that he no longer needs to report on me.'* If that is not enough then look here where he writes, *'Rabban Gamaliel is wondering how many times he has to physically punish me for my contrary and undefended opinions.'* But I even like this admission better. *"Today I asked Rabbi Nehanya the Great, what is it that you did or is so meritorious that you have been blessed with and exceedingly long life? His servants and students began to beat me and I was lucky to escape them by climbing a date palm tree.* A curse upon all their heads." Are you beginning to finally know this Rabbi who claims that he is one of you? The tally of his sins exists in this book, and I can tell you sincerely, I don't believe he has any regrets for all the evil things he has done. You all loved Rabbi Eliezer Ben Hyrcanus, a man that was truly one of the great sages of his time. A man whose reputation was so great that it even extended to us in Babylon and we mourned his death. When he expressed his dissenting opinion from the other Sages leading to his being deposed and excommunicated from the Council, we all wept. Even Rabban Gamaliel said that Israel had lost one of it greatest scholars that day. But someone had to deliver that message to Rabbi Eliezer that he had been excommunicated. In respect of his greatness, everyone refused to volunteer to deliver the message. No one except one Rabbi who cared little for how great a man Eliezer ben Hyrcanus may have been. Let me read what was written by the man that volunteered. *'I dressed all in black as if I was attending his funeral. I wanted him to know he was dead to all of us.* Arriving at the home of Eliezer ben Hyrcanus, the rabbi was already confined to his bed, the stress of his fight with the Council making him ill. When he saw me dressed in black, he knew right away that I was welcoming his death. *He then asked me why in all the time we had known each other, why I never in that time chose to serve and befriend him. I told him that there was never the opportunity or reason to do so.* After delivering the message from the Council, *I asked him if he thought he was going to have a natural death.* I knew that the news of the excommunication would likely be enough to break his heart and accelerate the onset of his death.' Here is your hero of B'nai Brak. A man that takes obvious delights in the death of his brothers and his superiors. It is obvious that he not only enjoyed delivering that message to Eliezer ben Hyrcanus but in so doing he knew it would hasten his death.

This is a man that you all think you know, but in reality, you know nothing about him. He is an enigma that has fooled you completely for years and preyed upon that very ignorance of innocence. This is the Akiva that came to Alexandria and decided he would defy God's will because as you can see, he has been defying God's will for years and the Council has been covering for him so that the people would not become aware of his constant hypocrisy. Because if they did not cover for him, you, the people would question how the Council could ever have come to ordain such a man in the first place. And the day that happens, is the day you begin to realize how fallible the Council really is and then you may begin to resist all their teachings. They cannot afford to let that ever happen. So, they will cover, and they will lie."

"This is all nonsense," Akiva attempted to interrupt and defend himself. "We are all guilty of writing or saying things that we don't mean and have no intention of doing or making public. How many of you can say you have never had an evil thought, but you are not guilty because you never acted upon it. We cannot judge each other on what we say but only on what we do. Did I have disagreements with my fellow members of the council? Of course, I did. It would be a rare day that we agreed on everything. That does not mean we did not respect one another. It does not mean we disliked each other. It does mean that as people we do not always get along every day and all the time, but when it is necessary, we do come together to make the proper decisions. Who here has never held an evil thought in their head that they may have accidentally said aloud but never acted upon?"

A few people in the gallery raised their hand but the vast majority remained silent and motionless.

"See," Akiva continued, "Almost all of us are guilty of such things but we should not hold others accountable for our thoughts. When I said such things aloud did I get punished for them? Yes, because my brothers would not tolerate even the thought of such matters. So, my back bears the stripes of every stray thought I may have had or shared. Do I resent my brothers for it. No, I do not, I forgive them for their lack of temperance, but I did learn an important lesson to write things down rather than say them aloud. That is a lesson you should all remember." He wagged his finger at all of them, in the manner of a parent making a point to their child.

Making a jest of his punishments, Akiva managed to sway some of the people to align with his thinking. How much easier it is for people to believe that his problem stemmed from letting his mouth talk before he gave his brain a chance to think on the matter. I realized we could go back and forth like this all day, with my quoting excerpts from his book and him simply dismissing it as meaningless dribble that escaped from his unthinking hand. My current strategy was not gaining me any ground in convincing people that Akiva's actions in Alexandria were intentional. If I could not convince the people, then it meant that the judges were probably equally unconvinced. It was all talk on his part, and as he told everyone, it didn't matter what he said, what only mattered was what he did. The only way I'd ever get the people to hold Akiva accountable was if I could find something he did that everyone could agree was unacceptable behavior. I needed to find something that he admitted doing, which I could amplify and then confront him with. I racked my brain to review every page I had read in his book. Some items I had read but dismissed immediately because I considered them to be too unrelated to the court case. That no longer mattered. I just needed an episode of Akiva acting improperly that he couldn't deny. Then it hit me. Nehardia!"

"Akiva," I raised my voice to catch his attention. "Some things exist only in the mind and are never manifested into reality. That is what you are saying. I think we all must admit that is true. But people in positions of power are in the unique position that they can say something, and it will become reality. Would you not agree? Their words have power, whereas the majority of people will never experience that level of authority where they will speak, and things will happen as a direct consequence. Akiva, you are one of those people that I speak of where your words can manifest into our reality. We merely need to look at Nehardia to see a perfect example of what I am saying."

I could see Akiva's back stiffen as soon as I mentioned Nehardia. The word obviously did not sit well with him, and I got the desired reaction to tell me that I should press on.

"Praetor, I object to the prosecution bringing up Nehardia. It has nothing to do with any of the charges of this trial. I cannot even fathom how events in Nehardia twenty-five years ago could even be connected to the tragic war we have just endured."

Yehonatan motioned for me to approach his table. Speaking in hushed tones he asked, "Is there a reason you wish to talk about the Defendant's days in Nehardia. As Akiva says, it can hardly be related directly to Bar Kochba. Perhaps you should reconsider this line of questioning."

I had no need for hushed tones. I wanted everyone in the courtyard to hear my response. "Praetor, some of the judges may already know what transpired in Nehardia, but the public I suspect is ignorant of the events. But Nehardia is the defining evidence regarding the character of the defendant. When tied together with other alleged offenses that took place in Ginzah it will demonstrate why this man cannot and should not be believed in regard to anything he says. It will also clearly define the true relationship he had with his superiors because the public has been falsely led to believe that they all loved Akiva, whereas the truth is that they feared and may even despised him. That being the case, then revenge is certainly a motive as to why he said the things he said to the Emperor."

"Revenge against who?" Yehonatan wanted to know.

"Anyone and everyone that stood in his path. Every voice that was ever raised against him. Every action that was ever taken to remind him of his lowly birth. Every stripe that lashed his back. Trust me when I say that Akiva was not lacking for individuals upon which to seek revenge."

"Praetor, this is utter nonsense," Akiva pleaded. "Let me call my witnesses now and they will show you how much I was loved by my fellow sages. Don't waste the courts time with this unproven drivel. The High Priest only seeks to tell lies because he knows the truth only serves to vindicate me."

"If they are lies, then let him prove it," I argued. "Let him look Abba Saul in the eyes and say to him it is all lies because I know for a fact he has had the story told to him by Rabban Gamaliel."

Yehonatan looked towards Abba Saul and watched as the grave digger nodded his head, confirming the story was true. "I will let the Prosecutor proceed with this line of investigation after which time the Defendant can summon his witnesses to disprove the statements if they can."

"Praetor," Akiva pleaded again, "This is grossly unfair. You are allowing me to be condemned by hearsay."

"We have heard nothing as yet," Yehonatan dismissed his complaint. "Let us hear it first and then we can decide what is to be considered fair or not. Elioneai, you have the floor."

"You may sit if you would like," I offered Akiva the opportunity to sit back in his chair but he did not budge. "After all, this may be quite a strain on you to hear of your actions in Nehardia raised against you once again." He still remained standing in front of the rope. "All right then. Stand if you wish. So, correct me Akiva if I'm wrong but as I recall it was around the twelfth year of Trajan's reign that you came to Babylonia, visiting a lot of the cities where we had established our schools. Is that correct?"

"Twelfth, thirteenth, around then," he muttered.

"And the purpose of this trip was to learn, I suppose?"

"At that time I was already one of the respected Sages of the Sanhedrin, so it wasn't as much a trip to learn as it was to exchange ideas," he corrected me.

"So, it had nothing to do with the letter we received from Rabban Gamaliel and his son Simon asking us to see if we shared any concerns regarding your behavior and qualification as a Sage?"

"That is ridiculous," Akiva exclaimed, "There was no such letter."

"Then this doesn't really exist," I reached beneath my tunic and began to extract a rolled parchment from one of the internal pockets. "Shall I read it for you?"

"Alright, there may have been a letter," Akiva conceded. "It was a long time ago. But it never said all the things that you are going to cite against me."

"How do you know what I am going to cite? This was only a request by your superiors to our Council in Babylon to see if their suspicions had merit. If any accusations were to be made, Gamaliel wanted it done through our legal system so obviously the Council in Judea would not have to take the blame. Should I present the letter to the court, Praetor?"

"If you do so, then it will be considered to be your fourth witness."

"But your honour," the defendant has already acknowledged that the letter exists. Therefore, it is not separate testimony. Merely confirmation of his own statement."

"Then in that case why do you think you need to present it," Yehonatan presided with logic. "But if you do present it, then it will be admitted as the statement from the witness that signed the letter as a separate statement and therefore considered to be one of your witnesses."

As there was no other way to have the letter admitted into the court record, I slid it back beneath my tunic, very relieved to do so. I had gamboled on Akiva acknowledging that such a letter from Rabban Gamaliel existed at one time. This was merely a copy of the letter providing a timeline of Akiva's visit but without specifically stating the reason for his coming. Sometimes a little exaggeration and taking a gamble is the best tool you have available as a prosecutor.

"I cannot afford to lose a witness, Praetor, so since it is clearly acknowledged by both parties that the letter to the Council of Babylon from Rabban Gamaliel exists, then I will not submit it."

"If you do not submit it, then I will deny it exists," Akiva saw an opportunity to eliminate either testimony or else one of my witnesses and he seized upon it. Having placed the limitation on the number of witnesses each of us could call was my own fault.

"Praetor," I requested, "Please check your notes and confirm that the Defendant already admitted that such a letter may exist."

Fortunately, Yehonatan was scribing details of the case as it unfolded and when looking back on previous statements made, he saw this denial by Akiva was nothing more than a slight of hand. "Since you have already acknowledged the existence of such a letter, then the court accepts that as an admission statement and cannot accept your denial of its existence at the same time. And since the prosecution does not wish to submit the letter for loss of a witness, then the court cannot acknowledge the accuracy as to the admission of its existence. So as Praetor I will exercise my right to seek clarification of this matter in a suitable manner that will satisfy all parties to the court. Abba Saul, is it true that you also have knowledge of this event in Nehardia, is that so?"

"Yes it is," the tall old grave digger replied.

"Do you also know of this letter which the Prosecutor holds in his possession?"

"Know of it!" Abba Saul guffawed. "I practically wrote the whole darned thing. I was Rabban Gamaliel's closest companion in his old age. Almost every night I cooked for him and his son. How else do you think I would have known of everything they did?"

"So, is it accurate to say that the letter was written as a request to the Babylonian

Council to make a judgment on the suitability of Akiva to be both rabbi and sage?

"That and much more," Abba Saul had to say.

Praise be to Abba Saul for coming to my own defense. Either it was too long ago and he didn't remember exactly what was written in the letter or else he did and he was just as eager as I was to level charges against Akiva.

"I don't understand his reasoning," Yehonatan admitted. "Why would Rabban Gamaliel ask the Babylonian Council to pass judgment on Akiva when they didn't even know him in Babylon that well? It would seem the Council was abdicating its own responsibility. That is not what I would have expected from our esteemed Council. From my perspective, I must admit, it doesn't make any sense."

"Exactly, your Honour," Akiva interjected. "It makes no sense now and it certainly made no sense then."

Yehonatan turned to flash a threatening look that forced Akiva to be silent. "You will talk when I say you can talk," Akiva was warned. "Interrupt me again and I will see that you are strapped to the Defendant's chair and gagged when it is not your turn to speak." He then turned back to Abba Saul, "Please continue."

"It does when you are afraid," Abba Saul attempted to clarify the confusion.

"Afraid?" was all that Yehonatan could say in response, somewhat dismayed.

"Yes. Very afraid. Akiva had twenty-four thousand students. These weren't merely students they were adherents, practically worshippers, totally under Akiva's control. They were almost fanatical when it came to fulfilling the whims of their Master. None of us had ever seen anything like it, and I don't think any rabbi will ever be able to achieve the likes of it ever again. It was a veritable army and already Akiva was using that strength behind him to force decisions in the council and bend the will of the other members. Those that had stood in Akiva's way were very anxious. How many times was it proposed that he become President of the Council and how many *times was he rejected because the sages said his pedigree was not pure enough.* His heart, it was said, was not free of sin enough. How many times did they take the whip to him, both the first Simeon and his son Gamaliel, because Akiva violated this law or that one time and time again, without any sign of remorse and certainly giving no indication that he was willing to repent. *Rabban Gamaliel nicknamed him Am-Ha'Eretz, so all would know he was deemed to be an ignorant man.* When it came to the blessing of the sages, Rabban Gamaliel gave the following pronouncement, *'Blessed is Johanan ben Neri for he is fearful of sin, Blessed is Reb Ishmael for he seeks only wisdom, but woe is to Akiva who only fears being chastised and woe until Eleazar ben Azariah who only dreams of riches and greatness.'*

"But did he actually believe Akiva would do him any harm?" Yehonatan still found it hard to believe that Akiva would intentionally threaten his teachers.

Sitting upright, his frame even seated towering above other men, Abba Saul made himself evidently clear as to what he believed. "Who is dead and who is alive, Praetor? Rabban Simon and his son Gamaliel were killed by the Romans years ago. Reb Ishmael and his son murdered by the Romans recently. Rabbi Ben Neri is dead by the hands of the Romans during this war. And yet, Rabbi Eleazar ben Azariah, an associate of Bar Kochba has been spared by the Romans. And of course, Rabbi Akiva, the very man who we are here to judge if he instigated this war has been spared by the Romans. Don't you think that is extremely odd? I would think that Rabban Gamaliel had good reason to think we may have all been in serious danger from within our own ranks.

"Nothing but more nonsense and ridiculous gossip from a bunch of old women," Akiva retaliated. "Rabban Gamaliel loved me like a son. He told me so many times."

"Did he say so on the day *he asked you to recite the blessings over the meal and you took all three blessings, blended them into one and began to eat as soon as you finished. When Gamaliel began to condemn you for your blatant disregard of the established blessings, you threatened him by asking if he would dare to stand between food and a hungry man. All Rabban Gamaliel could do was ask if it is always going to be your intention to cause dispute among the sages.* That is not love, that again is fear that you would disrupt everything that we hold dear and sacred." It was clear that Abba Saul had a long litany of accusations he could make against Akiva.

"Praetor," Akiva addressed Yehonatan, "How can you expect me to have a fair trial when clearly this judge is prejudiced against me?"

"For the same reason that you have five of the judges prejudiced in your favour. I didn't hear you complain when your five students were placed on the tribunal. Clearly, you are only offended when the situation is not in your favour. I declare that this matter of Nehardia will be heard."

"Thank you Praetor," I responded. "Perhaps now, Akiva, this would be a good time for you to take that seat. This story could take a while." This time Akiva did return to his table and sat down disgruntled in his chair. "So let me paint this picture correctly," I said directly to Akiva. "You would have been late forties, almost fifty, at that time, if I'm correct."

"Yes, about that," Akiva answered gruffly, angry that he could not stop me from revealing events from Nehardia, twenty-six years ago.

"Perhaps even younger," I suggested, "Because none of us really know how old you are. You have no recollection of the Temple, so you couldn't have been much older than five or six when it was destroyed, otherwise like Abba Saul, or my father, you'd remember something. And it has long been said that if anyone saw the Temple, you could never forget it. So perhaps you were only forty-five when you came to Nehardia. That sounds more correct, doesn't it?"

"It is possible," Akiva didn't disagree. It was obvious he was growing tired of this discussion regarding his true age. For years his colleagues have been trying to guess it.

"A young, energetic man in the prime of his life, his wife and children left behind in Judea, and here you were, free to explore the sights and infinite pleasures of Babylonia."

"I was there solely on behalf of the Rabbinical Council," Akiva resented my last insinuation.

"Yes, you were," I played to the crowd. "We've established that. Something about having the Babylonian Council perform an assessment on your abhorrent behaviour because Rabban Gamaliel feared to do so here. But you didn't care. As far as you were concerned, you could do no wrong. After all, weren't you the one that said, *'Anyone that does not serve the sages has no stake in the world to come.'* That sounds to me like you believe you are above the law and us minions are merely here to serve you."

"Yes, I said that, but you are twisting my words, it is not what I meant," he protested. "You are taking it out of context."

"What other context could it have? It certainly sounds like you are demanding subservience, and no one will be permitted to argue against you." I held out my hands placatingly, offering him the opportunity to provide a better explanation.

"I was actually saying that one of the best ways to be rewarded in the afterlife is to assist the sages and help support them."

"So, the implication that you be served or else they will be cursed, we should just ignore that. I guess that is once again your mouth saying things before your brain had a chance to think about it."

This time my joke at Akiva's expense got a very good response from those standing within the peristyle. From the grimace on Akiva's face, it was obvious that he hated being mocked and laughed at. That was a weakness in his personality that I recognized could be exploited to my advantage during the trial.

"You were fortunate that when you arrived, the Babylonian Council had such a strong relationship with the Pashah of Babylon at that time. When he heard that we had a guest from Judea that was a young man of such fine upstanding moral character, he decided to reward you with a gift few are ever offered. *He dressed up two of his most beautiful concubines as brides and sent them to your room to spend the night.* That is a gift so rarely offered in Parthia and only to men they hold in high regard. A lucky man indeed! *From what the two young women said the next morning, they undressed you, massaged you,* did a variety of things to you that all of us gathered here can only imagine*, but you remained stolid, preserving your moral standing and refused to have intercourse with them.* We don't need the letter to prove that took place as your write about it in your own book. The next day the Pashah declared that you were a man of exceedingly strong character. Or so the story goes."

"I did not have sexual relations with either of them," Akiva insisted. "I did nothing immoral with those two women."

I leaned over the rope to talk directly with a few of the men on the other side. "I don't know about you, but if I had two beautiful women doing a variety of erotic massage manipulations to my body all night, I'd probably be too tired for sexual intercourse afterwards too." Those assembled in the gallery went wild with laughter as soon as I said that. I had to wait a few minutes for the laughter and rambling talk to die down.

Akiva rose out of his chair, furious that they were laughing at him. "I did nothing wrong," he shouted. "They tried to force me to lay with them, but I refused. As God is my witness, I did nothing wrong."

"Yes, you did nothing wrong," I laughed. "And you certainly didn't have either of the two women escorted from your room at any time during the night either. No one recalls any shouts or appeals for help from you. In fact, you never left the room all night. Perhaps you were paralyzed by fear. Or maybe these two young, beautiful women had overpowered you and were holding you prisoner." The laughter raised on octave as it spread throughout the crowd. The veins in Akiva's neck began to bulge and pulsate, his face flushed bright red as he grew infuriated by the ridicule and spurts of laughter at his expense. "And here's the best part of the story," I drew everyone's attention as to what would be the climax. "When the Pashah *asked Akiva the following morning why he refused to have intercourse with the women, he responded that he didn't like their smell.* I wonder exactly what it was that he was smelling?" The courtyard erupted into absolute chaos, with screams of laughter, a cacophony of other indescribable sounds, as well as the obvious heckling that could be expected as soon as they started visualizing Akiva with his nose in places it shouldn't be."

Somewhere in the noise I could hear Akiva banging on the table and demanding that everyone be quiet and settle down to listen to him. It wasn't going to happen. People were already running from the synagogue into the streets of the town to pass on the details of the story. By midafternoon, I suspected everyone would have heard of Akiva's night time adventure in Nehardia. By evening, it would have been retold so many times that I wouldn't doubt if it was said Akiva outperformed Solomon with his three hundred wives.

Praetor Yehonatan recognized he had lost control for the moment and decided it was best to call for a recess. Ordering my guards to take the defendant back to a room that acted as a holding cell, he dismissed the rest of us until the afternoon, when I would continue from where I had left off. As we emptied out of the courtyard, our departure was hardly even noticed by those in the gallery. At some point, once they finished cackling, hooting, snickering and ridiculing their perceived notion of what Akiva must have been doing all night they would realize we had left and return to their homes until the afternoon session. But for now, they were clearly having too much fun. I considered that a win.

Chapter Twelve

The Trial: Day 3 The Afternoon

As they led Akiva back into the courtyard, the fiery Rabbi was still furious from the embarrassment caused by the morning's session. Before he even sat down, he was yelling at the crowd, attempting to shame them for even daring to scorn and slander his character. He probably should have thought more carefully about what he was about to say, because decrying that *'Jesting and levity will only lead you all into lewdness',* was probably the most inappropriate condemnation at that time that anyone could have threatened them with. Instead of filling them with dread, it only served to start them laughing further. Fortunately, the merriment of the morning had practically exhausted them and this time the round of laughter did not last too long.

Waiting for relative silence to be restored, Yehonatan signaled for me to begin my discourse again. "Why did I tell you that story," I asked everyone, not expecting answers but some in the crowd felt compelled to give their opinion any way. A few even threw out the question as to which one smelled worse. Others wanted Akiva's opinion on what a Jewish girl smelled like. It was clear to me that this afternoon session was going to be a challenge to complete, but I pushed on nevertheless. "I told that story because I wanted all of you to truly appreciate what the Torah teaches us. I am certain it won't be necessary to repeat the biblical story about the Garden of Eden because I'd be very surprised that you don't know it. But what you may not know it that the story had a second meaning which was intended to be understood as well. As a Zadokite, you all are aware that I have no belief in a Hell and therefore Satan to me is nothing more than God's servant, a lesser being, whose sole purpose is to question God and thereby ensure God acts in the best interests of all creatures and not just Himself. Because even God knows that when a being exists that is all-powerful, all-knowing and omnipotent, then it is very difficult to understand mankind's thinking which is less than perfect, often ignorant and which wields so little control over our own world. As an intermediary, this angel known as ha-Satan, the accountant, challenges both God and man by enticing mankind to respond to its basest of instincts and in so doing, God can evaluate the success or failure of his most beloved creation. Satan merely whispers in a man's ear and depending on the nature of the man, God can judge how successful mankind is in finding His holy pathway. If you can appreciate this concept, then you will fully and completely understand that it is not ha-Satan that is evil, but that the wickedness pre-exists within the man that is being enticed to do an evil thing.

Therefore, the snake living in the Garden of Eden was not to be considered evil. He was there for no other purpose than to enlighten God as to the nature of this creature called man. And it was the innate wickedness in man that was activated, thereby becoming an important lesson that taught God that under the influence of evil thoughts and amoral purpose, even the best of mankind can be led astray. Under the guise of seeking knowledge, for the purpose of increasing the quality of life, and both the pursuit and obtainment of power, man will forsake even Paradise. The serpent has always resided alongside with us, in every society we have built. He is one of us, constantly whispering in our ears, preaching of a better life if only we do what he suggests. The serpent speaks with a sly. devious and convincing tongue, swaying many to his cause and does this for no other reason than to prove to God it is time for Him to conduct another correction. And as we know from the stories of the tower of Babel, the flood and even Sodom, God is not adverse to performing these corrections for our sake.

The role of the serpent is well defined. It is to confound and confuse, telling us to do as he instructs because he will not perform the inappropriate actions himself. But then, when mankind is caught performing an evil act or deviant behaviour, then the serpent will preach while mocking us, that we, as God's children should have followed his example of inaction and not have listened to his words. These precise statements are written in that very book that now sits on the Praetor's table as evidence of Akiva's guilt. In it, you will find that Akiva has written the following: *'The Torah is not learned by practicing its laws but by seeing the law as it is embodied in the gestures and the deeds of the living sages, then you will learn the Torah.'* A harmless statement you might think at first when you glance at it. How can this be the same as what I've told you about the serpent. until you analyze the slippery words spread by the forked tongue of the serpent. In other words, he says, 'Don't learn the Torah yourself. Don't educate yourself in what God requires of you. Just believe that whatever I say to you is right and follow it without question. And blindly, so many of you have done exactly that, abandoning your own learning of the Torah in order to emulate what Akiva says and you think God will consider that to be sufficient to earn the Lord's favour. He is that servant, suggesting you follow his actions, his suggestions, and don't bother to interpret God's words for yourself.

If you sincerely believe that Akiva is correct in his statement, and emulation is still the best way to live your lives, then let me expose for your sakes what the serpent that dwells amongst you has also written in this book which he expects you all to follow blindly, instead of the Torah. *'The father brings the child into the world, but it is the sage that brings him into the next world. Therefore, it is the sage that is owed the honour that is normally given to the father. The sage is above the father and closer to God!'* Now I ask you all to search within your hearts and your souls. Is that what you think God truly wanted from us when he had Moses inscribe on the tablets as one of His commandments, 'honour your mother and father?' Nowhere that I know of did God ever write honour the Sage more than your own father. I think it is because He knew that many of these sages would turn out to be the descendants of that snake in the Garden of Eden. The snake challenges you and you still go astray from following the Torah.

In Babylon we saw the face of this serpent and we challenged it and proved that it spewed words of deception. Perhaps it was our own failure, but we permitted the serpent to return to its home and continue to whisper in the ears of the ignorant and easily misled. No where was it more obvious than when we took the Defendant to meet the college students in Ginzah, just outside Babylon. The students were invited to ask the visiting Sage from Judea questions that would test his knowledge. It is no secret that we consider our teaching in Babylonian schools to be superior to that of those that remain in the Holy Land. I won't make any apology for saying such a thing. You have to remember that for those that did not return with Nehemiah and Ezra over six hundred years ago, had to establish an educational system that could preserve the strength and faith of our people without wavering in any direction because we did not have the great Temple or the Sanhedrin present to guide us. So the schools in Mesopotamia have a long history of understanding and implementing the laws as proscribed strictly in the Torah.

As for Akiva's test, one of the students prepared several different dishes of fish from the river and the sea. On one side of each platter was the prepared fish, and under cover on the other side of the platter were presented clear examples of each of the fins, tail, as well as the skin removed from that same fish. The student proposed the following question for Rabbi Akiva; *'Rabban, Ih ave all these fish laid out before me and I do not know which ones I can eat according to the Torah. Can you tell me which are acceptable according to our dietary laws?* To which Akiva provided the standard answer that if it has fins and scales, then according to our laws it is acceptable. The student pulled away the concealing cloth from the first tray, revealing all the fins and what looked like rudimentary scales buried deep in the skin.

Akiva took a moment to examine all of the appendages and skin. "I would not eat this one," Akiva replied. "There may be scales but they are not formed properly and do not present as a protective armor for the fish as required."

Exposing the next tray, the student asked, "Teacher, what do you say about this next fish?"

Seeing the fins and seeing lines of sharp small plates in rows on the skin, Akiva said, "This one is acceptable," and he took a piece of flesh from the tray and swallowed it to demonstrate that he stood by his verdict.

As soon as he made that declaration, the next tray was presented with several small, prepared fish laying on the tray. Exposing the other half of the tray, Akiva acknowledged that there were satisfactory fins present but he could not see any scales on the skin. In fact, he felt the skin and said to the student, it feels like velvet. If skin feels so soft to the touch, then this fish cannot be eaten.

Then examining the next tray, it was clearly evident that this fish was long and bony. *The fins were obvious, and the skin was coated with row after row of small dark scales which were more readily apparent on the cloth but had peeled away from the fish.* Akiva took a piece of the fish and ate it, commenting to everyone that it was delicious and most certainly acceptable.

The last tray contained a large fish whose white flesh was baked to a golden brown. The fins were quite large, multiple in number and it had a broom like tail, but the scales were tiny and black, yet still distinguishable. Akiva took a long time to make his decision regarding this last tray before finally plucking a piece of fish between his fingers and popping it into his mouth. 'This one is acceptable,' he drew his conclusion. 'As you can see, I have carefully weighed out my decisions according to the law and I am right,' he advised the student.

"Teacher," the student intentionally and obviously avoided referring to Akiva as Rabban. "The first fish you saw was from the sea. It is known as tuna and we eat it all the time. But you would not eat it because you considered it to be unclean and therefore are opposed to our sages. The second tray contained a fish known as sturgeon. Our Rabbis say those are not scales but what they refer to as scutes. They advise us that we should not eat this fish because we cannot say for certain scutes are scales, but you declared that fish fine to eat. Again, you are in opposition to our sages. The third tray was mackerel. The scales are so small and interlocked so tightly that the skin of the fish feels almost soft to the touch. Once again it is a fish that we eat all the time but you condemned it as unfit. The fourth fish was an eel. Unlike other fish the scales are on the inside of the skin and you won't see them until the skin is removed. We are still debating whether or not this fish is acceptable as the Torah does not specifically say the scales must be external, but you immediately gave it your approval. The last fish was cod and throughout the world we have already ruled it was acceptable to eat."

So you are probably wondering what this great Sage had to say regarding these repeated errors in judgment? Here is what he said in his letter of excuses that was sent back to Gamaliel, 'Perhaps we are not in agreement as to what constitutes a scale and what does not, but today I made my decisions based on my interpretations and be it known that *before I tasted anything I recited a blessing. If God thought my choices to be incorrect then I know and believe that the Almighty, blessed be He, would have given me warning and therefore my decisions should not be scorned or rejected as God permitted it. Everything we know is foreseen by God, but freedom of choice is granted.* As such, had God foreseen my falling into sin, surely He would have interceded.' We know this not only because the letter is preserved by the Sanhedrin but because Akiva recorded it once again in his book as part of his own defense.

But that was not the end of the tests. No sooner had that student bowed his head and departed, then the next scholar stepped forward. '*Moreh, I have a question for which I need an answer. If I am given clay vessels that I know belonged previously to a Gentile, am I permanently prohibited from using them?*'

Rather than answer the question, Akiva began to ask his own set of questions. 'Were there any images painted on the vessels?

Was the clay porous in texture? Do these vessels have a handle or not? If so, are there one handle or two? Is there a lid to the vessel?" And so on and so on. It was obvious to everyone that he could not answer the question directly, so they invited the next student to step forward.

All this is simply old history for you, isn't it Akiva. We shouldn't be surprised because as you have written in your book, you instructed the Council that *if a chair has two consecutive broken boards, then it must be removed as it is considered defiled before God.* Of course, no one agreed with your ruling because God doesn't build chairs and we don't eat off the surface of a chair but we do prepare our food in clay pots. Therefore, we do have a ruling of a full week for the clay vessels to remain unused. It is not permanent as they tried to test you. You should have known. You attempted to avoid answering by confounding the issue with further questions. No matter how you try to explain your reasoning for doing so, it was obvious to all that you did not know the answer.

But let us proceed, because then came the next question, *'Reb Akiva, if the fast day falls on the Sabbath, what is the minimum number of hours we should fast?'* A pretty basic question," I addressed the crowd. "One that a true sage should have been able to easily answer. Am I not correct? So, what did Akiva say? He responded by first trying to talk around the question. *'I remember one time, Rabbi Yehuda saying to me on a day when the ninth of Av fell the day before the Sabbath and he saw me eating an egg well before the twenty-five hours of fasting had expired that I had violated the rules of the fast. I reminded him that it was forbidden to be hungry on the Sabbath.'*

'But what about the fast day that falls upon the Sabbath day,' the student insisted on knowing.

At that moment Akiva responded that he would not answer until he consulted with the Council back in Yavneh, explaining that one ruling could not satisfy all the different fast days.

'But should we violate the laws and requirements of the Sabbath if it is Yom Kippur that falls on the same day?' The student was not willing to let Akiva avoid providing an answer.

"I cannot answer because I do not know!" Akiva responded angrily, silencing the student once and for all. "One more question and then this is over!"

Finally, an admission on your part that you are actually ignorant of the Law, especially when it pertains to our most solemn of days, Yom Kippur," I admonished him. "But they were not finished embarrassing you yet, were they? With some hesitation, perhaps it was even trepidation, the last student stepped forward. *'During the seven-day inauguration of the Tabernacle, what clothes did Moses wear?'* Do you remember what happened next? You should, because you wrote about it in your book. Apparently, you had reached his limit of tolerance and patience, standing up at that point and berating the student for asking such a pointless and useless question. You declared that you were done with this nonsense and the questioning was over and you made your preparations to leave Mesopotamia, as you had enough of what you considered foolish games.

The report from the Babylonian Council regarding your failure to pass the tests arrived in Judea days earlier than Akiva, but apparently after reading it, Gamaliel was still reluctant to take any action against this wayward sage and strip you of any recognition," I explained to the enthralled audience. "Why do you think that was?"

"Because not knowing answers is not a crime," Akiva shouted out. "Why take action if there was no crime committed!"

"Perhaps not but that did not stop Gamaliel from having you whipped anyway because of the tremendous embarrassment you caused his Council and all the schools in Judea. To not know that Yom Kippur is the Sabbath of Sabbaths and therefore supersedes the regular Sabbath was unforgivable. To not remember that as the equal to Aaron, Moses would therefore be wearing the same white linen clothing as the high priest meant you haven't mastered the Torah. You claim to be a Torah scholar, but you don't even know the simplest of truths presented in our Holy Book. So why weren't you stripped of your recognition and dismissed from the Council. That's the real question. What was Gamaliel afraid of?"

Akiva insisted that his trip East, despite all the evidence, was not an attempt by Gamaliel to have him disgrace himself to the point that he had no choice but to resign from Council or be dismissed, and to surrender his recognition as Sage. "If all this were true," he ranted, "Why was I not excommunicated? Why then did the Great Rabban Gamaliel as well as his son Simon the Nasi, continue to tolerate my actions and teachings long afterwards and furthermore his son continued to honour me? Surely the Babylonian Council have recommended my removal? What was to be gained by my continued presence if your stories were all true?"

"Exactly the questions I'm currently proposing and hope you will answer," I declared in response. "Why did they tolerate you? What were they afraid of? I think we all want to know the answer to those questions."

"There are no answers," Akiva replied, "Because my status was never in question."

"A scholar that doesn't even know the answers to the most basic of questions? What I think is that Rabban Gamaliel valued peace over the in-fighting that would have resulted if he pushed for your immediate expulsion. We all know that Rabban Gamaliel if anything, was a man of peace. The Council in Babylon couldn't do it because you weren't under their governance. They could only make a recommendation, which in hindsight appears to be a major failing of our system. Had you been stopped earlier, perhaps our half million dead would still be alive today because you would not have had the authority to compel anyone to listen to you."

"I request time to call witnesses that can vouch for my character," Akiva demanded from the Praetor. "You've permitted the Prosecutor to sully my character with fables from Babylon and I have the right to defend myself."

"And so you shall. That is your right and it has never been denied," Yehonatan agreed. "Could the prosecution please bring to a close this line of questioning for today and afford the Defendant time to present his case."

"Of course, Praetor," I agreed. "So let me wrap this up quickly for everyone. Essentially, we have never left the Garden of Eden. We still live in a world where many of us our naive and gullible. Where this man can come along and say to us, '*As the day is first dark and then lightens up, so too will the darkness be followed by light,*' and we are stunned into silence thinking it is the most profound statement we have ever heard in our lives. If you don't believe me, you can read that quote and similar ones in his book. You don't need a Sage to state idioms like that. My grandmother would recite them all the time and in most cases, they were far more clever." The crowd chortled at my little joke. "But it's true. God sends the serpent to test us repeatedly and more often than not, we fail the test. I believe Akiva is such a test. He had a purpose to lead us astray and take us to the point where our continued existence teeters on a precipice. If we should fail to recognize exactly who he is, and we don't punish him for the crimes he has perpetrated against our people, then I am afraid there will be no pulling back from that precipice and we will cease to exist. If you are not convinced yet, then I assure you by the end of this trial you will be."

Having finished my remarks I returned to my position and sat in my chair, permitting Akiva to take possession of the floor.

"So far today you have heard them describe me as a fornicator, a liar, a provocateur, a fake, a serpent, a scoundrel, a traitor, a simpleton, and irredeemable. If not for the slanderous nature of these comments, they would be laughable. But I ask you, how could one man be all these things and still be considered a Sage, a scholar, an educator, righteous, honourable, charitable and incorruptible. There is no doubt I have other characteristics which tend to offend some people. I make no attempt to hide the fact that I may be somewhat arrogant, that I flaunt that the Lord has showered me in wealth and opportunity, that I consider myself somewhat more clever than my peers, but none of that in any way interferes with the love in which I hold my people, the Children of Israel. *Beloved are Israel for they were called the Children of God.* Those are truths that can never be denied. It would be incongruous for me to have this love in my heart and to be guilty of all the matters for which I am being accused. Yet here you have this so-called vaunted High Priest of Israel, this stranger to our land, saying all these horrible things about me and because of his status among our people you are supposed to automatically believe him. Why should that be? Especially when we have our own High Priest who stood alongside Bar Kochba throughout the war, who fought with us every minute in our struggle against our enemy. Who never abandoned us. Who I am proud to call my colleague and my friend. Who was the youngest man ever to serve as President of the Sanhedrin. Who passed more laws in a single day than any other leader of our Council has ever done. Let my first witness speak the truth about me and put an end to these foul lies. I call the rightful High Priest Eleazar ben Azariah to take the witness chair."

I watched, admittedly with some disdain, as my cousin strutted confidently into the courtyard through the entrance directly from the synagogue, where he obviously had concealed himself all this time, rather than walking through the peristyle surrounding the gallery. Just like a peacock, he was dressed in a muti-coloured striped robe trimmed with fur, the train of his robe flowing behind him like a bird's tail feathers. A golden tiara, similar but not identical to that worn by the High Priest, sat across his wrinkled brow making a mockery of our ancestors. If it had not been for the fact that we were sitting in a court of law, I would have knocked it off his head. I know I am sounding petty and jealous but that is not the case. Normally it was not my nature to be so aggressive but something about this trial was pushing me over the edge.

As I recall, Eleazar must be between fifteen to twenty years older than me, and actually my father's second cousin, but we had little contact over the years. He was never interested in the priesthood, only the money such a position could garner. Of all the family lines, and there were still several, his was the last that would ever be considered fit to wear the High Priest's tiara. After my grandfather's murder, the role passed on to his cousin, Phineas ben Habta. Had he known the Zealots would cut his throat soon after his acceptance, I doubt Phineas would have considered accepting it. The next in line should have been Ishmael's son Elisha but he was still too young at the time. My father was next, but he had already escaped to Parthia, so was not available but even so, he was still too young to accept, even if it had been offered to him. There was only two other family members left, the younger brother of Ishmael, named Azariah and another cousin of theirs known as Reb Ishmael. But Azariah was so firmly entrenched with the Romans that even if he was the last of the family line left on Earth, I doubt he would have been offered the position. They say he had his hand so far up the Emperor's ass, clutching Roman gold that not even a surgeon could separate them. That Azariah was Eleazar's father and this son of an undeserving and scorned family member somehow managed to rise in the hierarchy of the Council, not only to be appointed President of the Council, but even managed if only for the briefest of times during the war, to be acclaimed as the High Priest of Israel. This man is the ultimate insult to my family and heritage. As mentioned, the only other person that could rightfully make that claim would have been the cousin known to the Council as Reb Ishmael but he was killed along with his son and my father being too old, that title was now mine and mine alone. As far as I was concerned, Eleazar ben Azariah was nothing more than the pariah of our nation and an embarrassment to the family. Yes, my disdain for him may sound petty but it is the truth.

To no one's surprise, the questions that he was asked by the Defendant

185

were purposely generic, having no in-depth purpose other than to praise Akiva and describe how wonderful, righteous and saintly a person he was. Akiva ensured that the people heard exactly the words that he wanted them to hear and nothing more. That was his right and I acknowledge it. Eleazar spoke on endlessly of how close the two of them were in their overseeing the responsibilities and conduct of the Council. Eleazar talked about Akiva's role during the war, how he worked side by side with Bar Kochba, approving strategies and advising on what were God's expectations at any moment. I let it drone on and on, not even bothering to make objections, even when Eleazar made outlandish statements, such as how during the re-dedication of the Temple Mount, following the liberation of Jerusalem by Bar Kochba in the second year of the revolt, while he was standing on what would have been the site of the Holy of Holies, he heard God say to him that Akiva was His servant. I thought it best to let the people make their own decision on how credible any of this testimony might be. As if God would waste his time in such a manner. Nor did I intercede his monologue when he claimed that the Lord showed him a passageway beneath the platform of the mount where he beheld the Ark in all its glory. It would have been easy to ask him then why he didn't retrieve it in order to secure our victory. Those of us that are descendants of the last High Priests that served in the Temple knew that particular artifact had been lost to us a very long time ago. Closing my eyes to the nonsense, I just waited for my turn to cross examine the witness, unperturbed and oblivious to all the superfluous words and descriptions that my distant cousin chose to shower upon his good friend, Akiva.

Finally, when he had grown silent and there was no more history to recount of how the two of them transformed the Council for the better, passing their rules and regulations that only made the worship and religious practices of Yahvu less burdensome for the average Jewish family living in Judea, and how they were now working on their greatest project, this Talmud that Akiva spoke of being able provide everyone with the Codex of Laws that God intended us to live by but never included in the Torah, I heard the voice of Praetor Yehonatan calling sharply in my ear and snapping me from my state of near slumber.

"Would the prosecution like to cross examine the witness?" he asked gruffly, seeing that my eyes were closed. My guess was that he had already asked that question and was impatiently awaiting an answer from me.

"Yes...yes I would," I shook the cobwebs loose and forced myself out of my chair. I walked over to where Eleazar sat and stood beside his chair so that I towered over him. It was not that I was tall, but the fact that Eleazar was so short. I'm guessing he was about five foot four, potbellied from a life of extravagance and confident that money could buy anything and everyone if you have enough of it. And everyone knew Eleazar ben Azariah certainly had enough, being rumored to be the richest man in all of Judea. Richer even than the Romans. It was no secret that before the war he was a favourite pet of the Romans, just like his father, being invited to all the right parties of the elite and aristocratic classes and reciprocating heavily in kind and cost with a deluge of lavish Roman style parties and feasts of his own. That alone should have made anyone suspicious of how he could go from Roman collaborator to being Bar Kochba's chosen High Priest. I know it certainly had me wondering about what would have had to have been a strange string of events to make it possible.

"Why are you still alive?" was the first question to pass through my lips. It was time that I became blunt and make these people answerable for what was seemingly impossible. It was time to find the facts that had been eluding me thus far.

The question took Eleazar by surprise. Coming out of the blue, it was not what he had expected to hear. "What do you mean?"

"What do you think my question means, Cousin?" If I could make him anxious, I knew he would say a lot of things he never intended to. "It is in perfect Aramaic, is it not? Or would you prefer I phrase the question in Hebrew? Why are you still alive?"

"It sounds like you believe I should be dead," he responded nervously.

"Well, shouldn't you be." I reached beneath my tunic and pulled out a silver shekel that Simon Bar Kochba had minted during the rebellion. "I couldn't resist purchasing one of these from one of the locals," I told him. "The fact that the Romans are trying to gather them all up and melt them down, tells me that it is going to be a scarce and rare item some day in the future. I'd make certain you have some to pass down through the generations of your family. Wouldn't you agree?" I asked as I put the coin down on the table in front of him. "That's you in the legend, isn't it? It is a beautiful coin even though I don't recall them ever reporting there were four columns standing outside the Court of the Temple. I thought there were only two, Jachin and Boaz. But I guess it didn't matter if the artist got that wrong, as long as he spelt Eleazar the Priest correctly. That is your name, right? Now, I admit the lulav on the reverse is well done although the legend 'For the Freedom of Jerusalem' is incorrect as it is was a little premature at the time and now it seems an impossible dream. So, let me repeat, that is your name on the coin, is it not?"

"It could be..."

"Oh, don't be so modest Cousin, it's not like anyone else is parading around as Eleazar the High Priest of Israel. I'll just slip this back into my pocket. I'm certain you have a collection of them already and don't need another. So let me ask you once more, how is it you are still alive?"

"I didn't fight in the war," he responded. "The Romans know that."

"But you didn't need to, Cousin. You're right here on these coins. You are the spiritual leader of the revolt, a symbol of the resistance to Rome. Your name inspired hundreds of thousands to die for the cause. Besides Simon Bar Kochba, you are the living embodiment of the resistance as recorded on this coin. I just can't believe they would let you remain alive. Don't you think that's an incredible oversight on their part? I know if I was the Emperor of Rome and I had the opportunity to parade one of the leaders of the revolt in my triumph back in Rome, I'd have you there on the next boat and afterwards your head would be on the chopping block so fast that you certainly wouldn't be sitting here, all dressed up as if you still are something you're not, telling everyone about your good friend Akiva, who was also instrumental in launching the war against Rome. So, let me ask you once again, how is it that you are still alive?"

Everyone else listening to my questioning certainly thought it was certainly an incredible mystery that needed a plausible answer, after they had lost so many family members for a multitude of trumped-up charges and crimes against Rome during the war. How no one else bothered to ask this very same question before this trial of Eleazar was equally as incredible. Suddenly, you could sense what could only be described as a palpable anger swirling and suddenly rising from the gallery now that they had heard the question finally being asked. They all wanted an answer, and they wanted it now.

"I guess I have just been fortunate," was the best that Eleazar could respond.

"Fortunate!" I exclaimed loudly. "That must be the understatement of a lifetime. Perhaps even of the millennia. That would be like telling Rabbi Torta, may God have mercy upon his tortured soul, that he was unfortunate. What was his crime other than telling Akiva, *'grass will grow from your cheeks Akiva and still the Son of David will not come.'* He opposed this war, he opposed Akiva and somehow he is one of the many that was turned over to the Romans for execution."

"Truly unfortunate," Eleazar agreed.

"I just find it truly amazing that almost everyone who was a proponent of peace with Rome was either executed by the Romans or was forced into hiding, whereas you and Akiva, two of the most obvious and prominent Rabbis that not only advocated for war but actively participated in it, causing the death of thousands of Romans, just continue living your lives as normal; openly, defiantly, and with not a single Roman even harassing you. The word fortunate doesn't even come close to describing both of your situations. The word certainly doesn't do it justice. Incredible, unbelievable, impossible, that may be more accurate. Can you explain how it is even possible you weren't even arrested, let alone you are still alive."

"I can't explain it but Rabban Simeon ben Gamaliel would most certainly tell you that I have done nothing wrong and perhaps God is protecting me," Eleazar evoked the name of the Nasi of the Council as if it was a blessing that would save him from all harm. Only problem was Simeon ben Gamaliel had gone into hiding a year ago and still hasn't been seen.

"Wherever he may be right now, I doubt he cares enough to reveal himself in order to provide you with an alibi. Nor do I think the Romans believe in our God that they would respect His protection afforded to you" I instructed him. "By all logical reason, the Romans should have come for you first because you are technically a symbol of the revolt. Simeon, like his father, only wanted peace with Rome and he's a wanted criminal. The only way I could justify your freedom is that you traded it for a price. I'm just curious what that price actually was and whether the deal was made before, during or after the war."

Little beads of nervous sweat appeared across Eleazar's forehead and he wiped them away with the fur-trimmed sleeve of his robe.

"Are you implying that I'm a traitor to our people?" Eleazar tried to appear genuinely irritated by the accusation, as if it was absurd to even think it possible, but it was obvious he was feeling the pressure as he looked over towards Akiva with a look of haplessness, pleading for intervention.

Akiva rose to the occasion, coming to the defense of his ally. "It should be obvious to everyone," Akiva announced, "That as God's anointed High Priest, Eleazar ben Azariah has been safe-guarded and rendered as being untouchable by the Romans. He has the Lord's divine protection."

I just shook my head in disbelief. "Really, Akiva? Is that the best you could come up with? Has God made him invisible too, so the Roman's don't see him? That is about the poorest defense I have ever heard from anyone. Now let's get back to being serious and one of you needs to tell us what you offered the Romans so that they don't touch either of you. God didn't make you untouchable, but something or someone else certainly did."

"Are you suggesting that in some way I bribed the Romans," Eleazar feigned shock and disgust but neither look was convincing to anyone in the courtroom.

"No, but if you wish to carry on in that direction then you likely have enough money to make anything possible. So, I believe there was a price paid. I'm just not certain if the currency used was money or blood. Either way, I am certain it was a hefty price to spare your life. After all, that's how you have lived your entire life; buying whatever it is that you wanted. Is that not true?"

"I resent that accusation," Eleazar took offense to my comment.

"You wanted to be the President of the Council so much that you managed to buy the position when you were only eighteen. Eighteen! A child with about as much knowledge as a rock!"

"That's not true!" he protested loudly.

"Perhaps not, the rock my have been more intelligent. What does the Torah say on this matter? Let me quote, a leader or priest should not be in a position of power until they are at least twenty-five for they know nothing until then and they should be removed from power by the age of fifty because they no longer are able to member everything they have learned." I reminded him of what the law actually had written. "You and your council violated our sacred laws!"

"There was a miracle," he proclaimed loudly. "God knew it was outside of the law, s*o that night after my election He turned my hair white so that I would be older than my chronological age.* Everyone saw it. Everyone knows that it is true."

Leaning over the witness, I sniffed his hair. "Mmmm... still the faint trace of wood ash and tallow," I speculated.

"That's impossible!" Eleazar shrieked. "I stopped using those years ago!"

It wasn't until he completed his sentence that he realized what he had done. He just let everyone know he was in the habit of bleaching his hair with an alkali solution to keep it white. It was a practice used for centuries by the Greeks and Romans but one which was less commonly known in the Middle East. He had fallen into my trap because of his own vanity.

"So you have admitted you faked your miracle. Obviously, you weren't acceptable but somehow you still managed to obtain the presidential position. Must have been the money as there is no other justification. How much did you pay?"

"That's not true!"

"No? Then why was it written in Akiva's book? Here, let me show you what he wrote." Retrieving the book from the table I opened it to the desired page. "Here, read it for yourself."

Taking the time to read it thoroughly, I could see that Eleazar was becoming both infuriated and flustered, his face turning red with anger. No sooner did he finish reading it, than he began to read it again, which only inflamed him further. "Akiva," he shouted, "How dare you right such drivel! This is not how a friend writes about another friend. A curse upon your head, you traitorous lech." As much time as Eleazar had spent heaping praise upon Akiva, earlier, apparently it did not take much of an effort to have him turn on him like a pestilent harpy.

"Shut-up Eleazar, he is manipulating you," Akiva tried to dissuade him from saying anything further.

I stepped forward and took the book from his hands and began to read out loud the passage to those in the courtyard, so all would know what was written. *'It certainly is not that Eleazar ben Azariah knows more Torah than I do, but only because he is descended from greater men than I am. Happy is the person whose direct ancestors are the only ones to have deserved and gained all the merit for him to take for his own. Happy is the person that has a wooden peg from which they can hang.'* I think it is pretty clear what your friend Akiva thinks of your becoming President. For those of you that may not remember, let me remind you that when Rabban Gamaliel was forced to step down from the position of the Presidency, the Council needed to elect a new president in his place. They recorded their deliberations on the matter. *They said Rabbi Akiva was too Greek to be nominated, lacking a proper pedigree*, but for some reason others pushed for your election. If Akiva was too Greek, then you were most certainly too young. There's only one way you could have changed their minds, but bribery is such an ugly word. And it certainly doesn't surprise Akiva because he says it right here, *'Who's insides are not like the outside.'* That is what Akiva thinks of you. You may dress pompously and put on airs of superiority but on the inside you are empty, shallow, a fake. You are nothing but an empty shell. I especially like this part where he talks about your inability to govern the Council and your authority and knowledge being so weak that *you invited the displaced Gamaliel to resume the presidency three out of four weeks of each month.* Not even fifty percent but seventy-five percent of the time. He was laughing so hard that he says, in an effort to record your own idiom by which to be remembered for perpetuity by the students, the best you could come up with was, *'Where there is no bread, there is no study of the Torah. Where there is no Torah study, there is no bread.'* Only Eleazar could try to tie the study of the Torah to food and fail miserably in doing so, he says."

"Akiva is nothing more than a pathetic and evil liar," Eleazar blurted for all to hear. "You cannot believe anything he says. We all knew it, but we tolerated his lies and distortions because he promised he would make us all great men of Israel."

"Great as in being the supposed High Priest, Cousin. Is that what he promised you?"

"Yes, yes, that and much more!" he proclaimed.

"But Rabbi Aha, even though he was one of your little gang that were actually manipulating this war, he wasn't happy about your being named High Priest, was he?"

"How is it that you know of that?" Eleazar ben Azariah sounded surprised by my intimate knowledge of some of their inside dealings.

"Because after Reb Ishmael and his son were suddenly turned over to the Romans and summarily executed, I'm guessing Reb Aha had a change of heart and knew that something about the entire affair smelled rotten. As neither I nor my two sons were going to use our positions as High Priest to support Bar Kochba, then the next obvious and only viable option on their list for assuming the position of High Priest would have been our cousin Ishmael. Since my family were from Parthia, and far away, our refusal could be easily overlooked but Ishmael was part of your own Judean community. He could not be overlooked so easily. And after him, it was his son that would have been next in line for the position. We all knew that. But as advocates of peace with Rome, they both became obstacles as soon as they refused, didn't they? No way you could be offered the position as long as they were still alive. It must have been a relief when they were suddenly arrested with no warning at all prior to it happening. And then when they were executed, well that would have been totally unexpected considering that they had committed absolutely no crime against the Empire. Nothing that would lead to execution. But someone knew exactly what their fate was going to be. The path would suddenly be cleared for you to take the position and I'm guessing Rabbi Aha knew something bad was going to happen to both of them, as well when he wrote me his message because he wanted no part in it. This is what he wrote to me because his conscience was feeling guilty about what was being planned, *'You are holy to the Lord and therefore the vessel is holy. Just as one who makes use of the vessels commits sacrilege, so too does he who makes use of the priests commits sacrilege.'* At first it may sound like a riddle but you understand what he was warning me about?"

"He thought Akiva was using me," Eleazar suggested.

"Not only that," I responded. "He also thought he had a hand in the executions of Reb Ishmael and his son even though he did not sanction it. Do you know anything about that? Was Reb Aha right in thinking that in some way your unholy little cabal was responsible?"

"No I didn't," Eleazar sounded frightened. "I just considered it as being a terrible tragedy. I never thought of it as being anything more."

"A tragedy that coincidentally opened up the clear path for you to be anointed as High Priest. But since I am not a believer in coincidence, then I say to the court, this was premeditated. I may not be able to prove it yet, but I hope to soon," I concluded. "I have said all I needed to say to this witness, Praetor. He may step down."

"I can go?" Eleazar was unsure that he was being dismissed and free to go.

"You are just a hat to be hung on a family peg Cousin, just as Akiva said. You served a purpose and I doubt you even recognized everything that was happening. Nothing more than a puppet on a string. I only pray that you will be a more honourable man in the future and restore that honour that once belonged to the House of Phiabi. Praetor, I return the floor to the Defendant."

Without hesitation, Eleazar ben Azariah was out of the chair and in a matter of only a few seconds Eleazar had fled from the synagogue, through the same passage by which he had entered. It was evident he wanted to be long gone before Akiva could begin berating him regarding his statements.

"Does the Defendant wish to call further witnesses?" Yehonatan asked.

"Not at this time your honour," he replied somewhat solemnly, "But I would like to address the court regarding statements from the previous witness who I was not even given the opportunity to cross examine."

Yehonatan waved Akiva over to where he was seated in order to exchange a few words privately. Complying, Akiva approached the Praetor's table. "You understand that was your own witness," Yehonatan reminded him. "If you start claiming he is unreliable, then that applies to everything he said earlier as well."

"I understand that Praetor but as much as his testimony became hostile, I must clear the record because the Prosecution has created confusion."

"That is what you should have anticipated him to do," Yehonatan stated the obvious to Akiva. "After all, you are on trial and that was one of your character witnesses. Did you actually think he would give him a pass and let your character remained unsullied."

"I just need to clarify a few of the things that were said, Praetor," Akiva was now nervous that his request would be refused.

The Praetor just shrugged his shoulders and stared skyward. "Do what you think you must," he warned Akiva, "But be aware that you could be creating more damage than you think you can repair."

Akiva approached the rope divide. "Most of this afternoon you heard the High Priest, whom I remind you was appointed to that esteemed position by the Council when Bar Kochba reclaimed Jerusalem, heap praise upon praise upon me. He did so because he truly believed those things to be true. Then you saw the Prosecutor use his bag of tricks to make the witness believe that I had deceived and discredited him over the years by twisting a few words I had written in a book. You also saw what we all should consider as a normal response from Rabbi Eleazar when he believed that he had been ridiculed by me. I cannot blame him because it is a very normal reaction when any of us think someone is talking behind our backs. We strike back, and we say things we shouldn't because we are hurt. As I said, it is a normal reaction by any of us, and I cannot and I will not hold it against Rabbi Eleazar for reacting in that way. He is a good man, with whom I bear no grudge, and I cannot blame him for how he repsonded."

"That still doesn't mean you're innocent or excuse you of stabbing him in the back!" someone shouted from the crowd.

Akiva chose to ignore the comment. "The Prosecutor asked why he is still alive. I think the answer is simple. It is because he is a good man. Lots of good men died at the hands of the Romans and lots of good men have escaped thus far. That does not mean we will not meet our fate tomorrow and therefore we are only living on borrowed time. I don't know what the Prosecutor was trying to prove this afternoon, other than display his own jealousy that someone else was named as High Priest in his place because he refused to stand by his own people and support us in our hour of need. He chose instead to sit on the sideline and watch as many of us died, whereas Rabbi Eleazar had the strength of character, the bravery of his soul and the belief in Almighty God in his heart, to stand up and fight for our cause by joining with Bar Kochba. He showed himself to be the true High Priest of Israel, not this impersonator from Parthia that stands before you. Praetor, that is all I have to say. I will save my next witness for the morrow."

"You have the final word, Elioneai," Yehonatan advised.

"Your Honour, I object to this offer to the prosecution," Akiva exclaimed. "Why should the Prosecutor receive any more time. He has already dismissed the witness."

"For the same reason you were given the opportunity to redress the tribunal. What is fair is fair," was the Praetor's final word on the matter.

"I know this is difficult for everyone to absorb properly," I acknowledged there was confusion. "Who is good, who is bad? At times like these, it is hard to say because there is that high degree of confusion in our minds. But I remind you, this was not about what we think. This is about what the Romans are thinking. So, I need you all to think, even if just for a few minutes, like Romans and say to yourselves, who do I want to punish? Who do I want to execute? Those that were working with me or those that were against me? I think the answer should be quite obvious. So, when you see those that were definitely known to be fighting in the war and opposed to the Romans walking about freely, while those that attempted to find a peaceful solution executed, then you can say without hesitation, something is definitely wrong here. This is opposite to the norm. This is not making sense. Something else is playing out here and it all appears to be turned inside out. But don't be fooled or misled. The Romans do nothing without reason, and they spare no one without legitimate cause. That much we do know. That is all I have to say; that is all I ask that you think about until we meet again tomorrow."

Chapter Thirteen

Evening: 12th of Adar, 3896

The evening meal was exceedingly quiet on the third night of the trial. The silence was hauntingly quiet. "I know you are all dying to say something so you might as well get it off your chests," I told them..

"But you said we cannot discuss any details regarding the trial outside the courtroom Father," Joseph reminded me of my own rules.

"True, but surely you have something else that you want to say that isn't case related. That means any other topic is fine. I think some of the issues concern my personal handling of the trial.   Is that not so?"

"I was wondering Father, why you attacked Akiva all morning but in the afternoon it was as if you purposely held back and let him take control.   I could not understand your strategy," Joseph searched for a possible explanation.

"And which did you think was most effective, the morning or the afternoon session?" I asked.

"The morning of course," Joseph replied.

"And you?" I turned my attention to Azariah.

"I agree with Joseph, Father.   The morning you had him at a disadvantage.   The people were beginning to ridicule him.   He had lost all their support and much of their respect."

"And as strange as this may sound to you, that is the exact reason why I will tell you that the morning was the least effective session.   If it was my goal for this trial to merely humiliate Akiva and have him ridiculed with scorn, then I will admit that the morning was effective.   But that is not my goal for this trial.   Humiliation doesn't put a noose around his neck. I don't want the people laughing, I want them angry and shouting. To win this case I must prove that not only did he betray Bar Kochba, but that he betrayed all our people but most of all that he betrayed God! Making him the centre of everyone's jokes and having him exposed as a fornicator and a very poor scholar does not in any way help me succeed in proving my case. In fact, it draws everyone's attention away from the real issues."

"So why then did you pursue it all morning, Father," my sons asked.

"Because even though I knew it was not helping my case in any way, I realized that he was unable to control his emotions when he is aware that people are laughing at him. I thought if I could get him to a point where he was emotionally unstable, he might make comments that he would regret and to our advantage. Everyone knows that he and Rabban Gamaliel were like two clashing mountains that would never cease their antipathy towards each other even after death. If he became angry enough, I hoped he would first say something disparaging regarding Rabban Gamaliel and then possibly go on a rant regarding the war. But he was too smart to ever accuse Gamaliel of having been anything but an overly zealous, harsh disciplinarian despite all the lashes. The only time I made any headway today was when I asked why those that were allied with Akiva all seem to have survived the war and were never arrested by the Romans, while all those opposed to Akiva and the war were either executed or forced to hide. Clearly there is a connection there and I will have to exploit that venue more in depth tomorrow."

"Well isn't the answer obvious," Joseph had already made up his mind.

"If I was to tell you that the obvious is not necessarily the truth, would you accept that argument?" I challenged both my sons to answer.

Joseph was convinced he was correct. "If something is obvious then it should be accepted at face value," he argued.

"And what about you, Azariah? Do you believe the obvious is always true?"

"I suppose it would advantageous if you can gather a few facts that support the obvious. Then the odds are that it will be proven and accepted as true." Azariah was essentially agreeing with his brother but was clever enough to know that there was something more behind my question, so he added a few stipulations before saying yes.

"My Dear, if you will assist me in demonstrating my explanation, please. Can you come and stand beside me." Deborah rose from the table and took a position standing by my right side. She was very familiar with my habit of acting out scenes from trials from my many years of doing so back in Babylon, so this request came as no surprise to her. "Alright boys, I want you to listen carefully to me. My Dear, please forgive me if I should say or do anything that might offend you. You know that I love you."

Deborah laughed off my concerns. "Eli, if I don't know you by now then I doubt anyone else could know you better."

"Alright boys, I want you to look at you mother and I as we are now and then close your eyes." They did as I instructed. "Keep your eyes closed. Pretend that is the last sight you saw when you left our home in the morning. Now imagine that you are coming home in the evening, after being away all day, and you see your mother lying on the floor bleeding from a wound in her chest. Standing above your mother is a man with a knife in his hand. You look closer and see that the man is you father. Now open your eyes."

As soon as they opened their eyes, they saw the scene being played out as their mother lay on the floor pretending to have been stabbed. I am standing over her with a knife I took from my plate in my left hand. "Now close your eyes again."

A minute later I told them to open their eyes. When they did so they saw their mother sitting back at her seat at the table and I was using the knife to cut into the piece of chicken on my plate.

"Now tell me about the crime that you think you had witnessed," I opened the discussion while I continued to eat. "You first Joseph."

"The scene in the morning was a false front; a mask. It is a falsehood of what you try to project to the world. A happy and loving couple that has no issues. But during the day you get into a heated argument and in a momentary fit of insane rage you stab your wife and kill her."

"That is how you imagine it," I asked him? "You've known your mother and I all your life and that is the decision you come to. That I killed your mother?"

"Oh, that's different. I didn't' realize that it was actually both of you that I was discussing. I thought it could have been any couple."

"No," I said to him. "I told you specifically to take a look at your mother and me. So now you want to question the obvious because you now know it is us you are referring to. What was obvious before is now suddenly not so obvius."

"It's different now," Joseph suggested.

"How is it different."

"Well, you two love each other. You would never harm Mother."

"Based on what?" I pressed him.

"Well, I know you both," he insisted.

"So, you are suggesting that because you believe that you know us intimately, you are now suddenly willing to overlook the obvious murder and treat the crime scene differently. Is that what you are suggesting to me?" I know I was pressing him hard and embarrassing him a little in order to make him think properly about what he actually saw but this lesson was important.

"You wouldn't do it. I know you," Joseph protested.

"The people all know Akiva. They practically worship him. Is that enough to say that he didn't do it?"

"That's different," Joseph tried to explain but knew he was in a losing battle.

"How is that any different? Focus on the facts. Just because I am your father shouldn't be allowed to influence your judgment. You want to make assumptions or do you want to uncover the truth. The facts say I have a knife in my hand and I'm standing over the victim. Why is it not obvious?"

"It's not in your nature," Joseph argued. "If you are going to commit a crime, then there should be evidence from your history that shows that you are capable of committing murder. I would usually see a trend or a behaviour that proves you have the capability of doing such a thing."

"Better, much better," I commended him. "Not there yet, but keep going."

"So, I look for evidence of past behaviour that supports the obvious. Such as a history of violence or threatening actions to support my conclusion."

"And if you can't find any past behaviors to support your conclusion?"

"Then I have to find other supporting evidence between the time that I left in the morning until the time that I returned home that the crime could have been done in the heat of the moment."

"How will you do that?" I pushed him to elaborate.

"I find anyone that may have seen you both during the day. I must also examine the home to see if there are signs of anything else having been disturbed. There usually will be something else that preceded the crime that leads to the event taking place."

"What do you think about your earlier statement of the obvious being all that is required to prove the crime?" I asked Joseph.

"Perhaps it is not so simple," Joseph admitted. "Nothing is obvious until you gather all the facts to support such a claim."

"But, you certainly can make use of the obvious findings of what you saw in order to disprove the crime," I threw a fishhook into the scenario that I had presented.

"I'm not certain I completely understand what you are intimating," Joseph shook his head. "Are you suggesting there was no murder?"

"The knife," Azariah suddenly spoke up.

"What about the knife, Azariah," I encouraged him to continue.

"It was in your left hand."

"So what?" I commented.

"You are right handed. It is very unlikely you would have stabbed anyone with your left hand."

"Excellent," I praised him, at which point Joseph gave his brother a playful punch in the shoulder.

"So, now you need to hear my side of the story. As is the right of any defendant, no matter that you think their guilt is beyond any doubt and you believe the case to be 'obvious'. The scene you witnessed happened as follows. Consider this my alibi. Having returned home myself, I found my darling wife laying on the floor having been stabbed. I bent down and picked up the knife off the floor, which happened to be closest to my left hand and then stood up in shock, realizing there was nothing I could do to save her. I am so confused and stunned by the situation, I have no idea how long I was standing there until such time that you came home and found us in that position."

"Exactly what I was thinking all along," Azariah claimed, a huge grin on his face, only to receive another punch from his older brother.

"The lesson that I intended for you both to learn is that you can know in your heart, who may or may not have perpetrated a crime but that doesn't matter unless you can prove three things you will have trouble convincing others.   And by now you know exactly which three things I'm referring to."

"Motive, Opportunity and Benefit," Joseph and Azariah recited.

"So now I hope you understand my reaction to today.   Until I can clearly understand beyond a shadow of a doubt what it is that motivates Rabbi Akiva and how he used this opportunity of the war to benefit I will not condemn a man simply because I have a strong feeling. I don't expect either of you to base your decisions on merely a feeling either. It does not matter if you vote against me when you pass your judgment, as long as I know you came to your decision based solely on the facts and evidence as they were presented.   If I should fail in providing a clear understanding of the crime and proof that Akiva did as I say, then I expect that both of you will vote for his acquittal.   Do we have an agreement?"

"But Father, what if the evidence is not conclusive but is so voluminous that it certainly suggests it must have happened as suspected?"

"Then you have to ask yourself, 'how confident am I in the evidence I did hear?'   If I have eighty percent confidence in one piece of evidence but only thirty percent in another, then I cannot claim to have sufficient confidence in the evidence.   But if every piece of evidence I look at provides a confidence of seventy percent, then I think I can be confident in accepting it as proof of commission of the crime. As much as I would like to say that everything should be black and white, the truth is we live in a world that is always shaded in gray."

"But some things are black and white," Joseph was quick to raise a point.

"Are we going to argue this one over again," I laughed.

"I know Father that you always say peace is the best pathway to follow, but what choice did Rome leave us.   We had to declare war on the Empire.   Otherwise, we would have been eliminated as a people."

"You are young, Joseph and I know that even in my youth, I challenged my father in the same way when it came to the Kittos War against Trajan.   I couldn't understand how my father could so easily write to the communities that we had only one choice and must pursue the path of peace with Hadrian, even after his predecessor, Trajan had begun his pointless war of conquest against Parthia. When he offered up the two leaders of the revolt in Judea, I felt as if we betrayed all of our people and robbed them of the opportunity to be free. Even when my father attempted to explain that the lives of two people against the loss of tens of thousands, had the revolt continued, it was not enough to stifle my shame I bore for my father regarding this matter for the longest time. It wasn't until I looked at the evidence regarding the consequences of the revolt, recognizing that they were far more severe in those other regions where we rebelled, even though we claimed that we had won, that I realized he was right. In the cities of North Africa, the Jewish populations were expelled from those cities that they had essentially burnt to the ground. In Alexandria, every Jew was rounded up and sent into exile. In Cyprus, two hundred thousand Jews simply disappeared, and Cyprus declared itself free of Jews. That's when I understood that it was never about the actual war but about what happens when the war is over. Unless you can sustain perpetual war and have a population that exceeds your enemy's so many times over, you will never win. So instead, you must seek compromise, but compromise must be from a position of strength."

"In that case, what did you see as our position of strength from which we could negotiate, Father? Help me to understand. I had friends that fought and died for Bar Kochba while I sat comfortable in Jerusalem using our status as foreign dignitaries to keep us safe and out of harm's way. My friends are dead and here I sit knowing I did nothing to help them."

"I understand your pain son, far more than you can ever appreciate. I lost so many I cared for as well, friends, family, but as long as we are here, we represent Parthia and we were not permitted to engage in anything that Rome would consider Parthian interference. You understand that?"

"I understand it but it doesn't mean I like it. And it certainly doesn't make me feel any better we let so many die and we said nothing. You say there was a chance of compromise, so why didn't we do anything about it?"

"Who says we didn't try? Even though my role was limited, and my direct involvement forbidden, it doesn't mean I wasn't there to listen and provide comments where I thought it was advisable. There were even times I was allowed to attend some of the Council meetings. It was no longer the Sanhedrin since so many of the members had been already taken by the Romans or were in hiding and they could not meet the required number of seventy, but even this depleted Council, weak as it may have been, still retained a level of authority. Though they forbade my having a direct voice, Rabbi Tarphon remained a close friend and ally willing to convey my sentiments. I recall there was a meeting to which Simon Bar Kochba had been summoned. The war had raged for just over a year and when we looked around, we were amazed that all of Judea was suddenly free of the Roman presence and both Tarphon and myself agreed it would be the best time to approach the Romans to negotiate a treaty to end the war. Doing so from a position of strength that I was speaking of. Even so, the Council remained split between those seeking peace and those that I can only describe as fanatics or Zealots, thinking that it was somehow our mission to liberate the entire Middle East of the Roman yoke.

It was time for Rabbi Tarphon to address Bar Kochba directly and as he rose from his chair, he cleared his throat repeatedly in order to gain everyone's attention. "On behalf of all our people, we owe you a tremendous debt of gratitude Simon Bar Kochba, and it is clearly evident that God has blessed you and has shone His light upon you. You have rid the nation of Rome's presence and right now they shiver and quake in Alexandria, paralyzed with fear and unable to decide exactly what they should do next. We should not let this opportunity pass but should take advantage of their indecision. If they do not know what to do, then we should inform them what is their best option and in their own best interests. Now is the time for us to send representatives to Alexandria and offer them peace. But peace on our terms!"

Simon didn't have an opportunity to respond before Akiva was out of his chair and challenging Tarphon's opinion. "What kind of peace are you proposing," Akiva wanted to know, though it was clear he had already made up his mind on the matter and he didn't want to hear any more on any ensuing of peace. "We have fought and we have won. Which part of our victory are you so willing to sacrifice to your Roman masters? Look around you and witness God's miracle. We have regained Jerusalem. Now is the time we should be thinking about rebuilding our Temple. We should not be tucking our tails between our legs and begging the Romans for anything."

"We need peace with the Romans and their cooperation if we are ever going to rebuild the Temple.," Rabbi Tarphon replied. You cannot build if your young men are constantly fighting a war," Tarphon responded. "You think only of what you won, rather in terms of what Rome has lost! She has lost legions, she has lost this province, but most of all she has lost honour and prestige and that terrifies her most. If other nations catch wind of our success, then it will ignite the entire Empire on fire and Rome cannot and will not permit that to happen."

"You even admit she has lost, so why quit now," Simon spoke up. "Why not let the Empire be set on fire?"

"Because Rome is not a country, or a place, it is an idea. And men will not let their ideas die that easily. She is like the mythological creature called the hydra. We have cut off one head, but you will see, two will grow back to take its place. And if we cut off those two, then next we will face four, in a never-ending battle. Let's give her the opportunity to grow back that single head rather than escalate this further. Let us take a place at the table as part of her Empire, willing to compromise and be a strategic partner in the Middle East. Let us offer her friendship and assurance that we will fight for her security in this part of the world but do so as a free people under our own banner. Let us guarantee no further loss of life and honor on both sides and become masters of our own destiny. Be our king but rule as a wise king, that is all I ask of you. Remember the Hasmoneans. Remember our King, Simon the Just. No sooner had he defeated the Syrian Empire under Antiochus, he was suing their king for peace. And that peace lasted for over a hundred years until Rome arrived on our shores."

Before Rabbi Tarphon could even return to his seat, Akiva was already up again and speaking. "Shall we forget that we had many enemies in our past. There were the kingdoms of the Philistines, the Assyrians, the Babylonians, and the Greeks long before these Romans came. Peace was a hollow word with all of them. And where are they all now. Crumbled to dust and crushed beneath our feet as we tread upon the same sands of our land that they once walked on. And why is that? Because we let the Almighty do our negotiating. All those nations that rule by force, died by force. You all know that is God's plan for our enemies and he has never told us to negotiate with our enemies. He has always told us to believe in Him, have faith, and he will lead us to total victory. Let there be no doubt, the soul of Rome is dark and cruel and no piece of paper will ever guarantee us this peace you speak of Tarphon."

Rising to his feet once again, Rabbi Tarphon recognized that the real enemy to peace was not Bar Kochba but Akiva. "There is no denying that the two of you have achieved God's miracle," he began with praise. "No one could ever have imagined the success that has been achieved here when you first picked this man out from a row of thieves and robbers and said that God has anointed him as the messiah. Few believed you but you proved us wrong. You will always be known as the warrior and the Rabbi that conquered Rome but let us remember you more as the pair that brought us peace and put an end to needless death. Enough hardship. You cannot gain peace through continuous war."

"Nor can we gain peace through peace," Akiba replied. "When Rome first came to our shores, they came in peace. We welcomed them as brothers. And within ten years of their arrival, they were meddling and interfering in our politics. In twenty years, they were already deposing and appointing our kings. In sixty years, there were no Jewish kings and they were directly governing us. After seventy years were they not torturing us and treating us as nothing more than peasants and slaves within our own lands? Tell me that any of this is not true! Rome does not know what the word peace means. God has shown me that this man is our King. He is the Lord's chosen messiah. You either stand with him or you stand against God!"

Akiva's words sent the council into turmoil. To say that a continuation of the war was our only option, and to vote against such action would be an offense to God, effectively split the council in half. The shouting and screaming at each other went back and forth within the chambers for a long time, as I remember.

"There is a plan," Simon bar Kochba shouted loud enough in that booming voice of his to eventually silence the infighting. Mark my words, he was a very talented orator even though he had no formal training. Waiting until the perfect time when he managed to catch all their attention, he then repeated his words but this time more softly. "There is a plan. It is not as if we thought we could continue to take on the Romans forever on our own. I have sent a letter to the Parthian king asking him to send us troops as reinforcements in our war against the Romans. We will get the Nabateans and the Syrians to fight with us as well. Parthia will become our protectors and ensure that Rome no longer has a foothold in this area of the Levant."

I could not restrain myself any longer, as I began to clap my hands together to applaud such utter ignorance and stupidity."

"Who is it that dares to mock me!" Simon Bar Kochba was obviously insulted by my overt display of disrespect.

"One who is the servant of the King of Parthia," I answered succinctly, "And knows exactly what Parthia's presence in this land will mean."

"You have no right to speak here," Akiva challenged me. "You are our guest but that does not permit you to participate."

"Let him speak, let him speak," a chant was raised in the chambers and was not going to stop until Akiva agreed to let me speak. As stubborn as he was, he finally submitted to the demand.

"I think everyone knows me, but to those who may not, I am Elioneai ben Yosef, the true High Priest of Israel. I am here in your part of the world as a representative of King Vologaeses III, or maybe today it is Mithradates IV. It is hard to say because I was originally sent to Judea by King Osroes. Kingship in Parthia tends to be like a horse race, always changing position, and you never seem to know who will be king tomorrow in the Empire. That is the reality. So, if you were to ask me how significant is your letter to the King of Parthia, I would simply say to you, was it received by yesterday's, today's or tomorrow's king? It is worthless because even if one agrees to support you, the next may not. Nor, as some of us who are older and recall the lesson we learned some twenty years ago, the Parthian Empire is in no way prepared to fight a sustained and protracted war against the Roman Empire. We withdrew and withdrew until the Roman supply lines were so stretched that they could extend no further, and only then did we retaliate. Not to defeat Rome, but only to take back what was rightfully ours. Now you also seem somewhat confused as to the state of Jews in Parthia. Yes, we have our own court system, with a King and of course, a priest, represented by myself, but where is our kingdom, where is our seat of government, where is our temple? We have lived in Babylon for seven hundred years and yet we have none of those things. Why do you think that is? I will tell you. It is because they know that if we were to be given the physical realities of statehood, they would be at war with us at some point in time. Why? Because every kingdom wants its independence, and every king wants to be free. All your letter says, no matter which king receives it, is that you are willing to trade one master for the next. It is a clearly evident that whomever suggested it to you has no better grasp on world politics than you do. I agree with Rabbi Tarphon. Seize peace whenever and wherever you can and pursue it until it is no longer feasible. Then and only then does war become an option. As long as there is a chance of peace, then war should not even be considered."

Having said my piece, I made my way to the door and didn't bother to stay and see the outcome of their Council meeting. Clearly it did not go my way as the war continued for another couple of years with the eventual slaughter of our people. No sooner had the Roman forces returned to Judea, they began to immediately round up the voices of reason. That is the peculiar oddity of this court case. Those rabbis that had advocated peace and for that reason never even bothered to hide, like Rabbi Tarphon were some of the first they seized. Without even the merest hint of a trial, he was convicted and executed. That was the time I first became suspicious that there was more behind the sudden turn-around of Roman victories. There was something strange that I couldn't account for. Even after those first defeats at the hands of the Romans, there was still an opportunity to negotiate a treaty, but that window was closing rapidly with every subsequent victory by Julius Severus.

I suspected then that the Roman General was receiving information as to Bar Kochba's deployments and reports of unit strengths in each of the villages where he garrisoned his men. Severus never seemed to make a mistake, always picking off the units in order of the weakest to the strongest. No general in any war has that much luck or success. You would only be able to do that if you already knew what you would find in each town and could deploy the correct size and strength of force to overrun their defenses. Severus reduced the size of Bar Kochba's army at a steady pace until all that was left were the men of Beithar.

So, you asked me son, 'Why didn't I try?' I have to think and believe that I did try. I also think that so many like me tried as well. Should we have tried harder? I don't honestly know the answer to that question. Maybe, perhaps not. It still plagues me. I believe that the only reason I am still here is because the Romans refused to test the Parthians as to whether or not they would retaliate for the sake of one of their diplomats, because I am certain my name was on the same list as Rabbi Tarphon and all the rest of the rabbis that advocated peace and whom are no longer alive."

"I'm sorry Father," Joseph apologized. "I did not know."

"How could you know," I patted him on the shoulder. "These past four years only proved that if you knew too much it would be dangerous for you. To protect you, I was forced to keep many secrets. As long as you remained out of their political affairs you were safe. As your father, it was my responsibility to ensure that you both remained safe even if that meant keeping you unaware of all the events transpiring."

"Obviously you think Akiva was tied to Tarphon's execution," Joseph was still trying to pick my brain on the subject.

"That night I realized who was the puppet and who was the puppet master. Tomorrow, I hope to be able to prove that with my fourth witness."

No sooner had I mentioned the word 'witness' there was a knock on the door.

Deborah opened the door, and I could hear her greeting Jacob warmly.

"Come in Jacob, come in," I beckoned him. "Still plenty of soup in the pot if you would like some. It will take the chill off a night like tonight."

"I would appreciate that greatly Excellency. I had no opportunity to eat all day."

"Then sit and tell me what news you have. Did you get a reply?"

"Yes, Excellency."

"And… out with it."

"They said they would be here on yom shishi."

"That's cutting it to the bone. It's the final day of the trial," I was worried.

"It was the only time they could come Excellency.

"Then I leave it in God's hands. By His will there will be sufficient time. Now have some of this delicious soup before the fast starts at sunset. It's one of Deborah's best I might add and your favourite."

Chapter Fourteen

The Trial: Day Four, 13th of Adar 3986

Prior to the morning swearing in of both myself and Rabbi Akiva, Praetor Yehonatan said that he had an announcement to make to everyone that was present for the morning session. The timing seemed fortuitous because there was a much larger crowd than had been there the previous day. I'm guessing word of our feisty encounters from yesterday had attracted those more gossip inclined for today's events.

"I remind everyone that today's tribunal will be ending early in the afternoon so that you can all be at home tonight in plenty of time to break the fast, Now, some of you have asked me to say a few words on the meaning of the Fast of Esther, considering we have just come through this terrible war. It is my understanding that you want to know how we can tie the experiences of that past event to what we have just endured and experienced. Therefore, let me begin by saying that we are fasting today because we wish to share in the horrible predicament in which Queen Esther found herself during those dark days of Haman. And in some ways, it might be more meaningful this year. I mean this sincerely. Let me explain:

Married to a man that was the most powerful man in the world at that time, King Artaxerxes, Ester had never told her husband that she was Jewish. In all likelihood, even if she did tell him, he probably had no idea what being a Jewess even meant. It was not that he was a stupid man, but because it was a belief system or faith that anyone in power had no need to understand. And it most certainly was because the King had no knowledge of Judaism, not even knowing who was a Jew, or perhaps even what was a Jew, that he had just signed the request by his vizier to have his soldiers attack the Jewish areas of the city, permitting them to rape, rob, pillage, and kill any that may resist because he was told these people would not recognize his sovereignty. Even though the Jews in Persia were some of his most loyal citizens, he was told that they all scoffed at their king, and swore that one day they would be free of him because their God would redeem them.

As you can see, the situation was not that different from where we were six years ago. We had a king that called himself Emperor, that knew of Jews but did not know Judaism. He had advisors that told him exactly the same things that were said to Artaxerxes. That the Jews scorn him and swear their God will destroy him and free his people from the yoke of Roman oppression.

We are told that Esther had no idea as to what she should do. As a wife in his harem, she could only come before her husband at his request but if she didn't violate that rule, then everyone she held dear would likely be killed. But if she did break this law, then she would likely be killed immediately, and her death would have done nothing to stop the senseless slaughter of her people. So, she fasted and prayed for God's help to see her through this terrible dilemma, because no matter which perspective she looked at her problem from, she could only envision disaster ensuing. She had no hope, she had no power but because she turned to God. she heard His voice saying to her that He would protect her when she entered into the King's chambers without being summoned. The rest of the story we all know. The King didn't kill her for violating the rules. She did soften the King's heart and although he could not rescind his command, he ordered the armories opened in all the towns, so that the Jews living in those towns could defend themselves. We survived not because we took up the sword that day but because of a single woman's willingness to confess the truth and tell her husband her secret. But understand this very important fact that we all seem to overlook. For all those years that she had resided in the palace and served the King, she had concealed her true identity, so that he would never know that she was a Jewess. Greater than her fear of God, was her fear that the King would find out that she was different. To do so it meant she had to abandon her faith, avoid practicing any trace of her religion that would reveal the truth and it was only when the guilt of her surviving while everyone else that she knew and loved, such as her uncle, would be put to death, that she finally revealed the truth about herself. But she was very clever in how she revealed the secret she had been hiding all that time. She did not enter the throne room and blurt out 'I am a Jew.' Instead, she said, let me prepare a banquet for you and your Vizier Haman. For two nights she did this and when the King finally said, what gift can I give to you in gratitude, she asked for her own life. A strange request because he knew of no one that threatened her. But only when he said he would let no harm befall her, did she reveal the truth and explain that she was a Jew and therefore her life was in danger because, Haman intended to kill her. How the story ended, you all know very well..

I know you are all thinking, how do we connect what I have just told you to the situation we face today. There is a King that knows us not and the name of that king is Rome. And Rome has a Queen Esther, and that queen is named Judea, one of the many wives that resides in Rome's harem of nations; a harem so large and magnificent that it is filled with many beautiful queens stretching from Iberia to Armenia, from Carthage to Gaul. Compared to the greatness of some of these other wives, Judea is nothing more than a minor concubine. And if we are honest, probably not even as beautiful as some of the other queens that reside in the harem. This is the truth, but this queen Judea, she has some relatives and they are upset that this queen from their family, this jewel of their household is not the favourite of King Rome. And there are those that whisper into King Rome's ears that there is a family that refuse to respect you and say that one day their God will depose you and punish you by taking away your many wives because they have heard that they are upset that their Queen is not the King's favourite.

But here is where our story differs. Unlike Queen Esther, our Queen Judea did not go to her King and prepare a banquet for him so that he would be pleased and offer to grant her any wish that she desired. No, she would not debase herself to come as a beggar before her King. She made no effort to even explain the dire consequences of his actions if he attacked her family. She did not appeal to his heart and convince him to rescind his orders. Instead, she broke down the doors to the armories herself and she inflicted wounds upon her husband but no matter how hard she fought she could not kill him. Once he recovered from his wounds, he beat his wife soundly and he divorced her, casting her into the wilderness to die, thereby ensuring that she will never be a thorn in his side again."

"We had no choice," some of the people in the gallery groaned. "What else could we have done? If we did not fight, we would have been destroyed," the people in the gallery protested.

"Did you not just hear me tell you the story of Esther. Did you not listen to the part where she appealed to his heart after lavishing him with a feast. In order to get the desired end that she wanted, she outsmarted her enemies; she didn't outfight them. That is the true message. She found an alternative way in which to seize victory from what most certainly appeared to be defeat."

"There was no appeasing Rome," someone in the crowd shouted, met with the mumbled agreement of many in the crowd. "Hadrian was determined to end our way of life."

"Where is your proof of that? King Rome said you shall not build a temple to your God on the holy mount in Jerusalem! So, I ask you to look around you and ask yourself, 'Where am I standing today?' If this not be the spot where you regularly pray to God, then what is it? If God does not hear your prayer while you are gathered to assembly in this humble village synagogue, then why do you even bother to come here each Sabbath to pray? But if you were to say to me by means of challenge, 'Where is the sacrifice that must be performed by the priests as commanded in the Torah?' then I remind you that the Temple was nothing more than a pile of bricks and ashlars that the Romans leveled to the ground over sixty years ago and we have not made the priestly sacrifice since. Has God condemned us for our failure to sacrifice in all that time? The answer is no! He waits for us, but he does not condemn us. Show me in the Torah where God said you must construct for me a Temple? It isn't in the Torah; it is only in the Tanach that King David starts talking about building the Temple and insists that it must be associated with Mount Moriah. All that God ever instructed us to build was the Tabernacle. He never demanded from us a home built with stone and mortar. A Tabernacle that goes wherever we go. A Tabernacle that can never be destroyed by our enemies because it has no fixed place. We could have had our Tabernacle and our sacrifices for the past sixty years but instead we became obsessed with bricks and mortar."

"He wants to stop circumcision," another screamed out.

"And now you wish to cry out that the King Rome forbade us from the act of circumcision. There will always be an outcry against oppression. But is that what you truly believe? How do you think Rome intends to do that? Do you think they will have their soldiers going from house to house to check beneath your child's diapers, looking for a trail of severed foreskins that hang from our doorposts? I would think that even if the Emperor did have his men perform such checks we would be clever enough like Esther to find a way to evade such detection. Do you forget the story of Moses? Many times in the past our enemies have come looking for our offspring and every time we managed to survive despite their efforts to harm us. Why did you presume that this time would be different?

213

I know that there are still those among you, even after all we have lost that will continue to say that King Rome left us with no other choice but to take up arms. Yet, all I see are options that we never even tried to exercise. All I have witnessed was us dying in the hundreds of thousands because we tried not to be like Esther and find a way of appealing to the King's heart. We chose a path that had no other way of ending but in misery and death. God does not tell us to pick up a sword as soon as someone offends us. God does not tell us to sacrifice our lives if we can avoid it.

But now is not the time for me to chastise and criticize the decisions that were made by so many of us. We have all suffered terribly and I know that we all seek the answers as to why this happened. But to receive the answers, you must identify and recognize the proper questions that must be asked. That is what I hope we can find by the end of this trial and why I wanted to speak to all of you that have attended these past few days. We all may have different questions and therefore we may all be seeking different answers to explain our predicaments. Right or wrong, we have reached this terrible point in our lives because we felt there was no alternative but to take up arms and fight a war that perhaps we could not win. I have only one question that I have prayed would be answered by the time this trial concludes and that is whether or not we had our Esther and if only we had recognized her, could we have avoided all this death and misery. I need to know whether or not all the friends and relatives I have lost would still be alive, if only we had opened our eyes in time and saw that God offered us an alternative to war. I personally need to know if there was another way and we failed to see it..

I have no more to say. That is my discourse as to why this Fast of Ester should be considered very special and why we should pay special attention when we say our prayers to break the fast tonight. Tomorrow we are expected to celebrate our salvation from the Persians. But there is no joy in my heart with which I can rejoice. Purim this year will be a time of reflection for me and not a time of dance and celebration. I only hope that God will lift the veil of darkness that lies heavily on my heart and grants my wish that on the following day, when we return to this courtyard, I will have the answers I seek."

I must admit that I was impressed by him. The old Levite definitely surprised me with his skill to weave a sermon. Yes, I had liked him from the moment we met but I had no idea that he was capable of such oratory. He had passion and a gift to create a meaningful story from another well known tale. "I hope you don't mind Yehonatan but I would appreciate if you would let me use your sermon when I finally return to my home in Mesopotamia. You said it beautifully. I don't think anyone could have drawn both the comparison and the contrast between our present situation and what transpired hundreds of years ago any better."

"I would be honored if you were to quote me, Excellency." This time I was more than willing to have him refer to me by my title. With the trial already entering into its fourth day I needed the people to recognize there was a sharp contrast between myself and Akiva.

"If everyone assumes their proper positions we will begin today's session," Yehonatan instructed us. "I wish to remind everyone we will close our tribunal early today and we will not be summoned back into session until yom shishi. To both the prosecution and the defense, I remind you that will be the final day for the tribunal, so please prepare your presentations and witnesses accordingly. There will be no extensions granted. Let us begin," Yehonatan commanded. "I have a request from the Defendant that he be allowed to present his witness first. Do I have any objection from the prosecution?"

The ploy by Akiva was obvious. To deny the request might look petty. I knew exactly what he intended. As with his previous witness, he intended to drone on and on, consuming precious hours of the day, leaving me with little time to present my own witness because of today's early closure of the tribunal. Nevertheless, I decided to let him have his way. His ploy could just as easily fail because I knew there was only so much this witness would be able to say about Akiva's great and outstanding character before the comments actually began to sound rehearsed and redundant, thus rendering them meaningless. Then he would lose any interest and support from the judges he may have garnered. "I have no objection Praetor."

"The Defendant may call his witness," Yehonatan instructed.

"I request that the most honorable Rabbi Elisha ben Abuyah come forward and take the witness seat,"

Emerging from the first couple of rows of the crowd, an extremely frail, withered, and skeletal old man was helped through the dividing ropes and slowly hobbled his way very slowly towards the empty chair that waited for him. His forward progression was dependent upon the twin canes that he leaned heavily upon. At the rate he was moving, I became worried that the time which had been allotted by Yehonatan to the morning session might be fully consumed by what could only be described as this painful effort to reach the witness chair. His long gray beard extended almost to his waist, and the hooded black cloak he wore made him look more like the angel of death than resemble a living human. Some of the people in the crowd were shocked and horrified by his appearance, backing away from his presence, as if any accidental contact with his body or even with his dark woolen robes would immediately render them unclean.   It practically took forever for Elisha ben Abuya h to finally reach the witness stand, which I assumed was already known by Akiva.

Once seated, the questioning of the witness began. "We have known each other a long time, my friend, haven't we," Akiva asked, more as a statement of fact than an actual question.

Ben Abuyah's voice was frail, faltering, intensely fragile, making it all the more frustrating trying to hear and decipher his responses. As much as it was proving extremely difficult for me to hear, even though I was sitting but a few yards from his position, one can only imagine the thinking of everyone else. It would have been nearly impossible for anyone in the gallery to hear him at all.   But I actually felt that this could be used to my advantage.   As the people became bored, they would soon become restless. And once agitated and irritated, that emotion would carry easily through the air, affecting everyone to become restless and angry. That anger would be transferred into sentiments towards Ben Abuyah and Akiva. It wouldn't matter what Abuyah was saying, because it would be received as being purely.   Best to let this play out and see what would happen.

It was about an hour and a half that Akiva and Ben Abuyah droned on continuously, revealing their shared history from the time they both met, when Elisha ben Abuyah was still a fervent believer in God, only to wake up one day and question everything he had been taught regarding Our Lord.   A day that left him feeling on his own admission, far more liberated than he had ever been as soon as the restrictions upon his life had been lifted.   It was not that he suddenly violated every commandment that constituted our laws, but instead he began to make what he considered to be rational decisions based on his own perspective and moral convictions. He claimed he was in control to decide which laws were applicable and which were not in order to live life as a law-abiding human being and not just blindly follow what others had dictated.

At that moment I saw a golden opportunity to take advantage of what had been said. "So, you deny the existence of our God," I shouted so everyone would know what had been said.

"Praetor!," Akiva responded. "Remind the Prosecution that this is my witness and my time to question him. Not his. Tell him to be silent or else remove him."

Turning to me, Yehonatan admonished me with a simple warning and a wink of the eye. He could appreciate exactly what I had done. "Elioneai ben Yosef, you will not interfere with the Defendant's witness and will wait for you turn to cross examine.

And what I had done was draw everyone's attention back to the witness. Now that they were suddenly aware that he was a devout atheist, even though they could not hear his prior testimony, the were determined to listen to what he would say next.

Ben Abuyah felt compelled to defend himself against my accusation of atheism. Akiva had momentarily lost control of his witness and Ben Abuyah rambled on, making reference to his being a humanist, believing in the good of man and that if we all made a conscious decision to be better than we are, then we had no need for a god that actually served to divide us from our fellow human beings.

Those in the crowd definitely heard him this time. Akiva's close friend obviously blamed God for all the disasters that befell us. If he viewed God as evil, then what did that say about Akiva. Where most of my people saw unity through God, he saw division. Where we were taught that man essentially elevated himself by walking in God's footsteps, he saw nothing but mankind's continual failure to achieve an impossible goal. The only matter that Akiva managed to settle in the minds of everyone in attendance, from all of his monotonous questioning throughout the morning, was the undeniable fact that if Elisha ben Abuyah was his closest friend then they must have shared some beliefs in common.

Finally, it was my turn. It was certainly not my intention to proceed with a soft touch with Ben Abuyah no matter how delicate and frail he might be. As far as I was concerned, he represented everything reprehensible within our society and was an abomination that needed to be completely excised from our community. The reality that long ago, almost forty years now, the Rabbinical Council could not bring themselves to do that when he first became a heretic was just an indication to me of how weak and ineffective they had become.

"Elisha ben Abuyah, you are the one they call the Aher. Is that correct?"

"Yes," his voice croaked.

"And they call you the Aher or 'The Other' because…"

"Because I don't believe in God," his voice faded to the point that it was inaudible but I was not about to let that comment be ignored. He had already said as much when discussing his beliefs with Akiva but I didn't want the people to ever to forgive or forget his words begin spoken in defense of Akiva. This time I made certain that everyone would hear every word he uttered by repeating his answers loudly so they would be heard all the way to the farthest peristyle.

"What kind of man, would let others continue to refer to him as a Rabbi, when you don't even believe in the God of our ancestors. A rabbi is a teacher of God's message, and you no longer have any intention to do so. Even a pagan is preferable to you because you actually believe in nothing but yourself!"

"I believe in man as the centre of the universe," Abuyah answered meekly in his defense.

"Well mankind certainly hasn't achieved much in making this world a better place if that's all you believe in," I ridiculed his response. "How is it that you are still a member of the Rabbinical Council? Better yet, how were you even a member of the Sanhedrin? Help everyone here understand this. If you do not believe in the Lord, our God, Creator of the Universe, then you certainly don't believe in the God given commandments. Hence, you obviously don't believe that God gave us His laws through Moses. You don't believe in any of the miracles God employed to keep his Chosen People alive through the centuries. In fact, you don't even believe we are His Chosen People because as far as you are concerned, He doesn't even exist!"

"Praetor," Akiva objected strenuously. "The prosecution is out of order. He isn't even permitting or providing the witness the opportunity to answer any of his questions. In fact, he's answering them all for him!"

"Ben Abuyah, if you should disagree with any of the statements I made thus far then shake your head because I don't really care about your reasons for believing the way you do and I'm certain no one else here actually wants to hear your justification. The rest of us are committed in our ways but what confounds us is how you were permitted to be in a position of control over us without sharing our beliefs. Other than perhaps your loyal friend the Defendant, whom I question his Jewishness as well, now that I'm aware you are to be considered his dear and closest friend, it would seem to us that your presence as a leader of our community would be not only an insult to the people of Judea but more so, an affront to God. That perhaps we have been punished because of you and those that kept you in a position of authority, mocking God by doing so. Our Lord does not tolerate being betrayed and it is clear to me from the questions Akiva asked you that he obviously shares many of your beliefs in common. So, I ask again, how is it that you remained on the Council? Who was it that supported you in this regard and why?"

"Rabbi Akiva ensured that I remained on the Council," the Aher answered.

"You are telling me the voice of one man was enough to convince the Council of our Sages and greatest religious authorities, on such a matter that I'm certain many good people were opposed to, to keep you in a position of authority where you certainly did not belong! You seriously want me to believe that!" The grumbling from the crowd intensified to a point I was concerned it would drown out the rest of the testimony.

"There were others that wished I remain, thinking that they could convince me to believe again."

"But you knew that was not going to happen. They probably doubted it as well. Yet, you remained. Not only was it was hypocritical on your part to let them believe your conversion back to God was possible but in fact it was hypocritical for you to have any role on a religious council when you no longer had a religious bone remaining in your body!"

"Akiva can be very convincing when he needs to be," Ben Abuyah laughed.

"That is what frightens me. If he can convince the Sanhedrin and Council to keep a heretic as a member, what else is he capable of?"

"Praetor, I object to the prosecution suggesting that I am guilty of unspecified crimes. He is asking the witness to speculate on the unknown. This is like a man fishing in a rain puddle where there are no fish. He can't simply make up crimes where there are none." Akiva knew his witness's testimony was dangerous.

"Will the prosecution please refrain from leading the witness," Yehonatan warned me halfheartedly.

"Apologies Praetor. I'll rephrase the question. Elisha, why did the Council agree with Akiva's insistence that you remain a member of the Council? What could you possibly offer that he considered it imperative that you remain?"

"I am an expert in interpreting the law," he managed to say defiantly and loud enough that most could hear him.

"But our laws come from God, do they not?"

"No. Our laws were created by men. They are the laws by men, for men and to be enforced by men." It was clear that Ben Abuyah was not going to back down from his position of thinking it was his own importance that kept him on the Council.

"So if I understand correctly, you don't believe our laws came from God, in fact, you don't believe in God at all, but Akiva believed you should remain on the Council because he felt your views were important, which would suggest he might have shared your beliefs in some respects."

"I do not now," Ben Abuyah tried to excuse himself from answering directly.

"You must know," I argued. "He says you were close friends. Friends that shared their closest thoughts. You don't believe in God. You believe men created our laws and not God. And Akiva obviously believes in you. If he believes in you then he must believe partly in what you say. Yes or no?"

"I guess he must believe some of what I profess."

"As in man makes the laws, not God, perhaps?"

"It is possible," Abuyah nodded.

"And man is fallible, prone to error and guilty of sin," I stated. "Is that not correct?"

"Mankind strives to become better," he replied.

"That is not the question I asked. Yes or no! Man is fallible, prone to error and guilty of sin."

"Yes," his voice trailed off into silence once again.

"So by your statement, are you suggesting that all the laws that the Sanhedrin used to make when it assembled, as well as all of their final judgments, as well as all the rules and interpretations the Council of this land debated and argued over endlessly for days, months, even years, were for naught because they were or are inherently fallible since they never came from God."

"That was the very reason we engaged in debate," he attempted to explain, "In order to improve them since we know they may have been born in error."

"I understand this now!" I announced as if it was a huge revelation. "Akiva insisted that you remain on the Council and provide your expert opinion because he believes like you, God, whether he exists or not, made numerous errors in our laws and Akiva's purpose in life is to correct God!"

"Akiva cannot correct God because there is no God," Elisha ben Abuyah attempted to correct my statement.

"But essentially, that is what both you and Akiva have always been committed to doing. To correct the inherent errors of our laws, whether you think they came from God or not. Because as far as you and Akiva are concerned, your words are the equivalent of God's, since He does not exist. Is that not so?"

"Yes," Abuyah agreed.

"Can I have you repeat that," I rubbed my hands together. "Both you and Akiva believe that is it your task to rewrite our laws as they are written in the Torah because they are either incomplete or wrong because Akiva does not believe they came from God! Yes or no?"

"That is correct," he repeated.

"Hence, any laws that derive from Akiva's lips are the equivalent of those from God. As far as you and he are concerned, you are the equal of God in matters of ordaining law!"

One could feel the sheer power and force of the shock wave as it coursed through the courtyard, practically bowling over everyone there, as their jaws dropped, as they shook their heads in dismay. Why in the world Akiva would have ever called upon the Aher, a man despised by many, as one of his witnesses was beyond their reasoning. The man had just pronounced th at Akiva considered himself to be a god, a blasphemy punishable by death.

"Without going into why you don't believe, the fact is you are an atheist and therefore you consider all of us who do believe in God to be wrong. So, help me to understand something that has always confused me. You don't believe in our God, but you still refer to yourself as being a Jew. Is that also correct?"

"Yes," the Aher replied.

"By your standards, being a Jew has nothing to do with believing in the God of Israel."

"Being a Jew is purely geographical" he answered. "It is nothing more than a statement regarding where the generations of your family resided."

"On that basis, even though I believe in the God of our ancestors, you don't consider me to be a Jew. Is that correct?"

"Yes," he nodded his head.

"What am I then."

"You are a Babylonian Hebrew."

"And by this definition you adhere to, if there should happen to be a man from Ashkelon but he is from the Greek community that lives there, you would say he is a Jew. True?"

"Yes, that is correct," Ben Abuyah responded. "Because his family has been countless generations living in Judea, so he would be by nationality a Jew."

"So, in your mind he is exactly the same as you."

"Not exactly the same because obviously we look different but essentially yes. We are both Jews because our families originated from the same geographical regions in Judea,"

"Therefore, according to your definitions, when the Romans refer to us, meaning those that believe like me in the God of Israel, the God of my forefathers, no matter where we may live in this vast world as Jews, then they are wrong in doing so." Trying to unravel Ben Abuyah's mind was like trying to undo the fringes on my prayer shawl.

"Technically, they are wrong," he agreed. "But as a term of convenience, it is easiest for them to do so."

"Are the Idumeans or the Samaritans Jews?" I was curious.

"They are Idumean and Samaritan Hebrews," came the reply.

"What about the Mineans," I asked. "Are they Hebrews too?"

"Yes. Essentially, they share the same faith except they have also accepted Yeshua to be a prophet."

"Let me see if I understand this correctly. Therefore, you are saying, if a Minean lives in Judea, then he is identical to any other Jewish Hebrew as far as you are concerned."

"That is correct."

"That being the case, then if I happened to meet a Nazorean, who's family lived in our land of Judea for centuries and believed exactly as does the Minean, then he too is a Jewish Hebrew. Tell me if I am right n this thinking."

"That too would be correct," he said matter-of-factly and loud enough for everyone to hear. His response released a howl of curses from the gallery and angry shouts from those that had no tolerance for the Nazoreans that were becoming a plague within the Empire.

It was one thing to accept the Mineans as nothing more than Jews with a slightly misguided messianic view regarding Yeshua, but these Nazoreans, as they referred to themselves, they were an entirely different matter altogether. Essentially, they were nothing more than traditional followers of pagan beliefs attempting to merge Jewish traditions within their Roman heathen pageantry of heathen gods. I could sense the crowd was close once again to the point of becoming violent if I pushed this line of questioning too far. I could not afford to have the courtroom turn into a melee.

I signaled for everyone to calm down before I proceeded with any further questioning. I wanted them all to understand and hear where I was heading with this line of questioning.

"Is Akiva a Jew?" I asked.

"No," he replied without hesitation, "His family comes from outside Judea, but if he shares your faith then he is a Hebrew."

"An interesting choice of words" I immediately seized on what Abuyah had said. "You said 'if he shares my faith'. 'If' is a very subjective word. Does that mean you have your doubts?"

"It only means that Akiva must speak for himself. I cannot judge what thoughts exist in his mind."

"But you are his closest friend. If anyone would know his mind, it would be you. Yet, I think you question as well why he fought so hard to keep you on as a member of the Sanhedrin and the Rabbinic Council. I think you have your own reasons to believe that his beliefs may be more like yours than they are to mine."

"Praetor, once again I object to the Prosecutor putting words in the mouth of this witness," Akiva shouted in protest.

"And I object to what is now a known fact that the Defendant used this man, this atheist, this heretic, this non-believer, and admitted non-Hebrew, who denies our God, the God of all of us, to poison the Council all these years. The snake has definitely brought his poisoned words into the Garden of Eden. He has used the witness as a tool to spread lies and create dissent to all of our most sacred beliefs and traditions. To negatively affect the preservation and adherence to the laws as given to us by God in His Torah. If this pathetic excuse for a Jew can be the closest friend and ally of the Defendant, then there is no doubt in my mind that Akiva ben Joseph has been working against our people and attempting to destroy our faith in the Torah since the day he first came to study under Joshua ben Hananiah. How is it that we as a people of faith, a people of God and a people of the Law permitted this Ger and this Aher to rise to such powerful positions where they could so easily lead us into sin? I have one remaining question for the witness? Elisha ben Abuyah, what is your purpose?"

"I am not certain what you mean," he responded, his voice now as frail as it had been initially and barely audible.

"We all have a reason to exist, whether we recognize it or not," I explained to him. "For some of us, though you probably don't believe it, God gives us a purpose to exist. Others want to help people by providing health care and they see that as their purpose. Some wish to be powerful and lord over other people. That they see as their purpose. We all have a reason we believe we have been put on this earth. As such, I ask again, what do you see as your purpose?"

"If I had to speculate, then I would say to make people question in what they believe and realize we must guide ourselves to improve and not rely on a non-existent supernatural being in order to do so."

"In other words, you see your sole purpose, firstly, to convince us believers that we are inherently wrong in choosing to follow God, and secondly, to lead us astray by developing a set of laws based on the Torah but different in that you would consider them superior as a result of some misguided belief that you consider yourself capable by some means of improving on God's handiwork because as far as you are concerned, your words are equal to those of God. Is that not so?"

"Except they were never God's handiwork in the first place because there is no God," he corrected me.

"Assuming that was true, which I doubt anyone else here agrees with you, nevertheless, your good friend, Akiva ben Joseph, knowing this was your stated purpose in life, not only insisted but ensured that you would be kept in your position of authority and influence over us, where you could work towards achieving these heretical goals. You must have some thoughts on why Akiva would have agreed to this. You must have talked about this at length some time ago. You and he were the closest of friends. You can't honestly expect me to believe that he would have done so simply as a friend with no consideration of the harm he could be doing if this disease you suffer from was to spread through our people. And I call your thinking a disease because that is exactly what it is. A dangerous infection that requires you to be isolated and treated, not exposed to the public as Akiva has done."

Elisha ben Abuyah attempted to respond but a sudden unexpected wave of coughing prevented him from doing so. He grasped the left side of his chest and I was worried he would fall from the chair.

"As I said, most definitely a disease and I think we have heard enough about the Defendants true intentions and nefarious deeds from this witness. It is clear that Akiva shared this witness's intentions to undermine our beliefs and separate us from the love of God. The witness is dismissed."

I wanted to have Ben Abuyah removed from the court as quickly as possible. If he was to suddenly fall over and lose consciousness, it would destroy the advantage I had gained from his testimony, since the natural empathy of the crowd would make them feel guilty for despising a man that might die before their eyes. Fortunately, although Abuyah struggled to get on to his feet with the use of his canes, he still had the strength to move under his own strength. The crowd parted as he began hobbling towards them, their closely packed bodies splitting like the Red Sea. I began to think that after all his testimony, as much as they probably despised him now, rather than approach him to express their anger, they dared not move close, fearing the man and his beliefs as much as any other disease..

Yehonatan could sense that Ben Abuyah was becoming weaker with every step and also feared he would succumb within the sanctuary. "If I could have the Prosecutor's guards kindly escort the witness from the courtyard,"

My captain took up the task and ensured that he and his men carried Elisha ben Abuyah under his arms, through the back doors and directly to Akiva's house where he had been lodging. Once he had left the building, Yehonatan called for a recess before the court would return to hear from my next witness.

Chapter Fifteen

The Trial: Day Four Noon

Following the brief recess, while they managed to remove Elisha ben Abuyah, everyone returned to their positions. The tinge of anger that had been raised in the room by my questioning of the Aher, still had not fully dissipated during the respite. An attack on God, Akiva should have known would never have been taken well. I still could not fathom why he ever decided to summon Elisha ben Abuyah as one of his witnesses, when all he did was bring into question his own faith. Surely, he must have known how volatile any witness that was antithetic to our beliefs would have been met with resistance. Or am I missing the obvious that Akiva actually believed he had the God given authority to rewrite the sacred laws that had been given by God to Moses as he saw fit and that we would all acquiesce to his self-appointment as God's spokesperson. It couldn't possibly be that simplistic. Impossible. There is no way Akiva would be that big a fool, believing in his own greatness. Or could he? No, too simple. I had to be missing something important but as much as I racked my brains, I could not think what it could possibly be. If he had expected a favourable reaction from the mob in the gallery then he certainly miscalculated in that regard. But Akiva is a man that carefully calculates every outcome. That much, I know about the man. The fact that those present were still agitated made me wonder if that was his goal all along. Was he trying to provoke a riot and thereby have the trial postponed or dismissed. Did that mean he already knew he was in a no-win situation. If that was his intent, then what might be the gallery's reaction by the time I conclude with the questioning of my next witness. It might cause an all-out riot and I've just played into Akiva's hands to have the case dismissed.

Rising from his chair, Praetor Yehonatan announced that he had received a message from the Defendant that he would like to request a further witness prior to the handing over the floor to the prosecution. As this was most unusual, he asked both Akiva and I to step towards his table for a brief discussion.

"Elioneai, I need you to set aside your mistrust of Akiva and be patient. Bear with me and understand the nature of this request because it is outside your agenda but to deny the request might have some pronounce you as petty. I know that you can appreciate that according to the law, exactly as it was written, you both were given the opportunity to summon five witnesses each, and you both have made it clear that you would be exercising your privilege to have all five appear, But Akiva admittedly has not been granted the same opportunity as you to do so. He has been under house arrest all this time and therefore access for the purpose of contact and obtaining his witnesses has been limited, even if I did send messengers out on his behest. He managed to just hear from his son, Hunania, this very moment. The boy is here now and would like to simply say a few words on behalf of his father. I know it means forfeiting a bit more of your time, but can you imagine if word got out that you denied a man's own son to speak in his defense. To deny the request would appear heartless. I think you would agree that this would only be fair, considering the circumstances. So, I plead with you, would you willingly extend some leniency and grant Akiva this wish. I know you think he is a monster, but let the court decide that after witnessing both sides to the man."

Looking deep into Akiva's eyes, there was something there I had not seen before. I saw for the very first time since this trial began an element of fear. Perhaps the testimony of Elisha ben Abuyah had not gone the way Akiva anticipated. For all the bravado and strutting confidence he had effused at the beginning of the trial, the cross examination of Ben Abuyah had managed to strip away that mask and expose a man standing on the edge. Whatever he thought he would gain from the testimony of the Aher, it had apparently gone very wrong. Now I found myself suddenly looking into the eyes of a sheep that had been led into the abattoir and I could not refuse his request.

Yehonatan made the announcement for Hunania ben Akiva to step forward and take the witness chair. His son, like his father, was a handsome man, somewhere in his forties. The Greek features of his father were not lost in the passing of this one generation. The same light-coloured eyes and Mediterranean nose made it very evident whose son he was. He sat down in the chair and unrolled a parchment that he obviously had been carrying with him. The fact that he carried some prepared document, of which contents had not been reviewed in advance by the Praetor, made me wonder if I had just been tricked. "My name is Hunania ben Akiva," he identified himself.

Most of you know me as the second eldest son of my father and my mother Rachel bat Kalba Savuah. My family has always been well known to you. Many of you have even worked for my grandfather, just as my father did. I have been asked by my father to read the speech he gave at my oldest brother's funeral. All three of us younger brothers, Huma, Asa and myself looked up to Simon and his loss was a terrible blow to all of us. His funeral was attended by hundreds and my father's speech at that time we believed summed up the character of my father and the man that he was and is now. I would like to read it to you now:

> *Brethren of the House of Israel, listen to me. Not because I am a*
> *scholar have you appeared here so numerously, for there are those more learned*
> *than I, nor because I am wealthy, for there are those more wealthy than I. The*
> *people of the South honour Akiva but where do the people of Galilee come to*
> *know me. The men are acquainted but how is it the women and children*
> *come to me. Still, I know that your names shall be great for*
> *you have taken the trouble to do honour to the Torah in fulfilling a*
> *religious activity.*

"From this speech by which he thanked all of you that attended my brother's funeral, I know you will see that my father loved all the people of Israel dearly and the Torah was uppermost in his thoughts and prayers at all times. Whatever else may be said about Akiva ben Joseph, his devotion to his own children and to the Children of Israel is beyond questioning. Doing honour to the Torah was his passion and devotion. But my father would remind us that God gave us His precious gifts of his blessings and the Law not to be passed around lightly but for us to discuss as to how we could use them to be better than we already were. They were merely the tools provided to help the garden grow, not the endpoint but instead the beginning of our journey of faith. He would tell us the story of how he was sitting with the Procurator Tinnius Rufus and the governor asked, *'If the God of the Jews was so perfect in all that he created, then why didn't he create you Jews already born circumcised?'* My father replied, *'God did not create perfection but instead expected man to achieve perfection from the basic structure of all that God provided. Is it that hard to see man as a work in progress? Neither the horse or the donkey was suitable as a cooperative beast of burden, but man discovered he could take God's creations and from them achieve the mule, which was ideally suited for the tasks. God gave us rocks but a man with a hammer and chisel could reveal the marble statue hidden inside. It is man's duty to take that which God has given to us and unleash its inner beauty and strengths.'* That day the Governor of Judea was taught an important lesson about what it meant to be a Jew. A lesson that he resented and as a result made him jealous of us as a people. That jealousy fueled his rage and predisposed the Procurator towards war with us. My father didn't ask for war with Rome, he didn't instigate for the war against Hadrian, but he was one of the first to recognize that the call to war would be inevitable because he would never submit and diminish God's glory or greatness in the face of his enemies.

Even when it came to what was written in the Torah, he would never conceal nor hide the contents of our sacred book merely to appease an evil dictator. No, he would shout it at the top of his lungs for he would glorify our God above all others, no matter what the price he might have to pay for doing so. For the Torah, he believes is a light unto the world and that light must shine from one corner of the Earth to the other, shattering the darkness of evil. But even the Torah is like that block of marble, waiting for the sculptor to unleash its hidden beauty. It is a rare gift to see the beauty within the block of stone. My father was gifted with the ability of unlocking the Torah's secrets. The Aher is nothing more than a tool that my father uses in order to find the hidden doors that God has placed within his holy scroll. There are many that condemn my father for they are unable to see the beauty in the world that God has provided to us. Perhaps those others that condemn him are jealous that they did not share in the gift that God has given to Akiva ben Joseph. Woe to them that cannot see what Akiva ben Joseph sees. That is all I have to say Praetor," Hunania concluded.

"Does the prosecution wish to make a comment or ask the witness a question?" the Praetor asked.

There were actually a thousand questions I wanted to ask Hunania but I thought it probably best to say nothing. Yehonatan was right. To attack a man's son, even if it were for a just cause and in order to expose the evil of the father would not be well received by many in the gallery. It would look petty and shallow and at this point of the trial, I could not afford that perception of me. If I did ask any of the questions that came to mind, then they would have begun with, "How could he believe his father loved his children when he doesn't even mention the name of his beloved dead son even once during the short eulogy he gave? How can he even think his father cares about anyone but himself when words like 'I and me' are incorporated nine or ten times into a speech supposedly about his son Simon? Did he not even think it the pinnacle of arrogance to think people came only because he was a scholar, or a rich man, and not because they genuinely felt sorry for the passing of Simon, not caring less who his father might be? The mere fact that he provided all those reasons why he believed people would come to his own son's funeral and then penultimate reason he could arrive at was because he was present, spoke volumes. This show of narcissism was no different from his seeing himself as the artist that can unleash the beauty that God has created within the Torah. Never had I heard anything so egotistical but this was his son sitting in that chair and I would not disgrace any father in front of his child.

"No Praetor, I have no questions or comments. The witness may step down."

It was interesting to watch the interplay between father and son as Hunania made his way through the crowd to leave the courtyard. He barely even looked over at his father. Did he know something about his father that he wasn't disclosing and now he was just relieved to leave as quickly as he could having done a son's duty? I wondered if any of the judges had noticed the lack of exchange as well.

"Would the Prosecution please call it's fourth witness to take the chair," Yehonatan instructed.

"I would like to ask that Eleazar Bar Hitta come forward and testify."

Moving his way from the back of the gallery, the heavily set man with his portly figure made his way steadily towards the front of the courtyard, waiting momentarily as the rope was removed so that he could pass through and take the seat, looking very uncomfortable as he tried to squeeze his bulky frame into the chair that was obviously designed for a much smaller man.

"Please tell the court your full name and what you do as an occupation," I instructed him once he finally settled into the chair.

"My name is Eleazar Bar Hitta and I am a businessman from En Gedi."

"Businessman, Hah!" Akiba laughed. "He is a thief, that's what he is!"

Ignoring the interruption I continued with my investigation of the witness, "I assume you have had some possible dealings with the Defendant." The statement was obvious after Akiva's outburst and brough a round of laughter from the crowd.

"Yes, quite a few," he answered.

"And how do you know him?" I inquired.

"Years ago, he showed up on my estate in En Gedi. I am a wealthy landowner you should know. As such, my property took in a lot of the hill territory south of Masada and bordering on the Salt Sea."

"Which meant that a lot of the caves in those hills probably reside on your property. Am I correct?'

"Exactly," he agreed.

"So, prior to the war it would be fair to say that a lot of the rebel activity took place on your land, since they used the caves to hide from the Romans."

He nodded. "Yes, that would be fair to say."

"So, you knew some of these rebels," I suggested.

"Heck, I knew all of them," he corrected my assertion. "You might say that I was a procurer for them. They were my boys!"

Akiva could not hold back any longer, shouting once more at Bar Hitta a comment indicating quite clearly his resentment and that he was not very pleased with my witness's presence. "He robbed them blind. He sold them inferior materials at high prices. The man is a thief!"

"Praetor, please remind the Defendant he will have his time to cross examine the witness when I am finished. Until then, could he kindly keep quiet."

"Unless the Defendant wishes to be removed from this courtroom," Yehonatan warned, "the court requests him to be quiet from now on."

Displeased, Akiva grunted and grumbled as he folded his arms over his chest and glared at the witness.

"I think it is important to let everyone know that the witness appears today at great risk to his own person. His involvement with the rebels makes him a person of interest to the Romans. In fact, they would not hesitate to arret him if there should be any mention of his presence here. So, I beg all of you present to forget you even saw this man once he has provided his testimony. Most certainly, he is a true patriot and whether for the war or not, he deserves our utmost respect for the role he played during the war. He has come here willingly, and I think that on its own merits that is a statement to his stalwart character and to his personal integrity. There is no doubt in my mind that most men in a similar situation would have remained safely hidden from the Roman authorities rather than dare to be out in the open for no other reason that I requested his presence. I simply ask that he be afforded the respect and protection he deserves from all of us. Eleazar, please continue to describe the early events and how you came to know the Defendant."

"As I mentioned, it was my business to procure for the rebels. Food, horses, whatever they needed. These were my boys and I took good care of them."

"Weapons I presume as well?" I asked him to clarify.

"Well, the weapons were actually what we considered as the cast offs. You see, what I mean…"

"Don't worry Eleazar bar Hitta," I reassured him as soon as I sensed his nervousness. "Whatever you say in this courtroom will never fall upon Roman ears. You have my word on that."

"You see, at that time, all of the iron smelters located on my property were actually contracted by the Romans for the production of their weapons. They provided the ore and I made their weapons. I do admit I made weapons for them but what choice did I have. But they only bought those that met their quality standards. As such, any number of weapons that failed to meet their specifications were relegated to the scrap pile to be smelted again and reforged."

"And when you talk about not meeting their specifications what are you specifically describing, just so we all understand? Did I mean that these weapons weren't any good? Were they useless?"

"Oh, not at all. They were still very capable of killing an enemy just fine," he declared. "It's just that the Romans are very fussy about balance points, and the precise length of a blade. Pommels had to a specific diameter. Off a little bit this way or that, and they would immediately reject it. Things that others who weren't Roman wouldn't really care too much about. They were still effective weapons, just not for them."

"When you say the others, don't you actually mean the rebels?" I suggested. "And I'm presuming that there were probably always enough rejected weapons to keep the rebels happy."

"Yes, until he came!" he pointed directly at Akiva. "He turned our entire world upside down with his promises of greatness."

"Explain exactly what you're referring to," I instructed Eleazar.

"All right, I will try to describe our situation back then." He took a moment to reflect on the past and then explained, "Before the war, I have to admit my boys and their rebel forces weren't much to behold. A handful of leaders, each with their own raiders. Some were no more than a group of ten, others might have had up to fifty men. It didn't really matter. When necessary, if they needed more for an ambush, they would band together. All that mattered was it worked. And it worked well. Take out a Roman squadron here, a patrol over there. Perhaps even a supply train heading into eastern territories every now and then. Attack, plunder and then retreat to the caves in the desert. That's the way it was done. That was their way of life, and it was successful strategy for all of us.

The Romans provided me with a supply of ore to make their weapons, the rebels provided me with the swords and spears they took off the dead soldiers they attacked, which meant I could eventually resell the Romans their own weapons, and the ore they provided went into making more and more weapons for the rebels. Because the Romans paid for it all, I often described it as the perfect perpetual business model. Every successful mission, meant more young men would enlist with the rebel cause and what may have been bandits at the beginning, over time became seasoned captains that could command men. There were the likes of Ben Dromi, Jonathan ben Be'Ayam, Masabala ben Shimeon, Simon bar Kosba, Yeshua ben Galgaile, and Yehonatan ben Mhynym. Not to mention we had these two non-Jews, Aelianus and Thyrsis, sons of Tinianus. It didn't matter where they came from, they were all my boys. I'll admit the Jewish leaders fought for freedom, whereas the last two may have just liked killing Romans but still, they were good men and brilliant leaders too.

The Romans called them bandits because they had no overall strategy. Their goal was to keep killing pockets of Romans until there were none left to kill. Ten years, thirty years, perhaps even a hundred years. We didn't care and it really didn't matter because we knew eventually they would tire of losing their men and gaining nothing except holding on to a patch of scorched earth that meant nothing to the Empire other than being a causeway to Africa and the East. They knew it too, their garrisons continually striving against a people that they could never break the will of. In the end, we would win, and they would leave. It was just a matter of time."

"But you are suggesting then that something changed all that, aren't you," I decided to move this story along at a quicker pace before the court sessions ended.   Clearly, Eleazar bar Hitta liked to talk, even if an outlaw, but today was not the day for a long drawn out story. Perhaps some other day we would have had time to hear the entirety of his tale, but today I needed only the short version with the facts.

"Yes," he replied somewhat angrily. "Akiva happened. One day he shows up at my estate in En Gedi. He says he knows all about my affiliation and arrangement with the rebels and the operation I was running.   This sounded like a threat to me, so I'm naturally worried. He tells me to summon the leaders because he has an important announcement that he wishes to reveal to them.   At first, I deny having any knowledge of what he is talking about but then he tells me of certain dates of which he had knowledge of I had delivered a shipment of weapons to the Romans only to be followed closely by a transfer of ore to a secondary forge site that I had hidden up in the hills.   I don't know how he had this information, but he did and that made him dangerous. I'm thinking I might have to do something about him quickly, and I guess he senses it. He then declares he is no threat to me and all he wants is a meeting with the rebel leaders.   Truth is, a man possessing secrets like that is always a danger, because they always have a backup plan to protect themselves, so I knew I had no other choice but to cooperate and give him what he wanted.   I set up the meeting to take place several days later at a destination known only to the rebels and myself. Akiva had to first come to me and then I escorted him there. That way I could be certain that he wasn't betraying us and had arranged to be followed by the Romans.

When we get there, Akiva wasted no time in telling the rebel leaders that he had a vision in which he was visited by the Prophet Samuel who told him he must go and find the several warrior brothers in the desert and anoint one of them as the next King of Israel.   Under the leadership of this king, they would raise a great army and drive the Romans from our land. All of us began laughing, recognizing that we were wasting our time with one more lunatic rabbi whose brain had become addled from too much desert sun. Trust me when I say that we had seen enough of them over the years. We were preparing to leave when Simon bar Kosba said that he had that same dream. The others teased him saying that they all had dreams of grandeur at one point but got over it by the time they woke up the next morning, but Simon insisted his was not a dream but a prophecy from God of what was meant to come.   He truly believed it and no matter what we said, we could not convince him otherwise.

So, in the end they went along with this mystic nonsense and all the boys mockingly swore an oath that they would fight for their king to the death in battle. Really, what did it matter if one of the captains wanted to think of himself as a king. No one really cares what you call yourself going into battle. When you only have a hundred or so men in total, then every battle you engage in against the Romans is a battle to the death, meaning that kings can come and go on any day.

It began as a tease. 'Confronting the might of Rome, head on and winning, now that would be a miracle,' they joked at the time. 'Our hundred men defeating a legion of six thousand Romans. If this crazy Rabbi could make that happen, then you will have our commitment to fight to the death for you'. I mean, no one took it seriously. How could they? But then as soon as he heard them say that, Akiva said to them, 'I will bind you all to that oath that you have just sworn. I will give Simon twenty-four thousand men to lead into battle under his command. He will have to train them but then you all will fight for him. You have given your word and now you have been given mine. As God is our witness, there is no turning back now!"

"From what you are saying, it was Akiva that initiated this entire war when he committed all of his students to the cause and hence bound everyone to an oath that they actually began in jest. If I have followed your story correctly, as I see it, he sought you out, he selected Bar Kochba based on nothing more than a dream and then he bound everyone to fight for him by promising to deliver all of his students into the war effort. Did none of your rebel leaders not see something wrong with this plan?"

"Hey, you promise to give a rebel leader twenty-four thousand men and I guarantee none of them would have turned down such an offer. That is what they fantasize about, whereas the rest of us only want a beautiful woman. Of course, it was enough to start the war. Other than small garrisons spread out across the length and breadth of the country guarding specific strategic towns, what did the Procurator Rufus have? Nothing but the Legion IX Hispania, which had grown fat and lazy sitting all those years in Caesarea. It didn't really matter if those boys from Akiva could fight or not. I don't even think Akiva cared if they lived or died as long as they still retained enough to win the first few battles. You throw four times the number at even the best trained legion and you're going to win perhaps eighty percent of the time. It's not strategy. It's wholesale slaughter but ultimately the numbers are in your favour. Simon bar Kosba was well aware of that, so I can't really say he spent as much time as he would have normally training these new recruits.

First item on the rebel army's new agenda was to get enough weapons for twenty-four thousand new recruits. That's when things got interesting. Akiva insisted I had to make him twenty-four thousand new swords and a similar number of javelins. I guess he thought I could manufacture them out of thin air. I told him, you get me the ore and perhaps in six months' time I could hand you your weapons but that was the best I could do. There's only so much you can do with a single smelter up in the mountains. He didn't like my answer and I think that was the beginning of what I call the end of our relationship. Not that Akiva and I will ever on good terms. To be perfectly honest, I wasn't in to this whole doom's day war with Rome thing. Some raids here, an attack there, that gave us control over our situation. You attack, you fight, if you see that you're losing then you retreat into the hills and they give up searching for you after a few days. That way you live on to fight another day. But full scale military warfare is different, one mistake and there are no tomorrows if you lose. To me the risks were too great, and it wasn't that I didn't want to supply Simon with as many weapons as he needed, he was one of my boys after all, it was that I couldn't. I didn't have that much ore available and if it suddenly was made available and the Romans saw that much stock being manufactured at my other forges then they would have known immediately that I was the one arming the rebels.

That's when things got ugly. Akiva began accusing me of being sympathetic with the Romans, and I guess he already had his talons deep into Simon because then Simon, after all the years we had worked together accused me of betraying him. I was practically a father to him. The promise of kingship must have blinded him because he failed to see the enormity of what Akiva was requesting. But that Rabbi kept pushing, saying things like, 'God will ensure you get the weapons you need.' I couldn't fathom the urgency. If they had waited this many years to launch a bloody war, surely, they could have waited six more months for me to arrange the weapons."

"But he did manage to get those weapons for all of Akiva's students without your assistance," I reminded him.

"Because he did what he did best. He attacked a few garrisons and several outposts and after picking up a thousand swords here and a thousand there, he had enough to probably arm half of those poor students. The rest had to manage with whatever else they could find, which wasn't much; knives, clubs, staves, cudgels and even pitch forks. As I said, their training was minimal but it didn't matter. From what I saw, I don't think their so-called master ever expected to see them again. I think they were merely fodder for his war effort to get started. But like I said, you throw four times the number at a legion and even if all they had were sticks and stones they would probably end up winning but suffering terrible losses at the same time."

"And that's what happened, didn't it?" I pushed Eleazar to get on with his story.

"Obviously," he replied. "Governor Rufus led his legion out of Caesarea and marched the IX Hispania along the desert roads south of Jerusalem. Well, anyone with an ounce of common sense would have known not to take you legion into hill country where there's not a patch of cover available. Simon's men were waiting for them to enter a narrow valley where they could attack from both ends and crush them in the middle. Rufus barely escaped with a remnant of about a thousand soldiers but almost all of Akiva's students perished in the assault."

"Are you saying that it was quite unusual that the Procurator, even if he was the worst general in existence would have followed the strategy he did. Obviously, there were others, like his commanders who would have advised against it. So why do you think he pursued taking this route."

"I hardly consider myself a strategist, not like my boys were, but you don't do something like that unless you're either extremely ignorant or for some reason you're convinced you aren't going to find much resistance."

"So, you think he expected these students to scatter and run as soon as they were facing a disciplined, fully armored Roman Legion?"

"That would suggest that he had knowledge in advance that the major portion of Simon's army consisted of nothing more than raw recruits. Not even recruits, but even worse than that. He would have to know that they were nothing more than a useless, untrained bunch of Torah readers. I would guess if he knew that in advance, then it may have been possible that it affected his strategic judgement, and he was willing to take risks that he normally wouldn't dare. But that would mean that one of my boys had to reveal that secret to the Governor in advance."

"Do you think that was possible?"

"No way. Never! Impossible! Not one of my boys. I can tell you right now that they'd all fight to the death before passing on any secret to the Romans. Every one of them," he snapped back quickly. "They were committed to this war and they shared a brotherhood you could never comprehend. There would never come a day they would betray one another."

"But you admitted that you weren't committed to this war. You preferred the old way of doing things by constantly raiding. Any reason you could not have been the one that leaked the information?"

"Several reasons actually that should be pretty obvious. First one, to do so would have meant that I'd be admitting I had been working with the rebels all those years. All those Romans that died, I had shared in the responsibility for them. If I admitted to something like that, I wouldn't be here right now. Second, is that as much as they're my boys, I was still a businessman. Even after our little disagreement with the weapons, they were still my best customers. Now that they were an army, they needed even more supplies and more horses. I went from trading off the back of wagons to having caravans of supplies. No way I was going to give up that much business. And lastly, as much as we loved each other, if those boys ever got wind that I had betrayed them in some way, they would have spread my entrails all the way from Golan to the Negev. Trust me when I say, a Roman death would have been preferable. That Thyrsis knew how to make a man suffer for days without offering him the release of death."

"Then let us examine another possibility. This one may be more feasible. What if it was Simon bar Kochba who intentionally released the information in an effort to lure out the Romans. Feed the Romans the details of the army they're about to face, get them overconfident by telling them how weak you are and then they fall into the trap because as you said, even if you only have sticks, if you outnumber them four to one, you are probably going to win."

"To do that," Eleazar shook his head as he replied, "Would mean you would have to have a direct connection to the Romans. None of my boys have those. I was the only one that ever made direct contact with the Romans. To feed them information, you would require someone that already had a trust relationship with the enemy."

"And there was no other person other than yourself with that close a relationship?" I raised the question as to whether Eleazar still could have been an unintentional leak of the information.

"You're right, I could have leaked it accidentally through a chain of people that would have eventually passed the information on to the Governor but why would I say something so stupid unintentionally if I would do it intentionally."

"But a long chain of people between you and the Governor would have kept you a safe distance from the Romans knowing who leaked the information," I pointed out to everyone listening. "But you say you would never would have done it. Why?"

"Because I will tell you, there is no chain in this world that would ever be long enough to protect the source when the Romans start interrogating all those passing along the information. And as far as my boys are concerned, if one ever came to me with such a stupid plan as that, I would have kicked their asses from here to Galilee! You don't go telling your enemy, no matter how clever you think your trap that you're setting might be, 'Hey, guess what, I heard the rebels have twenty-four thousand religious students in their army that can't fight'. It's would sound so unbelievable that it would be dismissed immediately as a trap. Not even Tinnius Rufus is going to march his army into that canyon because he's going to say right from the start they're lying. He is going to believe the exact opposite, thinking that there must be at least twenty-four thousand well trained soldiers on the other side. The only way he would have believed it to be true is if it came from a trusted source."

"Someone close to him then?"

"It would have to be," Eleazar suggested. "Rufus had to believe it was the truth and it wasn't a trap and that's why he marched his men stupidly into that valley. Whoever told him the details probably assured him of an easy victory."

"But I still don't understand," I feigned ignorance. "Once again I remind you that you told us that you throw that many men at a legion even if practically weaponless, the odds are that they're going to win. Did you not say that?"

"Anyone with any military common sense would know that. Even with minimal training, a Torah student with a sword is still going to manage to inflict some heavy wounds. You don't launch an attack when you're that outnumbered."

"Rufus may not have been a military genius but he was no fool either. Right?"

"As I said earlier in my testimony," Eleazar completed my logical train of thought, "Rufus had to believe that they were all going to turn tail and run. Someone had to be pretty convincing to make him believe that was actually going to happen."

"Perhaps someone who knew the students very well and made a promise that they would turn tail and run, as you described it. That person would have needed to practically guarantee the students would retreat," I commented, letting the words linger, which suggested that I already had someone in mind. "Let's continue and figure that out later. I'm assuming that after that little surprise, Procurator Rufus knew he was in to a real war. So, what did he do next?"

"What every Roman governor has done in every other war against us when they made a mess of their first attack; they send word to the Legate of the neighbouring provinces to come and save their ass," Eleazar laughed as he recalled the sequence of events at the start of the war.

"So Certus Publicius Marcellus at the head of the legion out of Syria, and Haterius Nepos leading his legion from Arabia come to Rufus's rescue, if I recall correctly," They were names I knew wall having been resident in Jerusalem as the war took place. "Now your boys, as you call them, are about to face two very well trained legions. These are hardened soldiers, not anything like the force that came out of Caesarea. I would think now more than ever Bar Kochba would have needed a real military strategy. He just sacrificed his advantage in numbers by losing all those students. So, how could Bar Kochba go up against these superior troops?"

"You see, that's part of the war that so few know about and that's where it gets very interesting," Eleazar rubbed his chin, his fingers drawn through a scraggly batch of dark wiry hair. "Fortunately, Simon came to me to talk it over before making any hasty decisions. He may have accused me of failing him in the past for not providing the weapons, but he was still smart enough to know that when things got really, really serious, I'd always be there for him. He was concerned because of the pressure being applied by Rabbi Akiva. Simon was a warrior and he knew to trust his shield and his blade and it wasn't God that wielded his sword. He knew how to fight using the terrain to his advantage and he knew how to kill. But Akiva was insisting he had to stop everything and march into Jerusalem and make that city his headquarters. The Rabbi said God had demanded His city be liberated immediately and that it had to be restored as their capital. Simon knew it was the wrong move to make militarily at that time.   The walls of the city had been torn down a long time ago. In fact, it was that last war against the Romans, over sixty years ago when those walls were destroyed.   Since then, the city has had no defensive structures and no means of protecting itself from attack.   Much of the city still lay in ruin.   It was a death trap, open to every invader from all four directions.   Until   there   were   some   defensive   structures   rebuilt, making   the   city   of   Jerusalem   his   headquarters   was   the   worse   idea   that anyone could have proposed. It was so obvious, yet Akiva insisted.   Simon knew if he took his men to Jerusalem they'd be slaughtered by any approaching Roman legions."

"And what did you advise him?" I asked.

"I told him to tell Akiva to go to hell."

Having said that, a rowdy cheer went up from those standing in the gallery. It was as if they had been waiting a long time this day to say the exact same thing themselves.

Yehonatan banged on his table to restore the silence.   Once the noise had died down, Eleazar continued his testimony.

"I told him that he was the military leader that the men respected and any Rabbi that thought he knew better should sit himself on a horse at the head of the army and lead it himself.   Simon bar Kosba needed to fight wars in the manner that he knew.   That meant subterfuge, concealment, guerrilla warfare, the element of surprise. He knew I was always looking after his best interest. He took my advice and set up his administrative capital in En Gedi, avoiding Jerusalem all together."

"And that was the right decision, wasn't it?" I prodded him along.

"Of course, it was.   By the time Legate Marcellus arrived, Simon had enough time to increase his forces to over two hundred thousand men.   That early success over Procurator Rufus served as a rallying call and had certainly raised the spirits of everyone throughout the land. If I had been a younger man, I might have joined the ranks. They flocked to Simon like bees to honey.   That army out of Syria never knew what hit them. Legion III Cyrenaica was defeated almost as soon as the battle had begun. But during that battle what little had remained of Akiva's twenty-four thousand students was wiped out completely."

"Explain to us, how did that happen?" I asked curiously since it did not make sense to me. "They surely had enough time to be trained properly by then."

"Don't know," Eleazar answered. "Mystery is all I know. If Simon was still alive he could probably provide the details but I heard they refused to fight, preferring to become martyrs to the cause. Stupid nonsense if you ask me. You join an army, you fight. You don't just stand there and wait to be killed."

"You mean they willingly sacrificed themselves without raising a sword," I interpreted what he said. "Almost as if they had been told this was God's will."

"Guess you could say that. Just a bunch of fools. But after that Simon put into force a new policy. Anyone joining his army had to cut off part of the little finger of their left hand. If you had the courage to do that without hesitation, then you probably wouldn't hesitate when it came to plunging a sword into a Roman."

"That meant a lot of self-mutilation," I commented.

"That's exactly what Akiva said and condemned Simon for doing it. That's when the infighting began between the two. But by now Simon was beginning to have his doubts about Akiva's true intentions."

"Tell us more about that. Obviously, Simon had his reasons. What are these doubts you just mentioned. Did Simon bar Kochba ever come to you do discuss these doubts he had?"

"Not directly with me," Eleazar said apologetically. "Our relationship still was a little rocky I guess. Better, but still rocky. Akiva kept telling him that I was still trying to control my boys and keep him from becoming King, but that wasn't true. By that time, they had long outgrown any control I could exert. Akiva was now insisting that Simon had to become an observant Jew as if that would make a difference. But he said if he didn't, he would no longer have God's approval. You tell me how you can fight a war if you broadcast to the enemy that you will stop fighting on the Sabbath evening and not start again until the next evening. I asked Simon if he really thought the Romans would agree and take a day's rest as well. He knew they wouldn't, but now he was worried and confused, which only made him upset! He was afraid God would desert him. Then, Akiva insisted the only food the army could eat had to be approved by the Council. Where have you ever seen an army maintaining its own slaughterhouses and farms to ensure they don't eat anything unclean. As a soldier, you shove into your mouth whatever you can get and you hope for the best it doesn't make you sick the next day. In war, you can't have a picky appetite, but I did my best to ensure they had the proper food by sending my buyers out to scour all over the land for supplies. But no way in the world I was able to procure enough food if I had to ensure everything had been approved first by the rabbinical council first."

"You and Akiva are finding yourselves in opposition quite a bit from what you're telling me."

"You may not know it but I fought in the Kittos War," Eleazar gave away a bit of his own history. "We ate whatever we could find. An army only marches on a full stomach and if you can't feed your men, they will go elsewhere where they can get a meal. The demands from Akiva were constantly increasing and Simon was becoming increasingly frustrated. I couldn't blame him. There was an incident where the Romans were reinforcing the Temple Mount to provide some protection for their troops and as a result, the Tomb of Solomon collapsed in on itself crushing hundreds of them under the massive stones. Akiva claimed it was a Messianic omen and insisted that Simon had to go right there and then and capture the city immediately. He was constantly demanding that Jerusalem be taken. The demand was repeated endlessly, and Simon eventually acquiesced and launched an surprise attack on the Roman XXII Deitoriana under the command of Legate Nepos. The Romans held the high ground of the city but Simon was still able to take the city of Jerusalem as well as the mount but not without suffering some horrendous losses in the process. A waste of good men as far as I was concerned. I think any other military man would say the same.

But no sooner did Akiva have his precious Jerusalem, he demanded that Simon use his soldiers to start rebuilding the Temple. I heard from my sources that Simon became practically convulsive when he was told that. He wanted to know, and rightly so, who from among the Rabbinic Council was going to be fighting the war when the Romans legions returned in force because there was no doubt in anyone's mind that they would be back. Take his men away from the battlefield and they were all going to die. Akiva was unmoved by his rant, saying that it was what God demanded and if he was unwilling to do it then God just might withdraw his support from his appointed Messiah. There was no other way for Simon to interpret those words other than a threat and he made an equally rash statement in response that he would continue to fight the war his way, with or without God's approval. Akiva started shouting the word blasphemer and said he would no longer support Bar Kosba. If you ask me, that was the day the war was over and the Romans had won," Eleazar sighed.

"Why did you think that?" I wanted him to explain fully.

"Because it was obvious to anyone that heard Akiva say it, that was the day Simon's dream of a free Judea was shattered. As long as he thought God was on his side, he believed he was invincible. Unfortunately, he had misled himself into thinking that his success was the result of divine intervention. For some inexplicable reason in Simon bar Kosba's mind, and I don't know why, Akiva and God were practically the same thing. I constantly tried to warn him. I said right from the start, 'Don't ever trust this Akiva, he's no good if you ask me." but he kept insisting that Akiva was God's messenger and it was the only way he was going to hear the word of God. But as soon as Akiva took the word away, Simon became a lost soul."

"What did he do next?" I inquired.

"Simon moved his encampment from En Gedi to Herodium, just seven miles south of Jerusalem but he refused to enter into the Holy City again until the war was declared officially over. The rabbis and priests could do whatever they wanted in Jerusalem but it would be without his men. He said if they were no longer supporting him then they should be careful that he did not find them supporting the enemy in the future. They reached the point where they were exchanging threats."

"And that is when I presume he officially declared his relationship with Akiva a being over. Is that correct? Is that what you are telling us?" I wanted to clearly define and to establish the precise timeline of when their relationship became irreparably broken. This was the first time that I had ever heard that it had possibly ended this early in the war and that was important."

"That is the strange thing," Eleazar snorted with what sounded to be half a laugh and a deep breath combined. "Akiva still kept coming. Checking on things, Making certain that Simon remained observant in his religious duties and offering more of his criticisms of everything he didn't like. Meanwhile Simon continued to fight the war according to his own unique style. He selected about fifty towns throughout Judea that he fortified. He then dug an elaborate tunnel network beneath those towns so that they always had secret entrances and exits by which they could bring in supplies and move men about unobserved by the Romans."

"Aha, I see now," I needed everyone to hear about the tunnels as I nodded my appreciation for the clarification, "Essentially he turned these towns into larger and more elaborate versions of the cave systems he would use when he was still a rebel fighting against the small garrisons in the desert around the Dead Sea." You had to admire the strategy of taking what worked on a small scale and finding a way to expand it. "Very clever. I would never have thought of that myself."

Eleazar nodded his head as well. "Like I said, Simon needed to fight the war in the only way he knew how. He needed to be left to his own devices and not tempted into following a different path."

"Almost like fish have to swim," I muttered under my breath.

"What was that?" Eleazar didn't quite hear what I had said.

"Like fish have to swim," I said loudly this time so everyone in the court could hear. "It's something that Akiva wrote in his book, a record he keeps for writing the Talmud that he is planning. When I first read the story, I didn't know exactly why it was included in his book. I thought perhaps it was about ensuring that as Jews we should adhere to the Torah at any cost but that can't possibly be correct because it would be the antithesis of what Akiva is trying to convince us to do by proposing we adopt his Talmud instead. I'm beginning to think he is making a comment on Bar Kochba but disguising it as a parable or fable. I've heard about people that do this. When they are aware of their own guilt, then they are compelled to transfer their guilt on to someone else so they can feel better about themselves. I think that is the case here. I know I've digressed. I'm sorry to interrupt you like this but I need a few minutes for the court to hear what was written. I think it relates to what you were just saying. Praetor, if I may open Akiva's book again and have you read the section I marked to the court please." Moving towards Yehonatan I opened the book to the page I had clearly noted and spread it out before him.

The Praetor began to read. *"A fox was once walking alongside the river and saw swarms of fish panicking and swimming from place to place."* Looking up from the book and staring at me, Yehonatan appeared confused. "Are you certain this is the story you want me to read in the middle of your witness's testimony. A story about a fox and fish?"

"Yes Praetor, please continue."

"If you insist, though I remind you your time is almost done. '*So the fox* said to one of the fish, 'From whom are you all fleeing?' To which the fish replied, 'From the nets that people throw into the river to catch us.' The fox then said, 'Why don't you jump up on the land and they won't be able to catch you.'" Yehonatan looked up at me again, and I could tell that he was thinking I had lost my mind. I just shook my head and motioned for him to continue. "I will teach you how to live on the land.' The fish refused preferring to simply evade the nets.' That is all of it," Yehonatan concluded.

As I turned to directly face the attentive audience in the courtyard, I spoke directly to the townspeople. "I need you to listen carefully. I believe the fish in Akiva's story are none other than Simon Bar Kochba. The fox clearly announces what he is. He is a teacher, a Rabbi, the one that wants to teach the fish a new way to survive even though it will be far more dangerous for them; not to mention impossible. This is just like Rabbi Akiva with his Talmud. The people with the nets are obviously the Romans and they won't be satiated in their hunger until they catch every last fish in the river, which is not just Simon's army but the entire Jewish population. The fish, like Bar Kochba prefers to take his chances, doing what he has always done, evading the attackers, but which obviously annoys the fox. Akiva the fox, decides to deceive the fish, but did so not because he could eat them all, as that would be physically impossible, maybe one or two fish at best if he was really hungry, but because he wanted to put a stop to what they were doing which was surviving on their own. The fish would continue to evade the nets as they had done since the dawn of time and similarly, in the end, Bar Kochba's men would escape, continue their tactic to attack, retreat, evade and then hide, constantly replacing their numbers over time, just as the supply of fish would never be totally depleted."

Akiva could not remain silent any longer. "Praetor, that is nothing but a complete misinterpretation of what I had written," he disputed my explanation. "I was merely writing about how the Jewish people would prefer to study Torah, keep their religious observances and face death rather than convert even if it meant living."

I was not willing to let him explain this so easily. "And at first, I thought that was what you were saying too, but then there are these elements that don't agree with your analogy. You can't say that you wanted us to accept death, as the fox, who is obviously not Rome, was suggesting a completely different outcome by telling the fish to come on to the land as clear alternative that was available to them but would definitely end in death. Conversion would let them live, not die. Your analogy doesn't correlate. Perhaps you were saying that the fox was Bar Kochba and choosing war would lead to our deaths. But that doesn't make sense either because your story tells us to continue to flee just like the fish, even though our reality of the past four years is that you have been the fox that sent over half a million of your countrymen to our deaths by encouraging the war. Let us not forget, twenty-four thousand of those deaths were your own students that had absolutely a chance to evade the 'nets' but no chance to survive as warriors. You are that wily fox, that no one should have listened to, and I have no doubt you had an alternative mission in mind but this was your way of describing your own guilt. From the testimony we are now hearing and revealed thus far, you had a lot of demands for Bar Kochba but he would not listen to you. He was the one continuing to swim in the river and evade the fisherman and because he pursued his own tactics, you abandoned him. I have a feeling that sly fox was doing far more than just abandoning the fish. So, why don't you just sit down, be quiet and we will see if I can't find out exactly what that wily old fox was really up to."

"Praetor Yehonatan, the prosecution is being ridiculous," Akiva complained.

"I want to hear where this goes," Yehonatan responded. "The Defendant will please sit and wait his turn to question the witness."

"I apologize for my interruption Eleazar bar Hatti. My mind is just trying to draw connections between your testimony and what we know of the Defendant. So you were about to tell us what came next. Like the fish, I'm guessing the nets were still thrown into the river."

"You are right Excellency. The Romans kept moving more and more legions into the province in an attempt to subdue Bar Kosba. First came the Legion V Macedonia, then the Legion XI Claudia. Well, Simon bar Kosba made very short work of those two legions." Eleazar had a broad smile on his face when he mentioned those two successful battles. "Utilizing his elaborate tunnel systems, he was able to attack from almost any direction, whenever they were found encamped outside a town or village. And when they tried to give chase, his men would simply disappear into the tunnels just as easily." Beaming proudly, he puffed out his chest and said, "My boy really could work miracles. I'm telling you, if he had been left alone he could have kept doing that for years until he eventually wiped out every legion they sent against him."

"Left alone? How was he not left alone?" I asked.

"By the third year of Simon's campaign, it was obvious that matters had become a lot more serious in Rome. The Emperor, himself, became a lot more involved, realizing he was losing this war. He summoned his best general, Gaius Julius Severus, the Governor of Britannia and he put him on a boat and sailed him along with the equivalent of six legions to the shores of Judea. An additional thirty-five thousand Roman soldiers added to what was already here.

Simon, along with his guerilla tactics, was now fighting against Legions VI Ferrata, X Fretensis, II Trajiana Fortis and the III Galicia as well as the remnants of the XXII Deitoriana and III Cyrenaica and III Scythea. But it honestly didn't matter to my boy, Bar Kosba; they were just several thousand more Romans waiting their turn to die as far as he was concerned."

"But let's be truthful, it didn't go that way at all, did it?" I challenged his comment. "Therefore, he was wrong. You can't tell me that he could eventually be successful using his guerilla tactics."

"But it was," Eleazar insisted. "That entire third year of the war was a disaster for Gaius Julius Severus. Just look at the facts. Firstly, he divided his legions, a serious mistake, in an attempt to lay siege to all fifty or so towns that Simon was using to launch his attacks from. That gave Simon the advantage because without knowing the whereabouts of the extensive tunnel system, Severus had no idea where or when Simon's soldiers would appear. That third year was the first time I truly believed we were going to win this war. If he could just manage to eliminate half of Severus's forces, I was certain the Romans would sue for peace."

"That's a big expectation," I added. "You truly believed that he could eliminate half of the Roman forces."

"With all my heart," Eleazar bar Hatti placed his right hand over the left half of his chest. "As far as I could tell, it should have been possible. Let me say that better. It should have been inevitable because he was so close."

"Yet, it didn't happen, so why was that?"

"Honestly, I have no explanation for why it failed. I really don't know," he replied. "Severus withdrew his forces during the winter of the third year. I presumed that to be an indication of his resignation to the fact that Simon could not be defeated. By the beginning of the fourth year the Emperor arrived in Judea."

"Yes, I remember his arrival by boat at the port of Caesarea very well. Just as I remember the numerous times that I submitted a request for an audience with Hadrian, only to have it refused every time. It was clear to me that he had no intention to discuss a peaceful resolution to the war."

"Which should have been surprising, considering how much the Romans had suffered during the prior three years. We thought the Emperor had come to arrange a truce rather than lose any more men," Eleazar commented. When we realized that was not his intent, I thought the Emperor's attitude was bizarre. "It was as if he had been given some reason to believe that he could turn everything around. It was as if someone had provided his generals with a new strategy guaranteed to defeat Simon's forces."

"Which must be true, because they immediately turned the tide of the war," I concluded.

"No! That is the part which is so strange. Nothing changed," Eleazar seemed alarmed. "There was absolutely nothing new or revolutionary in their style of warfare. They did nothing different from what they did before. Severus returned with his men, built his encirclements, and laid siege to the towns just as he did before. But this time he was able to keep Bar Kosba's men trapped in each town, not permitting them to escape and wreak havoc. Somehow, he had discovered every one of their entrances and exits from the tunnels and was therefore able to capture one town after the other as if it was a game of sennet."

"All of them? How could he possibly know the location of all those hundreds of tunnels. They were spread all across the countryside." I couldn't believe the Romans could suddenly find every tunnel when they couldn't do it before.

"Not hundreds," Eleazar corrected me, "Perhaps closer to a thousand. Simon knew that every fortified place required an entrance and exit in every direction. North, south, east and west. The entry points dug leagues from the towns in each direction. That's how he was able to attack the Romans so easily and then disappear. But somehow Severus was able to locate all of them."

"Somehow, or someone," I corrected him.

"I cannot say with any certainty, Excellency, but personally it is my belief that there had to be a traitor that provided that information. Over the winter, the location of those tunnels and exits must have been passed over to the Roman generals and their tacticians and then they drew up their attack plans based on that information. That's why Hadrian became confident of a victory. I feel it to be true in my bones."

It was a lot to digest, a traitor in their midst, but I had the same belief. "Let us say there was a traitor," I postulated. "We are talking over fifty towns where Bar Kochba had garrisoned his men. How could any one man know of every tunnel and every exit in each of those towns. I doubt even Bar Kochba would have known every one by memory."

"And now you have broached the very reason I readily accepted your invitation to come and testify as a witness at this tribunal, even though my appearance outside my refuge definitely places my life in danger. I owe it to my boys. They would have done the same for me. It's well worth the risk if I can get them justice. I thought long and hard about that question of a traitor until my brain actually hurt. The quest for revenge consumed me. I concluded that the only way for the Romans to know about all the tunnels in every town was because they had someone that could move freely about Judea without any interference. Someone who could pass through the rebel security zones without any questions ever being asked. A person that could go wherever he wanted and do as he pleased inside the town because he had been given that authorization directly from Simon bar Kosba."

"Was there such a man?" I demanded to know the answer.

"Yes!" Eleazar cried out while simultaneously standing up and pointing towards the Defendant. "There was one. Akiva ben Joseph!"

No sooner said, those in attendance began howling and the gallery erupted into absolute chaos. Objects flew wildly through the air. I think we all feared for our lives as some of the people rushed the dividing rope, fueled with blind rage. I ordered my guard to form a wall between us and the insurgent mass of people. It wasn't until Jacob had no other choice but to order his men to draw their swords that the people fell back and there was a partial restoration of order.

"Men of B'nai Brak listen to me!" I shouted. "I feel and understand your anger and I agree that what you have just heard is quite disturbing but that does not necessarily mean that it is true. At this point, it is an opinion of one man and nothing more. And we need more! Let us not be hasty to pass judgment. It is our purpose in this tribunal to back opinion with fact and only when we can do so, can we say there is no doubt as to what happened. We are all hurting! I understand that. You have all suffered dearly from this war but we do not blindly hurt others without having proof that they are actually responsible. An eye for an eye! I agree with the laws as they were passed down to us but we cannot take an eye until we know exactly who was responsible for the crime and whose eye that must be forfeited. Give me the opportunity to see if I can identify a perpetrator of this crime beyond a shadow of any reasonable doubt. Let me do my job as your appointed prosecutor and let the justice mechanisms of this tribunal do its job to determine criminality! I believe we are getting close and I promise you, if we do find out that we have been betrayed then I assure you, that person will be made to pay a heavy price. I promise you that! So please, settle down and return to where you were standing. We are a people of laws. We hold the law to be sacred and we live by the law. All I ask is that you trust me to see that the law is upheld. If you believe in Our Lord then you know we will have justice."

It took some time, but the anger of the crowd was finally diffused. I almost feared continuing on with the questioning of the witness. It would only take a single spark to light the courtroom into an out-of-control conflagration. Just one more shock revelation from Eleazar, like the last one and there was no telling what the people would do. I knew I had to move tenderly as if walking on glass from now on. Those of us on the courtroom side of the rope were all nervous. None of us wanted to see what the people were capable of, if they rioted.

"Are you all right to proceed?" I asked the witness.

"I think so," came his response midst his rapid and shallow breathing.

"Are you absolutely certain that Akiva had access to go and come as he pleased in any of the towns?

"I'm Pretty certain," he confirmed his answer. "As I mentioned before, even though he said he was abandoning Simon because he could not get him to agree to rebuild the Temple and make Jerusalem his headquarters, he still would return every now and then to make ridiculous demands. Simon would complain to me about it whenever he became frustrated."

"Praetor, I must seriously object to any further of this man's testimony," Akiva was practically in tears. "You can readily see how this conjecture based on one man's hearsay, and we need to remember that is all it is, can fuel the people into a murderous frenzy. He can barely recall the details of which he speaks. What has he actually told us? That he is told something vague, in the heat of temper by Bar Kochba and that suddenly renders it true. Funny how lies can expand so much beyond their original telling," Akiva was insisting that it was all fabricated. "It is almost the same as sins. *In the beginning a sin is like the fine thread taken from a spider web but over time, in the end as it is entwined, layer over layer, it will become as thick as the cable that is found on a ship.* And I have sat here listening to these statements from a man that even Bar Kochba accused of betraying him and I can tell you with certainty, he has been guilty today of telling some huge lies, especially when he is talking about me."

"You will have your chance to cross examine the witness," I reflected on Akiva's protestation, "But you did raise a good point. Eleazar, you did admit that Bar Kochba felt you betrayed him as well. So, Akiva is correct in raising that as a valid point. It does seem somewhat unusual. That being the case, why would Bar Kochba still turn to you whenever he wished to relieve his mind?"

"As I said, those were my boys," Eleazar did not appear upset by the question at all. "I was like a father to them and they were like sons to me. We don't always get along with our fathers but we still turn to them for advice in spite of our differences. You use the word betrayal, but that is Akiva's word, not Simon's. It was more a case of his feeling that I let him down in his time of need. We may not have always agreed but he knew I would never steer him wrong. We had an unbreakable bond. We were family. In his heart I think he always knew I could not produce all those weapons unless I fired up all my smelters at once and that would have given ourselves away to the Romans. But with Akiva always threatening to pull away God's support from Simon, I think he began to doubt in himself, and that's where he felt the betrayal. The worst thing a leader of men could ever do was begin to doubt themselves. When they all were still nothing more than seven bandits raiding Romans in the desert, we had this saying, 'I don't care if God is for me, I just pray He isn't for my enemies.' There is no offense there but Akiva, still called it blasphemy."

"But let us talk more about the specifics regarding the tunnels or any insight to any strategies. Do you know for certain if Bar Kochba's men shared any of those details with Akiva?"

"I have no proof. I can only tell you that Akiva had access. Let me tell you of what happened in those last days of Beithar."

"You know what happened in Beithar?" I was shocked and surprised. "How could you possibly know? Anyone that was there was either killed or captured. As far as I now, you were never there." I was confused as to how Eleazar could make that statement and began to doubt some of his prior testimony myself. "Tell us, how you could possibly know?"

"Because what you may not know is that not everyone was permitted to stay and die in Beithar," he explained. "Akiva made certain of that."

"I'm confused," I admitted as I dwelled on his statement. "I don't understand what you are you trying to say?"

"As I said, Akiva went wherever he pleased."

"That doesn't answer my question. We know he was there, and it was his incredible explanation of being rescued by an angel that led to this trial, but we have no knowledge of anyone else that escaped. Either they were killed or they're now in prison camps in Hebron and Gaza being sold for the price of a horse. But sadly, the Romans are not permitting us to redeem any of our own people. So, we can't get their stories. Therefore, how is it even possible that you know what happened in those final days?"

"Because two of my boys returned home to me just days before the fall of Beithar."

"Are you saying they were deserters?" That was the only explanation I could think of for why they returned to En Gedi.

"Of course not! Don't be ridiculous. They were two of the bravest men I know," Eleazar ben Hatti sounded both insulted and wounded by my insinuation and I couldn't blame him. "I guess you've never fought in a war Excellency. Any one of my boys would have gladly given their lives to die alongside their brothers. The fact that they were forced from the city filled them with disgust, but Akiva made it impossible for them to stay. Things were quite desperate in Beithar. By then, every other town had fallen to the Romans and this would be Simon's last stand. Either they would all die in Beithar, or he would find a way for them to defeat the Romans. Those were the only two options available. And from what my boys told me when they returned, he had a plan. A good plan. Word had been received from the Galileans, the Samaritans, the Idumeans and the Nabateans while Simon and his men were barricaded within the city and it was good news. All those other people confirmed that they were willing to bring their armies to Beithar and join the fight against the Romans. They all knew that a defeat of Serverus's army at that time would be the end of Roman dominance in the entire region. After Severus there was no general left that Hadrian could throw at the rebel army. Everyone, not just us Jews would have their freedom, so they were eager to join the fight."

"Yes, we heard that already from some of the other testimony," I mentioned. "But it never happened. They never came."

"They never came because of him!" Once again Eleazar was pointing directly at Akiva, his eyes burning deep into the Rabbi with absolute hatred.

I found that hard to believe but I had no reason to doubt Eleazar. "How could Akiva have prevented these men from the other provinces from joining? It was not as if he knew any of their leaders to turn them away."

"He didn't have to," Eleazar's face became a deep crimson red with anger as he explained. "He still had his hooks into Simon. *'You cannot let any of those other people fight for God!'* he threatened Bar Kosba. They are nothing but heathens! *Dismiss them all, send them away and God will perform a miracle the likes the world has never seen.'* He fed him a lie and he swallowed it.

"You are certain that is what he said? No doubt at all." I thought about these words and all that came into view in my mind was seeing the fish hanging from a hook set by the fox. Here was the miracle of fish coming onto dry land and surviving. Abandon any military strategy that made sense, dismiss the offer of reinforcements from the other neighboring nations, and accept on faith a miracle will happen. Oh Akiva, what have you done?

"As certain as I am that both Aelianus and Thyrsis returned to me with some of their men with tears in their eyes and a hole in their hearts. Simon dismissed them because Akiva promised him this great miracle. For years they fought side by side, as friends, as brothers, as family, and to be told to leave like that, because they were heathens, unclean, and God would not grant victory as long as they were present in the city, at a time when they knew he needed them desperately, tore their souls to shreds. Dismissing them in his hour of need was the worst thing he ever could have done to his brothers-in-arms. Even now they still mourn. Not so much for their brother Simon but for themselves because part of them died that day as well. They feel they should have refused to leave. They know they should have defied his order, bore the consequences and fought on with their comrades. They regret that they never removed Akiva's lying tongue from his mouth putting an end once and for all to his influence over Simon."

This was all too hard for me to take in at once. I knew that if I was in shock, I could just imagine what everyone else was thinking. "Give me a moment here to collect my thoughts." I stood motionless. "So, let me see if I understand this correctly. Tens of thousands of troops from these other nations are willing to come to Bar Kochba's rescue and destroy the last of Rome's legions but because they weren't Jews, and trust me I had enough of that nonsense in an earlier testimony from Ben Abuyah, they were turned away."

"That is correct," Eleazar nodded his affirmation.

"And anyone that wasn't Jewish within the city was told to leave as well."

Once again he nodded in agreement while glaring at Akiva.

"And all this happened for no other reason than Akiva foretold that if these others fought for Simon, he would lose the battle, but if he refused their assistane then God would perform some great miracle and we would prevail."

"That is what my boys told me when they returned. As upset as they were, they had no reason to lie. Believe me when I say, they are still torturing themselves for having left his side. They told me that they tried to talk sense into Simon but he wouldn't listen. Akiva had affected his mind to such a degree that he actually believed there would be a miracle."

"This from the same man that had repeatedly told him that God was deserting him over and over again because he was a blasphemer." I kept shaking my head. "How could Simon believe anything Akiva had to say to him?"

"Remember, it was Akiva that declared him to be the Messiah. Akiva was the one that guaranteed his early successes. It is Akiva that claims he can communicate directly with God, Almighty, that he is blessed by God. Everyone in our land knows Akiva is considered to be one of the greatest of all the Sages, or so they say. By this time Simon had become a true believer and Akiva was his Master. The question had changed by this time for Simon and was now, how could he ever doubt anything Akiva would say. The answer is, 'he couldn't. Just as he had done to his students, Akiva was in control whether Simon liked it or not. And there was nothing that either Thyrsis or Aelianus could do about it."

I turned my back to Eleazar ben Hatti. There were tears in my eyes. Because Simon bar Kochba wanted so much to believe that Akiva was a servant of God, he failed to recognize that it was himself that was the true servant. He couldn't see his own greatness without viewing himself as being nothing more than a pale reflection of Akiva's own greatness. But now, worse of all, I was coming to realize for the first time that I may have been wrong and Simon Bar Kochba may have been the true Messiah and I and others like me, denied him the opportunity. It was possible that God was always standing with him, from the start of the war and he was given the opportunity to free Judea from suffering beneath the Roman yoke but he was never able to reach his full potential because he was restrained by a malevolent, petty, pathetic human being that had his own agenda.

I marched over towards Yehonatan's table and very calmly picked up Akiva's controversial book that had become a central focus of my court case. I flipped through the pages until I found one of the excerpts I had marked and in a voice that was already beginning to choke with my tears of regret, began to read several passages out loud. *'Samaritans are true converts from once fit priests that assimilated among them. Over the generations the Jews assimilated with these Samaritans, a people who have the status of Gentiles, and therefore it is only fit that we consider the descendants of those Jews that married Samaritans to have the status of being uncertain bastards. For, if a Gentile or a descendant of a Canaanite slave engages in sexual intercourse with a Jewish woman, then there should be no doubt that the offspring of that relationship are nothing more than bastards. In truth, the eating of Samaritan bread is worse than the eating of pork!* They are an unclean festering sore and since it is unknown how many over the years have intermingled within the Jewish population by laying down with Jewish women, who whored themselves to the men of this despised race, then we must cleanse the population by eliminating all those that are suspect." As I read those words aloud, I became consumed with rage. The accusation against the women of our nation, to label them as prostitutes and spread hate and division within our nation was too much for me to swallow and was and I let the anger consume my mind and my body. I could feel the weight of the book in my hand and without even realizing it I was racing uncontrollably towards Akiva. "You sentenced all those people to die because you could not accept those coming to their aid were better than you. You consider most of our people to be filth and scum. You dare to call our mother's whores!" I could hear the words ringing in my ears. I felt the blood splash against my face as I brought the book down upon his forehead. None of it seemed real. The wound on his scalp oozed profusely, then a red streak began to flow down to his ear. The splatter on my face felt warm and somehow comforting. My right arm kept rising and striking down repeatedly against every exposed part of Akiva's body. I could see him raising his arms, attempting to shield against the repeated blows but I was merely a spectator to a scene in which I had no involvement. "You are an arrogant, self-serving bastard!" a voice that wasn't mine screamed out those words, making use of my lips. "Not even fit to provide the bread of life. More generations of Jewish blood flow through their veins than the pathetic drops that you can ever shed." The book kept crashing down again and again. "You are not my servant Akiva ben Joseph. I reject you! You have failed my Children!" It wasn't me. Those weren't my words. The book smacked squarely across his jaw. In my ears, there was a ringing that sounded like the distant cries for help but the words were hollow, unnatural and distorted. All of this had become surreal; a pantomime in which I was playing a part. None of this was me!

"Captain, restrain you master before he does something he regrets," Yehonatan ben Matthias yelled, fearing I would beat Akiva to death.

I vaguely recall arms reaching out to grab my own, which restrained my hands. Someone wrapped their arms around my waist. I felt myself floating on air as I was lifted up and pulled from the room. I felt free, flying on angel's wings. Far off in the distance was a cacophony of sounds consisting of men's and women's voices surfacing from every direction. Indistinct, echoing, rising from a bottomless well, that tried to swallow me until I succumbed to the stark, cold emptiness that enveloped my being and I passed into a place beyond time and this earth. Into a world without Akiva.

Chapter Sixteen

Morning: 14th Day of Adar

"I don't understand what happened," Joseph admitted he was as confused as anyone else, as he spoke to his mother. "All I know is that I was wishing I could grab that book and strike a few blows of my own. This wave of emotion suddenly seized all of us. I swear to you mother, there was something else, some unworldly presence in that room with us. I believe it possessed all of us at that moment. That wasn't father any more, it was something else."

"I'm so afraid. I just pray your father will wake up soon," my wife was practically in tears. "I've never seen anyone so still and pale. So lifeless."

"Don't say that Momma," Joseph protested. Father will be fine. You will see."

"But it's true," Azariah confirmed. "He's hardly breathing. And when he does it's so shallow. This is something worse than death."

"What could possibly be worse?" I said as I sat up suddenly. "I'm fine and I'm hearing every word, so please stop talking about me a if I passed away."

"Eli!" Deborah screamed as she rushed to hug me and hold me tightly in her arms. "God has sent you back to us. Praise be to Yahvu."

"I didn't realize I was gone," I said, having little recollection of what happened. "What day is this?"

"It is Purim Father. You most definitely been somewhere else for almost twenty-four hours." The look of relief on Joseph's face told me that I must have had them all worried but I just couldn't remember how I even got home.

"You are a very lucky man, Excellency." There was a middle-aged man with a carefully cropped beard sitting beside my bed, informing me of something I already knew.

"And who are you?" I asked.

"Dear, this is the Doctor, Ishmael ben Hezekiah.   He has been tending to you ever since they brought you back from the synagogue."   My wife would not let go of my hand fearing that I would drift off again to wherever I had journeyed.

"As you may be aware," Ben Hezekiah began explaining, "Traumatic events are usually triggered by repressed memories that have been stamped into our memories but kept buried until they flood our minds like a tidal wave.   If that event exceeds the threshold of our ability for our minds to deal with the reality, then it will often have an adverse effect and our minds will shut down completely."

"Doctor, could you please just tell me what you think in plain Aramaic and not all this medical talk that I can barely understand."

"In other words, the shock of what you were dealing with overwhelmed your senses and the automatic reactions of your mind took over and for a period of time what you would refer to as your spirit was separated from your corporeal body."

"That is your medical opinion? That makes no sense at all. My spirit separated from my body?   Are you serious? You are suggesting that I had lost control of my own body and wasn't aware of what I was even doing," I regurgitated his explanation for what it was worth.

"Yes, that is what I am saying," he nodded.

"That's ridiculous.   I knew exactly what I was doing at the time."

"Then tell me," he urged me to continue, "What were you doing."

"I was…" I tried to remember but I could visualize anything regarding my last moments in the court.   "I think…no, that's not right…I was…I don't know.   What is wrong with me."

"Nothing is wrong with you," the doctor insisted.   "Your mind just wants to protect you from remembering the trauma."

"What trauma?" I had no idea what he was referring to.

"Father," Joseph rested his hand comfortingly upon my right shoulder, "I don't know how to tell you this, but you practically beat Rabbi Akiva unconscious with his own book."

"No...I couldn't have." But no sooner had he told me, the memories began to flood back in horrific details. "That wasn't me doing it," I tried to make him understand. "I can see it, but that wasn't me. I was watching it but that wasn't me." I held my face in the palm of my hands trying not to see it any longer.

"Our brains are a complex organ," the doctor attempted to explain it once again. "The function of our minds is to take in all the information gathered through our senses and determine if it is real or imagined."

"So you're saying I just imagined seeing my hand beating Akiva with his book?"

"No," the doctor answered, "That part is real."

I closed my arms firmly. "I can see myself doing it now and I think I was beating him to death," I responded. "That's more than just real, that's attempted murder. I tried to kill the man."

"In your mind perhaps you saw yourself beating him to death," the doctor explained, "But in reality you only hit him three of four times. He wasn't going to die."

"Impossible!" I reacted. "I can see the pictures in my head. There was blood everywhere!"

"It's true that there was some blood. It was only a little cut on his forehead and below his left eye," Ben Hezekiah advised. "Nothing serious at all."

I looked around at my wife and family and they were nodding in agreement with the doctor. "It is true, Father," Azariah confirmed. "Although I wish it had been more. A lot of people felt that way."

"It certainly felt like more," I smiled thinking about how it felt like it had been much more but everyone in the room took my smile as a sign of relief that I hadn't injured Akiva severely.

"Excellency, are you aware of your current surroundings now?" the doctor inquired.

"Is this a question regarding my health or is it just your curiosity, Doctor," I wanted to know.

"To be frank, it is both. I must let Yehonatan know about the status of your condition. I need to determine if you can continue with the trial tomorrow or whether it is necessary to confine you to your bed.

"To the first part of your question, I am fine and nothing is going to keep me away from taking part in the tribunal tomorrow. As to your second part, I think losing the last twenty-four hours of my life was long enough, so there's no way I'm remaining in bed."

"You must accept that you've had a very serious episode even if we don't exactly know what occurred. You were unaware of your episode but to everyone else here, they thought they had lost you and you had already passed on to the next world."

"Doctor, if you must know, it was like floating in a bath of warm water but there was no water. It was like the sun had burst into this blinding white ball that burnt my eyes but there were no lights. I was surrounded by voices but there was no one speaking. That's where I have been all this time, and I assure you, I have no intention on returning to that place."

"You say you heard voices? Do you recall what was said," he pushed for more information about this refuge in my mind that I had visited.

"Only that it kept repeating, 'Well done my son,' but little else," I mentioned.

"You think you may have been hearing your father's voice then, a visitation from beyond the grave," Ben Hezekiah surmised.

"Not at all," I dismissed his conclusion with a laugh and a backwards wave of my hand. "My father happens to be very much alive, and I'd like to keep him that way. And before you leave here and spread some ridiculous rumour that I was involved with necromancy and speaking with the dead, I have no idea whose voice it may have been and why it said that. All I can tell you is that it was reassuring. Now, ignoring this anomaly which I just told you, am I fit to go back to the courtroom tomorrow or not?"

"There is nothing I can find physically wrong with you," the Doctor concluded his examination and diagnosis.

"And as far as my mental state?"

"Nothing remarkable from what you've told me," he stated.

"And my passing out?"

"It is my opinion that it was probably just a stress related episode.   There was a lot of tension in that courtroom at that time," he commented.

"Then you are free to go, Doctor," I dismissed him.

Packing up the few items he brought to our room, the doctor rose and bowed to my wife and sons.   I waited until the door closed behind him.

"So, tell me now," I turned to my sons.   "What really happened in the court room. It all seemed so real.   I swear I saw myself killing Akiva with blow after blow. I had his blood all over me.   How is he still alive?"

"It was exactly as the doctor said," my sons confirmed.   "You hit Akiva a few times with his book and had several small cuts on his head. Nothing that serious."

"I don't know whether I should be happy, relieved or disappointed," I weighed the options and found the former better than the two prior responses.   "The scene is playing over and over in my mind. I had beaten him to a pulp and I couldn't stop myself from doing so."

"Personally, I'm a little disappointed Father," my youngest son expressed his opinion.   "After I heard Eleazar ben Hatti's testimony there was little doubt in my mind who betrayed them. If I had been you, I would have killed him right there and then with his own book."

"Then you must keep that opinion to yourself, Azariah. Don't ever let anyone hear you say that.   We have to defend the laws of our people, not make them. We cannot place ourselves above the law.   We cannot discuss this any further outside the courtroom.   I must apologize to Akiva tomorrow as I cannot permit any possibility of a mistrial."

"Akiva is already demanding one," Joseph let me know the latest news.

"Did he state upon what grounds…"

"Because he says you attacked him and tried to kill him inside a sanctuary, which violated our laws," Joseph filled in the blanks.

"Technically, the courtyard is not inside the sanctuary since it is a structure   extraneous to the synagogue but I can't say he's wrong.   What I did was a violation of our laws. In my mind I did kill him and I must bear that guilt. But if all he suffered was a few cuts, as you said, then as far as everyone saw it, I had no intention to kill him. I just have to prove to the court that if it was my intention, then he'd be dead. Since he isn't, I doubt Yehonatan will dismiss the case just because Akiva thinks he is in danger. After yesterday's testimony, there should be no thinking about being in danger because as a traitor his life is already over."

"You think there is enough testimony for a conviction?" Azariah questioned.

"Yes, I do," I admitted, "But we shouldn't be discussing the case. You're still both judges and have to make up your own minds as do the others. Until then, the trial is not over."

"Enough talk about Akiva, Dear," my darling Deborah had been sitting beside me on the bed, absorbing all that had been said. "I want to know about you. What really happened?" Knowing that normally I'm not a violent man, she felt it was time to ask the question that weighed heavily on her mind.

"It was bad enough when you have this convert, or son of a convert, we don't even know which, preaching to us who should be considered a Jew and who shouldn't because he considers someone to be nothing more than dirt beneath his feet, but when he reduced his argument down to a loaf of bread I couldn't tolerate his discrimination any longer."

"I don't understand why would talk of bread upset you so much Eli," Deborah sounded confused.

"Because bread is the essence of life! What do we pray every Sabbath? Thank you God for giving us the bread from the earth. Whether or not people accept the Samaritans as Jews, is a personal opinion that smacks of racism if they're denied their place among us. That is a sin in itself because God claimed right from the start of our nation that we were a mixed multitude. But ever you visit them you would see their baking of their bread adheres to the same laws of the kashruth from the Torah as ours do. The same bread of the earth that God has given unto them as well. To reject eating their bread is essentially rejected God. The same God that serves us both. It was a metaphor."

"A metaphor?"

"Yes," I knew that it was necessary to explain a difficult concept. "Akiva wasn't talking about bread. He was talking about the essence of life as it has been gifted to us from God. The bread of life given to Jew and Samaritan alike. Ask any Samaritan you meet about his faith and he will tell you that he considers his beliefs to even be stronger than our own because unlike us the Samaritans have had little exposure to the outside world. Essentially, they practice our religion as it was handed down a thousand years ago. We, those of us descended from the southern tribes are the ones that have progressed and changed over the years. As such, his bread, or his faith in God may fact even be purer than ours. We are bound therefore to break bread with them. Rejecting them is no different than rejecting God's gift. As such, in making his declaration, Akiva was saying he is above God. His words outweigh that of the Torah. He is the ultimate determination of what is deemed acceptable and what is not. I know that probably no one else understood what I did but in this case, if bread be the basis of life and faith, then Akiva considered himself to be the final arbitrator as to who is blessed. That is why his words infused me with such rage but as for what followed, I was the instrument of some other unworldly power. Whatever took possession of my limbs at that instant wanted Akiva to pay for all the wrong he has done to our people."

Deborah nestled her head into my chest and wrapped her arms about me. "Eli, even if it was your heart that filled with rage and inflicted those wounds upon Akiva, it does not matter to me. I never have doubt in your righteousness. I know you are a good man and if you feel the need to strike out it is as God's servant and for no other reason than to do his work. You do not need to feel ashamed for striking another man."

I could tell that my wife didn't completely believe my explanation that it wasn't truly me that had raised my hand against Akiva. She thought I was merely covering up for my personal guilt. It didn't really matter because the truth was, that knowing he had been struck sorely actually made me feel better. I admit, it was not a feeling I was accustomed to, but it was one that I could appreciate as having its time and place when necessary.

"I love you, Deborah. I guess I haven't told you that often enough, and certainly not much recently with all that is happening, but I want you to know that."

"Eli, you never have to remind me of that. I always know it in my heart. Look...you've embarrassed the boys," she said softly.

"I think it's time they get married and have their own beautiful wives to tell how they feel. Right boys?" which only embarrassed them more.

"Not going to happen," Azariah was defiant. "Joseph is still the oldest, so he has to be married first. Until then, I'm going to enjoy my freedom."

"Enjoy it why you can," I cautioned them both. "But when the time is right, your mother and I will tell you when your wedding day is going to be." I winked at my wife and she laughed. We had our own little secret that we hadn't shared with them.

"Any ideas as to what we should do now?" Joseph asked, swiftly changing the topic.

"I think now we should go out into the streets to celebrate the festival and see if there are any treats that the townspeople made for Purim. Let them see that I am restored to my health and tomorrow will be a trial day once again, just in case they had any doubts."

"I thought you told the Doctor you would stay inside and rest," Deborah challenged my suggestion.

I tilted my head nonchalantly. "No, I never said that. He advised it but I never agreed. So technically, I'm free to go out."

"I will go tell Jacob to summon the guards to escort us," Joseph advised.

"No." I stopped him. "No guards. We are the High Priests of Israel, whether the rabbis in this land wish to accept it or not, these are our people no matter where we reside. It is time that the people see that we have not abandoned them and even though the Temple no longer exists, we are still the living embodiment of that sanctuary, and we are here to help them. They have suffered much over these past few years. Let us see if we cannot provide them with at least one day of some hope and happiness by just walking among them. So everyone, into your best clothes and let us greet the people."

It didn't even take half an hour before we were all walking through the streets of the town and enjoying an afternoon in the spring sunshine. I had convinced Jacob to tell his men to remain at their camp outside the synagogue, but he refused to remain behind with them saying it was his duty to guard us and I would be shaming him by insisting otherwise. I couldn't convince him, so I eventually agreed but told him that he had to blend in which meant he couldn't carry any weapons. After negotiating for several minutes, I finally agreed that he could still carry a small knife but it had to remain concealed. He was satisfied and we were on our way.

The attitude of the people we met along the streets was surprising. I had not expected to find so many with their spirits uplifted, even though the festival of

Purim is intended to be a joyous and happy day. I think it was the town's children that impressed me the most when I saw them. Resilient and strong, they remained seemingly unscathed by the horror and devastation of the war. Many had lost parents and siblings, but despite the absence of those loved ones, they still retained the capacity to play and explore the world about them with never ending curiosity of unbridled youth, the way that children were meant to do. Rome may have defeated us but it did not destroy us. We were not broken. We would come back, and we would be strong once again. Of that I was certain. Seeing their happy faces restored my faith in our future.

I think it was seeing these children frolic and play that helped me to ignore some of the other things that Akiva had written in his book that I never mentioned to my family. Yes, his writing about the bread was what brought out my rage at that instant but there were other things he wrote. Many other things. Paragraph after paragraph that actually filled me with fear and trepidation Purely evil things such as his writing that he believed that he and his fellow Rabbis, meaning those that were subservient to him, *could control the omnipotent power of the Torah because they would find the key to mastering its contents. Once they found those keys it would give them the power to issue blessings and curses, create men and animals, have mastery over witchcraft, spells and incantations, and manufacture amulets that bestowed special powers. With that power they would commune directly with heaven.* More than ever, I was certain Akiva saw himself as God's equal and I knew it was up to me to stop him. Akiva saw the Torah not as a guidance to live a better life but as a tool to use to set himself and others on a pathway to perhaps becoming a god. A malevolent spirit disguised as a holy Sage. Nothing could be further from the truth. As much as I was reluctant to admit it, I had come to the realization of just how easy it was for the people to be led astray by a gifted snake with a smooth velvet-like tongue, lurking in the Garden of Eden.

Now it was up to all of us that remained after the war to protect this next generation from falling prey to the fox that watches the fish swimming in the river. In their innocence, they are no match for the wily fox, unless there are those of us to safeguard them and protect them from being preyed upon. As we sat down in the central square of the town, watching the children dance around us, I tilted my head towards the heavens and nodded, acknowledging my understanding of the present situation to the Master of the Universe and the understanding as to why He made me select this out of the way route through the countryside over two weeks ago, even though the Kings highway would have been faster and smoother for the wagons to traverse. These are the way of the almighty God. It had always been His intent to have me pass this way and resolve this unfinished business.

In a short time, around a dozen of the town's children had gathered around my feet, their parents and guardians watching tentatively a short distance away, still not confident enough to approach me directly because of what they presumed was my lofty and therefore distant status. But what parents don't do themselves, they often let their children proceed with in their stead. Children don't have an issue with status or caste. It is simply beyond their understanding. They don't see others as being anything other than equals. If only the world could always see itself through a child's eyes, so many of our problems would disappear, but sadly that is not the way it is. "Tell us a story. Is it true you served in the Temple? Are you as old as Methuselah? Are you a Maccabee?" they asked, or should I say demanded to know, because that is what the elders are supposed to do on Purim. Tell the children stories.

I had to laugh, because not only did I share in their enthusiasm, but for the first time in a long time I felt as if Judea did have a future. I asked them what in particular they would like to hear, knowing full well from their first questions that they didn't want to hear a story about Purim. I guess they already heard the tale of Esther too many times over the past few days to want to hear it again. At least not for another year.

"I know," I said clapping my hands, "How many here know the story about Nimrod?" I was in luck, very few raised their hands. "Good!", I expressed my satisfaction that we had agreed so quickly that this would be the story to tell. I waved my hands for the adults to come and sit with their children and stop standing at a distance which I felt was unnecessary. No sooner had the parents sat down, when it seemed like the entire town had poured into the square and were now sitting in a circle around myself and my family.

"Long ago, in the Kingdom of Babel, their lived a mighty man named Nimrod. He was the son of Cush, who was the son of Ham, who in turn was the son of Noah. We all know who Noah was, don't we," I asked. The children responded with a resounding 'YES'.

"On his twentieth birthday, his father gave him a very special gift. The animal skins that Adam and Eve had worn in the Garden of Eden when they first covered their nakedness. These clothes were magical because whoever wore them could turn invisible and they also endowed the wearer with great physical strength. Nimrod loved to hunt and because he could now turn invisible, none of his prey ever saw him stalking them and he gained a reputation of being a great hunter. And because he had great strength, he would challenge the largest and strongest of men in the kingdom to a wrestling match, but he would always win because of his magic clothing. The people saw his accomplishments and appointed him as King over their kingdom. But as king, he believed his kingdom was too small for his greatness and so he decided that he wanted to rule the world. So, he attacked all of the neighbouring kingdoms and before long he ruled the world, the first man that could ever made that claim.

As his power and fame grew, a very common thing happened as it usually does to all men that seek to conquer and rule harshly over others, so too did his wickedness grow. He told his subjects not to waste their time praying to God but to pray to him instead. He would say to them, "Did God give you victory over the other kingdoms?" to which they all would answer 'no'. "Did God hunt all the wild venison and cattlebeasts of the forests that fill your stomachs each night so your families do not know hunger?" to which they would say 'no'. "Did God raise the massive stones used to build your houses and your cities?" to which they would once again answer 'no'. "Remember, I gave you all those things," he reminded them. "I lifted those stones on my own back to build you your cities," he told them. "Why should you trust in some god you do not know, if I was the one that delivered to you all of these things?" And the people listened to his words and they turned away from God. They said, "Nimrod is a mighty hunter of men and beasts, let us pray to him,"

I looked at the children's expressions in reaction to my story and I could see that they were horrified by the thought that any man would consider himself an equal of our Lord.

"But still this was not sufficient for Nimrod as he wanted all men to pay him homage and divine honours, throughout the world. So, he built a tower made from a round rock and on it he placed a throne of cedar wood, upon which were stacked four more thrones. One of iron, a second of copper, another of silver and then gold. But on that golden throne lay a round precious stone that served as Nimrod's seat of power. He then sent out word to all nations that they must come to his city and pay tribute if they did not wish to be conquered. In response, men from all nations came and paid him divine honour, bowing before his throne. The gifts will pile like a mountain before him as he sat on his throne, but still Nimrod was not satisfied. "Where is God?" he asked. "Why has he not come to pay me tribute as I rightly deserve. "Why can I not see my equal? Is he so afraid that he hides from me? If so, then I will go see him." So, he told his people he needed to have his throne set higher and six hundred thousand men began building a tower that would extend into the heavens.

Can anyone imagine how tall that building would be?" I asked the children.

"Big," was the most common answer they shouted.

"Bigger," I responded, "It was huge. How many have seen the mountains?" Quite a few raised their hands. "Well, by comparison, the mountains were like step stools next to the tower that was built." Their jaws dropped on hearing how tall and massive Nimrod's tower was.

"Many years passed until the tower was nearing its final stage of completion. The tower was so high that it took a year for anyone to climb all the stairs to the top. From the dizzying height men would shoot arrows heavenward, seeing if when they fell back to their feet, if they were covered in blood. One day the arrows fell back and there was a red covering upon their tips. Seeing what they thought was blood they yelled out that they had slain God and they began to celebrate and revel in what they had done. As they drank well beyond their fill because they lost all reason, many fell from the great heights of the tower. Because when men drink too much the alcohol they become drunk and lose all sense of balance. So, a warning to you all when you grow up, not to drink too much wine or ale." I wagged my finger at the kids warning them about the evils of adulthood.

"Others began shooting more arrows into the sky to see if there were other gods or heavenly beings to be slain. Their arrows crashed back down to the earth, slaying those less fortunate that happened to be standing beneath the tower. God watched and said, "This Nimrod still thinks he is more than a man" and blew a cold wind across every province of the Kingdom so that all men caught a chill and lost their voice. But upon regaining their voices every man found himself speaking a different language so that those working on the tower could no longer communicate with each other. They became so frustrated that they began striking one another with their iron tools. Others abandoned their posts, going in search of anyone else that might speak the same language that they now spoke.

Does anyone know how many languages there are in the world?" I asked them.

"Ten" one of the children answered. "Maybe one hundred," said another.

"Well at that time," I told them, "God thought he had to make it impossible for them to ever strike with their weapons at the heavens again, so he made them speak several thousand languages. He did so purposely, so that it would take them months before they would ever find someone else that spoke the same language. Fortunately, we don't have as many languages now, but we still have a lot. I would think there is probably close to a hundred if I was to guess," I pointed to the child that gave me that answer, then gave her a thumbs up of approval

"As for Nimrod, the same wind that infected the people with different speech, blew a gnat up his nose. The gnat ascended into his brain and began to eat away at Nimrod's intelligence. For forty years it ate away at his brain until Nimrod became no smarter than the beasts he once hunted. Afterwards, he would run through the forests living no different from the other wild animals. One day, Esau, brother of Jacob was out hunting, as he was the greatest hunter of his time. There was a rustling in the forest, and he saw what looked like an animal moving between the trees. Remember, Nimrod still wore the animal skins from Adam and Eve that his father Cush had given him, so he would have looked like a wild animal to anyone hunting. Knocking an arrow to his bow, Esau drew back the bowstring and let the arrow fly. And thereby, the legend of Nimrod, the first man to rule over the world came to an end.

Would anyone like to tell me why this story is important today," I asked.

One brave boy in the crowd raised up his hand and I swirled my finger, signaling for him to speak. "Because we still have bad men today that want to rule the world," he answered.

"Yes, we do," I agreed with his insight. "And what else do we learn."

"In the end, God will punish them," he replied.

"Very good," I congratulated him. "When you study the Torah, you will see that our entire history is about others that have tried to rule the world, including us, but all of them have failed. For thousands of years, kingdoms have come and gone. Empires have lived and died on the same battlefields on which they were born. Kings and queens and even those that called themselves emperors are now nothing more than the dust of the earth. As we walk these roads that crisscross our land, we trample the enemies of our past under our feet as if they never existed. Assyrians, Egyptians, Babylonians, Greeks, their blood has all soaked into the soil that we walk upon every day. And that means that throughout all that history, there is one thing that has always remained constant, always existed and continues to survive throughout all the changes of history. Does any of you know what that constant is?"

One little girl was eager to answer, waving her hand frantically in the air.

"Yes," I pointed towards her.

Proudly she stood up and smiling gave her one word answer, "God!"

"Yes, that is true," I told her. "God is definitely never ending and will always be there until the end of time. His love for us is constant but do you know what else is always constant?" I asked her.

She shook her head.

"We are constant," I answered for her. "Just as Nimrod had special powers that were derived from the skins that Adam and Eve wore, so too do we, the Jewish people have similar powers that are derived from God. Our special power is we 'survive'. No matter what they do to us, we will survive, and we will still be here when all of our enemies and these other civilizations have faded away and have become nothing more than forgotten memories. And you know what else?"

They all shook their heads.

"You all have that special power too. Never forget it!"

Chapter Seventeen

Trial Day 6: 15th Day of Av, 3896

There was a nervous energy radiating from every corner of the courtyard this sixth morning of the tribunal. There was a sense that something significant was going to occur, a breakthrough revelation, based upon the testimony from two days ago. To many that were in attendance, it was becoming clear that Akiva had betrayed our nation and was possibly responsible for the deaths of hundreds of thousands. The onus was for me to provide an excessive burden of proof and regrettably, I had not been able to do so yet. I know that I still had left an element of doubt lingering in people's minds and I knew today would be my last opportunity to eliminate any uncertainty that may still persist. I also knew that there would be some people that thought I had come very close to convincing them, only to lose their support once I started beating the witness. All that did was to garner sympathy for a defendant, including Akiva, that he most definitely wasn't deserving of but no one wants to see a defenseless man attacked in a courthouse. Not to overlook the immediate impression of such absurd visuals presented by such an attack, which also weren't in my favour this morning once the guard led the defendant through the courtyard, as Akiva's right forehead sported a long, scabbed and ugly gash and the left side of his face was discolored and swollen. He could barely open his left eye. Joseph said I had hardly touched him, perhaps nothing more than a couple of blows, but from what I could see, I had beaten him soundly.

"I wish to remind everyone gathered here today," Yehonatan ben Matthias began speaking, "That we will be concluding this trial earlier today, as is our custom, several hours before the actual sunset so that all of you will have time to return home and prepare for the Sabbath. So gentlemen of the court, I would appreciate if you could conclude your statements and inquiries this morning as soon as possible, so that the afternoon can be used by the judges to deliberate their final decision."

"Your honour," Akiva didn't even wait for Yehonatan to tell us to return to our stations before pressing the Praetor for a dismissal. I knew it was coming. I would have done the same in his situation. "I would like a ruling on my request to have this case discharged from the courts. Surely the injuries I have sustained at the hands of the Prosecutor indicate there is a malignant prejudice that has infected the body of this court and I will not receive a fair judgment."

It was obvious that Yehonatan was expecting the motion as well as he hardly even batted an eye when Akiva spoke up. Anticipating the request, a response had obviously been prepared long in advance although he had never consulted me about it. He began by saying, "I will admit that the Prosecutor overstepped his authority at the time, but I know that he has regretted his actions and if the defendant is in want of an apology then I am certain that one will be provided."

"Praetor, this was not a simple minor insult as you are making it out to be. Take a good look at my face. This was a terrible and deadly assault using a dangerous weapon." The weapon assertion was met with a sprinkle of laughter by those that had witnessed the attack two days ago.

"Oh, no! It was a deadly double-edged book," someone shouted and the people in the gallery began to laugh.

Akiva ignored their tittering and persevered with his demand. He was not willing to let his request be overturned. "The only apology that would match the gravity of the crime performed by the Prosecutor would be a dismissal of this case. You know that to be true, Praetor!"

"Your request is denied, Rabbi Akiva ben Joseph," Yehonatan ruled, waving it away as casually as one shoos away a fly. "I will have the Prosecutor apologize and see to it that he makes some form of financial restitution for damages, but this case will continue. The scribe will duly make note of the denial of the request, please," he instructed the synagogue administrator. "It is the court's rationale is that there was reasonable provocation for the attack The Defendant's insistence that foreign troops could not enter the war eliminated any military chance of survival the defenders of Beithar may have had. If this is proven to have been deliberate, then the minor attack you suffered will pale compared to the consequences of being found guilty."

"Am I to be judged by God's desire not to have our army defiled by the presence of the unclean," Akiva fired back. "God was willing to perform miracles for us but only if we truly believed and Bar Kochba was no longer a believer.

"How could he remain a believer?" Yehonatan asked. "Your enforcement of the ban and threat to remove the Lord's divine protection may have directly influenced Bar Kochba's to react negatively and against common wisdom of warcraft."

I didn't have to say anything, It was as if Yehonatan was already presenting my case, but at this point of the trial, there was no need for any of the judges to remain impartial. They already were deciding the case.

"I would think the subsequent refusal of acceptance of aid offered by various nations outside Judea, may have been a direct result of your influence," Yehonatan continued. "It is such a highly charged matter, that if it were true, then the reaction from the Prosecutor may have been nothing more than a spontaneous outburst activated through high emotional stress of losing loved ones, that was shared by many of us in this courtroom. Although it does not make the Prosecutor's actions defensible, it does provide us with reason to see that it does not happen again. Violence in the court is not to be tolerated and I will repeat an apology with restitution from the Prosecutor will be offered to you."

Praetor Yehonatan's coal black eyes pierced though my outer garments and burrowed deeply into my flesh as he awaited my apology. It was clear that I didn't have a choice in the matter either. My behaviour had been irreprehensible, and an apology was in order. But having assessed my adversary this past week I was expecting Akiva's combination of foolish pride and general arrogance to make him refuse any offer of apology as being too little and too late. I was right on both accounts.

"Bah!" Akiva made a deliberate and exaggerated motion with his hands as if he was brushing dirt from his sleeves. "Keep your apology. It would be meaningless anyway."

"Then Gentlemen, swear your oaths to God and then let us get back to our court proceedings. As I have heard from the Defendant that he has no further request to present witnesses, it behooves the Prosecution to begin their final presentations and evidence. Can you please call your remaining witness to the chair."

"But Praetor," I pleaded, "My final witness has not arrived as yet and it is most essential that they have the opportunity to speak at this hearing. This early session was intended to be the Defendant's time to call witnesses. There was no warning that we were changing the timetable. Hence, I will need the Court to accept that my witness's appearance before the court will be delayed."

"Elioneai, we were all aware of the time frame for this trial. In fact, you were the one that set this time frame at the onset. But we also agreed that should either the Defense or the Prosecution not use their allotted time, then we would see to it there were no unnecessary delays in the proceedings. I don't have the authority to extend this trial into perpetuity so that your final witness may or may not present themselves. At best, I will give you a reasonable time for them to arrive but there must be a point during the day at which time I will say it has been long enough and you must present your concluding statements even if it means you do so without your final witness. Is that understood? Have I made myself clear?"

"Perfectly Praetor." I had no other choice but to agree. "May I ask what might constitute a reasonable time?"

"Before the noon break. That shall be considered reasonable. Now, if I can have both of you swear your oaths to our Lord, we will begin."

Once again it was time for us to swear our oaths to God to keep the truth and pass no false testimony from our lips. I knew of my sincerity but how was it possible for Akiva to so easily recite these words when I knew for a fact he was concealing the truth. I repeated the words from the oath automatically, but in my mind, all I could think of was how I would be able to stall this trial as long as possible until my witness arrived. I looked over at Akiva and thought I saw a subtle smile buried beneath his heavy beard. Perhaps he could sense my desperation or knew something I didn't.

He wore the marks from the assault like a badge of honour, knowing that thus far the case against him had only proven him to be an immoral human being, at worst a man with despicable racist tendencies, and a hopeless womanizer at best, but certainly not a traitor, even if he was the only man that had easy access to all of Bar Kochba's fortresses, I still he had not proven that he used that access to gain knowledge of the tunnels and inform the Romans. The only punishment he would receive would be a decline of respect from the people, a slap on the wrist from the tribunal, and perhaps a stripping of his recognition as Sage by the Council, but absolutely nothing in regards to the crimes I knew deep down in my soul that he had committed during this war. I closed my eyes and said a silent prayer. 'God if there was ever a time I was in need of your help more, I don't remember it. Please aid your humble servant, Son of Abraham, Son of Isaac, and Son of Jacob. Son of Aaron and son of Zadok. I pray you give me the insight and strength to deal with this matter strategically and speed my witness on their way."

"Before beginning, I would like to remind both parties that it is the Defendant's right and entitlement to present the final words and counter any accusations made by the prosecution. That being the case, as soon as the prosecution closes his presentation, it will be the Defendant that has last word and there will be no further rebuttal. I now declare this court is back in session."

In my mind all I could hear were the words 'stall, stall, stall' being repeated over and over again. My witness had been granted until noon to arrive, but that meant I couldn't close my arguments any time before their arrival or else it would become the Defendant's time and I would forfeit the opportunity to put my witness in the chair. The problem was that I had run out of things to say to fill the few hours if necessary. But then I remembered that Akiva had a lot more to say in his book that I had not mentioned as yet and much of it had to do with my final witness. It was time to use his own stories and make it last as long as I could until my witness arrived.

"Praetor, at this time I would like to recite a passage from that book in front of you that we all recognize by now has been filled with so many insights and comments by the Defendant that it is difficult to know exactly where to start and which ones need repeating. But there is one that springs readily to mind that is practically screaming out to me to be read to those assembled here. Permit me to access the book to the appropriate page so that you can confirm that what I am about to tell the court is a true rendition of what is written and that I am not fabricating any part of it through the addition of my own words." Walking over to the Praetor's table I picked up the book and as I did, I noticed the cover stained with dried blood which made me shudder. Opening the book to the right page, I pointed to the paragraph for Yehonatan to follow along as it dictated it from memory.

"I need everyone to picture this scene in their mind so they can appreciate what I'm about to say. *There are these two Rabbis sitting in the square of the Lower City of Jerusalem. One of them is the defendant, Rabbi Akiva and according to what he wrote, not being very specific about names, the other is Rabbi Simeon.* I'm assuming he is referring to Rabbi Simeon ben Gamaliel the Younger, the Nasi. At the time, I'm also assuming Rabbi Simeon is much younger, perhaps in his twenties, because the two of them are not discussing some passage in the Torah but instead are practicing the age old art of girl watching.   As we are well aware, Rabbi Akiva will never be too old to give up that art, especially as seen with the Queen of Ethiopia, but Rabbi Simeon was married at a young age and I have to assume this was before his marriage, or else he would have been in big trouble. "

The comment was met with a short outburst of laughter but nothing in comparison to the laughs that were received earlier in the week.   It was obvious the crowd had grown somewhat insensitive to the constant accusations against Akiva regarding his sexual proclivity.

"Along comes this extremely beautiful woman with her reddish hair, strolling through the lower city. Her pale white skin, her beauteous features and extremely curvaceous body do not go unnoticed.   She is dressed in her best finery, jewels adorn every part of her body and it is most obvious that she was a patrician of Rome. A very wealthy Patrician lady.   *They recognized her immediately as the wife of the Procurator, the Lady Rufina. Upon seeing her magnificent beauty, Rabbi Akiva spat on the ground, began to cry and then laughed out loud. Rabbi Simeon was confused by this behaviour and asked Akiva for an explanation.   Akiva told him, 'I spat because from such a simple drop, this beautiful woman was born from a drop of semen exchanged during the sexual act.   I cried because how cruel that such beauty was wasted on one not of our people but also because eventually, she will be buried in the ground and the worms will consume her flesh and her beauty will be wasted.   But I laughed because I knew at some point I would have the pleasure of such a beauty as my wife.'*   Did I summarize his statements correctly Praetor?"

Yehonatan nodded.   "Yes, that is exactly what Akiva has written."   I think it was the fact that Akiva made the final comment regarding making her his wife that shocked everyone that had heard his words.   The sheer audacity that he would even suggest he wanted to have a physical relationship with the beautiful wife of Procurator Tinneus Rufus, probably the most despised man in all of Judea, astounded them.   Truthfully, that would have met the very definition of sleeping with the enemy in a traitorous relationship.   Compounding their astonishment was the knowledge that Akiva had been a frequent guest at the Governor's palace in Caesarea.   Some of their favourite stories as told by his students had been the supposed debates between Tinneus Rufus and Rabbi Akiva over a variety of Jewish customs, in which Akiva always won and Rufus had to swallow the distaste of his defeat. Perhaps now the prize for winning those debates was a little more understandable if Akiva was being rewarded with something more personal than the Procurator's continual contempt and animosity. Was there an actual secret relationship?

"These are your words, are they not Akiva?"

"We have been over this several times Elioneai, I don't know why you keep wasting this court's time. Yes, I am a lecherous old man if that is what you are trying to prove to your followers. Where is my sin? I admire the female sex and I believe them to be one of God's greatest creations. Do you think after God created Eve in the Garden of Eden that he said to Adam, don't pay her any attention. Of course not! Some of my colleagues on the Council may wish to believe that sexual intercourse is in some way a perverse and sinful act but I prefer to believe that it is one of the greatest pleasures God has granted us. When else can we fulfil one of His commandments to go forth and multiply and at the same time receive such personal satisfaction? The reward is instantaneous and for that reason I believe it was the Lord's intention that we seek it whenever and wherever possible. God did not forbid us from having more than one wife and I believe it is because he understood a man's cravings. So, if you wish to believe I have sinned because I openly expressed those cravings, then I care not what you think, only what the Lord believes matters and He does not care at all."

Strangely, there seemed to be a lot of whispering and muttering in agreement coming from the people, particularly the men gathered in the courtyard.

"But I will remind everyone," I interrupted Akiva's dissertation, "That at some time after this event that you wrote about in your book, you also introduced into the Sanhedrin a new law that said the following; *any man could immediately divorce his wife without just cause, other than the fact that he has seen someone more beautiful that he wishes to marry.* Is that not also true?"

"And the Council voted on it and approved it, so it is obvious that it is the will of God and I only stated that which most men desired."

"Therefore, am I correct in saying that you feel justified in passing such a law?" There was a purpose to this line of questioning even though it may not have been obvious to most, at first.

"If the Council members thought this was not as God wished it to be then they would have voted it down," he suggested. "We have been over all of this Praetor, why should we have to repeat this again? The prosecution has proven its point that I am a lover of women. If that is a crime, then I am guilty."

"I must agree, Elioneai. It is not a crime for a man to admit he is a womanizer, I think you will be surprised to find that Akiva is not alone," Yehonatan accepted Akiva's objection. "Move on to something different Elioneai as the court does not need to go over this again and again."

"Then let me be more specific. You know the Lady Cornelia Metalla Rufina, do you not?" I asked.

"Your Honour," Akiva objected once again, "How is this question moving on to something different? It is just a continuation of what was asked before."

"Praetor, please if I may be indulged in this matter. We have not discussed the specifics of the relationship with the Procurator's wife at any time during this trial. We have flouted it being nothing more than a fanciful story, but we have only touched on the interest the Defendant may have had with her, but I believe it is their actual relationship which is crucial to deciding the outcome of this trial."

Yehonatan looked very suspiciously at me as if he was judging whether or not to censor my comments any further. "You actually believe that you have proof of an actual relationship?" It was evident that the Praetor didn't believe me.

"Your Honour!" Akiva couldn't withhold himself any longer. "If the Prosecutor is only interested in knowing if I had sex with the wife of the Governor, then let me make that clear now. The answer is no! I will state that unequivocally now so we can be done with this foolishness once and for all."

"You are certain you wish that to be your final statement on the matter and written into the transcript of this trial?" I challenged him.

"As I said, the answer is No!" Akiva was adamant.

"Let the court record show that the defendant has stated that he has never engaged in any sexual act with Lady Cornelia Metella Rufina, wife of the Governor," Yehonatan proclaimed. "You now have it recorded, Elioneai. But you better be clear on what this is all about?" Yehonatan was losing his patience.

"You Honour, as mentioned, I beg the Court's indulgence. We are focused, are we not, on whether or not there is irrefutable evidence of a crime of treason that can be laid upon the Defendant. Is that not so?"

Yehonatan nodded his head, but he was confounded by my question. "That is the original purpose for holding this entire tribunal," he agreed. "The original accusation made was that Akiva had betrayed our people. This was not about some imagined affair he may have head and I must admit the court is losing its patience with this line of questioning."

"What if the two conditions were one and the same? As such, it would be a terrible, heinous crime if it should be proven to be true. That the pursuit of sex led to a man betraying his own people. It exceeds our wildest imaginations to even conceive of such a justification that a man would do such a thing in the name of lust. But treason, like any other crime, must have a motive. A motive requires the guilty party to want something they sorely desire, so much so that they will do the unthinkable. Usually, it is something they don't already have in their possession, and they are desperate to obtain it at any cost. The inconceivable reward that drives them to proceed with the crime until the abominable act is completed."

The Praetor shook his head in disbelief. "Surely you are not suggesting that Akiva desired the Procurator's wife and for that reason he betrayed an entire nation? I am sorry, but I cannot believe such speculation and I will suggest to you, Elioneai, that such an inference is ridiculous, and the Court is not amused by this waste of time."

"Is it really that ridiculous?" I asked the Court. "Do we not think a woman can drive a man to behave in a manner that is completely unnatural to his normal self? Show me a man that has not bent his self over backwards in order to please a woman!"

"But to commit treason, Elioneai, that is on an entirely different scale," Yehonatan objected. "Really? You wish to pursue this argument?" Yehonatan was prepared to shut down any further discussion of the matter.

"If I must, then I will justify it through our own Tanach and the stories given to us by the Almighty. Was Samson's desire for Delilah so ridiculous that he would not betray his oath to God? Clearly, it was not! By doing so, he betrayed his duty and obligations as a judge of Israel. Was King David's desire for Bathsheba so ridiculous that he would not commit the ultimate sin of having his loyal and trusted general murdered so he could take his wife and thereby break two commandments of both murder and being covetous at the same time? We know the answer; of course not! Was Solomon's desire for the Queen of Sheba to lay with him in his matrimonial bed so ridiculous that he did not raid the treasury of the Holy Temple to shower her with irreplaceable relics to take back with her to Ethiopia along with the son of their relationship? Again, we know this to be true. Was Ahab's desire for Jezebel so ridiculous that he would sacrifice both his throne and kingdom in order to excuse all the evil that she did? Shall I keep on going, your Honour or do you still believe the betrayal of an entire nation for a woman is impossible?"

"Granted, you have made a point, Elioneai, but unless you can provide some proof, then this is nothing but hearsay," Yehonatan cautioned. "You may continue this line of questioning a little longer but do not take too much time before revealing the truth or I will shut it down!"

"Let me rephrase my last statement so that it is abundantly clear," I addressed Akiva. "You are willing to stand by your statement that you have not engaged in any sexual activities with the wife of the Procurator Tinneus Rufus and you swear so before God, that he may strike you down if you should be found to be lying."

"I told you already, it never happened. I don't deny it may have been wishful thinking on my part but that is not a sin." Crossing his arms over his chest it was obvious Akiva had nothing further to say on that matter.

"It is true that you were seen and known to spend a lot of time with the Lady Rufina, is it not?"

"Everyone knows that she was coming to me to learn about Judaism. She had a passion for our culture and wanted to understand us better. That is not a secret and I never made it out to be one," Akiva defended all the times he had been seen with the Governor's wife.

"I agree with the fact that you did the exact opposite in that regard," I commented. "Not only did you not keep it secret, you made certain that everyone was aware of her visitations because it had become so obvious that she was visiting you. In fact, these visitations were a fairly regular occurrence and transpired over a number of years, including during the war years. Is that correct?"

"As I said, she was very passionate in her learning. Not

even this war provided a sufficient reason to prevent her from pursuing her studies."

"Why didn't you just give her the books from Flavius Josephus?" I asked. "A copy of his **Antiquity of the Jews** would have told her everything she needed to know, and you wouldn't have needed to see her so regularly or privately for that matter. That is what a smart man would have done. I suspect that her interests went beyond history. I think most would agree. I doubt that you could have added any more to that fine work that Josephus wrote, so perhaps there was more to her studies that you haven't mentioned or disclosed?"

"But in her thirst for knowledge, she also wanted to learn about the Torah and Tanach," he explained. "Those are issues not explained in any detail by Josephus. They required my explanations."

"An interesting point," I emphasized. "Aren't those the two areas that you and your colleagues in the Council *forbade to be taught to the female offspring of our own people.* That was the Council's decree, was it not? That seems a little unfair, don't you think?" You declared that it was alright for you to teach a Gentile woman, as stated in your own words to Rabbi Simeon that in time you would eventually convert and make her your wife, the religious insights to our heritage, yet you are not willing to provide that same education to a Jewish woman. You went so far as to have it classified as a sin to do so. Make me understand. How do you justify it for the Lady Rufina."

Clearing his throat, Akiva prepared to defend his position. "You must understand that when a Gentile asks to learn about the Torah, then that is a very special situation that deserves special consideration. God considers our efforts for the conversion of a Gentile to our religion to be a great blessing."

"And you consider that to mean either a Gentile man or woman. No difference! And as such, you would say that a non-Jewish woman is far more deserving of recognition and respect than a Jewish woman. Does that summarize exactly what you are saying or did I hear you wrong?" I made certain that everyone in the gallery could hear my question.

Akiva suddenly found himself having to defend his opinion on Jewish and Gentile women, which as anyone knows is a hopeless situation once any man from within our community has been caught by his wife looking at one of the many beautiful heathen girls that live among us.

"It was not that simple. There were other factors. This was not any Gentile woman. This was the wife of the Procurator," he tried to use her title as a defensive justification for his unacceptable actions and in order to explain why she was given this exceptional treatment. "You cannot refuse the request of a woman in her position. To do so would invite death. I could not, nor would I, and I believe most will understand my reluctance to die," he explained.

Considering how much the people of Judea hated and despised Procurator Tinneus Rufus, Akiva's decision to personally educate her in our religion was hardly a wise choice. I think most would have taken the option of a swift death.

"I could not refuse her," he continued. "For the Lady Rufina to make such a request could only mean that she was being guided by the hand of God! I was doing God's work," he boasted.

Blaming God for his obviously bad decision to provide her education wasn't well received by the people. "Akiva Goi Ahuva, Akiva Goi Ahuva," they started chanting repeatedly as an insult. It certainly summed up their perspective that Akiva was a Gentile Lover. Yehonatan was desperately trying to regain control over the gallery but his voice had weakened over the course of the trial and he was easily drowned out by their chant.

"How dare you accuse me of such a thing," Akiva shouted but to no avail.

"The Ger loves a Goi," I made certain my voice was heard above that of the people. "What else would you expect from a man that Gamaliel suspected wasn't even a Jew! Who in his heart was never a Jew. How many times did he meet with the Lady Rufina? Ten, twenty, perhaps even a hundred times. Even during the four years of warfare, she was seen frequently visiting Akiva in Lydda and even here in B'nai Brak from what I've been told by reliable sources. Some of you even recall seeing her at Bar Kochba's encampments so she could continue her special lessons from Rabbi Akiva. I don't know about you, but that surely isn't what I would expect from a casual acquaintance?"

Finally, I had achieved the goal I was longing for since he trial began. I had set a fire in the hearts of the people. It was as my wife had advised me. Focus on his two obvious weaknesses. His love for money and for women. More importantly, tie both of them together, she suggested. Between their intense hatred for the Procurator Tinneus Rufus and this new knowledge that the sage had been unusually close to Rufus's wife, there could be no doubt left in their minds that something other than lessons in Judaism were behind these visits. But I couldn't stop yet. It was essential that I kept stoking the fire.

"It is said that there must always be an intense motive for a man to betray his own people. I will say to all of you, if a crime of passion is not intense and reason enough to commit treason, then I don't know what else will be more of a motive. I don't know about Akiva being a Gentile lover in general, but I will tell you that I believe he was in love with this woman and would have done anything for her! Even betray his own people. Perhaps he doesn't even think of us as being his people as I see no evidence that he does. And as we know, Akiva writes about his own guilt and includes it in this book in an effort to justify his actions. It is his way of seeking absolution. The inclusion of this story in his book is his way of confessing to his crime of loving her! And when I reviewed his writing, I don't think it was merely wishful thinking of his that she would become his wife. I believe he has already lain with her as if she already was his wife!"

"That is a lie," Akiva shot out of his chair and began screaming. "Prove it!" he shouted. "Or else be condemned by your own lies to this court," he demanded. Those who were still fervent supporters of their beloved Rabbi began the chant, "Prove it, prove it," and would not let up.

"I ignored their chants. "Your sons, your husbands, your fathers and your nation all died because Akiva sacrificed them willingly for a beautiful Roman woman and his own words, written down by his own hand, in his own book are the only way he knew of confessing his crime. That should be proof enough to anyone that reads it. It is his personal confession and obviously his blatant attempt to ask for the Lord's forgiveness without exposing the degree of this crime to the public. His days of hiding his sins are over. What he once had buried, through the divine light that descends from the heavens, Almighty God, in His pursuit of justice, has provided me the insight to raise the sinner's crimes into that light. He swore here before God that it did not have sexual relations with that woman, and I say that is a lie! He swore in vain in God's name and I say that is punishable by death!"

"Prove it, prove it," the chorus from his supporters intensified in volume.

"Elioneai, I warned you not to go too far in making statements you cannot prove," Yehonatan ben Matthias cautioned me. "You have no proof. These statements are inadmissible and the court is bound to admonish you."

I looked to the back of the room but there was still no sign of my Captain Jacob. "By the end of this day Praetor, you will have your proof. That I swear by God above. You will have your proof!"

Yehonatan was not satisfied by my answer but it was definitely enough to pour naphtha on to the fire, as the crowd that accepted my accusations against Rabbi Akiva as being the truth, took up a chant of 'Death to the Adulterer. Death to the Roman lover!'. There may have only been a hundred and fifty people crowded within the peristyle today but the amount of noise they could generate shook the heavens. It was obvious, should I have agitated any further, the rope barrier that divided the gallery from the courtroom area was not going to hold them back. I could see from the concerned expression on Yehonatan's face that he was praying that I could keep the people under control after what I had started. My words had the desired effect, but I didn't know if I could restrain the reaction. Many that had once loved and idolized Akiva, were now filled with intense resentment because of his relationship with the Procurator's wife. It was as if he had cheated on them personally. Not even his supporters would challenge this mob. Yehonatan clasped his hands together as if in prayer, shaking them nervously towards me, practically begging that I do something quickly to restore calm to the courtroom.

"Listen to me! Listen to me, everyone! We are not like that," I shouted above the din of their noise. "From the time of Moses, we have been a people of laws. And if one of us has broken the law then he will be held accountable according to those same laws we revere. Never forget that we are the Children of God, his beloved Israel, and as his Chosen People we will not behave in the same manner that the Gentiles do. Until such time this man is proven guilty beyond a shadow of a doubt, we will not lay a hand upon him and we will not undertake any sentencing where there is a lack of evidence to prove our case undeniably."

"See! See! Listen to what Elioneai, your false High Priest has said," Akiva shouted. "There is no proof! The Prosecutor has lied to you."

I ignored his claims and continued, "Because that is who we are. That is who God has made us to be, and we will do nothing that casts a shadow upon our loyalty to the Law. Until such time that I have a witness stand in this courtroom who can point a finger at the defendant and declare that they have witnessed him laying with the wife of the Procurator, in a sexually provocative position, then even I who sincerely believe him to be guilty of such a crime, will have no other choice but to declare him innocent of such a crime. But know this, I would not say these words and swear my oath unless I believed I can deliver such a witness and I ask only that you be patient and bear with me. You will have your proof!"

Upon saying that last line, the court again erupted into a chant against Akiva, but we were all relieved to see that it had lost its intensity and the risk of the mob taking control had been reduced sharply.

"Until then, I will not let the law be abused by anyone, even if they feel vindicated in their actions. We are Jews, and no matter what the truth may be, we will always behave as Jews. We all share a mission to uncover the truth. Emet, is all that we seek. A simple word, but one formed from the first, the middle and the last letters of our alphabet because God tells us that truth must be the same from every direction that we look at it, otherwise it cannot be called the 'truth'. These judges that are sitting here will be the final arbiters of that truth and they will be the ones that decide upon the sentencing. Not you! Not me! And certainly not as a result of any expression of anger that any of us may harbour. I told you all that I will provide you with the truth. I will now take another oath. If I fail to provide that proof, then I place myself into the hands of your judgment. My life is yours to decide!"

My willingness to let my fate be decided should I fail to prove my case was a shock to most. They had not expected it but it was enough to convince most that I must have the proof I talked about. It was a gambit, but it had proven itself to be effective. The intensity in the courtyard lowered significantly and a reasonable level of calm had been restored. I was as relieved as anyone else on our side of the rope that I was able to restore an element of calm. Perhaps Akiva most of all who had turned as white as a ghost at the height of the crowd's vehement display. He was slumped in his chair, suddenly looking far older than when he arrived at the courtroom this morning. I suspect for a moment, his life had flashed before his eyes.

"This was a despicable and disreputable display by Elioneai ben Yosef," he complained to the Praetor, Yehonatan ben Matthias, as soon as he caught his breath and some colour finally returned to his face, even if he still looked quite pale. Sitting upright, he raised his prior concerns as I had expected. "I believe all the judges will certainly agree that it was completely unacceptable that the prosecution fueled the crowd with his own hatred, prompting them to seek vengeance even when there was no provable crime. I have already given my solemn word to this court that Lady Rufina and I have never engaged in any illicit behaviour. If the prosecution has any evidence to prove differently then I insist that he presents it now and not later as he suggests. Otherwise, he must apologize to this Court and I expect the Court to declare this entire affair to be a mistrial based on the presentation of his false and unsupported evidence. I have the right to be protected from slander and threats. That is within our laws. This court has proven itself incapable of protecting me and securing my personal safety. As such, I demand that the Praetor addresses my legitimate concerns immediately and holds the Prosecutor accountable! He has offered his life to be judged by those present in this court and I expect him to fulfill that promise."

Yehonatan acknowledged that Akiva had raised a sound and reasonable motion for dismissal of the court case because of the Prosecutor extending his rhetoric beyond the facts of the case and possibly delving into the realm of fiction, creating a situation where the defendant did not feel safe any longer. He had no other choice but to present it, because for all intent and purpose, it was true. "What have you to say regarding this charge," Praetor Yehonatan asked me pointedly.

"First, let me apologize to the court if they feel I had placed anyone's life in danger. It certainly wasn't my intention and I believe that is the only grounds for a dismissal. The defendant must prove it was my intent and I think the fact that I was able to restore the calm and quiet of the people shows that it was never my intent but only a result of evidence coming forward in this trial."

"Evidence without proof is not evidence at all," Yehonatan corrected me. "His demand that you present your evidence immediately is not unreasonable. Do you or do you not have such evidence?"

"I have the evidence and I have sworn this to be true before God. I asked those in the gallery to bear with me and be patient as I wait for it to arrive. I ask the same indulgence from the Court as well." I quickly looked to the back of the room but still no sign of Jacob.

"What are we waiting for," Yehonatan sounded angry at my delaying tactic.

"If the Court can please remain patient, Praetor. It will be my next witness that provides such proof. If that witness says that there is no evidence of such a liaison, then I promise you that in front of this Court, I will admit to my guilt of slander and defamation. I will also admit to my guilt of swearing an oath in God's name in vain. I will place myself in the hands of the people and my life will be forfeit. I will not shy away from this promise."

"Hah," Akiva scorned my comments. "What possible witness could you have that would know anything about a non-existent relationship with the Lady Rufina? Their words will be a lie as well. There is no one with such knowledge, and if someone should show claiming otherwise, then I will accuse them of being a liar too. Your Honour, this is obviously a poorly planned charade by the prosecution, and I wish to save the Court the embarrassment of indulging in this deception any longer."

"Let the Court worry about whether or not it embarrasses itself," Yehonatan admonished Akiva. "All I need from you is whether you agree to wait for this final witness Akiva?"

"Let Elioneai call whomever he wants," Akiva sounded confident. "It makes no difference. They know nothing and I tell you all now that it is only a waste of time. It's all a poorly designed ruse on the prosecution's part. I will wait until the closing of the afternoon session as we agreed to do."

"Therefore, I declare this morning session will continue until a half hour past the midday position of the sun and if the prosecution's witness has not arrived by that time, then Elioneai ben Yosef, you will be held accountable for making false statements to this court," Yehonatan hammered his decision on the table. "After that time both the prosecution and the defendant will present their summations at the start of the afternoon session. Are we clear on this?"

We all agreed as Yehonatan laid out the timeline for the rest of the day

"If we are clear, then let it be also agreed that we are an hour away from the half hour past midday. Your time is running out quickly Elioneai. If I were you, I would use that time wisely and retrieve your final witness," Yehonatan advised.

Chapter Eighteen

The Trial; Midday Day 6

"It is pointless to wait any longer, Elioneai," Yehonatan advised. "The people are already becoming restless to leave so that they can eat their noon meal. If we don't let them leave now, It will delay the afternoon session and I'm afraid we won't be able to conclude the trial as scheduled. I believe it is time to make your apologies to the Defendant and throw your-self at the mercy of this Court for obvious statements where you slandered Akiva. If you can't continue at this time with your final witness, then I will clear this Court for the noon day meal and most likely declare a mistrial when we return in the afteroon."

"So, my choice is to not even wait until the half hour past noon as we have agreed, and instead declare my guilt to the Court that I have perjured my testimony and maligned the witness. Or I can say nothing and you will still rule this case to be a mistrial.   That's what you are saying?"

"You leave me with no other choice," Yehonatan replied. "By your own statement you said you would throw yourself at the mercy of the people in this court if you could not prove your statements."

"You do have another choice," I argued.   "Just give me a few more minutes until the half hour after midday, Praetor, I am begging you.   I know for a fact that my witness is coming.   They gave me their word. They promised. Just a matter of being a little more patient," I pleaded.

"This will not be the first time someone promised to appear in court and then failed to show," Yehonatan advised. "You know that to be very true."

"A few more minutes at best," I pleaded with him again.

"If I could stop the sun from traversing across the sky, you know I would," he declared, "But I don't have that power and neither do you.   I would suggest you accept that your presentation has drawn to a close and you can continue with your closing summation when we return in the afternoon. This case is to be closed today. I have no control over that. If we are going to make this afternoon's deadline, then you have to begin wrapping up your arguments now."

I looked up at the Defendant sitting with a smug look on his face, that concealed that inside he was grinning from ear to ear. I had this sudden urge to grab his book and beat him over the head all over again. He knew that I had run out of time and it was obvious that most of the evidence I presented would be considered at most circumstantial, much of it being nothing more than hearsay. But worst of all, he would declare my most crucial statements as being intentional fabrications and I would pay the price dearly. Oh, how the tables had turned, with myself soon to be found guilty of giving false testimony and slandering Akiva in the process. He would walk and I would be the. one receiving judgment. How was that even possible. There was so much evidence already piled up against Akiva, but I must admit much of it had been circumstantial.

Had I been too overconfident when I first established this tribunal? I had ensured that there were enough judges that were affiliated with Akiva that I could not be accused of weighting the final judgment in my favour. Now I could see that by being so generous I had done the exact opposite. I knew it, Akiva knew it, and it was exactly what he had counted on happening in the end. Did my arrogance and hubris blind me? Did he always know that I would never be able during the week to provide sufficient evidence that clearly proved him to be guilty beyond a shadow of a doubt? Any lingering doubt would prove ultimately to be his salvation.

Seated behind his table, Praetor Yehonatan called for order, preparing to close the morning session. The people in the gallery jostled and pushed for position, readying themselves to exit through the doorways to return to their homes for their noon time meal.

"Is the Prosecutor ready to agree that we close this morning session?" Yehonatan directed his question towards me, but my mind was still a thousand miles away, thinking of how best to deal with my failure. I walked as slow as I could towards his table, making each step last several breaths. I could see no other choice but to agree.

"Praetor, I…"

"The Romans are coming, the Romans are coming," someone on the outer ring of the courtyard was overheard shouting. A look of panic spread across the faces of the crowd. The all too familiar shout of the 'Romans are coming' over the past few years had become associated with imminent death.

"Everyone relax," I shouted but I don't think anyone heard me, as they were frightened and too concerned for their own safety. I decided I better try another tactic. "How many can you see?" I attempted to attract the attention of the young man that first sounded the alarm.

"Just a handful," he replied. "Perhaps nine or ten at most. And a carriage."

"Thank God!" I thought I had spoken to myself but I must have said it out loud because several people turned to look at me with quizzical expressions on their faces as to how the presence of Romans would be something I was grateful for.

"Calm down everyone," I shouted at the top of my voice. "Praetor, may I present my final witness. Everyone be calm." If they thought my previous comment on being grateful for a few Roman soldiers was strange, they certainly thought I had lost my mind when they heard that the presence of the Romans meant my final witness had arrived.

"Elioneai, what is going on here? What have you done?" Yehonatan demanded to know. "Have you betrayed this tribunal to the Romans?"

"Praetor, I wish to announce this morning session is not officially over. My final witness is now present, and I apologize for the delay but I request that either their testimony, which we all agree is crucial, be presented and heard now, or else the witness's time in the chair be reallocated to the agenda for this afternoon. I leave the decision to the discretion of the Court."

"This is most unusual," Yehonatan remained confused by the announcement.

"Perhaps then we should leave that determination to the people assembled in this courthouse to decide. Shall they depart for their meal, or do they wish to stay and hear what the witness has to say now."

Before Yehonatan could even agree to the latter, the tumult of noise and excitement from those assembled within the courtyard overwhelmed everyone with what sounded like a unanimous decision. No one wanted to leave. Food was inconsequential. It was as if time for everyone was suddenly frozen and no one dared to move a muscle in an effort to leave the courtyard, their eyes glued to the unfolding scene. As the door to the carriage swung open, Jacob, the Captain of my guard, extended his right hand to assist the occupant down the steep and narrow row of steps that unfolded from beneath the carriage, until she was standing firmly upon the ground. Her face, perfect in every manner, could have been easily mistaken for that of an angel. It radiated with beauty so divine that the Romans must have considered her to be a goddess. Her long red tresses were wound high atop her head and held in place by a golden tiara. Draped around her long neck was a string of precious stone the size of walnuts, that contrasted perfectly with the paleness of her pinkish hued skin. Every feature of her face, from her brow, to the delicate turned up nose, and the fullness of her rubied lips suggested she had been carved from marble by one of the Empire's greatest artisans.

As she stepped towards the portal of the courtyard, the people parted as if they had become the Red Sea, clearing the way as they watched in awe, their jaws dropping down to their chins, while remaining speechless. After a full week of the constant drone of noise and excitement, the lack of sound in the courtroom was almost eerie. The train of her silver embroidered dress flowed behind her, resembling angel's wings. Gracefully, she moved towards the front of the courtyard, and I released the rope so that she could pass through unhindered and take the chair that had been reserved as the seat for the witnesses. Turning to her escorts, she ordered her guards to return to the carriage and wait for her there. At first the captain of her own guard refused, concerned about her safety, but she would not hear of it, insisting that they all leave and that Jacob would ensure her safety. I don't know what relationship or knowledge they had about my Captain but it was enough to satisfy them and they returned to the carriage.

As much as I was ashamed to admit it, even I found myself captivated by her phenomenal beauty and the way she wielded that magic so effortlessly. It was rumored that she was well into her fifties, but I would swear she did not appear to be a day over thirty. Not a single line creased her brow or her cheeks. Her chin and neck were firm and showed no signs of sagging with age. Truly the Lord had blessed her with the gift of eternal youth, but I could not help but wonder why. Was she part of some vast eternal plan that only God was aware of, and she was here to play a part in a play of which I still could not appreciate the storyline. Had all these events, even this tribunal been preordained by God, as was her appearance and we were merely playing out our roles no choice of our own? Or was she just another mystery of our universe that neither I nor any member of mankind was ever intended to resolve? And for the first time since reading Akiva's words in his book, I could appreciate how a man's mind could be twisted by a single glance upon a woman and he would become convinced to betray a people. Truthfully, what mortal could ever fully understand the ways of the Almighty in lavishing such beauty on a woman that wasn't even one of His chosen?

I noticed how she never looked directly across at Akiva who sat to her left once she took the witness chair, intentionally avoiding any prolonged eye contact with the Defendant. Perhaps she was ashamed of her presence here and what she considered to be her betrayal of him. Oh, how the table turn when we play the game high above our station. When she first entered the court area, I noticed that she winced upon seeing his bruised face but quickly bit her lip, forcing herself not to give it a second thought. His reaction on that first exchange was quite different. Since then he could not help but stare constantly at her, never removing his eyes from her presence, with an expression that I could only describe as defeated, dejection, perhaps even capitulation, but at no time could I detect any hatred, which I had thought might be a normal response when feeling betrayed, even between lovers. Whatever spark of life he possessed earlier in the day when he thought he had overturned my case, now appeared to have deserted him, his soul numbed by her unexpected arrival. Akiva ben Joseph, in the presence of the Lady Rufina was no more than an empty husk, the lights of his soul extinguished.

It was time for me to bring the prosecution's case to an end. "As my next witness, I would like to introduce her Excellency, the Lady Cornelia Metella Rufina, wife of the Procurator of Jude…", I stopped myself before I had completed the final word. "I mean wife of the Procurator of Palestina." I couldn't afford to have anything recorded incorrectly as part of this testimony. "On behalf of this court in B'nai Brak, I wish to welcome Lady Cornelia and tell her how much I appreciate her stepping forward as a witness in this case. I know it has been difficult for you to make this decision and I appreciate how hard this may have been on your conscience but I swear to you my Lady, I had no other choice."

Yehonatan interrupted me at that moment, "Will the Prosecutor please approach my bench and explain to me what in God's name is going on here." Clearly he had finally snapped out of the trance. I could tell from the look on his face he was concerned that somehow I had crossed the line but he couldn't precisely identify where that line might have fallen.

I walked calmly to where Yehonatan was sitting and leaned over, my hands firmly planted on top of his table. Whereas the last time I stood here I was resigned to defeat, this time I was enthused with confidence.

"Can you explain to me what the wife of the Procurator is doing here?" Yehonatan asked for an explanation as he whispered.

"She has come to testify," I answered also in a whisper.

"I can see that," the Praetor was not satisfied with a simple answer. "Why is she here?"

I continued to speak in hushed tones so that only the Praetor could hear what I was saying. It was not intended for the ears of the judges. "This witness has vital information regarding everything we have discussed and disclosed at the trial this week. Give me the chance and I will demonstrate that everything I have presented is true."

"I understand all that," Yehonatan shook his head, "But what I don't understand is why the wife of the Procurator of this province is sitting in this court and testifying at all. Why did she even bother to come? Did you do something I should be aware of that forced her to appear today? Are we in any danger? Her presence here is most unusual and highly dangerous. Did you somehow force her to be present?"

"I wouldn't use the word force," I danced around his assumption. "I am more inclined to use the word 'convinced'. I convinced her to attend this trial and give her testimony for the sake of future peace in this land."

"And you wish me to believe that despite her being a Roman, that she has any concerns or feelings for this land or the people living in it."

"By the time she finishes her testimony, I hope that I will have succeeded in making you believe that she does have feelings for our country, even if those feelings are the result of her relationship with one man."

"You play a dangerous game, High Priest," he warned me.

"As do we all, Yehonatan. But sometimes it is the only way."

"And how are we supposed to communicate with her? I don't speak Latin," Yehonatan was concerned that her testimony would be misinterpreted, rendering it invalid."

"Treat her like everyone else," I advised. "It should be no surprise that she is fluent in Aramaic, so she understands anything that will be asked of her. There won't be any issues. She converses better than a lot of native speakers."

"Good," was all that the Praetor had to say.

"So, if it pleases the Court, may I get back to the questioning of the witness?" I determined that time was running short.

Waving his hand to dismiss me from his table, Yehonatan gave the command, "The prosecution may proceed."

"Thank you Praetor," I bowed my head and returned to where Cornelia was seated, taking a position to her left side so that she remained in full view of everyone watching from within the peristyles. "I would like to start with some simple questions if that is all right with you," I commented.

She agreed with a simple 'Yes', in a voice that was soft and delicate like drops of falling rain.

"Although I know you will not swear in the name of our God, and if you did it would be a meaningless exercise, but regardless of that, may I replace your promise to tell the truth by a binding oath to whatever gods you do pray to? Do you promise to tell the truth."

"I do."

"Do you know the Defendant, Akiva ben Joseph?"

"I do."

"How long have you known him?"

I rotated my head until I could look over my left shoulder in order to see if there was any noticeable reaction from Akiva. There was none. He just sat there with his face buried in the palms of his hands, signifying he could not bear to hear her testimony. He obviously knew where my line of questioning would be taking her. It was as if all his nightmares had descended upon him all at once.

She took a moment to think about the question. "It would be about ten years now."

"And where did you first meet the defendant?"

"It was in Alexandria. Egypt. My husband and I were there as part of the official hosts from the provinces, welcoming Emperor Hadrian on one of his earlier visits. Tinnius Rufus had just been appointed as Procurator so it was important the we attended."

"That being the case, I presume the defendant was there as part of another delegation representing either the Sanhedrin or the Rabbinical Council from Yavneh at that time. Not as an official representative of the province as you were."

"I can't recall precisely for that visit but there were other meetings in Alexandria and some of those times, he was there as part of a group," she confirmed, "But I must confess I didn't pay much attention to any mission's official designation."

"Still, he must have made quite an impression on you if you can recollect a particular Rabbi from among an entire group of Rabbis," I suggested. "Personally, when I look at a group of Rabbis, they all look the same to me. It's like a baker's bread mold, they all come out of the oven looking the same. Same beard, same dress, same mannerisms, even the same way of speaking. The only way to tell them apart is sprinkle a little sugar on one, cinnamon on another. Perhaps even some salt." Although everyone in the courtyard was nervous because of her presence, my little joke managed to get a few laughs and ease the tension in the courtyard.

Even Cornelia relaxed a little bit as she heard the ripple of laughter. "I don't know, maybe it was because he looked so different," her head tilted on an angle, and you could tell she was reflecting on her past memories.

"I concur," I confirmed her comment. "I may have not known him for ten years, but I do remember him just over six years ago. He had a lot more hair then, I must admit. Perhaps not as wrinkled, but those blue-green eyes of his, they were so deep and intense. He was a real eye-catcher. I'm certain with those eyes and that blonde hair he once had, he must have had a lot of women take notice of him in his younger day. Wouldn't you say so?"

I could see that Cornelia was feeling a lot more comfortable with our conversation and was prepared to say a lot more if I asked the questions correctly.

"So, let me rephrase my question. You saw him among this group of Rabbis and probably thought he certainly stood out like a stalk of corn in a wheat field.   Am I right?"

"You are certainly right," she said with a girlish little laugh. "I looked at him standing among all those old shriveled up prunes, all of them hunched over in their prayer shawls like they were carrying the weight of the world on their shoulders, all of them waving their hands about frantically in the air whenever they wanted to express themselves and make a point and I wondered to myself, 'How did no one not realize someone had switched babies between cribs when they were not looking. There was no way I could convince myself that he was a Rabbi. I thought maybe he was their interpreter, or their Roman banker and they decided to dress him up as one of their own for the purpose of their mission or perhaps even as a joke."

Another spurt of laughter greeted Cornelia's comments on the possible mishap of exchanging babies to account for Akiva's marked differences.

"In other words, your curiosity became aroused, and you simply had to find out more about him. It is a typical human reaction when we notice something which appears strangely out of place. It is an impulsive reaction and then you find out he came from a family of converts and suddenly it all makes sense."

"Exactly," she agreed, her voice sounding bubbly. "You must simply find out how he could be so different or else it would drive you mad," She laughed again with that little girlish twitter and I swear almost every man in the courtyard probably fell madly in love with her at that moment. There was something very special about this woman that rendered her irresistible. "I pointed him out to my husband, the Procurator Tinnius Rufus, and he was also intrigued, saying we definitely must find out more about this very different looking Rabbi."

"As such, you wouldn't describe your relationship with Akiva ben Joseph as a casual acquaintance, a one-off circumstance that rarely happened again. In fact, both you and your husband took a particular interest in the Defendant. Perhaps it was a simple business-related arrangement, or maybe I could suggest you even found each other's company stimulating and enjoyable and as a result, over time it managed to evolve into something stronger, one might say even more personal type of relationship between the three of you. Would I be correct in suggesting that?"

"You are absolutely right," she agreed with my assessment. "My husband detested talking with the Council from Yavneh. It was always a case of them wanting this or they needed that. They were never satisfied, always demanding more. Whatever he offered was never good enough and they were constantly sending their complaints directly to Rome, accusing Tinnius of numerous crimes. But when he saw Akiva, he immediately had a change of heart and said to me at that time, 'Perhaps I can find a way to work with this one. He looks like one of our own and should therefore be more rational and reasonable in discussion."

"It would be a reasonable assumption. And I presume he was he right?" I questioned.

"Yes, Rabbi Akiva became a regular guest at our palace in Caesarea. Whenever my husband had a problem concerning the Jewish population, he would immediately summon Rabbi Akiva and see if they could manage it together."

"From what you're saying, it sounds like they had a good working relationship. A strong friendship possibly, if I might say so. So, that being said, how did we manage to have so many problems arise when it should have been obvious that these two leaders of our two communities were dedicated to working together in an effort to find compromise and solutions. You would think it would have created a much better environment between our two people. I can't see how it couldn't work!" The more I could keep her talking freely, the easier it would become to reveal the information I needed without her even realizing it.

She leaned forward in her chair indicating that she was about to say something keenly important. "It worked very well at first. Akiva would visit the palace with a list of demands from the Council and one by one, he and my husband would go through it identifying those that could be easily ratified, those that would need to be reworked in order to make them acceptable, and then the last pile of items that were rejected outright and would never see the light of day."

"And pardon my asking, but you were physically there, sitting with them at the table, all the times they held these meetings? You can attest to the fact that this was really the case. That your husband worked closely with Akiva to deal with all the issues."

"At my husband's request of course," she replied. "He felt my presence made Akiva more agreeable in their discussions."

"Do you think that was that true?" I wanted to follow up more on this train of thought.

"Was what true?" she asked, not fully understanding my question.

"Did your presence make Akiva more cooperative? I would have thought as a Rabbi he would have asked your husband to dismiss you from the room. After all, as a rabbi, they don't really believe it is a woman's place to be involved in matters of business or law. They think you should remain where you belong, cleaning, cooking and making babies."

"That does not sound like the dear Akiva I know, at all," she shook her head, not believing he could agree to something like that. I don't think she even realized she had said 'dear' Akiva'. I hoped it registered with everyone else that heard it. "Well, it's true," I advised. "He even wrote something similar to that regarding a woman's place in his book. But you are saying he actually wanted you there and your husband was probably right in thinking that you were a positive influence on Akiva when it was time to negotiate."

She smiled broadly, and I thought I could detect hearing another series of sighs coming from the men in the crowd as she did. "I mentioned to you my husband is a very shrewd and clever businessman. If he says he detected that Akiva was more likely to negotiate more leniently when I was present, then in most likelihood, Tinnius was correct."

"It still strikes me as an odd relationship," I expressed my opinion. "It is no secret that Quintus Tinnius Rufus is certainly no lover of the Jews. For me to envision this picture of him sitting down for these regular meetings with Akiva ben Joseph, this hardly portrays the image of someone that despises the Jews. In fact, it would suggest he was actually attempting to be a good administrator, while from the records kept on his rule, it can be said that is certainly not the case as far as anyone that examines it. I really need you to help me reconcile these two contrasting images."

"I assure you that it is not that difficult," she informed me as if the answer was obvious, and perhaps it was to her. "Although the two of them would often come to a tentative agreement, it still required Akiva to return to the Council and acquire their final approval for each and every agreement. But because it was Akiva presenting these changes to the laws or rules, they were often rejected by y our own leaders because they despised him. Everyone knows that. Akiva would tell Tinnius when he returned with the unsigned agreements that it had nothing to do with the Governor but was because they would claim Akiva didn't have the birth-rite and thus privilege to represent the Council. That he had overstepped his place. Others would say that he thought himself too clever and they would simply refuse in order to take him down a peg or two."

"That is the explanation that Akiva provided to your husband. That in order to teach him his proper place, and humiliate him, the Council would dismiss the agreements because he arranged them without their permission, even if refusal of the agreement was detrimental to the population."

"That is exactly how Akiva would describe it," She concurred.

"That certainly would agree with some of the disagreements he described with the Council that he has written into his book," I pointed out to her with a smile of my own. "Let me paraphrase what you are suggesting. Even though the Governor and Akiva had developed ways by which they could deal with some of the major issues in the land, even those which were direct benefits to the people, their solutions were denied because of jealousies from these other rabbis. That probably made your husband very angry?"

"Not so much angry as sad. My husband could sympathize closely with exactly what Akiva had to say, because so many of his excellent suggestions were also rejected by the Senate back in Rome."

"Yes, I can see how the two of them naturally gravitated together," I commented.

"Both men shared many similarities as to what they desired and what they were willing to do in order to achieve their goals. I believe that is why they got on so well together," she justified their relationship. Tinnius Rufus, my husband, should have been made governor of one of the provinces that actually contributed significantly to the Empire. His appointment to Judea, as it was called at the time, was not taken well. He considered it an insult and certainly was not based on his demonstrated abilities, which should have earned him a province like Syria, Greece or even an Iberia. Instead, his appointment here was most likely a result of the aristocracy in Rome looking down their aquiline noses at his lowly breeding. Many were jealous of him. We had assumed his marriage to me, as a member of the Caecllia Metellii family, would elevate his status among the aristocracy but instead it did the opposite and lowered mine. Quintus Tinnius Rufus had intelligence, money and a respectful marriage but in the end it served him very little."

"Yes," I agreed, "It sounds like a very familiar story as we already established earlier during the trial. One might even say, two peas in a pod when we examine Akiva's and your husband's histories. When you talk about all that your husband had to suffer and endure, I could very easily replace his name with that of Akiva ben Joseph's and their lives would almost be identical."

"Indeed, they were very similar," she agreed. "Two men capable of doing so much more but trapped into positions of lower power and recognition because others despised their origins."

"It was certainly lucky that Procurator Quintus Tinnius Rufus had you then," I commented. "He may not have had the position of power that he wanted, or even the ability to rise further in the ranks, but he most definitely had the most beautiful woman in the Empire to help support him along with her aristocratic background." I knew it was that beauty that brought those two men together as well and why Tinnius Rufus may have had something that Akiva felt he was far more deserving of. It is no surprise that when two men have similar backgrounds, one is always going to be jealous of the other if they think life hasn't treated them equally. It's basic human nature. I knew that I had to explore this possible jealousy further without overplaying my hand.

Her cheeks blushed as soon as she heard the compliment, but it was more than that, her face was practically glowing. "You are much too kind for being the High Priest," she complimented me in return. I knew exactly what she was intimating, having been obviously informed that priests in the eastern kingdoms with our desert God, tended to behave more like asexual monks than those in the Roman priesthood. She was testing me as much as I was investigating her. It was obvious that she knew she had power over men and more certainly, she knew how to use that power. But I could play this game as well.

"The truth can never be a lie," I continued, "Especially when standing in a House of the Lord. I am forbidden to lie when I'm in a holy house. And I don't think that there is any denying that other men would have desired you greatly and yet here was this poorly born, low level government official being able to say that you were his wife."

"He was always very proud of me," she added.

"Had he been the kind of man to think in a more malicious manner," I suggested, "He probably could have used your beauty to make fools of all these other so-called high-born aristocrats. For example, he could have encouraged them to fall in love with you and then find ways to expose and embarrass them afterwards. That is if he was a man predisposed towards doing such things. A man like Nero, whom I heard tale of his doing that all the time in order to control the senators." When she did not respond to my suggestive intimation immediately, I was worried that perhaps I had been too direct in my statement, too clever for my own good.

"Oh, he definitely would do that," she finally broke her silence and didn't even bother to deny her husband was capable of such blackmail. "He'd wait until some of them would send me lavish gifts, at which time we would confront them or otherwise see to it that their wives received my thank you note."

"A very clever man, indeed," I congratulated her, but must admit that I was somewhat surprised that she revealed that fact. "But weren't you concerned that some of these men, whose only crime was being infatuated by your beauty, would have their careers destroyed by your husband's acts of revenge."

"It was only a game," she described it innocently, "Don't you think they deserved it?" For a fleeting second, I thought I saw her grin devilishly at me. For a moment I felt like a fly in a spider web. Obviously, she had no regrets or second thoughts regarding Rufus's and her actions. What lay behind that beauteous mask was not as innocent as one might think.

I knew I had to be careful with my next question. "What about men that could be used as steppingstones in your husband's career? Did he ever use you to lure them in order to arrange a better business deal or perhaps to receive a recommendation?

There was a subtle transformation of her features that those close enough may have seen if they were looking closely. I noticed it right away. Whereas previously she emitted an allure of almost childish sweetness and innocence, now there was this slightly harsher hue to her visage that lacked that trace of guiltlessness she had presented seen earlier.

"Elioneai," she became direct, using my name without any title, "Why don't you just ask what it is that you want to ask? Let's save ourselves both some time."

"And that would be?" I was uncomfortable by her directness, but she had taken control of this interrogation.

"You want to know if my husband at any time in the past, ever suggested that I use my womanly wiles on Akiva in order that he would do certain favors for my husband. Isn't that why you summoned me to testify at this trial in the first place?"

I cleared my throat, a little embarrassed to speak. "Yes, that is the reason you were brought here but for your sake I was trying to be a little more delicate and discrete in my manner of presenting the questions to protect your reputation."

"From what I have seen and learned over the years since my husband was sent to the backward province, regarding your people's attitude towards Rome and its citizens, I have no reputation remaining that needs to be protected. You are cursing me from the moment the sun rises until it sets each day. So, let us be quick and blunt, as I have no intention of staying here longer than I need to in order to settle this matter between us.

We knew from the time we first met Akiva that he probably had more in common with us than he did with those he considered his Jewish compatriots. Do you even know the degree to which he had been mistreated by his colleagues on the Rabbinical Council? I bet none of you know. I doubt any of you care. Have you ever seen his back? Any of you? I have. It still bears the scars from the countless lashes he received from your so-called religious leaders. No matter how much greater his intelligence on matters of the law might have been, he would always be that ignorant convert that had ambitions and pretenses of being president of your Sanhedrin one day. But alas my little Akiva was too naive to realize they were never going to let that happen. They'd let him preside over the Council every now and then, but that would be the limit of his recognition. As you can see, my husband and Akiva had much in common. It was just a matter of letting Akiva know that the possibility of his seeking revenge was not an impossible dream. They were not two peas in the same pod. They were the same p ea that just happened to be split between two different worlds."

Suddenly, there wasn't a single sound that could be heard within the courtyard, neither from the judges nor the stunned crowd as everyone had become petrified like statues, hardly believing their ears regarding what they had just been told by the Procurator's wife. My guess is that some of the men were more bewildered than shocked, probably wondering where that sweet angelic creature that first stepped through the gates of the courtyard had gone. But she was right, the best possible idea was to wrap this up and get her testimony quickly and then have her safely on her way before anyone fully realized what she was saying. I couldn't afford to have her harmed by the people."

"I presume that means you both were able to manipulate Akiva?"

She laughed upon hearing the question, but this time it was not the soft titter of a young woman. This time it bore an evil and malevolent tone. "Oh my! You make it sound like he was tortured. Akiva didn't do anything that he never had any intention of doing. It was just that my husband was able to make it all happen sooner than later."

"In what way did you motivate him," I had to know.

"It was obvious Akiva was enamored by me. When we first met he could barely take his eyes off of me. Tinnius joked that the lust could be seen steaming from Akiva's ears. Perhaps the blood has run cold in most of your other religious leaders but with Akiva, it was clear that he still possessed that hot Mediterranean blood from his parental stock. You men think it is all about your charm, but I will tell you, it is fairly easy for a woman to identify a man who is a womanizer and Akiva was undeniably one of those men. But a fisherman still needs to have the fish on the hook before he can reel it in. My husband suggested we find out Akiva's routine and habits, so we might know at any time where he would be and what he was doing."

"And this was important to whatever you were planning?"

"If we knew when and where he would be, then you do what every woman does that is seeking a particular man. You make certain that the law of coincidence works in your favour."

"Forgive me if I don't understand," I apologized. "I guess as a man, I'm not familiar what you do to make it work in your favour."

"Do you really think that when you are young and you happen to see the same girl at different times and different places that it is purely by accident? That when you finally begin to talk with one another it is a miracle that your God arranged it all by ensuring that you did find one another only through happenstance? It is the oldest trick in the world that is practiced by women. We find out when and where you are going to be, pretend we don't see you when we go there, and then make certain that you actually bump into us, purely by accident. Then at first we pretend that we don't want to talk to you, perhaps even ignore you but by the third or fourth time of our paths crossing we will say to you something to the effect, 'It was obviously meant to be' and so we start talking with you and you get all excited thinking you are the luckiest and most blessed man in the world."

"And this is what you did with Akiva," I recognized exactly what she meant now. "Now I understand. This is why he wrote in his book that when *he was sitting one day in the lower city of Jerusalem with Rabbi Simeon ben Gamaliel, he commented upon seeing you and that you had to be one of the most beautiful women that he ever laid his eyes upon and that he would eventually convert you to Judaism and make you his wife.* Correct me if I'm wrong but I'm guessing that wasn't the first and only time he just happened to 'accidentally' cross paths with you without your husband being present. You made him believe that all of those times that he had these chance encounters with you that it must have been God's way of sending him a message and why he said to Rabbi Simeon he thought you would eventually be his third wife. I can see why he thought so, but what I don't understand is what made him so confident to think you would convert?"

"It was actually Tinnius's idea," she declared. "He suggested to me that we had to find a way that I could be seen publicly and alone with Akiva without raising any suspicions. As I mentioned, my husband was very clever and he realized that Akiva would never refuse me if I asked him to teach me to read and study the Torah."

"The perfect alibi," I admitted. "Yes, it was very clever, except that Akiva was the one preaching to the Rabbincial Council that they must never teach Torah to a woman. He was obviously saying one thing to them but doing another when it came to you. How did you manage to convince him?"

"Or perhaps he was simply trying to resist, by raising shields against falling in love with me, but in the end, he succumbed and couldn't resist any longer," she winked at me, as if to suggest she could have any man she wanted, even me. I suddenly felt like that web was getting tighter and tighter.

"Yes, I guess he did finally succumb and that would also explain why he had the council pass a ridiculous law that *a man can divorce his wife immediately if he should find a woman that is more beautiful,*" The Procurator must have been delighted that you had Akiva, an insider on the Council, dancing wildly to your song. I have no doubt that you are obviously the reason he proposed that law. I'm guessing there have been a lot of men doing your bidding. It's clear he had become obsessed with you!"

I scanned the faces of everyone, from the judges to the crowd within the peristyle to see how well they were processing the information. From the looks of shock and dismay I could detect, the only answer I could arrive at was 'not very well'. The entire week I had thought I had prepared them for the reality of discovering that everything I had said was true. But only now, hearing it directly from the Procurator's wife, they could no longer dismiss it as being simply a possibility. It had all become very real.

"Would you say that the word 'obsessed' describes his situation appropriately?"

"I would like to believe it was far deeper than an obsession my dear," she challenged my thinking. "I would like to believe he was madly in love with me."

The combined sounds of the gasps from the crowd was like a wind passing through the mountains.

"What could you possibly need from a rabbi on the Council that you would go to this length to bring him under your control? What was your husband seeking to do?"

"We needed someone on the Council that could exert control over the others," she admitted.

"But you said he was never going to the Chief Rabbi. How does that serve your purpose."

"We didn't need someone that could control the Council, we needed someone that could disrupt it. We had no idea when he proposed his law on divorcing a wife simply because she was no longer beautiful, that everyone else was going to agree with him. It just made us realize that they all had weaknesses that could be exploited and Akiva would be a very useful tool."

"That it?" I questioned. "He was merely a tool to you."

"Of course there were mutual feelings of love," she answered, "But that wasn't how it started."

"Are you saying that you love Akiva."

"Of course I love him," she replied as if she could love a hundred men and it wouldn't make a difference.

"But at first, what was it that you actually wanted from him?"

"Now you're finally asking the right questions. We needed him to start a war," she answered rather calmly and matter-of-factly.

"And how was this going to serve your interests, may I be so bold to ask?" I was unable to grasp her line of reasoning. "Without wishing to be critical or cruel to you, because I don't doubt you have these amazing powers that can sway men to your will, but how does one even go about starting a war? Who do you have to insult in order to get one nation to revolt against another. And I certainly don't wish to diminish your husband's position of authority, but even if Procurator Tinneus Rufus was to pass some abhorrent law that infuriated the Jews, they would have done what they always had done before, which was dispatch a letter to the Senate in Rome, raise a complaint against your husband, and just like before, have the law rescinded. And since this was becoming such a common occurrence when it came to your husbands governing of Judea, I suspect the Senate would have eventually had Rufus removed from this posting and then you and he would have disappeared to that place where failed governors all go."

"Clever boy," she purred. "You think you have it almost all worked out. Of course, I will admit that you are partially right in your basic assumptions but there's so much more. If Tinnius Rufus was to devise a law that infuriated the Jews, then, just as you thought, it would have been one law too many to have the Senate excuse it again. I don't mean to insult you, but you have no appreciation for just how clever Tinnius Rufus can be. My husband knew that the only way this would work was if it wasn't a law directly from himself. It needed to be a law from the Emperor."

"But the only time Hadrian established a set of laws that interfered with our way of life was six years ago and that was in Alexandria when…" My mind was swirling at the thought. Could the three of them have been involved in what everyone had described at the time as an apparent accident. Suddenly I had my doubts as to whether it was an accident at all. Perhaps it was simply a case of murder. "Are you suggesting that the drowning of Antinous was not an accident?" To even think that it was possible to have murdered the lad and gotten away with it was mind boggling. Why would she be telling me this? One word to the Emperor and both she and her husband would be in prison awaiting death.

"Of course it wasn't an accident," she immediately set me straight on what she thought. "The precious boy sacrificed himself for the sake of the Emperor," Cornelia replied.

"And why would he do that?" Her explanation failed to make any sense to me.

"Earlier that summer, there was a monstrous and ferocious lion that was terrorizing the people living on the outskirts of Alexandria. Hadrian and the boy decided to go hunt the animal. Antinous as most people knew, was an excellent hunter. Very few were better with a bow or spear than he. When they first encountered the beast, the Emperor launched his spear, striking and wounding the animal, which only served to drive it into a wild rage. It launched itself at the boy, who was unprepared for the attack, sitting high in the saddle, trying to gain a better perspective. The attack came so swiftly that Antinous didn't have a chance to even raise his spear. Seeing his young lover in peril, Emperor Hadrian charged towards the lion, leaped upon its back and plunged his sword into the beast's beating heart. But what most people don't know is that there is a law in the Book of the Dead from Egypt that says when death is cheated of a life that clearly belonged to Anubis then another life must be offered in its place. There was no doubt that Antinous was intended to die but Hadrian intervened and cheated Anubis of his soul payment. The priests in Egypt explained that if the debt was not paid soon, then Anubis would come to collect it directly from the Emperor."

"Why would the priests tell a young, impressionable eighteen year old boy something like that," I was shocked to think they would say such a thing.

"Of course not, Hadrian would never let the priests tell Antinous such a thing. He would cut out their tongues first."

I pursed my lips as it dawned on me. "So, you and your husband did. Am I correct?" I started putting the puzzle pieces together.

"I merely told him of the legend that existed," she said calmly. "It's not as if we pushed him into the river," she dismissed herself of any responsibility. "We didn't tell him that he had to kill himself."

"He was merely a boy," I reminded her.

"He was a paidika," she waved off my concerns as if they didn't matter. "Antinous was already eighteen. That's older than most. How much longer do you think after his body changed and became that of a man, Hadrian would continue to love him. Do you not think Antinous was aware of that? Paidkikas know exactly how the system works. His lifeline was already on a shortened thread. At least in this way he became immortalized and deified for his sacrifice. He knew that Hadrian would love him forever!"

"And then you persuaded Akiva do the rest by saying it was a punishment from God because Antinous was a Bithynian Jew, and therefore as a homosexual he had to die."

"Oh," she sounded surprised. "I see you have already discussed this. It did not take much persuasion to have Akiva repeat what he sincerely believed."

"Yes, I had already determined that part, I just never understood why Akiva did it. Now I understand it completely. It was all part of a ploy the three of you had arranged."

"And as a result," she concluded her story of Antinous, "we had our war."

"But I think if we learned anything from the past four years, it was that none of us gained anything from an extended war. You didn't, we didn't and certainly Rome didn't. All we have on all sides is death and destruction and the power equation has not shifted at all. What did either you or your husband actually gain?"

She smiled at me and for some reason, it sent a shiver down my spine. It may have been that same sweet smile we all saw before but now I can detect a far more sinister reason behind the rubied curvature of those perfect lips. The fly, I imagined, could now see the eight legged terror moving towards it.

"Imagine if it had been only a brief war," she proposed. "A small flare-up lasting a year, maybe two at most, that swung in favour of the rebels at the onset, taking out a few garrisons and cohorts around the province, but then the procurator at the head of the legion puts it down swiftly and completely, breaking the back of the resistance in Judea once and for all."

"Tinnius would have been declared a hero," I conjectured, "And depending on how successful the victory, it might even earn him a Triumph in Rome, especially if he could say his one legion took out an army five times greater in size."

She winked at me for putting together the fate of Akiva's students that were never intended to become warriors after they enlisted.

"Suddenly, he would have some respect and they might even assign him to a more prominent part of the Empire to govern," I surmised. "Granted, that might have happened, but what would Akiva have gotten out of it. After all, he would still be seen as the one that started the war as soon as he appointed Bar Kochba as the messiah. His students were the soldiers taking on the Roman soldiers. You couldn't ever confess to the Emperor that it was all a setup, otherwise Rufus wouldn't be having a triumph but instead his own execution. Akiva would have to take the blame."

Sitting up straight in the chair, she held up her right hand and rolled out her thumb. "You aren't thinking," she advised me. "Firstly, the removal of all those that prevented him from achieving his rightful place as head of the Council."

"Which just also happened to be all the rabbis that were against the war in the first place." I suddenly realized how easily they had achieved her first point and for what reason. "Any opposition to beginning the war is quickly removed simply by accusing them of being the instigators to the Romans. Your husband knew they weren't but he was more than willing to dispose of them. Was it Akiva that made the request to have them eliminated? We have a right to know." I wanted to know exactly who turned them in to the Roman authorities.

"It wasn't so much as a request as it was just a matter of making a list of all the known peace lovers that might stop the onset of the war. Akiva probably didn't even realize he was composing a list until it was too late. Once Tinnius had the names he knew what had to be done with them."

"But as the one pushing for war, how could he not have known he had compiled a list of all those that opposed him. That meant Akiva must have known its intended purpose," I answered my own question.

"Not necessarily," she answered slyly. "Akiva would endlessly talk about all those other Rabbis, all those he considered less deserving, that stood in his way of achieving the success that was his by merit. He was a lot like Rufus in that way. He would talk endlessly with Rufus about the nature of those that were reporting his behaviour to the Nasi, after which he would be whipped severely. From the descriptions he provided, it wasn't difficult to determine which of those Rabbis that were reporting on him were also the true Roman sympathizers. Akiva didn't have to point any fingers at anyone, it was obvious from his complaints."

"I guess two peas in a pod share much in common. I would not give Akiva that much credit that he was oblivious to why they were being arrested."

"Perhaps not," she replied, signaling that I was beginning to understand. Next she rolled out her index finger. "Second, a pardon from the Emperor in recognition of his misguided error in appointing the Messiah. As soon as he realized his mistake, he was to pull his support and that of your God from the one you called Bar Kochba and then starts preaching a message of peace and reconciliation."

"And why would Hadrian do that," I questioned.

"Because very few Romans would be killed and Akiva would hand over Bar Kochba to Rufus on a silver platter. A life for a life!"

"But something went terribly wrong with your plan, didn't it?" I countered. "You were willing to sacrifice a few cohorts and a garrison or two, but what you didn't count on was the people flooding to join Bar Kochba's army as soon as he had those first few successes. Instead of a few thousand foot soldiers, he had an army. You underestimated the Judeans as you always have in the past. To your own surprise you found out he wasn't some mere bandit forced to hide in the Judean desert for years but instead he was a real leader of men. A true warrior and a man capable of commanding an army of hundreds of thousands. Just like that slave Spartacus that you underestimated a couple of hundred years ago. Your first mistake was that Akiva picked the wrong man."

"He intentionally picked someone young and not as seasoned as some of the other rebel leaders. Who could have known that this Bar Kochba had a natural ability to command?" she defended Akiva, which suggested to me that she did have some honest feelings for the old Sage. "Perhaps your God really did choose him," she surmised.

It was hard to tell if she said that sincerely or was simply mocking us.

"It must have been quite the surprise when your husband rode out at the head of the legion expecting an easy victory, but instead encountered a vastly superior army that annihilated his troops even with the burden of those twenty-four thousand students. You and your husband ran to Alexandria in Egypt to lick your wounds and sent word to the neighbouring governors to come to your rescue. But that meant leaving Akiva behind with an army that was drunk on its first victory and he was unable to control their leader. These rebels weren't his usual group of scholars that he could bully into compliance. He was out of his depth and he didn't have you available to advise him. Am I piecing this together correctly?"

"It was a setback," she agreed, "But we had planned on a contingency. We didn't run to Alexandria because we were frightened. We went there because we knew if we failed to put this Bar Kochba down quickly then there was a very good chance it would escalate from the level of a limited provincial revolt to a full scale regional war. That meant we had to gain the Emperor's attention and we could only do that from Alexandria. We informed Hadrian that we had a man on the inside. From that summer three years earlier in Alexandria, he already knew Akiva, and judged him as being compliant and therefore a Roman asset. The Emperor was willing to let Akiva continue working within the rebel party, while a siege based strategy was being formulated by General Julius Severus."

"But that can't be all of it. I think Akiva's compliance demanded something more at that time. There is no way that Hadrian would put that much faith in a common man, especially some minor Jewish Rabbi, to deliver a victory for Rome. Your Emperor is not that big a fool. Is that not so? If Bar Kochba became too successful, there was no guarantee Akiva would rip his support away from him. Akiva is like a leach that will latch on to whomever he thinks will be the ultimate winner. As I see it, there had to be more to ensure his willingness to betray Bar Kochba. I believe in order to work, you had to be complicit in this plan as well. You and Akiva became the key. Only you could secure his loyalty and adherence to the plan."

"It would appear that you have already worked out many of the details already," she commented on my deductive skills. "You are right, in order to succeed, Akiva and I would have to become far more involved. The Emperor was already disappointed in my husband, blaming him for the start of the revolt, and Bar Kochba was proving himself to be a far better strategist than we had thought."

"Akiva certainly didn't need gold or money. He had plenty of that. Power, well it's debatable but in his mind I believe he also thought he had enough of that. The only thing he desired and didn't have was you. You can roll out your fingers and tell me how this was all part of your plan, but I don't believe any woman wants to sell herself into prostitution but you didn't have a choice, did you?"

"As you said, Hadrian is not a stupid man," she replied. "He had his own spies in Judea and already knew that we were behind the appointment of a messiah for the Jews. This was our doing. It wasn't that he disagreed with our plan, he saw how controlling Akiva could be key to ending the rebels for good, but now that we had created this mess he demanded that we also put an end to it." She took a deep breath and sighed. "His spies also told him how Akiva absolutely adored me and would likely do anything if he could have me."

"And you agreed to sell yourself in this manner?" I had to ask.

"Not at first, but when the choice is between that or the execution of my husband, there really was no way to refuse."

"It's all beginning to make sense now," I postulated. "Let me know if I'm right. I think the way this worked is that Akiva would arrive at the villages before they were under siege and of course, being so close to Bar Kochba, he would be permitted to enter without any second thoughts by the sentries. At some point, perhaps days or weeks later you would arrive at the same village, explaining that you were invited, and Akiva would have you escorted past the Jewish sentries to his quarters and no one would even question such behaviour. As he intimated, no one would even think twice about it because he had convinced them that your willingness to study Judaism and the Torah, as a dedicated convert, was actually a tremendous blessing. And of course, both you and Akiva made certain that the story of your pending conversion was out in the open and widely circulated. Any rabbi that could convert the wife of a Roman governor must be a great rabbi. No doubt about it. Meanwhile, he wasn't tutoring you but instead was providing you with all the information he had garnered during the time in the village, regarding all the secret tunnels in exchange for the pleasures you offered him. I must admit, I was originally confused why Tinnius Rufus would have permitted it. Why he would let you wander about the countryside during a time of war. He must have heard all the rumours about your conversion. The story was widely circulated. It really didn't make any sense at all, and he should have been furious with you. Personally, I think it would have been the most embarrassing cuckolding any Procurator had experienced, let alone try to explain to his superiors. I should have realized it was all part of your plan."

"You are such a clever man," she cooed. "You now see how easy it was to exchange the information. As you said, a little pleasure and some men will

313

offer up their souls. Akiva provides all the details of the town's defenses and I carry all that information back to Caesarea. My husband then passes that information on to Julius Severus and the general takes the city. It was all so simple and happening in front of Bar Kochba's eyes.."

"And that truly is the sad part of it," I agreed with her. "It was all so utterly simple. So simple that I'm certain Akiva even had himself convinced that someday in the future you would be his wife. But there had to be some suspicion. I am certain that not everyone could have been fooled that easily," I questioned her. "Surely Bar Kochba had to question the coincidence of your arrival in a town only to have it fall to the Romans shortly afterwards."

"The best way to earn trust," she schooled me, "Is to give up something they think is of value. When I arrived in each town I would tell the generals about the Roman troop placements and where there were weak points in the Roman siege walls. It was useful information but had little impact on the outcome of the battles. It just meant that when Severus's men finally laid siege to the town, the would seal off the tunnels immediately, preventing any Jewish sallies, and the few Jews that did manage to escape were able to do so because of the information I provided."

"And then these handful of escapees, so glad and grateful to still be alive, would flee to the next fortified town, thinking that they owed you a debt of gratitude for their survival and told everyone about how you betrayed your own people in order that they could be saved. Feel free to stop me at any time if I am off track and getting this wrong," I advised her.

"You are doing amazingly well Elioneai," she congratulated me on my insights. "What they didn't realize was that it was part of Julius Severus's overall plan. He was herding the surviving rebels into one town, where they would become a burden on the food and water supplies, and when it came time to make their final stand, they would be defeated once and for all. It was all very simple, don't you think?" Now I know she was taunting me.

Those assembled in the gallery also sensed they were being taunted and were growing quite agitated. The truth was obvious to them by now. Akiva was the one who had been providing all the details concerning the labyrinth of tunnels and the exit points beneath each town, and Cornelia was permitted to simply deliver that information to the Romans without interference. So when Severus finally launched his attacks, he knew exactly where to position his troops to avoid any surprises as, well as to seal off the escape routes.

"But I'm guessing you also gave specific information to Akiva," I suggested. "Obviously he had to be told by you in advance the exact day the Romans would be breaking the siege and launching an attack. In that way he would always manage to leave the towns well before that day arrived. True?"

"Of course," she reaffirmed. "Our plan required that Akiva remained alive. He had become the Roman army's greatest asset."

There were angry shouts coming from the crowd, as they vented their anger against both Cornelia and Akiva. The insults began flying about the courtyard and I could sense the crowd was reaching a point where they'd soon be out of control and do something rash.

"Silence, everyone. Do you want to get us all killed?" I turned on them. "Have you forgotten there are ten Roman soldiers just standing outside this courtyard. How many of us do you think they can kill if you were to do anything stupid? I'd predict that could take out half of you before you got the better of them. Afterwards a full legion will appear and your entire town will be put to the torch. Remember, this woman is here as a witness and therefore is under the protection of our laws and my personal protection as well. It doesn't matter if you don't like what she is telling you. What is done is done and there's no turning back time to correct the errors of our ways. What we need to know is how it happened so we can prevent it from ever occurring again. She is a Roman. Therefore, she does what Romans do. We are not here to judge her for that. But when one of our own betrays us, that is what we are here to judge and until I have every last detail of what he did, I will not let you lay a hand on him. Now everyone be quiet or I will have my own guards throw you out of this courtyard to face the Romans."

Sometimes it takes a dose of reality and fear to get everyone to cooperate. Once they realized that they had a good chance of being killed if they took any action against the wife of the Procurator or against Akiva, it quieted them sufficiently for me to continue.

"I must admit that my only surprise is that Bar Kochba didn't figure out what you two were doing until it was too late, and he found himself trapped in the town of Beithar. I presume it was the miraculous disappearance of Akiva, choosing to leave rather than die along with the men that finally woke Bar Kochba up! He experienced first-hand what his officers in all the other towns had experienced. The disappearance of Akiva just before the Romans launched their attack. A tell-tale sign but I'm guessing none of those officers ever survived after their towns fell to tell Bar Kochba what had transpired. And then once he finally knew, that's why we have word from the few survivors that did escape Beithar that he was roaring like an angry lion screaming to the heavens that he had been betrayed. And that's why he kicked Rabbi Eleazar Ha'Modai to death. Because there was no way in this world that Ha'Modai could not have known what Akiva was up to, considering they shared their sleeping quarters. Ha'Modai was left behind to pay the price for Akiva fleeing and revealing all the tunnels to the Romans."

"It appears that you knew all this already, so why did you require that I come and testify," she was curious.

"I had my suspicions, but not the proof. I needed someone to tie Akiva directly to the crime. I needed to hear it directly from you."

"I'm surprised that you are the only one that questioned his loyalty. I think it should have been obvious," she stated a fact but it sounded more as if she was ridiculing us for being ignorant.

"We have this misguided belief that a Jew will not betray another Jew, even though our entire history is one story after another of being betrayed by our own people. It has always been our downfall."

"But that is the very definition of betrayal," she seemed amused. "It is always one of your own that betrays you. Otherwise, it would not be called betrayal."

"A point well taken," I conceded. "It is not that it doesn't happen, it just usually doesn't happen on a scale of this magnitude. But you never finished telling me what Hadrian was offering Akiva for undermining the war effort and betraying his own people?"

"Rolling out her middle finger she recited the next promise. "Akiva would be given that which he desired most in this world."

"Was that really going to happen?" I questioned.

"It doesn't really matter at this point in time, wouldn't you agree," she raised a valid point.

"You're probably right," I agreed. "There will be no future for Akiva if this court has its way. Even if you did love him."

Cornelia smiled but remained silent. As to this last point she was not prepared to reveal any more secrets.

"That's all right. You don't have to say anything. I know that a lot of that gold and treasure he has stored in his home came from you. I suspect that his wife, Rachel was likely wearing jewelry that you once wore, but she never bothered to ask him where it came from. I just wonder if she would have been so happy to display it publicly if she knew that you had been wearing it first."

"I had more than enough jewelry," Cornelia defended her gifting it to Akiva. "It was impossible to wear it all and some of it was out of fashion. Better that it was gifted to another woman that could appreciate it than let it sit in boxes never to be worn again."

"A nice sentiment," I commended her, "But such generosity is not what I would expect if Akiva was nothing more than a mere pawn in your plan." Giving her possessions away to another man meant she had placed herself at tremendous risk if discovered. "I'm certain when your husband suggested you study Torah alone with Akiva he did not intend for you to start paying him for those services as well!"

At that point the Lady Rufina became upset by my talking about payments. "You promised me that we would not talk of such matters in your letter" she tried to remind me of the message I had sent with Jacob.

"I promised not a word of this would be spoken to your husband by me and I will keep that promise. The same way what we found in Akiva's possession will never be mentioned to Rufus. I just need these judges to understand that there were a variety of gifts provided by you personally to Akiva and that is the primary reason why you are here today."

"What are you implying?" For the first time since testifying, Cornelia Metella Rufina looked flustered and worried.

"I implying nothing," I assured her, "They will not be mentioned any further." I already knew the answers to all the questions I had not asked. I merely needed to look over in Akiva's direction, saw how destroyed and distraught he appeared and I knew everything I needed to know. "But I do have one more question which I hope you will answer. Why four thousand gold aureus?   I still don't have the answer to that riddle."

Cornelia was resigned to the fact that I knew all of hers and Akiva's secret.

"It is the bridal weight.   Are you going to ask me to explain it further?"

"No, that is sufficient.   I have no further questions from the witness Praetor."

Yehonatan looked immediately to his left and was about to ask Akiva if he wished to cross examine the witness, but he could see from the Defendant's condition, who still had his face buried in hands, that he appeared to be well beyond any ability to talk.   It was obvious Akiva was willing to forego asking any questions.

"The witness may step down now," Yehonatan ben Matthias consented to dismissing Cornelia Rufina form further testimony.

The mood of the people on the other side of the ropes was still quite belligerent. They were no longer in awe and shock as when she first entered the courtyard.   Their mood now was one of wanting an eye for an eye. They had just been informed that the entire war, through which they had all suffered tremendous losses, was nothing more than a crafted manipulation of their own leadership.   Yes, I had made them fearful of the Romans outside, but it would only take a small spark and even the threat of death would not stop them from venting their anger against Akiva and Cornelia.

"Yehonatan," I caught the Praetor's attention, "I think it will be for the best if I personally escort the Lady Cornelia Rufina from the courtroom." Extending my right hand, I helped her rise from the witness chair and together we approached the rope dividing us from the people standing in the gallery.   Those standing on the other side refused to move out of our way to let the Lady Cornelia Rufina pass. "I will warn you all once more and not again," I bellowed.   "I have promised this Lady my protection and if any of you so much as touches a hair on her head I will call down the wrath of God upon your households.   You won't have to deal with only the Romans but with my guards and God's holy legions as well.   Now let us pass!"

Some of them moved out of the way but others still refused.   "Jacob," I commanded, "Prepare your men!" As soon as my Captain Jacob heard my command, he signaled for his men to unsheathe their swords. The all to familiar sound of iron sliding on leather as the swords were withdrawn was enough to change the mindset of those still blocking our way.   They stepped aside, leaving an empty aisle down the center of the courtyard. I did not hesitate, escorting the procurator's wife outside as quickly as possible before they had a chance to reflect on the fact that they vastly outnumbered my own guard. As soon as she was safely beyond the synagogue's main building, her armed escort surrounded her to protect her the rest of the way. I continued to walk beside her until we safely reached her carriage Before climbing the steps, she turned her head to pass on her final words to me before parting. "You said you already knew the answer but just so you know it was true, I do love Aggi in ways I could never explain to you. Reassure me that you will never mention the gifts to my husband."

"Rest assured that I do not give my word lightly, my Lady. I promised to keep your secrets protected and I will never let them pass from my lips. Your husband will hear of none of this, and those items that we spoke of will disappear so that they will never see the light of day to be used against you again." I smiled, giving her the reassurance, she required.

"I thank you, Elioneai, you are truly a man of honour. I wish you could have thought the same of me, but what I did I did for Rome."

I let out a sigh as soon as she said that. "If I was truly a man of honour, then I would have found a way to have ended the war before it ever began. I failed my people and we have suffered terribly because of it."

Placing her right index finger across my lips she silenced me from speaking further. "You must learn that some of us are forces of nature and others are simply the trees waiting to be blown down. No matter what you wish, you cannot prevent us from being who we are."

They were words of wisdom that made me realize there was still far more to this woman than I had obviously seen today.

She spoke again, "Please, if you could do me one last favour?"

"Whatever I can do for you my Lady."

"Please ask Aggi to forgive me."

She turned her head back and climbed into her carriage. In a matter of minutes her carriage and escort were traversing northwest on the road back to her palace in Caesarea.

Chapter Nineteen

The Verdict:

Everyone within the courtyard stood in stunned silence. Most found it difficult to believe what had transpired. Was the wife of the Governor of Palestina really there or had they just imagined it. Did they actually all bear witness to hearing of the greatest betrayal of the Jewish people throughout our entire history by a man that had completely fooled all of them to the degree that they considered him to . be the saviour of their future. They were left wrestling with their demons all at once, wondering who was to blame, who was responsible, but more importantly, who would be able to repair the damage that had been done.

I had returned to my place at the forefront of the courtyard, where I found all of the judges had become numbed, barely able to react to what they had borne witness to. Over in his corner, Akiva still sat, grieving silently, his head still positioned exactly as when I had observed him last. Even Yehonatan appeared exhausted by the entire ordeal and appeared lost as to what to do next. I walked forward and stood before the Praetor's table. "It is time for us to draw this to a close," I told him. "I suggest we don't take a break and just move into the closing session."

Almost reluctant to say it because he feared for the worst, Yehonatan called for the closing remarks. "Will the prosecution please present at this time its closing summation. You may begin Elioneai."

Half of the courtyard was already covered in shadow, and I knew the sun had descended to a point that it was in the last quarter of its traversing the sky. That meant the people could not be detained much longer or else they would be unable to prepare for the Sabbath. The question in my mind was how I would be able to wrap up everything that we had heard in the past six days into a concise package that could be delivered in a few minutes. Then it hit me, I should use the past to guide me. Walking over to the chair where Akiva sat in silence, I attempted to gain his attention but he remained motionless. Shielding his face from the people, he was already signaling to everyone present that he had resigned himself to defeat, guilty of the crimes of which he was accused. I began to wonder if that was his true intent. If he could somehow convince the judges that he was remorseful and penitent, that might change the way in which they would decide the outcome of this case.

Standing beside the accused, I began my summation. "This is the man that at one time you were willing to call your second Moses. I want you to look at him now and say to yourself, would you have followed this man into the desert for forty years? Would you still believe anything that he carried down the mountainside inscribed in stone even if he claimed it was given to him by God? Because not too long ago you would have answered yes and that means you also must be held accountable for the recent events that have befallen us. He committed a tremendous number of sins, as we have established during the week, but none of them would have succeeded unless you were willing to give him that authority, willing to surrender yourself to all his demands, but most serious of all, willing to overlook what it said in the Torah and disregard God's own words! Yes, Akiva is guilty, but so are you!"

The panel of judges looked confused. They had not expected me to suddenly defend Akiva and lay the blame at the feet of the people of Judea. From the look on their faces, I knew that I was achieving the desired effect even though they had no idea what I was planning.

"You were all so mired in the hatred you held for the Romans, that you failed to examine the clear signs that were laying directly in front of you. While your lives became harsher, your losses intolerable, and the oppression under the Romans even more insufferable that you ever imagined, you never asked how was that through it all, Rabbi Akiva became richer and his freedoms even more generous to go anywhere he pleased in the land. He continued to gain while you all continually lost on every aspect of your lives. While the great sages like Gamaliel and his son Simeon, Ben Tarfon and Reb Ishmael, told you not to take arms against these Romans, even though these occupiers treated you as nothing more than beasts of burden, but instead to follow the path of peace, you never noticed that their voices of calm were the ones that were being silenced forever, yet the voices advocating war were permitted to live and speak freely. How could you not notice what was happening right in front of your eyes? How could you all be so blind to the reality?

When this man," at that time I pointed directly at Akiva so all eyes would focus upon him, "Declared Bar Kosba to be Bar Kochba, the Son of a Star, your living, breathing Messiah, you readily sent your sons, brothers and fathers to fill the ranks of his rebel army. You watched and cheered as Bar Kochba marched towards war accompanied with twenty-four thousand students that Rabbi Akiva released from his tutelage, none of whom were qualified to fight, none of them even equipped to wage war, and certainly none of them prepared to die so easily. At first God took pity upon our soldiers and provided us with early victories so that there would be time to reflect upon your terrible and hastily drawn decision to go to war, ensuring there was still time to approach the Romans with an offer of peace from a point of strength. But Akiva urged you to fight on and convinced you that your total liberation was at hand. How many of you even bothered to think regarding how this would all end? Did you honestly think the Romans, whose civilization is bred to fight, would abandon the war? Did you really believe they would stop sending legion after legion until they finally won? This was not a war against a handful of small kingdoms that dwelt in Canaan. This was a war against the greatest empire that the world has ever seen! Tell me of your expectations, let me understand you, where did you see this ending? How was it possible for you to convince yourselves that there would be a different outcome?

You ignored all the signs, convincing yourself that Moses had returned and his spirit resided in this pathetic shell of a man you see to my left. Read your Torah, Deuteronomy Chapter 34, verse three. See what it says! 'Never again did there arise in Israel a prophet like Moses.' The words of the Lord are eternal. They are meant to be read now and read in a hundred generations from now. Time is immaterial. No matter how or when you read them, they will provide the same message. There will 'NEVER' be another prophet like Moses.

And who was Moses? He was the lawgiver. Everything that constitutes us as Jews, the Children of Israel, was delivered to us by Moses. Akiva wants you to believe that there were two sets of laws. A written Torah and an oral Torah he is referring to as this Talmud. I challenge any of you here to show me where it is written by Moses that there was an oral Torah. You will not find any reference because it does not exist. Therefore, you should have known that anyone insisting there is such an oral law was attempting to lead you astray. But none of you objected. That oral law was nothing more than your golden calf and you all bowed down before it.

I showed you that after the first string of victories, God provided you an opportunity to change the course of the war and return to a peaceful path, but you chose to continue to dance around that graven image made in gold. And I can understand you were lulled into a false sense of security and superiority because Bar Kochba continued to win more than his share of battles. You became drunk on victory and neglected the fact that you can't live in perpetual warfare. Over the passage of time, it became evident, even to a skeptic like myself, that he most likely did have divine support. Another opportunity presented it to sue for peace. This time you could do so from an even stronger position, and I had no doubt Rome would accept. It was then that your new Moses made his decision to abandon Bar Kochba. Because you had elevated Akiva above all others, even Simon Bar Kochba saw Akiva's abandonment of himself as being no different from that of abandonment by God. But God saw the deception that was taking place ad how you had been misled by Akiva and so He made all the neighbouring nations stand up and voice their support for Bar Kochba and offer him their armies to command against the Romans. When have you ever seen all of our neighbours united to come to our aid. Of course, it was by God's will that such an event occurred. It was a miracle and you dismissed it because Akiva told you to do so. As you can see, as much as you desire to lay the blame at Akiva's feet for all your ills, the reality is that he merely provided the temptation but it was all of you that chose to bite into the apple.

But rather than recognize your own failings and guilt in these matters, instead of taking responsibility for these disastrous decisions, you still turned to Akiva and asked him why God had abandoned you. And true to form, he fed you the story that it was because Simon Bar Kochba had given consideration to accepting the offer of the Samaritans, the Galileans, the Idumeans and the Nabateans to fight alongside his army. And like the sheep you are, you all agreed that must be the reason for your failure. Not one of you stood up against this lie and saw the evidence that it was Akiva who forbade Bar Kochba from accepting their offers and then immediately afterwards turned his back on his chosen Messiah. Instead of recognizing the obvious, that God was offering these additional armies from your neighbors as a miracle to help you find a way to win the war despite all of Akiva's evil mechanizations, you still chose to follow Akiva over the truth. In order to do so, you needed to turn away from your misguided devotion to Akiva. But none of you could bring yourselves to do so! Not until I came and found you all dwelling in this pit of lies and deception.

And what did I find when I arrived in your town, only a couple of weeks passed? Did I find you grieving and mourning the tragedy of our people, the loss of our nation, the theft of our inheritance? No! I found all of you embracing Akiva ben Joseph, proclaiming his return to you as a miracle from God to be celebrated. Over five hundred thousand of your countrymen, your family members, and your children killed during three and a half years of bloody warfare, their bodies left to rot in the fields, forbidden even to provide them with a proper burial by the Romans, and you had the sheer gall to declare to me when I arrived in B'nai Brak that Akiva's return to you was a miracle from God. If that is the god you worship, then I want no part of this false deity. You worship a god of lies, a god of deceit, and a god intended only for the ignorant. You worship this god of Akiva and that false god brought you nothing but death. Right now I am tempted to pray to the one and only God in heaven, the God of my forefathers, the God of Abraham, Isaac and Jacob and ask him to pass judgment on this entire city of idol worshippers for you have become another Sodom and Gomorrah. You made Akiva your idol and now that I have shown you that he is nothing more than wood, you wish to tear the idol down!"

"No, Excellency," they shouted pleas for mercy from every corner of the courtyard. "Forgive us, Excellency for we have sinned. God forgive us our sins!" A chorus of prayers for forgiveness echoed throughout the courtyard.

"Save your prayers and don't ask me for forgiveness," I shouted at them. "Stop your praying to men of mere flesh and blood and pray instead to God Almighty, for he now holds your lives in the balance. Pray as you have never prayed before and convince our Lord that you were blinded to the sins committed by the serpent Akiva ben Joseph, even though that which is written in stone, should never have been discarded so easily. Ten commandments Moses carried down the mountain and yet all I see is a people that have forgotten all of them.

Let me remind you of our covenant with the Lord that you have so easily abandoned. The first, 'You shall have no other God but me,' yet you were willing to have him unleash this book he calls the Talmud, with these new rules of God according to Akiva and you made no effort to silence it. These are not the words from God but instead are the words from men and I say that Akiva has broken that first and second commandment sin the spirit of which they were intended.

The first commandment that you failed to adhere to and by which God shall judge you; "Thou shall not bring idols before Me," needs me to look no further. The fertility trinkets that I purchased upon my arrival, that he made and blessed for you to pray to clearly demonstrates that the first and second commandments have been violated.

The third, 'Do not swear using the Lord's name in vain,' and you all heard me provide to the Defendant the opportunity to retract all of his sworn oath but he chose not to do so. Every day of this trial he swore and oath to God and every day he violated that oath. Many within this assembly supported him in doing so, and therefore I say that in this House of God the third commandment has been broken.

The fifth, 'Honour your father and mother' yet until this week you knew not a thing about Akiva's family. He gave them no honour. He pays them no respect. When has he ever said a word of his father's conversion. No, he has buried them in obscurity and written them out of the book of life forever and yet none of you ever held him accountable. For that reason, I say unequivocally, the fifth commandment has been broken.

The sixth, 'Thou shall not kill,' but I say the blood from over half a million Jews stains the soul of Akiva and all of you that supported him forever. Those stains can never be washed away from your hands. Shall I remind you of the twenty-four thousand untrained, vulnerable, defenseless, misled students, commanded by their Master to go fight, even though he knowingly sent those young men to their deaths while also knowing he was going to betray them even if they survived. There is no doubt that the sixth commandment has been broken.

The seventh, 'Thou shall not commit adultery' and even though I cannot prove beyond a shadow of doubt that he did so with the Queen of Ethiopia, there should be no doubt by anyone that he has done so with Rufina, the wife of the Procurator of Judea. It matters not that he claims he has not fornicated with them because it was made clear during this trial that Akiva has his own definition of fornication. For those that do not believe me, I point you to a section in his book where he asks one of his students *whether you can accept the word from two witnesses in court that swear you had intercourse with an espoused maidservant over your own sworn declaration that you did not.* Do I really have to tell you who the espoused maidservant he was referring to might have been. But in telling this story he claims he can *deny having had sex because he does not complete the action.* By withdrawing early, he insists *that he has no guilt and has committed no crime.* That is why he was able to sit here so calmly and say that he has not had intercourse with the Lady Rufina.

You permitted him to write new laws and judgments contrary to our commandments. There is no requirement that says it is necessary to spill his seed within the woman before he can be found guilty. Whether he did or did not, he lusted after them and in whatever contact he had with the flesh, in his heart it was adultery. It matters not that these women were not Jewish, it is still the betrayal of his wife Rachel and the husband of the woman he is with. A betrayal of the wedding vows that God holds sacred. You learned this week that Akiva ben Joseph was an adulterer but most of you already knew this, and you permitted him to break the seventh commandment, while at the same time changing how we interpret the law.

The eighth, 'Thou shall not steal.' I will remind you there is a trail of gold and jewelry leading to Akiva's home that testifies to his theft of items for countless years. Need I remind you of the gold step-stool, dipped in the blood from those servants that Rufus killed, mistakenly thinking they had stolen his prized possession. And here it lay in Akiva's home, as a clear sign to his wickedness. I remind you of the four thousand gold aureus that Akiva took from a close friend and never accounted for. Yet, many of you were his guests, took pleasure in his accumulated wealth, but never once questioned from where it all had come. You turned a blind eye, though you knew it could not have been through legal means. There is no doubt that he has broken the eighth commandment but aided by your complicity.

The ninth commandment, 'Thou shall not bear false witness against your neighbour.' Akiva's entire life has been about bearing false witness against other people. From the time he betrayed his first wife in order to pursue the daughter of Kalba Savuah, that was not a decision based on love, but the promise of great wealth and he lied in order to obtain such a marriage. He wanted the title of President of the Council, which constantly eluded him until he finally devised a plan to eliminate all those that prevented him from achieving that goal by falsely accusing them and delivering them into the hands of the Romans. Where were any of you to raise a voice against such obvious lies. How could you not see that his gain was at the expense of others that were all better men than he was or ever would be. He clearly coveted the incredible wealth of Rabbi Tarfon, though rich himself, but preferring to use the Rabbi's gold to repay a debt, rather than sacrifice any of his own wealth and then lied about how the money was used, playing upon the generosity and idealism of Tarfon. All of these are clear indications of breaking the ninth commandment.

And finally, we examine the tenth, 'You shall not covet your neighbor's wife or his belongings.' Some of you may question what is the difference between this and committing adultery? One can commit adultery without ever actually desiring the woman. What you heard today and what is written in Akiva's own handwritten entries in his book that sits upon the Praetor's table is undeniable. Today you all saw the beautiful wife of the Procurator, the Lady Cornelia Metella Rufina and you might say that you can understand and appreciate how in his heart he may have coveted such a woman, but the fact that he pursued that relationship for over ten years, even though her husband was both friend and neighbour to Akiva meant that the tenth commandment has been most certainly violated.

Ten commandments and I have proven to you beyond a shadow of a doubt that this man that sits before you has broken nine of them. As for the last one, regarding the keeping of the Sabbath day, who knows if that one wasn't broken as well. We know that he forced Bar Kochba to accept the fourth commandment and in so doing, when he rested his men on the Sabbath Day, our armies suffered terrible losses. Did God really intend for us to die on the Sabbath?

But let me remind you, this is the man you dared to claim was the equivalent of Moses. This was the man you praised above all others and chose to heed his war cry as he marched you willingly to your deaths. This was a man that hated everything you stood for, detested everything you believed in, and most of all, as can be gleaned from the numerous pages of his own admissions, as written in his book and testified to by others, hated the Torah, which is God's manifestation on this earth. This is the man you chose over your own God, and you still wish to stand here in this holy House of God and consider yourselves to be innocent of the crimes that we have all heard and been witness to. How is it possible that we will condemn Akiva for all his sins without ever pointing a finger at our own involvement."

"We have sinned Excellency but we were deceived," someone cried out.

"We knew nothing of Akiva's betrayal," one man pleaded. "He fooled us all!"

"Akiva is the sinner, not us," a woman's voice sailed above the others.

"We lost our children. We have lost our future. He has lost nothing!" another voice rose above the din.

"Death to Akiva," the shout began with a few, only to become a chant picked up by the rest of the crowd. I let it continue for some time before holding up my hand and calling for silence.

"Fortunately for all of you, it is not up to me to bring to trial any more than the case at hand," I warned them. "Although you were not complicit in his crimes, as far as I can determine, it is undeniable that you still aided and abetted his efforts, permitting him to play out his role over these past few years. All I can suggest is that you live out the rest of your lives in fulfillment of God's laws and pray for His mercy. The Lord is a merciful God. He will hear your prayers if your heart is pure. As for Akiva ben Joseph, I rest my case and let the judges now decide his fate."

Concluding my statement, I walked slowly, my head held high, to the far side of the room, easing myself just as slowly into my chair and folding my arms across my chest for dramatic effect.

"The court asks if the Defendant has anything to say before the passing of sentence."

Akiva remained absolutely silent, never uttering even a single sound. One had to look very carefully to see that he was still breathing.

"It is now for the second time, that this court of law in the town of B'nai Brak asks if the Defendant has anything to say in his own defense." Yehonatan's request was still met with silence.

"It is for the third and final time, that this court of law, legally convened under the rule of God asks if the Defendant has anything to say in his own defense."

A single tear rolled down Akiva's cheek. Failing to receive any response, Yehnonatan instructed the judges that they could now begin their deliberations to determine sentencing. I was surprised when only after a few minutes of beginning the deliberations, Rabbi Meir said to the Praetor that he had a request to make of the Court. When Yehonatan asked the nature of the request and was told that the students of Rabbi Akiva would like to change the counting structure of the votes, the Praetor grew very concerned and asked for me to join the discussion.

"What is the problem," I inquired.

Rabbi Meir was obviously the student's spokesperson, coming from a distinguished family and being slightly older than the rest. "We don't think the system is fair," he explained.

"I have to argue that point," I objected. "I don't think I could have been any fairer towards you. Your votes are equal to every other person as a judge and juror and there are five of you in total."

Meir bowed to me apologetically, "I'm afraid I did not make myself clear. I meant that the current system of counting is not fair to you or to this court."

I must admit that his answer caught both me and Yehonatan off guard. "I think you need to explain yourself further," I instructed him.

"Talking among ourselves," he began to explain, "We realized that we all have recognized the guilt of our Master, but it is written that no student should be permitted or responsible for the denigration of their Master. If we were to vote separately it would forever be recorded that Rabbis Shimon, Yehudah, Yosi, Eleazar and Meir were responsible for the condemnation of one of the Sages of the Great Council. No one would ever trust us again. Our reputations would be destroyed. Neither the people nor our colleagues would ever let us teach again."

"So, what is your solution?" I questioned.

"We have a single voice, a single vote."

"What good will that do if you still vote that he is guilty. Everyone will still know that you all condemned your Master."

"But not if we vote to acquit," Meir waited to see my reaction.

I urged him to continue to explain himself in more detail.

"It's obvious to everyone how the other judges are going to vote. They don't really have any choice in the matter. The evidence is overwhelmingly tilted towards a conviction. And so, they will vote overwhelmingly according to the law and that will make five guilty votes and we will be the one vote for acquittal. Rabbi Akiva will still be found guilty by a majority."

"But not by a unanimous decision," I corrected him. "It will be considered a hung jury," and therefore the punishment will have to be decided by the Romans, who as far as we know may even free him because he is their puppet."

"It is the best we can do to still adhere to our vow and at the same time show that Akiva is guilty. As for our single vote, no one will ever know if it consisted of all five votes to acquit, or perhaps three votes to acquit and two guilty verdicts. And they will never know which student voted which way. We will be seen as not violating our oath as students to protect and revere our Master at all times."

"But if I agree to your request, the rest of our people will never see how justice was served because it was not a unanimous decision. It will make us look indecisive and uncertain, even after Akiva was found to be responsible for the deaths of so many of our people. We would be handing him over to the Romans without a solid conviction and even if they decide to execute him, people will begin to think that he is a martyr rather than the villain of this war." I was reluctant to have all of Akiva's sins erased so easily by ending with a hung jury. He does not deserve to depart this world with his slate wiped clean.

"Excellency, if I might be so bold to speak and explain as to why you don't want him branded as a criminal. To do so would be a terrible mistake." Meir obviously saw my struggle to agree to his plan. "If I may explain..."

"Please, go ahead and tell me why I should be thinking differently."

"We have just survived a terrible time. Perhaps the worst time in all of our recorded history. What the Romans are planning is no different than what the Assyrians did to the Kingdom of Israel in the north. They will disperse and scatter us across the globe, among all the other nations as slaves, servants, and beasts of burden. They will be transporting people from other lands to Judea, so that they can live in our homes and take our shops and farms to operate as their own. Already they have changed the name of our country, forbidding us to even mention the word Judea but I will die before I ever stop calling it that. Over the years they will make the world believe there was only Palestina, a fabricated name derived from our ancient enemies for an imaginary country, inhabited by a people that never belonged here and don't even know our God. Jerusalem is now referred to as Aelia Capitolina and we are forbidden to even enter the boundaries of our own capitol city. I certainly don't need to remind you that a statue of the Emperor Hadrian on horseback now stands where are Holy of Holies once stood. You have seen it yourself. A marble statue of a pig has been placed at Jerusalem's southern gate. They talk of erecting their own temple to one of their many gods on our holy mount and if they have their way, they will eliminate every trace of Judaism from the promised land. It will break our people once and for all, reduce us to a state of misery, leaving us nothing to believe in, nothing to hold on to except our belief that God will always protect us and deliver us from evil no matter where we find ourselves exiled. Perhaps not in a decade or a century, but sometime in the distant future, he will hear our tears and he will send us another saviour and bring us back home. But that can only happen as long as we hold on to that very thin thread that still binds us together as a people."

"You are saying that thread is our faith, and our willingness to die for what we believe."

"Exactly Excellency. We must believe that this war was not in vain. That our countrymen died because they refused to abandon their religious beliefs. That all of them preferred death before submission, martyrdom before assimilation and self-sacrifice before desertion. This is the legacy we must pass down. You have shown that we all bear responsibility for this devastating defeat. We made one mistake, let us not make another. We need to show that our leaders had to be strong, unrelenting and adamant in their solidarity with God and the people, even if that was not the case. These men must be seen as stalwarts in the fight against an evil world, yes, men not unlike Moses in their willingness to sacrifice everything for the sake of the Almighty."

"You are suggesting you can't have anyone destroying that narrative," I appreciated his concern, "But to let our future generations venerate a man that deliberately tried to destroy us, to praise him as a hero, when he sacrificed our one true chance for freedom for a woman that he could never have, you ask too much from me. Too much from all those that suffered because of his sins. Our people deserve to know the truth."

"If word was to get out," he continued, "That the man people referred to as our

331

greatest Sage, as one of the fathers of our religion, a man that they believed spoke with the angels, was a fraud, a betrayer, perhaps even more than that, even still more pagan than Jew, it would destroy us as a people. It will cripple our faith. Why should they believe in anything the other sages told them. They would condemn it all as lies and soon everyone would be like Rabbi Elisha ben Abayu, an atheist that believes in nothing but himself. By releasing the truth, you would be doing just as the Emperor had plotted to make us disappear as a people forever. It is our faith that makes us both distinct and separate people. Hadrian's goal will not be accomplished by what he planned with Akiva, but as a result of our own loss of faith because you will have exposed our gullibility and culpability in this disaster that befell us. Do you see the dilemma we now face, Excellency?"

"He betrayed us for the price of sex with a Roman woman," I protested.

"And Samson betrayed not only us but God as well for the price of Sex with a Philistine woman. Do we despise him or consider him to be a hero?"

"In the end he redeemed himself," I completed the story. "He destroyed our enemies."

"Did he really?" Meir questioned. "If he did, then explain how is it our enemies now call our country after the Philistine nation he supposedly eliminated and erased from history. This Palestina is merely a reminder that the Philistines still exist and still plague us."

"Ahhhh…" I released a long sigh. "As much as I hate to admit it, you have presented your points well. I can see your point and I cannot dismiss your concerns. But nevertheless, neither can I have Akiva surviving this trial only to spread his lies and hatred to those that never know what we have heard during the trial this week. If he is handed over to the Romans, then we must have a strategy that ensures that they execute him almost immediately. We know already he has been protected by them as their little lap dog and free to roam this country. They will try to protect him and keep him alive if they can. If I agree to your proposal, then I must have your assurances that he will not be afforded any protection and becomes a dead martyr and is not permitted to be a live hero. He is too dangerous to remain alive!"

"My fellow students and I have already discussed that possibility. Eleazar ben Shamoa will take Rabbi Akiva onto the Temple Mount. The present law is that any Jew found on the mount will be violating the edict forbidding our access and will be summarily executed for the crime of trespassing. There is no way that the Roman's can ignore an edict from their own Emperor. The Procurator will not be able to pardon him. His punishment will be swift and decisive."

"But doesn't that mean that Shamoa will also be executed?" I was concerned that there would be one more death of an innocent Jew.

"He is willing to accept that fate. He says being Akiva's student has made him unclean, and that he deserves no better than to share in the punishment of a Master that betrayed the people. E says it is his duty, as well as the fact that he says he has never been to the Temple Mount. He wants to see it and stand on it before he dies."

I could not help but look over at Eleazar ben Shamoa, and my eyes began to well up with tears. He smiled back at me, which only made me want to cry even more. I could feel my throat beginning to choke as I tried to speak. "He is probably the bravest of us all," I struggled to get the words out.

"Those like him are the reason we must spin the outcome of this trial properly," Meir commented. "We must preserve the faith."

"There was so much revealed in this trial, how can you possibly provide a cover over it all," I wondered.

"Shimon ben Yochai is a master storyteller. Already he is thinking of ways to obscure the facts.

"I think that will be an almost impossible task," I commented, looking at the facts from my perspective. "How do you hide the death of the twenty-four thousand students. Young boys that were unprepared, untrained and ordered to their deaths knowingly by their rabbinical master, Akiva simply to make it look like there was a legitimate army under Bar Kochba at the start of the war so that Rufus could receive the glory, fame and credit for defeating a force five times his number. It was all a sham. How does one hide that?"

"This is how, *'And in those days God sent a plague upon the students of Akiva because of the constant discord and disrespect they paid to one another,'* Who will say otherwise?" Meir related one of the covering stories that Ben Yochai had already prepared.

"A plague? Really? A plague that just targeted Akiva's twenty-four thousand students because they showed a lack of respect to each other. You expect anyone to believe that? Even if I had no knowledge of this trial I could never believe something so farcical. If that is the best he can do then I think we may still have a problem."

"Don't worry," Meir reassured me. "He'll work on it. By the time he is finished everyone will believe what is written. A hundred years from now it will be the only version of the story anyone will ever know."

"I will put my faith in you, young Meir. Whatever you do, don't fail me," I grasped his forearm to signify my agreement to his plan. "But tell Ben Yochai that it is still essential that he disperses the truth in these stories he weaves so that in the future, one of my descendants, if they find themselves in need, can still identify the truth behind what happened here. The truth must be preserved, even if it is to be concealed. There must always be a trail that leads back to the truth."

"It will be done," he agreed. "He will conceal the truth in plain sight."

"Accepted then! We will vote according to your plan. Praetor, let us proceed with the vote."

Yehonatan stood to make the announcement that the voting would commence immediately. Those citizens of the city that still remained anxiously within the confines of the courtyard moved closer to the ropes in order to hear the decision. Their concerns of preparing for the Sabbath had been outweighed by their eagerness to hear the final verdict.

"The students of Rabbi Akiva ben Joseph, who have requested and been granted a single ballot to be recorded, how do you vote?" Yehonatan asked.

"For the sake of mercy Praetor, we vote for acquittal."

No sooner had they cast their vote, the crowd erupted into a chorus of verbal abuse and swearing. This is not what they wanted to hear, not after I had inflamed them by saying they were just as guilty for letting Akiva and his Roman allies get away all these years with his nefarious plan. They needed a scapegoat to wipe away their own sins and to do so, they wanted blood.

"Silence in the court," Yehonatan shouted them down until a relative calm had been restored. Simon ben Zoma, how do you vote?"

"Guilty your Honour."

This time the shouting from the remaining crowd was more jubilant.

Simon ben Azzai, how do you vote?

"Guilty Praetor."

Ben Azzai's vote was met with a similar reaction to Ben Zoma's. As far as the townspeople were concerned there was no other vote possible.

"Abba Saul, how do you vote?"

"Guilty Praetor."

This time the shouts, cheer and round of applause were much louder and meant the people already knew how the deciding votes would end. They didn't understand even with a majority, it was still a hung jury because of my promise at the start of the trial that it had to be a unanimous conviction. I would not break my promise. Furthermore, there was no rule that my sons would necessarily vote according to my own inclination, but I guess there was an unwritten rule that they would not disrespect me by doing otherwise. An unwritten rule that governed Akiva's students as well.

"Joseph ben Elioneai, how do you vote?"

"Guilty your Honour."

The applause was continuous now, and Yehonatan had to proceed even if he could not get silence in the court.

"And Azariah ben Elioneai, how do you vote?"

"Guilty Praetor."

"Akiva ben Joseph, though you make no effort to demonstrate your cognizance," Yehonatan addressed the defendant, "The vote has been taken and you have been found guilty of the crimes for which you were accused by an overwhelming majority. But because the guilty verdict was not unanimous, you will be handed over to the Roman authorities with a request for execution for your part in the war."

As soon as the Praetor announced the sentence, I thought I could detect a small smile appear on Akiva's lips. It was the first sign of any emotion I had seen from him all afternoon. It was good to know that he was still alive. It was obvious he thought that handing him over to the Romans was the best he could have hoped for. Once he was handed over into their custody, he could invoke the Procurator Rufus to release him under their arrangement. I had my doubts as well that Rufus wouldn't honour their agreement. After all, according to my arrangements with his wife, the Lady Cornelia Rufina, I would not provide her husband with any of the evidence that her affair with Akiva was more than a sham. If he knew, I had no doubt he would have had her executed. My only hope was that Meir could deliver on his promise.

My guards led Akvia from the courtyard to the prison house. It was then that I think he realized for the first time that his life was certainly going to be different from now on, and the label of criminal was permanent, even if he thought he wouldn't be executed. He probably expected to remain under house arrest but that was a misconception on his part. Now that he was a convicted, he would learn to live in a prison cell no different from any other prisoner, until such time that he would be taken to Jerusalem. Rabbi Meir had indicated that would take place soon and I would make certain he fulfilled that promise.

Stepping towards his former students, I could not help but mention my concerns to Meir that I still had this strong suspicion that Akiva believes he is not going to be executed once he is handed into Roman custody. I reminded them that his connections go all the way up to the Emperor even if he is caught violating an Imperial decree.

"Excellency," Rabbi Meir addressed me with due sincerity, "Whatever it takes, whatever I have to do, I promise you in this sanctified House of God that Akiva will have his day with the executioner. You have my word."

"I will be returning soon to Babylon, but I want you all to know that I am relieved to know that whatever the future of our people in this land, which will always be Judea and never Palestina as far as I am concerned, from now until forever, is in your trustworthy hands. You have restored my hope that we will survive this disaster and we will be stronger for it. May God bless you and protect you all the days of your lives."

"And God bless the House of Phiabi," they said.

"I will remember you said that," I teased them. "Let's see if you can convince your colleagues to say the same," We all laughed at the private joke. Never will happen, I thought to myself. As far as these rabbis are concerned, the House of Phiabi will always be seen as a plague upon their existence. Perhaps they're right in fearing us. Who knows of what interactions there will be between my family and these modern Pharisees in the future. It can't be any worse than it has been.

Chapter Twenty

The Road North:

It was a beautiful morning on yom rishon, the day following the Sabbath, and we were already on the road heading north as soon as the sun had risen. The four of us, myself, my two sons and Abba Saul, decided it was too nice a day to sit in a hot covered wagon so we rode up front with the captain of my guard. Ben Zoma and Ben Azzai had decided to stay longer in B'nai Brak and help the town return to a semblance of normalcy following the tribunal. Whereas my sons and I were riding on our mules, our usual mounts, it was necessary for one of Jacob's men to offer up his seventeen-hand horse, as there was no mule that would have been able to move beneath the enormity of Abba Saul. Even standing seventeen hands high, the horse looked tiny beneath Abba Saul, and if it wasn't for the stirrups, he would have been dragging his feet along the ground.

"Perhaps next time we travel we should think about bringing along an elephant," I jested at Abba Saul's expense. My normally staid and unemotional guards couldn't help but laugh as well, as they looked over at Abba Saul and the awkwardness of his predicament. As uncomfortable as he may have looked, I knew exactly what my guards were thinking, "Oh my God, the poor horse."

"You know, there are bigger horses," Abba Saul responded.

"That happens to be the tallest horse we have available. In fact, it is probably the tallest horse in the province. I'm afraid the world was built on a much smaller scale than you require Abba Saul. You may have to ask God about that someday."

"Funny you mention that; I believe that day will be coming sooner than you think," he said jokingly about himself.

"But not until you've seen Babylon," I told him.

Azariah was practically bursting to ask a question, but he was unsure how it would be taken, seeing the usual dour face of Abba Saul. I already guessed what he wanted to ask. I gave him a nod to indicate he should go ahead and ask.

"Abba Saul," he said his name sheepishly, "May I ask if your parents were giants too?

The grave digger's scowl transformed into a wide grin and then he burst out laughing. "My mother was probably one of the smallest women you ever would have seen. Barely five feet tall," he continued to laugh. "You can imagine how people would stare when we'd walk together down the street. Even as a teenager I was almost one and a half times her height. They'd look at me and then my little sweet mum and the other women would imagine the pain of giving birth to someone like me. Of course, as a baby, I was no different in size than any other baby, but we didn't bother to tell them that. It was more fun watching them imagine the pain of the childbirth, and then move uncomfortably, squeezing their legs together as if they could actually feel it."

"What about your father," Azariah was still curious.

"Now, he was a tall man," as far as I remember. "A little taller than your father but certainly not like me if that's what you're wondering. No, Azariah, there is no one else like Abba Saul. The ancient Anakim are long gone from this world."

"Do you ever wish the race of giants still existed?" Azariah asked next, implying that Abba Saul was indeed descended from that extinct race of men.

"Not really," he answered. "When you read your Torah and Tanach, you get the feeling that the giants were not too well liked by the race of normal sized men. It seems any time men and the giants encountered each other, the giants always ended up on the losing end. They were seen as a threat I suppose. This way, as the only one, I'm not a threat to anyone."

"Certainly makes sense to me," Joseph waded into the conversation. "Mankind wants to destroy anything they don't understand. Just look at us. The rest of world doesn't understand us at all, so their natural reaction is to try and destroy us. I doubt they will ever leave us alone. Isn't that right Father?"

"I don't know about the timeframe of 'never'," I responded. "God did promise that one day we would illuminate the world and once everyone came to know our God then there would be peace and understanding."

"If this past week taught me anything, it's that we can't even find a mutual understanding that permits us to have peace among ourselves," Joseph's mind was still lingering on the events of the trial. "All our lives Father, you taught us the Torah is the only law we need, and as High Priests, that is the way we are supposed to think, but what if it is not enough for the modern world? After all, the Torah was written for a world thirteen hundred years ago. And the Tanach, well…it just tells tales of heroes and prophets and none of of those exist anymore."

"Just because the Torah was dictated by God over a millennium ago, doesn't mean that it doesn't apply to today or tomorrow and that the Lord didn't anticipate we'd have the same issues in the future. In fact, I think it may be more appropriate now than it ever was in the past. And don't be fooled, we still have our heroes today, although we seem to be better at tearing them down these days than praising them."

"How so?" both my sons asked.

"Well, let's look at some of the things that came up at the trial. What was the main reason Bar Kochba was defeated by the Romans?"

"Because he was betrayed, of course," Joseph replied without any hesitation. Azariah and Abba Saul nodded their agreement.

"Tell me how he was betrayed," I pushed for a more definitive statement.

"He needed the support of Akiva to be convinced that God fought with him and his troops on the battlefield. When Akiva abandoned him, he lost all hope and was resigned to defeat."

"If that was the case, then who was actually betrayed?"

"I don't understand," my eldest son wrestled with my question.

"You just told me that when Akiva abandoned him, Bar Kochba felt betrayed and lost all hope. At least that is what you implied, was it not?"

"Yes," Joseph agreed, "But you're going to tell me I'm wrong, aren't you?"

"Of course, I am, I'm your father. That's what fathers do," I teased him.

"Akiva was incapable of betraying anyone. So, the answer is no, he didn't betray Bar Kochba," I tried to correct his way of thinking. "Akiva had no power that he could betray anyone. Any authority that Akiva had was an illusion. That is what I hope you came to realize from the trial.

People readily gave Akiva power and authority over their lives. He wasn't deserving of it, he certainly didn't earn it, but they still gave it to him. You see, sometimes people are so eager to have someone lord over them, that they will willingly give away their freedom of choice and self-determination, and more often that not, they do so blindly only to regret it later. We all have a destiny, but we have freewill to accept or decline what God has prepared for us. Therefore, we only have one being in this universe that we should be turning to in times of doubt."

"I guess you want us to say that Bar Kochba betrayed himself," my eldest son came to understand my point.

"If we look to the stories in the Torah, we will read how God made that perfectly clear to Moses that he was in control of his own destiny and even punished Moses when he let his doubts and fears overcome his faith. God had already shown Simon Bar Kochba what he was capable of. He gave Bar Kochba wisdom to command wisely over thousands of men and make the right decisions at the right time on the battlefield. That strength and power resided in Bar Kochba, it didn't come from Akiva. It never came from Akiva but Bar Kochba didn't have the strength to believe in himself. So he attributed his successes to Akiva and let Akiva control his fears. If only Simon bar Kochba had given credit and praise for his victories directly to God, where it belonged and not to Akiva, then he may have actually won this war."

"I thought you said we could never defeat the Roman Empire," Abba Saul challenged my last statement.

"It all depends on how you define the word win. If you define it as destroying all the legions of the Empire, and seeing an end to Rome, that was never going to happen. But if a win was when Rome could no longer see any advantage in sending more legions into Judea, only to have them slaughtered, so it chose a different tactic, such as seeking a truce, then I think they would have settled on an armistice and returned Judea to the status of Kingdom under the rule of a Satrap."

"But by listening to Akiva and not to what God had already implanted into his heart and mind, he betrayed God! That is what you are suggesting," Azariah had arrived at an understanding of my meaning.

"Your both right," I congratulated my son. "Bar Kochba did betray himself, by not knowing where to place his faith, but most of all he betrayed God, for not listening to what God had already shown him and turning to Akiva for answers."

"Bar Kochba knew he needed forces that could attack the Romans from behind while they were attacking Bar Kochba's men confined to the towns and cities. Every fibre of his military thinking told him that was the only way he would defeat General Julius Severus. He had the Galileans begging to do so, the Samaritans willing to lay down their lives for their Judean brethren, and even the Nabateans and Idumeans offering to ride in from the desert to his aid. When has that ever happened? I will tell you, never! In all our history we have never been able to ally ourselves with our cousins in battle. Surely that was God's miraculous sign for all to see. You either had to be blind or a man without faith not to see the hand of God. Sadly, Bar Kochba may have been both. For the first time in recorded time, all the people claiming descent from Isaac, were willing to come together and fight alongside one another as one people, one glorious army under God, as we were always intended to be since the days of the Patriarchs. Severus would never have been able to withstand the onslaught from more than one direction. Bar Kochba knew it was the right choice, he knew that this was a miracle that brothers that have been at each other's throats for so long were willing to fight shoulder to shoulder, but he still sought approval. How could such an event been anything other than a direct sign from God, but as soon as he told Akiva of his plan, Akiva claimed God would abandon him. Akiva played on the one weakness he knew he could exploit in Bar Kochba, the man's ego!"

"I thought Akiva told him that God would not permit a victory to be won by those considered unclean," Joseph challenged my explanation. "What does that have to do with ego?"

"In order to plant the seeds of doubt, Akiva had to say more than just God does not approve of these other nations. He had to tell Bar Kochba that if he went ahead and accepted the aid from those considered as 'unclean' races then should they win the battle against the Romans, then they would be the ones claiming t he victory, not him and certainly not the God of the Jews. Bar Kochba was damned no matter what happened if he let the others fight with him."

"He was a fool to listen to Akiva," Abba Saul spat out the words.

"Well, that could be said for many of you as well. "What were all of you esteemed members of the Rabbinical Great Council doing for the past thirty years, if it wasn't listening to everything Akiva had to say, while at the same time kissing his converted Greek ass," I taunted him.

"Not me," Abba Saul denied it immediately. "Was never that man's ass kisser."

"Bar Kochba had a choice. Let those other nations fight alongside his army, and in so doing betray Akiva, or do as Akvia demanded and betray the miracle he was witnessing with his own eyes when those letters of assistance arrived. He chose to do the latter, a terrible decision, and as much as we would like to condemn him as a fool for doing so, we have just lived through a week of testimonies that demonstrated just how good Akiva was at manipulating people. I believe that for far longer than we are willing to admit, we all betrayed God because we chose to listen to Akiva ben Joseph ha Ger. Rather than look for our answers in the Torah and the Tanach, so many of us turned to Akiva for solutions that only served to lead us astray from God."

"We have suffered a horrible price for our blindness," Abba Saul admitted.

"One that the cost will take a long time to recover from, I'm afraid," I suspected that time would practically be an eternity.

"Then it was fortunate that you heard that rumor that brought us here," the grave digger added.

"Good fortune had nothing to do with it," I refuse to accept happenstance as an explanation as to why I was drawn to B'nai Brak. "Our Lord God made certain that I came here, much as he made certain that all the facts of the trial would come out as well, no matter how clever Akiva may have been."

"Truthfully, when did you become fully aware and convinced that Akiva was being coerced to work for the Romans?" Abba Saul wanted to know.

"It was when I read in his book where he and Rabbi Simeon ben Gamaliel were sitting in the Lower City and then said after they both saw the beautiful Roman woman in the street that he intended to marry her. It was not a coincidence that I opened the book to that particular section and it reminded me that it was the same thing Samson said after he saw the beautiful Philistine girl and later when he saw Delilah. No sooner did I read it, then a little voice in my head that I have come to know as belonging to God said, 'Can you not see, they are one and the same.' I realized they were definitely the same. One was a Danite, treated like an outcast by the more powerful Judahites but still wishing and believing he should be recognized as a judge over all the tribes, even though the other tribes were never going to agree that he merited it. He worked hard to establish his right to be a judge but in the end was willing to throw it all away for a beautiful foreign woman. We all know the story of how his pursuit of Delilah led to his betrayal of God by revealing his secrets to her. After reading that, it was just a matter of identifying Akiva's Delilah."

"And you knew then that he was having an affair with the wife of the Procurator Tinnius Rufus. That is truly amazing," Abba Saul was intrigued to know more regarding my insight.

"No, not then," I answered.

"I know, I know," Azariah thought he figured it out. "You knew they were intimate when Jacob found the golden bed stool and showed it to you. That's right, isn't it?"

"No, it wasn't then either," I informed them. "All I knew then was that he had stolen property from the Governor's house, but I wasn't certain how he obtained it. I may have had my suspicions, but it was when Jacob later pointed out some of the other items in Akiva's possession, especially the jewelry, that only could have come from the Governor's wife that I realized they had a close relationship but I still didn't know they were sexually intimate."

"Then it must have been when you read that story about *the foreign Princess throwing her treasure into the sea and Akiva finding it*," Joseph took his best guess at the timing of my revelation.

"What I interpreted that story as signifying was a guilty man realizing that sometime in the future someone was going to wonder how he had accumulated such massive wealth. It far exceeded what he gained from marrying Rachel and their inheritance from Kalba Savuah and it was also pretty obvious that Akiva certainly couldn't be recognized for his intelligence as an investor, since he was always losing money, so at some point he would needed to explain where it all came from. He wasted money and was known to be extravagant with his trips and failed enterprises and was seen to be overly charitable, yet there was never any shortage of gold and jewels. Yet no one ever asked. Not even you, Abba Saul.

He tried to conceal the truth and avoid discovery by converting fact into fiction. Having the added sense of hindsight, it is now clear to all of us that the foreign princes was undoubtedly the Lady Cornelia Metella Rufina and she was throwing her gold and jewelry into the sea because of her love for Akiva. I know for a fact that she did love him but at the time I began to understand this story, I actually took its meaning to indicate that they had not been intimate. The sea I thought was a metaphor, meaning that there was this great uncrossable divide between them. As far as his using the treasure to pay off serious debts that he owed to a foreign king, I understood that to simply be an excuse for never trying to return the treasure to its rightful owner. It justified in real life how he may have come into his tremendous wealth, stolen or else taken from others, but he never returns any of it, even though he apparently he insists one must return all found wealth to its rightful owner in the Talmud he was writing. So that wasn't when I realized it either."

"So, when was it?" they asked in exasperation.

"If you insist on knowing the answer, it was when Judah ben Tarfon mentioned the four thousand gold aureus."

"What did that have to do with anything?" Joseph asked.

"It was a very specific amount," I responded.

"Yes, so is one gold aureus, or ten, or even a hundred, but that doesn't mean that two people are lovers simply because they exchange a gold coin. What is the real story?"

"That is the real story, if you must know," I laughed at their shared disbelief.

"Impossible," Joseph refused to accept my explanation.

"All right, I will tell you," I finally submitted. "Now listen while I explain it to you. First, as I said, it is a very specific amount. You don't ask for four thousand gold coins unless you need four thousand gold coins for a specific reason. That being the case, then what things come to mind that cost that much?" I could see that they were stumped by the question. "Don't worry about trying to answer, I will tell you. In the old days of Rome, the rich families of the aristocracy would pay the dowry to the would-be-in-law by giving them their daughter's weight in gold. Over the years, rather than actually weighing their daughters, it just became customary to give four thousand aureus if the girl was petite, and an additional thousand if she was considered large boned."

"You mean fat," Azariah interrupted my explanation.

"Having seen the Lady Cornelia, you all know she is what we would all consider petite, hence a four thousand gold coin dowry. But since it has almost been universally the case of one Roman aristocratic family marrying another, all of them tending to be rich, this money never actually gets used but instead is just transferred one generation to the next by the continual birth of daughters. Control of the funds therefore would still remain with the daughter that was married and that also provided a significant safeguard if she was ever divorced by her husband, which I must say happens a lot in Roman society. In this manner the daughter retains control and can take that dowry with her into her next marriage, so even a divorced woman is still seen as desirable because with four thousand aureus, she is by all definition, rich.

On closer examination, you will come to realize that it is a perfect protection system by which the aristocracy of Rome can preserve its fortunes since the money never actually departs from circulation within their class structure but also serves to protect every women of their upper class society from financial hardship. But then let's say for some reason a husband becomes worried that his wife may have taken a lover and wants to know if she might have intentions to end their marriage. The first thing he could do is ask to have confirmation that the dowry has remained untouched. If it is all there, perhaps his wife may only have a casual lover but that would be nothing serious to worry about as far as the husband is concerned, since Romans don't think of fidelity in the same way that we do. But should he search for the money and find that it is gone, in part or all of it, that means his wife has considered this lover to possibly be her next husband and she is already showering him with gifts. It would be a silly thing to do as a rich and powerful husband would demand a heavy price for his wife's infidelity. That often meant the head of his wife and that of her lover if he wanted to be cruel. So only a woman that was seriously in love with another man and was likely to be physically intimate with her lover to the point that they felt committed to each other would ever dare to use the dowry money. She'd also have to have reason to believe her husband would never suspect her of such behavior and I'm guessing the fact that Tinnius Rufus told his wife to go out and actually seduce Akiva might be reason enough for her to think that he would never suspect them. But even the most uncaring and unloving of husbands at some time becomes aroused by suspicion and jealousy. That meant that the Lady Cornelia, if she had given away her dowry, would have run to Akiva in a desperate and practically maniacal panic, insisting that he needed to return all of the money immediately, all four thousand pieces so its absence would not be discovered. But of course, Akiva would not have the money available, because as I said, this was a man who loved to be impulsive and wildly extravagant, praised for his generosity of giving away money to numerous causes, schools and charities, especially because it didn't potentially cost him anything, not a single zuz, since it was usually someone else's money that he was spending. But this time, he had no other recourse but to request the money from Rabbi Tarfon, who like so many others never suspected Akiva of any sinful behavior."

"You were able to determine all that from the mention of four thousand aureus," Abba Saul was impressed. "So why did you ask the Lady Cornelia about it if you already knew?"

"It was simply a warning. I needed to remind her that she had no other choice but to cooperate with me and she shouldn't try not to do anything foolish after she returned to Caesarea. As long as she knew that I knew about the four thousand gold coins it not only guaranteed her full cooperation but also her silence regarding the trial. Don't be fooled by her beauty. In that heart of hers beats the soul of a Lilith. If she could think of a way to tell her husband an alternative reality about what we were doing and have all of us arrested and executed, while at the same time saving Akiva, she'd do it. I pointed out in my letter of invitation to her, requesting that she testify, that I had incriminating evidence that would make its way to her husband's desk if she did try anything."

"Ah...I understand," Abba Saul nodded his approval. "Blackmail has its place."

"I prefer to call it friendly persuasion. For everything there is a reason, my friend. Remember it is said, 'I find more bitter than death the woman, whose heart is snares and nets, and her hands as bands; who so pleaseth God shall escape from her; but the sinner shall be taken by her.' As I said, all answers can be found in the Torah and Tanach."

"Ecclesiastes, Chapter 7," Abba Saul recognized my quote.

"That book has always proven itself to be a source of wisdom for me," I commented. I honestly think if more people were to read it in depth and more thoroughly, as well as pay attention to its numerous messages, then we wouldn't need the Pharisees of this age insisting that God needs an interpreter."

"Well, I've read it," Joseph informed all of us, "And that's why I don't intend to get married."

"I may not have mentioned this to you earlier son, when you mother and I were briefly talking about marriage, but when we are back in Babylon, we have a few families we have already arranged to meet. It is time that your mother and I select a bride for you."

"Father, I'm only twenty years old!" Joseph pleaded.

"Sounds about the right age to me," I snapped back. "What do you think Abba Saul?"

"He's practically an old man already," the grizzled old graybeard expressed his thoughts on the idea of marriage.

Azariah started to laugh at his brother's predicament.

"Oh, did I not mention the reason we are looking at a few selected families is because we are looking for two wives."

Azariah lost his natural copper skin colour and turned as white as a ghost. "But…but…I'm not even nineteen yet," he practically cried.

"Another boy past his prime," Abba Saul criticized. "Why did you wait so long?"

I guess we all knew the answer to that question. Three and a half years of war tends to set back the best of plans.

Epilogue

The letter arrived a few days before Succot. I had not expected to hear any news from those I left behind in Judea, so it was a pleasant surprise to receive the missive. I decided that I would continue to call our ancient homeland Judea, despite the Romans banning the name and insisting we all refer to it as Palestina. After all, I live under Parthian rule, so who are the Romans to tell me anything. They are just one more empire to rise and fall, disappearing as dust on the wind, but my people will still be there when the Romans are long gone.

I noticed that the impression in the wax seal indicated that it came directly from Rabbi Meir in Jerusalem. I certainly had not anticipated receiving any messages from Akiva's former student. A feeling in my gut told me that it was going to say that there had been a problem. Somehow, I wasn't too surprised. It wasn't if I hadn't thought about it. Akiva was like a cat. No matter how many times you think he has met his fate, he always seems to find a way to escape death.

I opened the missive with some trepidation, breaking the seal and then slowly unrolling the single page of parchment. I began reading it, breathing heavily as I did so, careful not to make any errors in interpreting the facts as they had been written.

Greetings Excellency.

In the name of the Most High, a blessing upon you and your family.

I made a promise to you that I would see to it that Rabbi Akiva received the

punishment that he so richly deserved. Not long after you left B'nai Brak we escorted our Master to Jerusalem. Along the way we met Reb Pappos ben Yehuda.   When he inquired where we were going, he

grew very distraught after we told him what had transpired at the trial.   He told Eleazar ben Shamoa that he was not permitted to go alone to take Rabbi Akiva to the Temple Mount because he knew Akiva would fill his head with doubt and convince him that it would be a sin that he was committing.   Over the years, Reb Pappos said he had seen Akiva use his powers of persuasion to convince many people to do things that they swore they would not do. He feared that Ben Shamoa's youthful age made him susceptible to Akiva's will. Therefore, he proposed that he would accompany them both to the Temple Mount to pray.   He would see to it that there would be no opportunity for failure.

When we protested that it was not right because Reb Pappos is reputed to be free of sin and therefore to give up his life would be a repudiation of his legacy, he simply told us that he had committed years of sinning.   He reckoned that his greatest sins of all were due to all the years he spent engaging in religious debate with Akiva only to now realize that it was all for naught, and God has seen it as nothing more than idle chatter.   To pay for his sins, he insisted on assisting in taking Akiva to the Mount.

And so they did, and together they forced Akiva on to his knees close to where the Holy of Holies once stood. Singing their prayers together, voices so loud that even the angels in heaven would hear them, the Romans came and arrested them all.

We heard the news that Reb Pappos and Eleazar ben Shamoa were executed soon after their being taken prisoner, but Akiva remained in a cell and there was no date set for his execution.   We waited, and waited, and all we heard was that Akiva's fate had not been decided.

What was even more worrisome is that he began seeing visitors in his cell and was afforded comforts that others did not receive. This went on for months and I began to doubt that he would ever face justice.

I swore to you that I would ensure that Akiva would be made to pay for his crimes and my word means more to me than the fact that I would be complicit in the shedding of blood.

I travelled to Caesarea and asked for an audience with the Procurator. He thought it strange that I would actually be seeking to know when Akiva would be executed rather than pleading for my Master's life. He confided to me that the Emperor's protection over Akiva could mean that he may never be executed. This would be in recognition of all the support he had provided during the war.

But it was obvious the Procurator had no love for my Master and wanted him dead for reasons of his own. I think he always suspected the relationship between his wife and Akiva was greater than he was led to believe. He informed me that Hadrian would only rescind his order of protection if Akiva was to openly declare himself in opposition to Rome and the Emperor.

Hadrian knew that having Akiva treated like a guest in the prison would eventually break the spirit of the Jews and destroy any nationalism as more and more came to see that he had betrayed them. It was obvious that Rufus didn't care either way since he would not raise a hand to defy the Emperor's orders.

I knew I had to change the Procurator's mind. I told him where he could find his long lost golden bed stool. When he asked how it came to be in the possession of Akiva, I told him it was a gift from the Lady Rufina. His rage was indescribable. Now he had proof that his wife was not as honest and forthcoming as he thought but he did not suspect infidelity on her part. But now, he knew the truth and he wanted Akiva dead for stealing far more than a bed stool from him.

He had a plan and I was instrumental to its success. There was only one way for Akiva to be seen as being in opposition of Hadrian and that was to begin practicing those Jewish rites that had been prohibited. Together we decided that I would request that Akiva perform my ordination as a Rabbi, the primary restriction that Hadrian had ordered. At first, I was reluctant because I knew that I would be arrested as a participant in this violation of Roman law and probably executed as well. But Rufus understood my fear and removed one of the rings that he wore on his right hand. "This ring will guarantee you safe passage and prevent your arrest," he informed me. "Show it to the guards when they arrive." Taking the ring I left his presence and made plans to see Akiva in his cell. He was pleased to see me, as if all that had transpired during the trial never occurred. When I told him I wanted to be ordained he laughed at me. "You can't be serious", he said. "If I was to do that, they would definitely not hesitate to kill me. I'm sorry Meir but it is not going to happen." I had no choice but to tell him that I informed Tinnius Rufus of the relationship he had with his wife.   He needed to know that whether

or not he ordained me that his end was coming.   Better that his final act

be seen as performing a rite in the name of God rather than for having

sexual relations with a married woman.   Akiva saw the sense of my

argument, even though the outcome would be the same.

Perhaps he even thought he could gain a little of God's mercy and forgiveness

before he died if he showed some repentance in performing this final

act.   He agreed and it was done under the observation of the guards so that

we knew that the act would be reported and the punishment meted out.

Apparently his death was horrible.   I did not stay to witness it. Wearing

metal talons, Rufus had the flesh torn from his body until his entrails spilt

across the ground. There are stories that say I was a witness to this brutal

execution and perhaps with the Procurator's permission it

may have been possible to gain entry, but why would any man do so other

than by a morbid curiosity.   I have no such inclination and in some ways

I resent the story but Shimon ben Yochai has already perpetuated it and

even reports now that Akiva shouted out the Shema as he was dying. 'The

Lord is God, the Lord is One,' succumbing as soon as he recited the final word.

Of course, as I mentioned no one was there to witness his execution, but that

also means no one can rebuke this story.   Ben Yochai is very good at

weaving his tales.

How strange that the execution was conducted on the Day of Atonement, *which I consider a fitting justice as it was almost seven months after his initial arrest. It was time that he atoned for his sins!*

The irony, if there is one, is that my ordination by Rabbi Akiva failed to be recognized by any of the other Sages. I had to have it repeated by Rabbi Yehudah ben Babba.

Though Shimon ben Yochai will be able to obfuscate the real history of events for future generations, I guess this generation will not so easily forget or forgive.

Though I don't know if our paths will ever cross again, I want you to know that we will do our best to ensure that the Torah remains our true source of laws. Anything else will merely be commentary.

I am grateful to the Almighty that he provided us with the opportunity to see for ourselves the greatness of the Kohen Gadol.

Baruch Atah

Rabbi Meir

Rolling up the parchment, it was hard for me to determine how I actually felt at that moment. In some ways I was happy and relieved that it was finally over, but I could not help but think that it was only the beginning as far as the battles that my family might face in protecting the Torah from being misinterpreted and misappropriated by this growing class of scholars that lack the fundamental concept of the immutable word of God. Would we constantly be wrestling for the soul of Judaism? Only God knows the answer to that question. I am merely his servant and nothing more.

Letter From The Author

I am certain that there is a portion of my readership that is wondering why this book was written, considering that most of my other novels are stories about the actual events of war and not the aftermath. In fact, they may have actually bought this book thinking it would be the ultimate war story about Bar Kosba, who is referred most often to as Bar Kochba in this book because I want everyone to realize he was about as close to the 'warrior Messiah' as any man would ever get and the later reference as Bar Koziba or 'Son of Deceit or Lies' was only applied when the same people that cheered him on decided it was best to protect themselves from any association, lest they found themselves in a Roman prison.

When I researched the Bar Kochba War, or the Second Roman-Jewish War, as it is also called, the most outstanding accomplishment that I could discover regarding the series of battles was that technically Bar Kochba had won. Considering the disastrous outcome, it seems strange that I would say that, but there was a point during the war, where Bar Kochba could have requested negotiations with the Roman government and established a semi-autonomous country similar to what Simon Maccabee had done with the Seleukid monarchs after the defeat of Antiochus IV. And in all likelihood, the request for such a truce would have been granted. Because of that realization, I decided to investigate all the reasons why it didn't happen. Not too surprisingly, the answer was in the Talmud, that compilation consisting of three separate sections, the detailed laws known as the Halachah, sayings and commentary in regard to the law called the Mishnah, and stories, memoirs and histories referred to as the Gemara. It is in this latter section, the Gemara, that the rabbis of the period kept recording their so-called exploits. And just as Rabbi Meir mentioned and promised my ancestor, Elioneai, the various rabbinic editors of the Talmud, over the years would rework many of these stories for the sake of preserving their religious content and the preservation of Judaism, but rather than eliminating many of the events from the historical record that were of a cruder or contrary nature, they would simply hide or obfuscate the facts so that it would take anyone seeking the truth behind these events a lifetime of detective work to assemble them into their proper place of relevance and importance.

But that is exactly what I had; a lifetime. For those that are unfamiliar with my story, I was trained in an orthodox Jewish school system known as Eitz Chaim (the Tree of Life) and was being groomed to transition into the Yeshiva and life as a Rabbinical Scholar. This was despite my family background of being Karaite, even though more than the occasional ancestor crossed over every now and then to become a Rabbanite. It just goes to prove not even my family can claim to be perfect. As they awarded me with scholarships, made me the valedictorian and begged my mother to convince me to remain in their system, there was always this little voice inside my head, just like the one Elioneai could hear, that kept saying, 'Something is definitely wrong here.' I learned at a young age to listen to that inner voice and over my lifetime it has never steered me wrong.

One of the issues I obviously had was with the Talmud. I make no denial of my innate prejudice against that book. Nothing more than a collection of argumentative discourses, often presented by inexperienced, uneducated scholars (there's an oxymoron for you), that had absolutely no right to offer an opinion on anything worldly or historical, especially when it came to explaining the wisdom of God, since it was obvious they were anything but open-minded. As Karaite, I knew that everything I needed to know was in the Torah and the Tanach. How to live my life, how to be good to my fellow man, how to find and pursue justice, and even how to recognize whether my life was travelling along the correct path or not. But the Talmud, it just raised red flag after red flag as I studied it because there were so many issues which I found unacceptable within its pages that I condemned it for being nothing more than the words of petty men, craving greatness that they never deserved. The more that I delved into these rabbinical teachings, the more I realized they would have never come into existence and achieved subsequent acceptance if Jerusalem had been rebuilt and the Temple still stood. As long as the priests were still adhering to their Boethian and Zadokite teachings, the Talmud would be viewed as irrelevant, perhaps even as blasphemous. Zadokite and Boethian teachings that are at the heart of Karaism and therefore the very antithesis of the post-Temple Rabbanite religion, would have been dominant.

If the above hypothesis was true, as I believe it to be, then anything that would have meant a resurgence of the Temple cult would have been perceived as a threat by some, if not all, of these rabbis. Their authority only existed as a default mechanism of a vanishing priesthood, resulting from the destruction of the Temple, and certainly not because these men merited the positions of authority and scholarship that they claimed from the vacuum. So, if their origins, as related to the Talmud relied on the basic premise of my hypothesis, then that meant there would have always been someone from their ranks that wanted to ensure they would never lose their power and therefore would do anything to guarantee the failure of Bar Kochba's revolt.

Thus, the second hypothesis was born, that there must have been a traitor, a true Benedict Arnold, that worked tirelessly to prevent the rise of a Jewish Kingdom ever seeing the light of day. And because of my years training under the Rabbis, I also knew they could never remain silent about what they considered their achievements, even if those perceived successes were less than honourable. They would often gloat to me that there were secrets that remain untold to the student, shocking secrets, that are only revealed once one joins the fold of being an Orthodox Rabbi. But their confession of having occult knowledge only convinced me, that what they held true today amongst themselves, was almost certainly very true two thousand years ago as well. The old adage that a leopard never changes its spots applies equally to the rabbinical cult. and our history has consistently suffered for twenty-two hundred years because of it. Wherever Jews have suffered, you will always find there was a betrayal of one sort or another, most often committed by these 'self-appointed' wise men that we refer to as rabbis. One only has to read my book *Zutra* to see the truth of this statement.

Knowledge can often be a source of emotional grief, because when the truth is revealed, we often realize we may have been better off when we had the gift of immunity offered by ignorance. By attacking one of the sacred heroes of Judaism, I know that I am inviting the scorn and hatred of many within the Jewish community. I may be cheered on by my Karaite brothers, but population wise, we are probably no more than fifty thousand in a sea of close to twenty million. I'm also positive that those that are secular Jews, as well as atheists will read this book and see it as supporting their agnostic or godless world perspective along with their homocentric beliefs. Nothing could be further from the truth regarding this book. The story as presented, is a message that repeats itself over and over again; 'If only we had listened to God and not to men.'

I only ask that those that will be so bitter and aggressive in their attacks, to take just a portion of that energy and simply review the facts which are presented that I have drawn from the Talmud itself. If you have been wondering why there were certain paragraphs or sentences written in *italics* scattered throughout the book, it is because those are either direct quotes from the Talmud and thus incorporated into the storyline by the people that actually said them, or they are stories taken directly from the Mishnah and Gemara and applied exactly as the speaker had intended them to be, even though their context had been obscured. So, before condemning me, take the time to check for yourself that I have lifted these quotes and stories directly from the Talmud as they were written and brought them together as they were intended, coalesced into the story from which they were derived. If I am to be condemned, it should only be for plagiarism, because I have not altered what the original authors of the Palestinian Talmud wrote almost two thousand years ago. As Rabbi Meir promised, these events and truths of that time, even though them may be incriminating, would not be erased, but at the same time, Rabbi Shimon ben Yochai would do what he did best, obfuscate the facts.

There are parallels between what happened in the time of Bar Kochba and what is happening right now in the 21st century. There are Jewish leaders today that will bend over backwards to appease their Gentile masters. Men and women that are so concerned about concealing their Jewish heritage that they will stand with every other societal and worldly cause except their own, even if those causes call for the elimination of the State of Israel and an end to the Jewish homeland. They will let antisemitism infuse their racist tropes and discriminatory rhetoric while at the same time these pseudo-Jewish leaders shout anti-racist slogans for every other race but our own. We must learn to take care of ourselves first, and any Jewish leader, no matter in which land, or for which government of whatever country they serve must swear by only one mantra of 'Never Again' or they must bear the consequences of their betrayal and failure before God Almighty. If we learn anything from this story, it is that our greatest enemy is most often the one standing beside us.

There is a great war epic waiting to be written about Bar Kochba but it will never be more important than our understanding of his betrayal by a man that has been practically elevated to sainthood within Rabbinical Judaism. We must learn to be introspective and recognize that for centuries we have been fed upon lies and mistruths by the very people that benefit from keeping us in the dark. People that have accused me openly of trying to perpetrate the misleading of our people through the presentation of revisionist history tend to know very little of our history. As far as I am aware, the only revisionist history that I have witnessed, is that which has been filtered through the mouths of those committed to our elimination as a people. It is presented in an unscrupulous media, every day by those wishing to deny that our war against Roman occupation ever took place in a land known both then and now as Judea. That we are the occupiers and we have no ties to the land in which we spilt our blood for thousands of years is the ultimate falsehood.

Establishing our history and our unbreakable ties to our homeland involves dissecting out the true history of our people from the Talmud. It is there but it is well concealed. We merely have to look at what the Talmudic scholars write themselves about the need for the Talmud. They call it *'a serious and substantive effort to locate in trivialities the fundamental principles of the revealed will of God."* They took it upon themselves, as their responsibility to read a few lines of the Torah, translate it according to their own insights, and then invent some homilies, not necessarily an accurate recounting, by which to teach it. I think we only have to look at two aspects of their intentions, two words that sum up their teaching and you will then have a good appreciation of my concerns. The two words I refer to are 'trivialities' and 'homilies'. Much of their time was focused on trivialization and because of it they failed to see the elephant standing in the Room. If you have read this book cover to cover, the entire Bar Kochba war was lost as a result of trivialities and a failure to focus on God's true intentions. For a group of scholars to freely admit that they were obsessed with uncovering the mysteries and secrets behind trivialities and in so doing, thinking they will discover fundamental principles, is in itself a confession to the uselessness of their ineffectual and eccentric activities. To state further that they will then express these irrelevant and insignificant findings by way of homilies, might as well be saying that they have fabricated it all into a false history or stories to suit their own purpose, because what is the definition of homiletics if it is not to say tedious, moralizing preaching and sermonizing presentation.

Where the insights for my books come from is no secret. It is that small voice inside our heads that all my ancestors have referred to. Sometimes it may be a few words, whereas other times it might be as if I'm watching an entire movie of events. I never question why these visions or insights appear; I simply write them down. When I originally approached this topic, it was my actual intent to write a historical battle novel that would be the ultimate war story attributed to Bar Kochba, since none actually exists. I had not even been thinking about Akiva's role in the story other than his selection of Bar Kosba and then his admission at the end of the war that he made an error in judgment. That was my intent but as soon as I sat down to type my first sentence, that little voice shouted out to me that this was all wrong. There was a story here that desperately needed to be told but it was not about Bar Kochba. He was not the driving force behind the war. That voice said, 'there was a history concerning the last Roman-Jewish war that had been intentionally concealed but purposely seeded throughout the Talmud so that it could be pieced together over time with some concerted effort' and I merely had to find it. I started to do so, and soon I came to realize, there was a much larger and significant story than I could have ever imagined.

Dr. Allen E. Goldenthal

Avrom Aryeh-Zuk Kahana

Descendants of Phiabi

Descendancy Line of The Author

Phiabi
160 -

Ophiabi

Seth
(Sis)

Avan

Jonas

Eleazar

Mathias

Jonathan

Theophilus

Mathias

Nebedaeus

Hezekiah

Ananias

Eleazar

Ananus

Ananus

Amoth

Joseph Caiaphus
(Art-Marthias)

Joshua
Damneus

Maxima

Menaham

Jonathan
Caiaphus

Eleazar ha
Cayef

[1]
Joshua

[2]
Martha

Jonathas

Joseph

Elioneus

Azariah
113 -

Eleazar
140 -

Joseph ha
Cohen
117 -

Judah
Cayafa
186 -

Mar
Sharafa
180 -

Joseph ha
Cohen
215 -

Sharaf
259 -

Judah
Mar
280 -

Azariah
313 -

Kahana
340 - 414

[2]
Martha

[1]
Joshua

Gamaliel

Jonathas

Jesus

Ishmael

Phiabi II

Amariah

Eleazar

Ishmael

Ishmael II

Elisha
190 -

Rab
Ishmael
228 -

Haben

Phineas Ben
Haben

Rab
Hanina

Ba-Fiuhas

www.ingramcontent.com/pod-product-compliance
Lightning Source LLC
La Vergne TN
LVHW091213080426
835509LV00009B/966